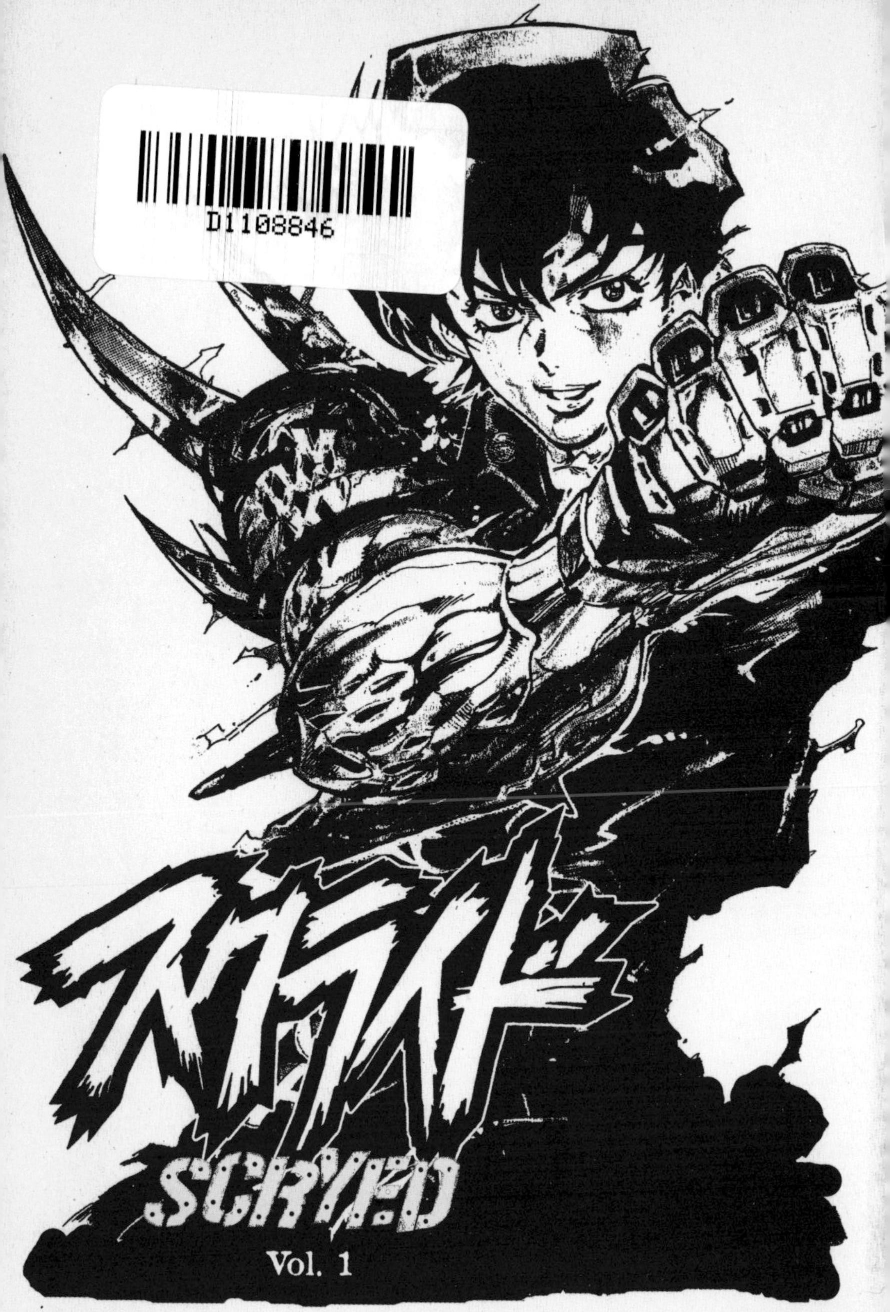
SCRYED
Vol. 1

ALSO AVAILABLE FROM TOKYOPOP®

*INDICATES TITLE IS IN THE RIGHT-TO-LEFT FORMAT

MANGA

ACTION

ANGELIC LAYER*
CLAMP SCHOOL DETECTIVES* (April 2003)
DIGIMON
DUKLYON: CLAMP SCHOOL DEFENDERS* (September 2003)
GATEKEEPERS*
GTO*
HARLEM BEAT
INITIAL D*
ISLAND
JING: KING OF BANDITS* (June 2003)
JULINE
LUPIN III*
MONSTERS, INC.
PRIEST
RAVE*
REAL BOUT HIGH SCHOOL*
REBOUND* (April 2003)
SAMURAI DEEPER KYO* (June 2003)
SCRYED*
SHAOLIN SISTERS*
THE SKULL MAN*

FANTASY

CHRONICLES OF THE CURSED SWORD (July 2003)
DEMON DIARY (May 2003)
DRAGON HUNTER (June 2003)
DRAGON KNIGHTS*
KING OF HELL (June 2003)
PLANET LADDER*
RAGNAROK
REBIRTH (March 2003)
SHIRAHIME: TALES OF THE SNOW PRINCESS* (December 2003)
SORCERER HUNTERS
WISH*

CINE-MANGA™

AKIRA*
CARDCAPTORS
KIM POSSIBLE
LIZZIE McGUIRE
POWER RANGERS (May 2003)
SPY KIDS 2

ANIME GUIDES

GUNDAM TECHNICAL MANUALS
COWBOY BEBOP
SAILOR MOON SCOUT GUIDES

ROMANCE

HAPPY MANIA* (April 2003)
I.N.V.U.
LOVE HINA*
KARE KANO*
KODOCHA*
MAN OF MANY FACES* (May 2003)
MARMALADE BOY*
MARS*
PARADISE KISS*
PEACH GIRL
UNDER A GLASS MOON (June 2003)

SCIENCE FICTION

CHOBITS*
CLOVER
COWBOY BEBOP*
COWBOY BEBOP: SHOOTING STAR* (June 2003)
G-GUNDAM*
GUNDAM WING
GUNDAM WING: ENDLESS WALTZ*
GUNDAM: THE LAST OUTPOST*
PARASYTE
REALITY CHECK

MAGICAL GIRLS

CARDCAPTOR SAKURA
CARDCAPTOR SAKURA: MASTER OF THE CLOW*
CORRECTOR YUI
MAGIC KNIGHT RAYEARTH* (August 2003)
MIRACLE GIRLS
SAILOR MOON
SAINT TAIL
TOKYO MEW MEW* (April 2003)

NOVELS

SAILOR MOON
SUSHI SQUAD (April 2003)

ART BOOKS

CARDCAPTOR SAKURA*
MAGIC KNIGHT RAYEARTH*

TOKYOPOP KIDS

STRAY SHEEP (September 2003)

SCRYED

Story by Yosuke Kuroda
Art by Yasunari Toda

Vol. 1

TOKYOPOP®

Los Angeles • Tokyo

Translation - Jan Scott Frazier
English Adaptation - Jan Scott Frazier and Luis Reyes
Retouch and Lettering - Monalisa J. de Asis
Cover Layout - Raymond Makowski

Senior Editor - Luis Reyes
Managing Editor - Jill Freshney
Production Coordinator - Antonio DePietro
Production Manager - Jennifer Miller
Art Director - Matthew Alford
Director of Editorial - Jeremy Ross
VP of Production & Manufacturing - Ron Klamert
President & C.O.O. - John Parker
Publisher - Stuart Levy

Email: editor@TOKYOPOP.com
Come visit us online at www.TOKYOPOP.com

A **TOKYOPOP** Manga

TOKYOPOP® is an imprint of Mixx Entertainment, Inc.
5900 Wilshire Blvd. Suite 2000, Los Angeles, CA 90036

ISBN: 1-59182-228-9

First TOKYOPOP® printing: March 2003

10 9 8 7 6 5 4 3 2 1

Printed in the USA

History

22 years ago, a seismic phenomenon struck the Yokohama region of Japan, driving the highly populated district miles into the sky. This caused not only wide-scale death and destruction, but it also effectively cut the area off from the established institutions of Japan-- its political systems, social welfare and, perhaps most crucial to the survival of society, law enforcement. Yokohama descended almost immediately into a lawless dystopia and became known as the Lost Ground. However, over the two decades since the catastrophe, some citizens of the Lost Ground have been able to rebuild a small corner of Yokohama. The resulting cities have been protected from the wasteland beyond by well-guarded walls, stirring resentment between the well-to-do within and the desperately poor without.

The seismic phenomenon also triggered a strange biological abnormality in the population. A fraction of the newborns in the Lost Ground have developed the power to manipulate matter. This power is called Alter, and those who possess it are known as Alter Users. Just as a schism has arisen between the citizens of the cities and the denizens of the wasteland, Alter Users have fallen into two camps: those who choose to aid humanity and those who choose to exploit it. The latter have become cynically termed Native Alter Users.

SCRYED

Vol.1

Contents

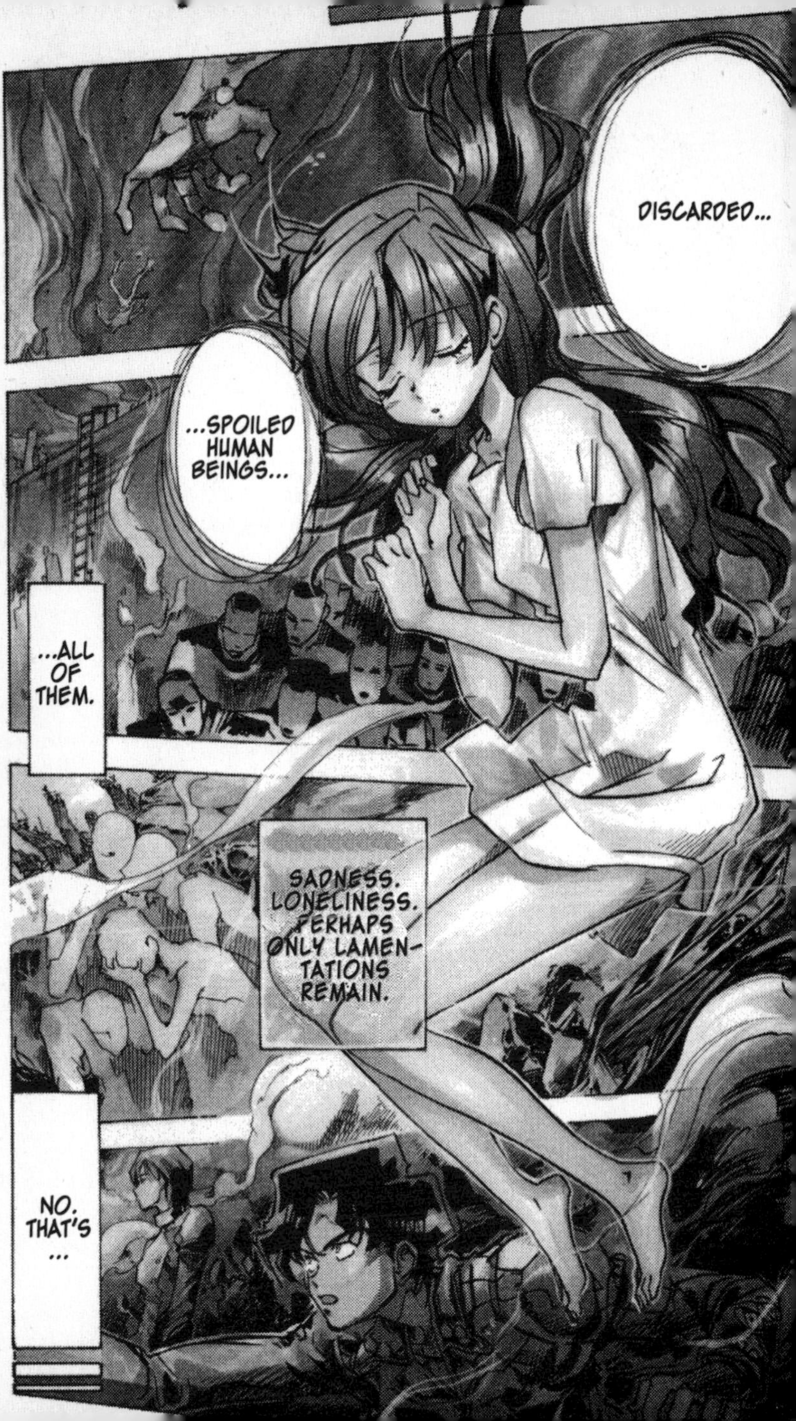
DISCARDED...
...SPOILED HUMAN BEINGS...
...ALL OF THEM.
SADNESS. LONELINESS. PERHAPS ONLY LAMEN-TATIONS REMAIN.
NO. THAT'S ...

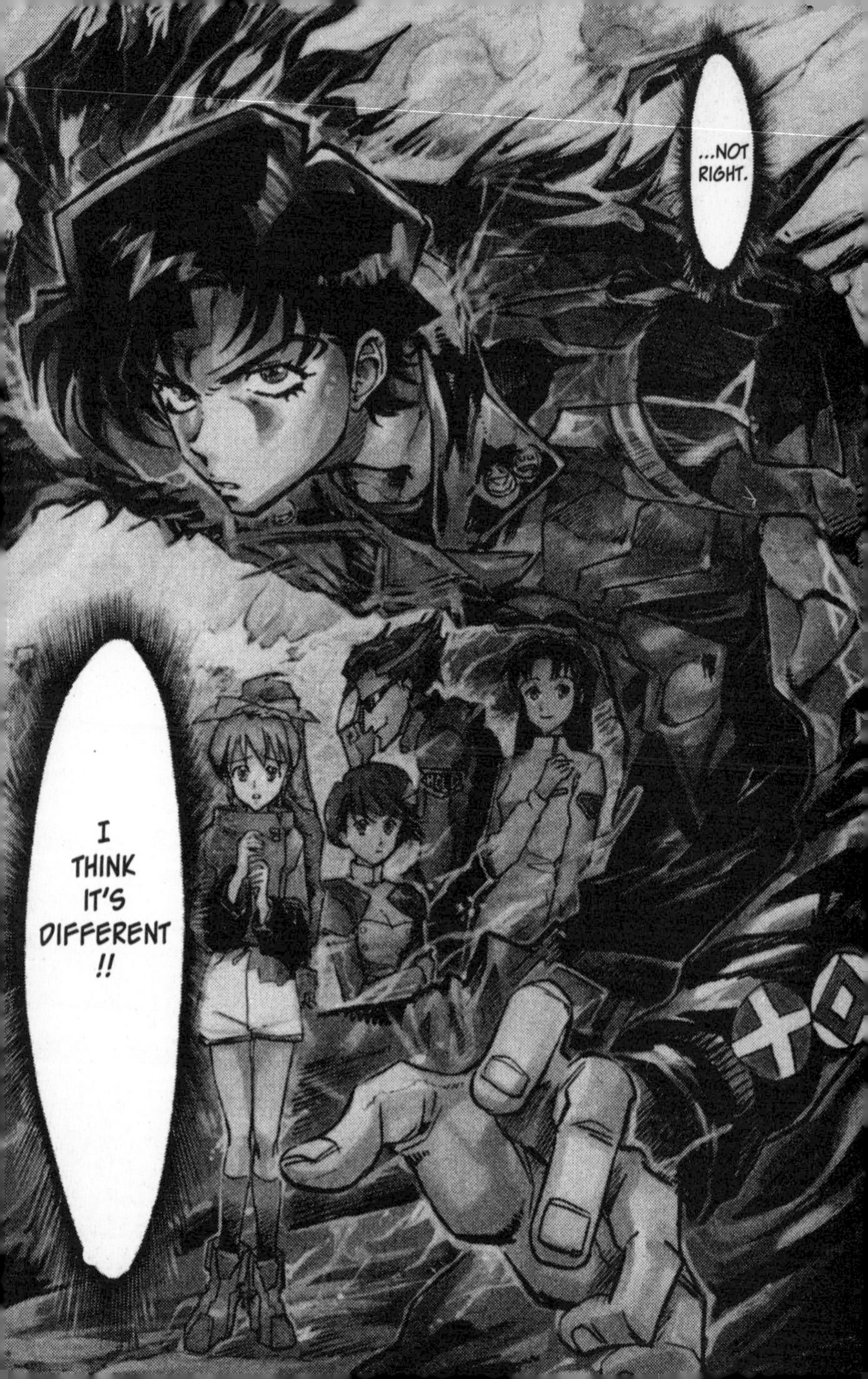
...NOT RIGHT.
I THINK IT'S DIFFERENT !!

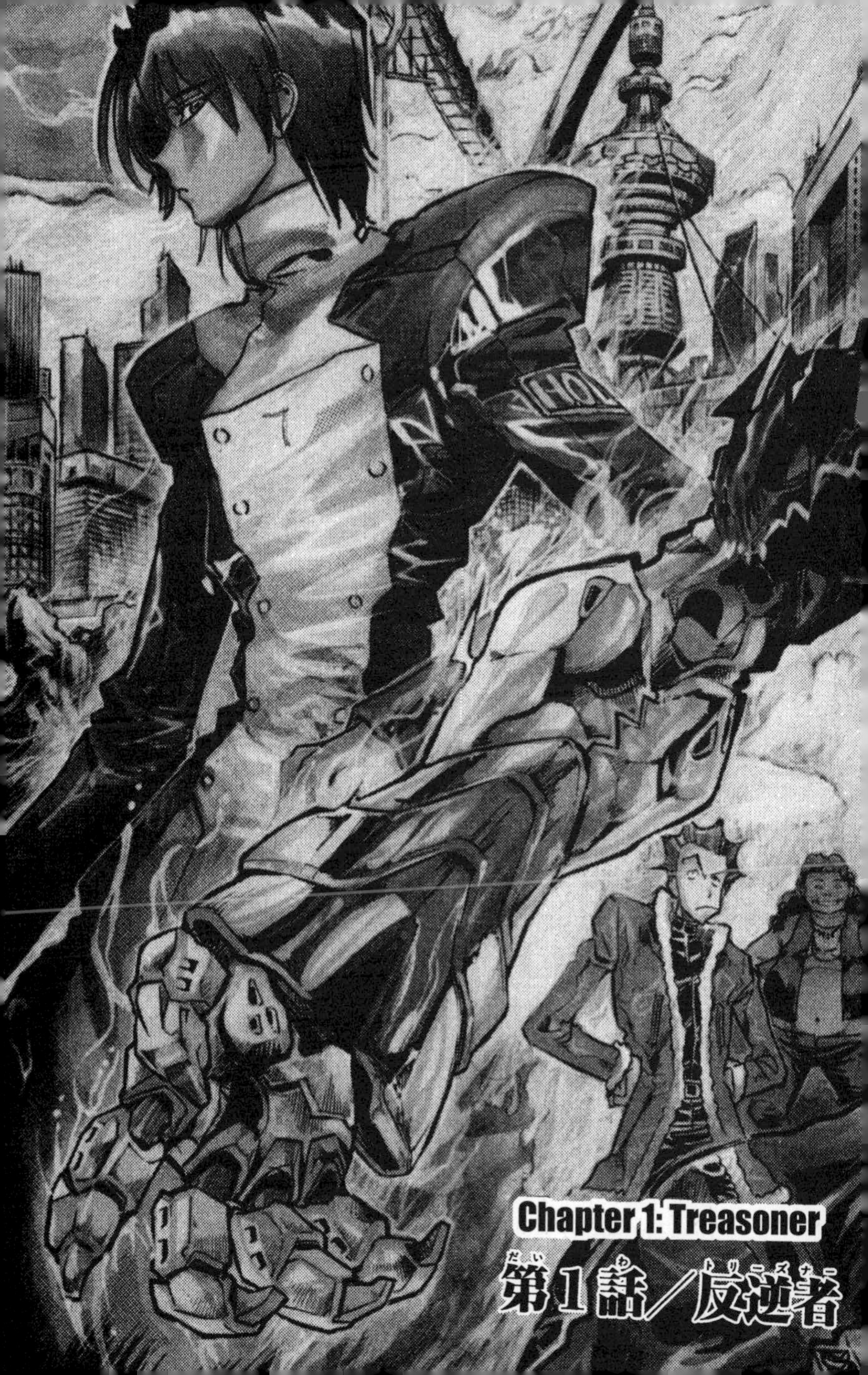

Chapter 1: Treasoner
第1話／反逆者

SCRYED

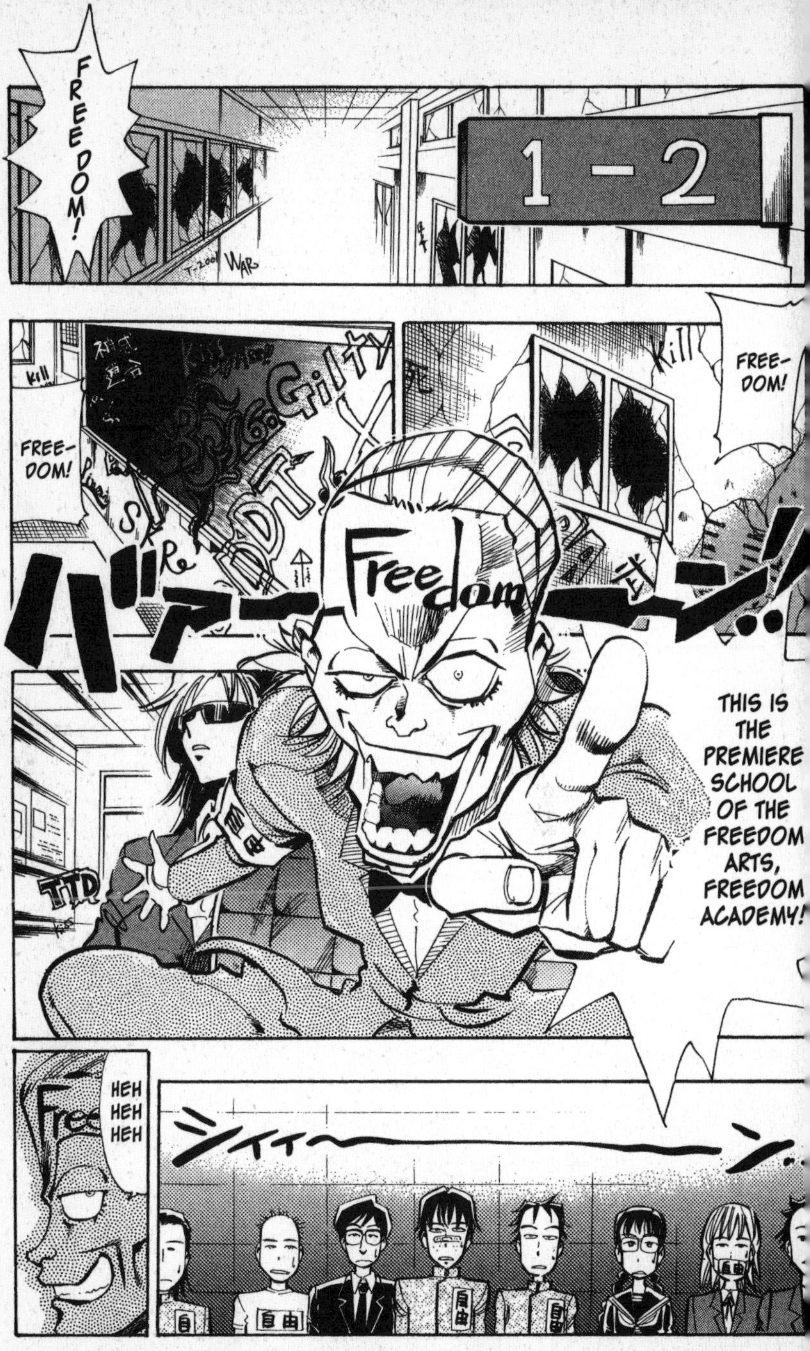
FREEDOM!
1-2
FREE-DOM!
FREE-DOM!
バアーーーン!!
THIS IS THE PREMIERE SCHOOL OF THE FREEDOM ARTS, FREEDOM ACADEMY!
シイイ〜〜ン...
HEH HEH HEH

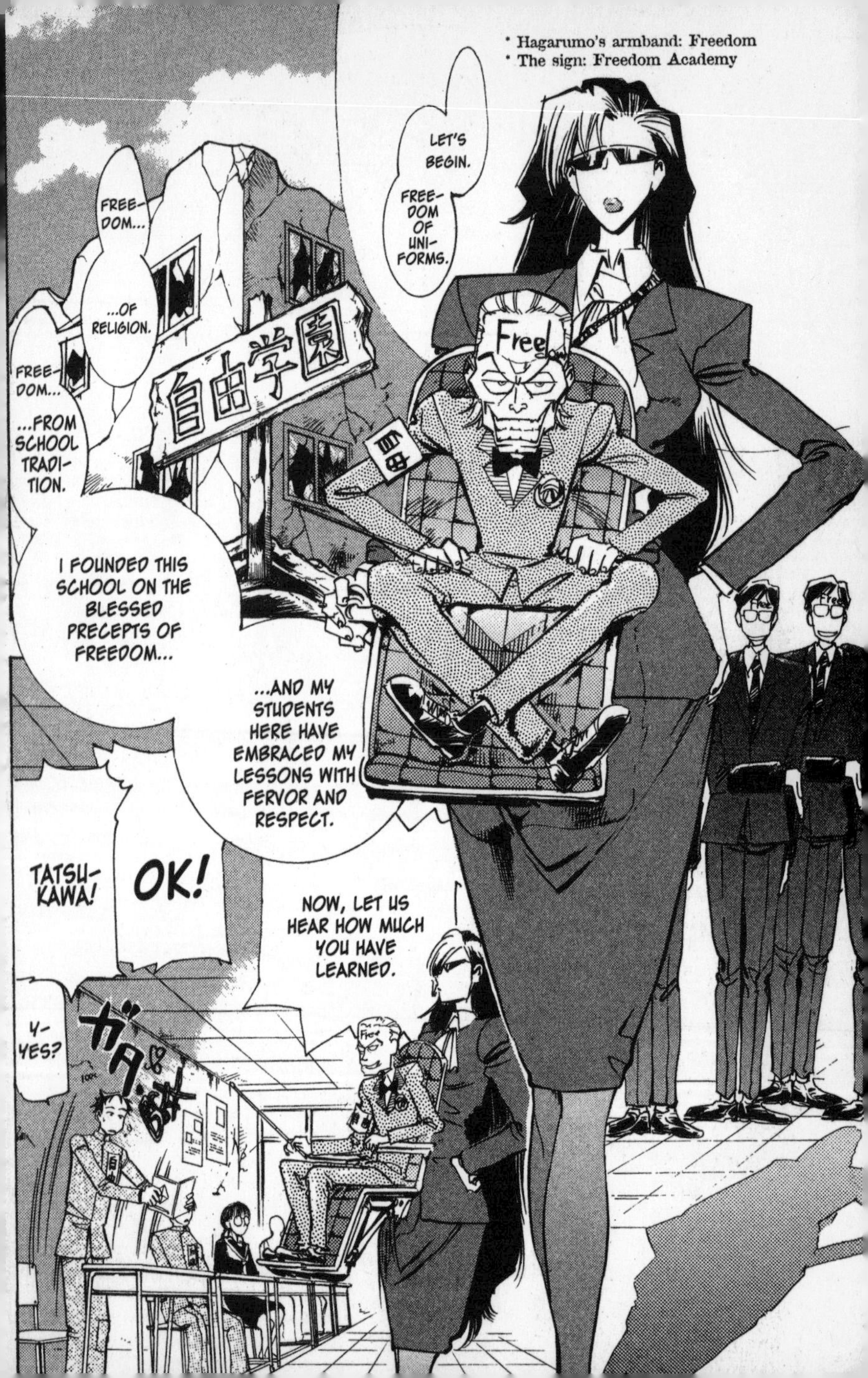
LET'S BEGIN.
FREEDOM OF UNIFORMS.
FREEDOM...
...OF RELIGION.
FREEDOM...
...FROM SCHOOL TRADITION.
自由学園
Free
I FOUNDED THIS SCHOOL ON THE BLESSED PRECEPTS OF FREEDOM...
...AND MY STUDENTS HERE HAVE EMBRACED MY LESSONS WITH FERVOR AND RESPECT.
NOW, LET US HEAR HOW MUCH YOU HAVE LEARNED.
TATSUKAWA!
OK!
ガタ
Y-YES?

* Hagarumo's armband: Freedom
* The sign: Freedom Academy

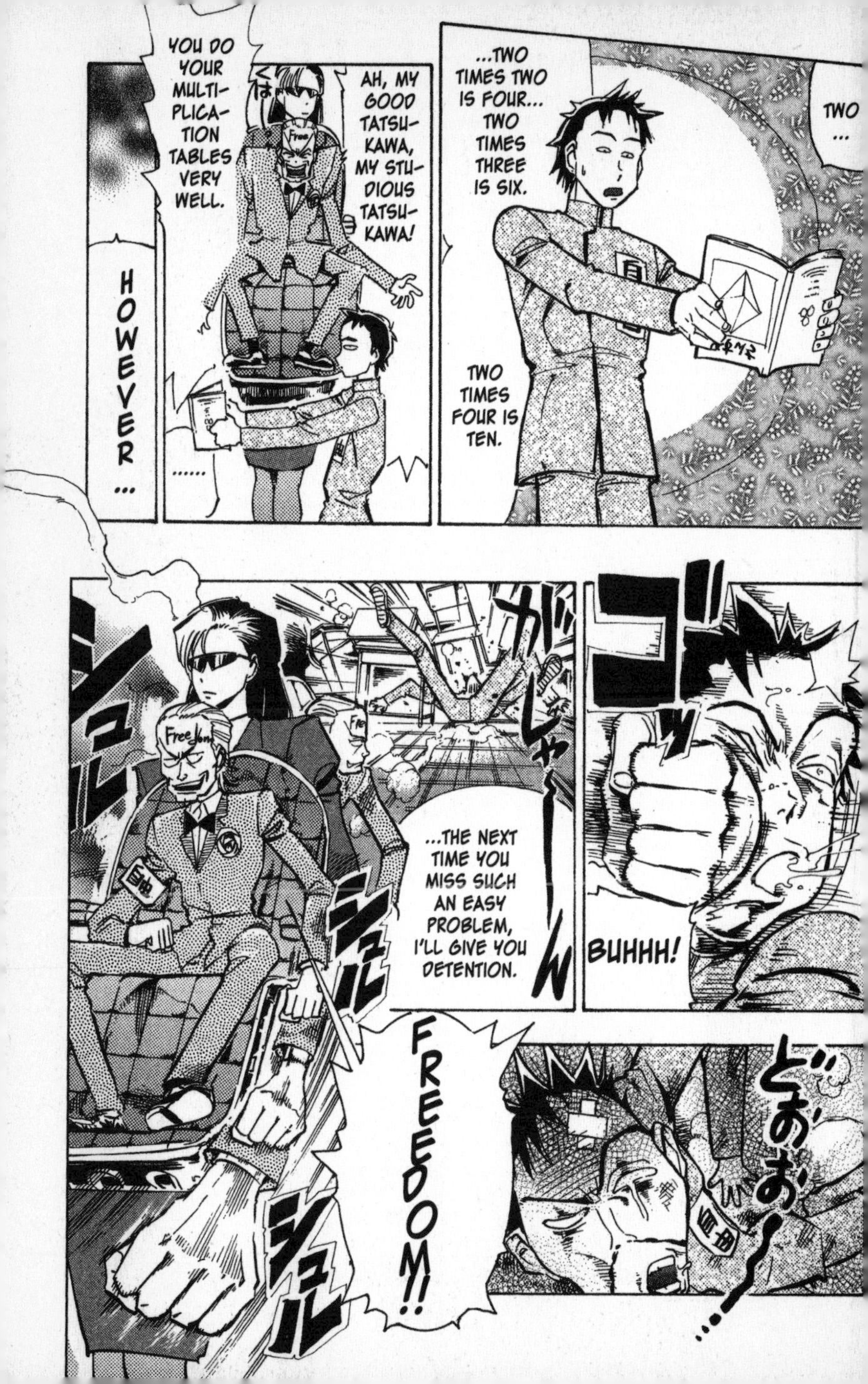
TWO ...
...TWO TIMES TWO IS FOUR... TWO TIMES THREE IS SIX.
TWO TIMES FOUR IS TEN.
AH, MY GOOD TATSUKAWA, MY STUDIOUS TATSUKAWA!
YOU DO YOUR MULTIPLICATION TABLES VERY WELL.
......
HOWEVER...
ゴッ
BUHHH!
がしゃ～ん
...THE NEXT TIME YOU MISS SUCH AN EASY PROBLEM, I'LL GIVE YOU DETENTION.
FREEDOM!!
どぉぉ～…

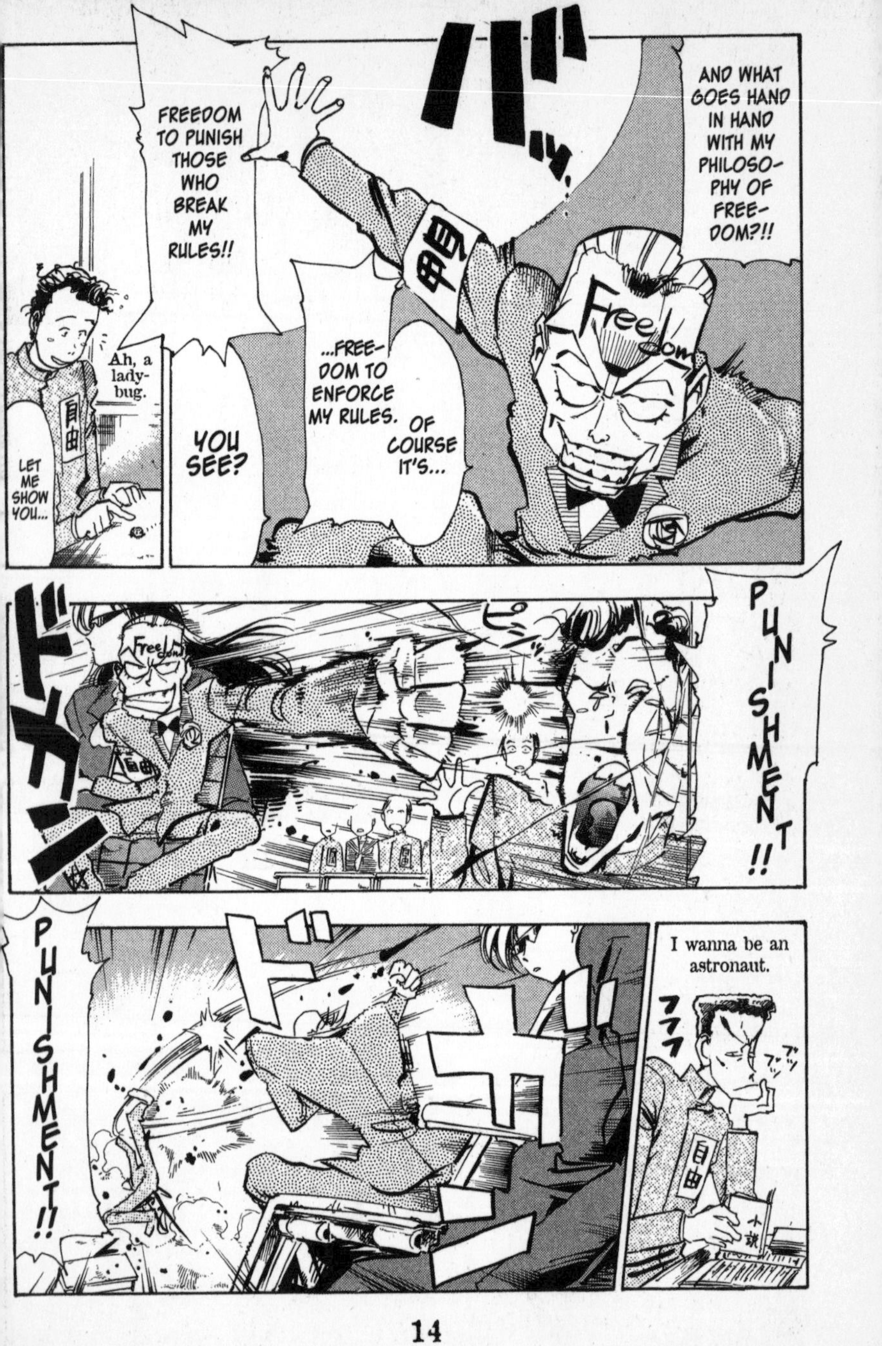
AND WHAT GOES HAND IN HAND WITH MY PHILOSOPHY OF FREEDOM?!!
OF COURSE IT'S...
...FREEDOM TO ENFORCE MY RULES.
FREEDOM TO PUNISH THOSE WHO BREAK MY RULES!!
YOU SEE?
Ah, a ladybug.
LET ME SHOW YOU...
PUNISHMENT!!
I wanna be an astronaut.
PUNISHMENT!!

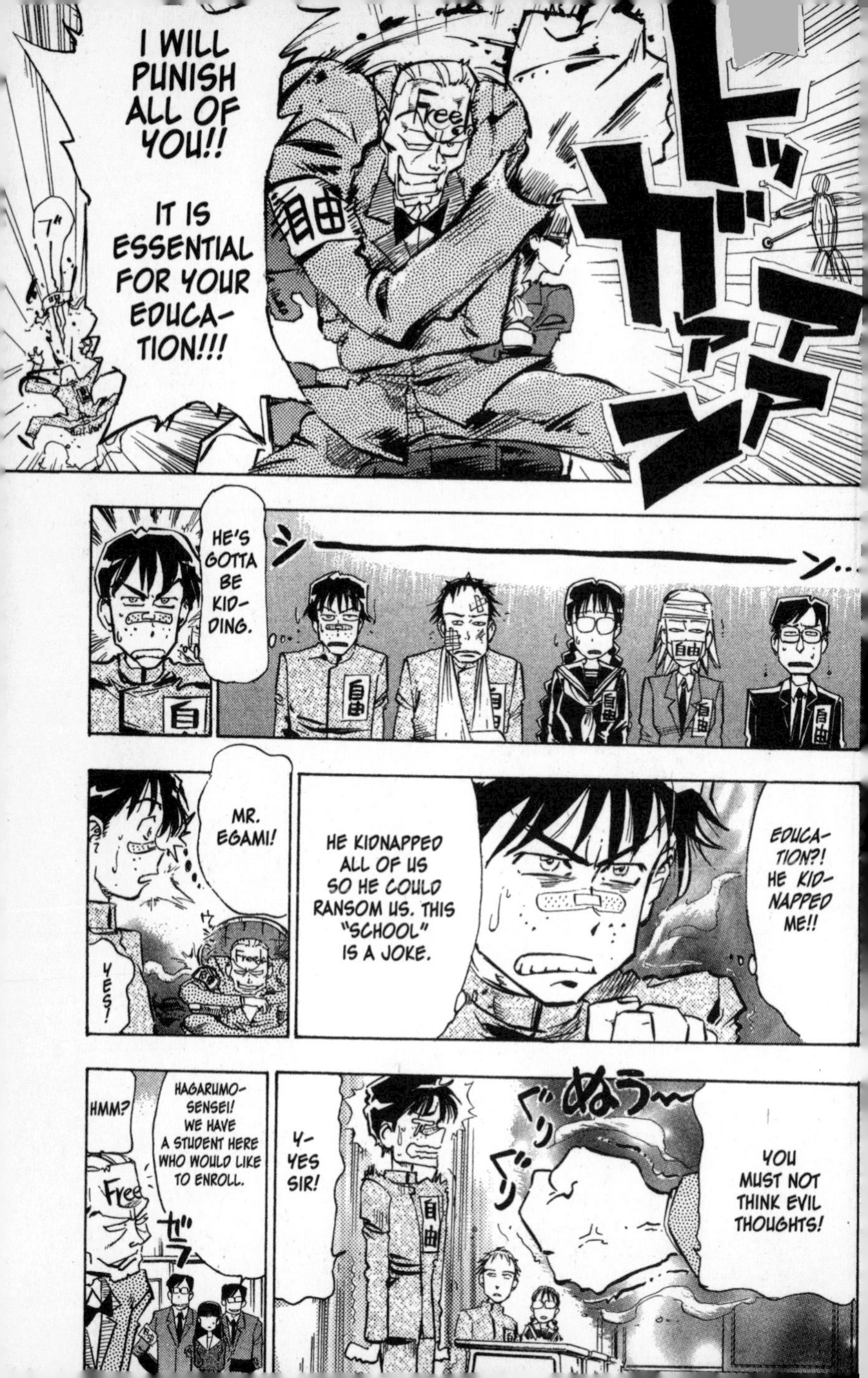
I WILL PUNISH ALL OF YOU!!
IT IS ESSENTIAL FOR YOUR EDUCATION!!!
HE'S GOTTA BE KIDDING.
EDUCATION?! HE KIDNAPPED ME!!
HE KIDNAPPED ALL OF US SO HE COULD RANSOM US. THIS "SCHOOL" IS A JOKE.
MR. EGAMI!
YES!
ぬう～
ぐりぐり
YOU MUST NOT THINK EVIL THOUGHTS!
Y-YES SIR!
HAGARUMO-SENSEI! WE HAVE A STUDENT HERE WHO WOULD LIKE TO ENROLL.
HMM?

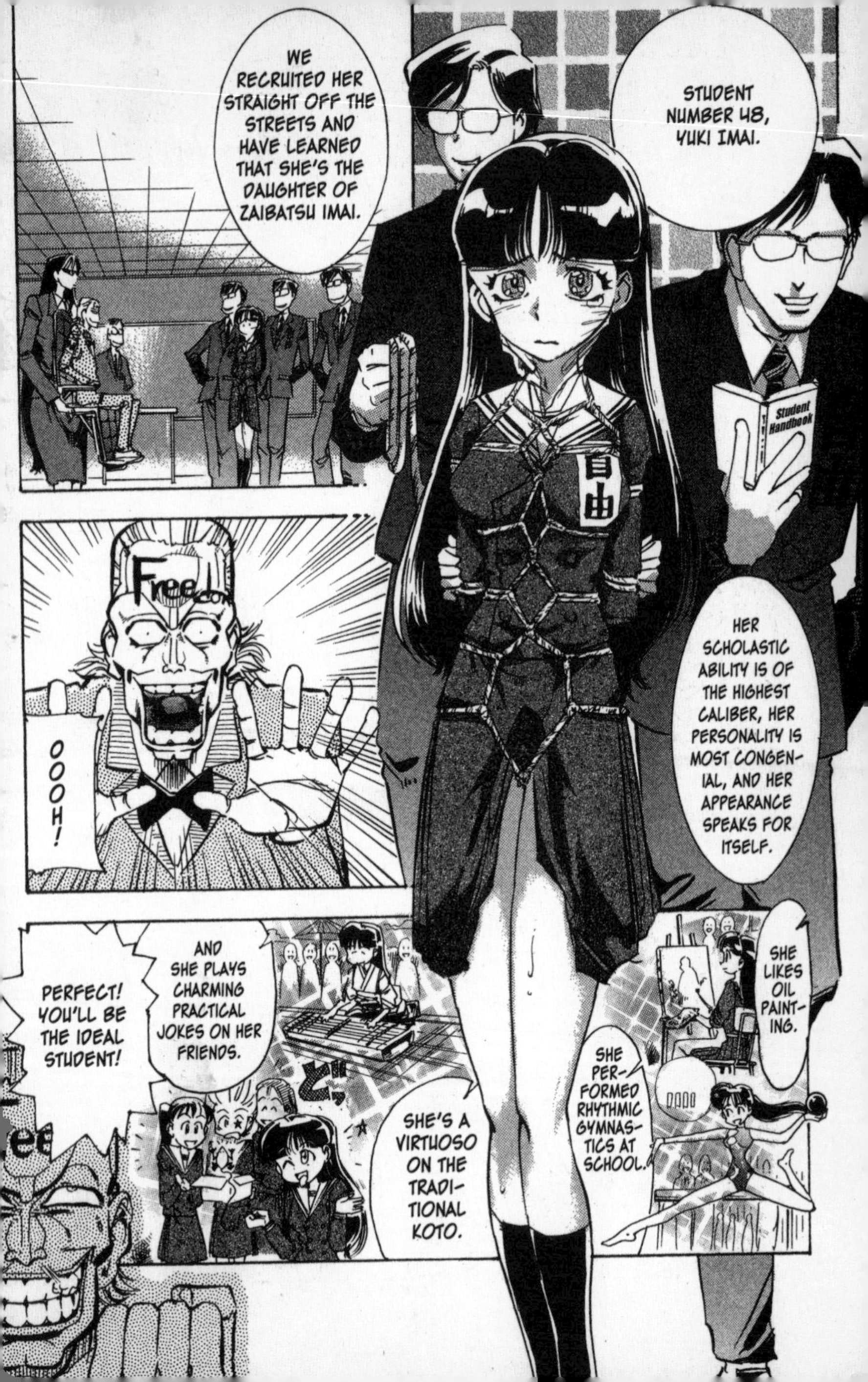
STUDENT NUMBER 48, YUKI IMAI.
WE RECRUITED HER STRAIGHT OFF THE STREETS AND HAVE LEARNED THAT SHE'S THE DAUGHTER OF ZAIBATSU IMAI.
Student Handbook
自由
HER SCHOLASTIC ABILITY IS OF THE HIGHEST CALIBER, HER PERSONALITY IS MOST CONGENIAL, AND HER APPEARANCE SPEAKS FOR ITSELF.
Free
OOOOH!
SHE LIKES OIL PAINTING.
SHE PERFORMED RHYTHMIC GYMNASTICS AT SCHOOL.
SHE'S A VIRTUOSO ON THE TRADITIONAL KOTO.
AND SHE PLAYS CHARMING PRACTICAL JOKES ON HER FRIENDS.
PERFECT! YOU'LL BE THE IDEAL STUDENT!

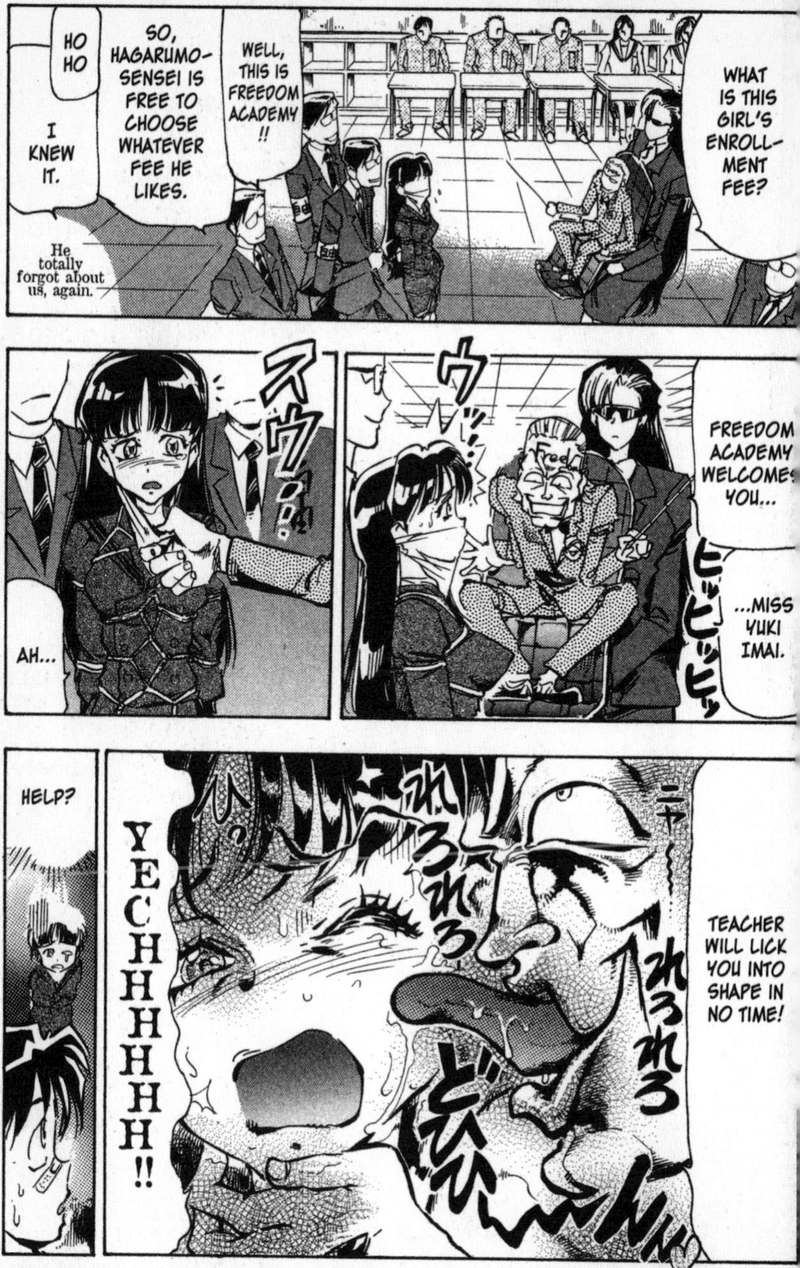

WHAT IS THIS GIRL'S ENROLLMENT FEE?
WELL, THIS IS FREEDOM ACADEMY!!
SO, HAGARUMO-SENSEI IS FREE TO CHOOSE WHATEVER FEE HE LIKES.
HO HO
I KNEW IT.
He totally forgot about us, again.
FREEDOM ACADEMY WELCOMES YOU...
...MISS YUKI IMAI.
Fred
AH...
TEACHER WILL LICK YOU INTO SHAPE IN NO TIME!
YECHHHHHHH!!
HELP?

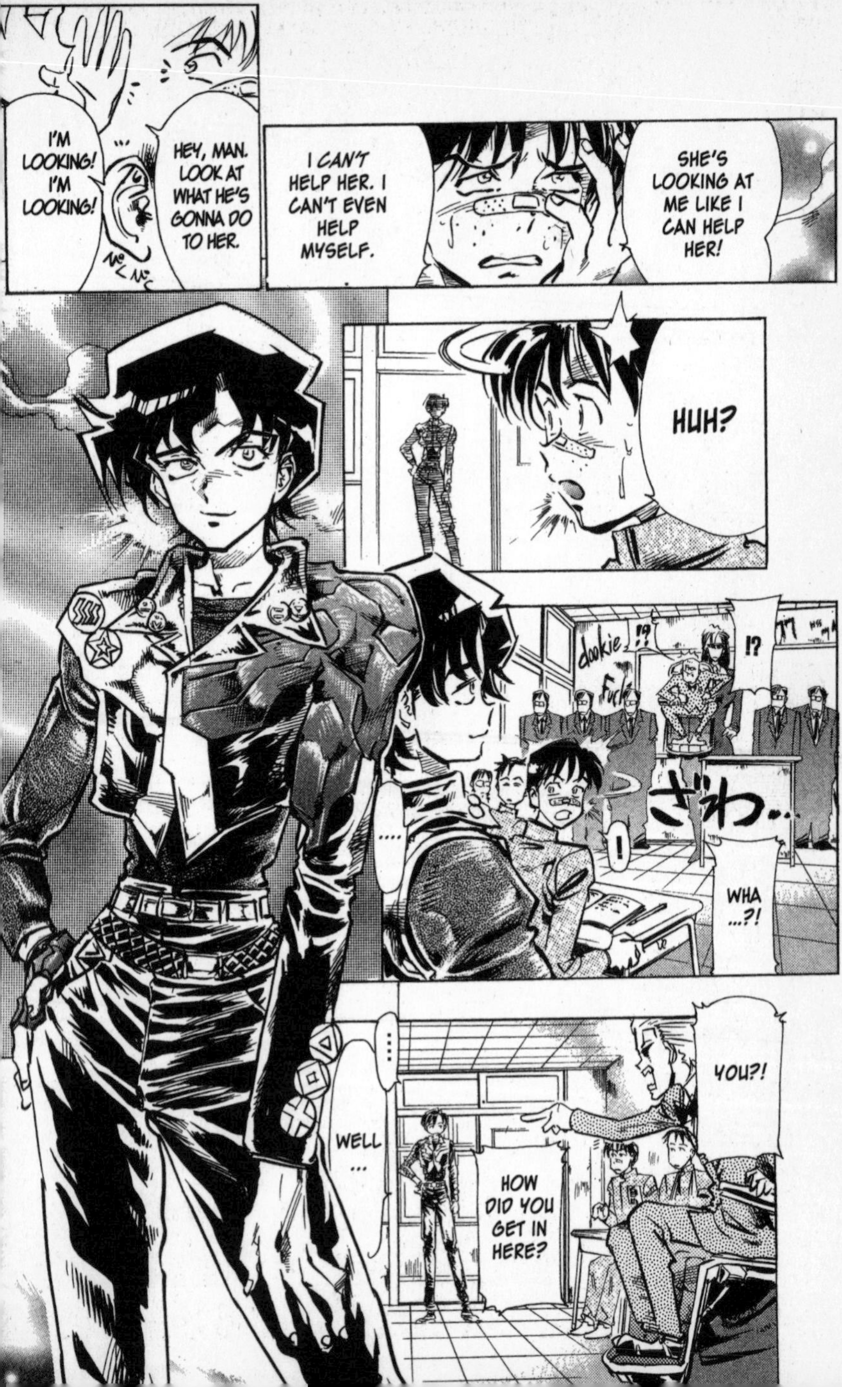

SHE'S LOOKING AT ME LIKE I CAN HELP HER!
I CAN'T HELP HER. I CAN'T EVEN HELP MYSELF.
HEY, MAN. LOOK AT WHAT HE'S GONNA DO TO HER.
I'M LOOKING! I'M LOOKING!
HUH?
!?
dookie
Fuck
!?
ざわ...
!
WHA ...?!
....
YOU?!
HOW DID YOU GET IN HERE?
WELL ...
...

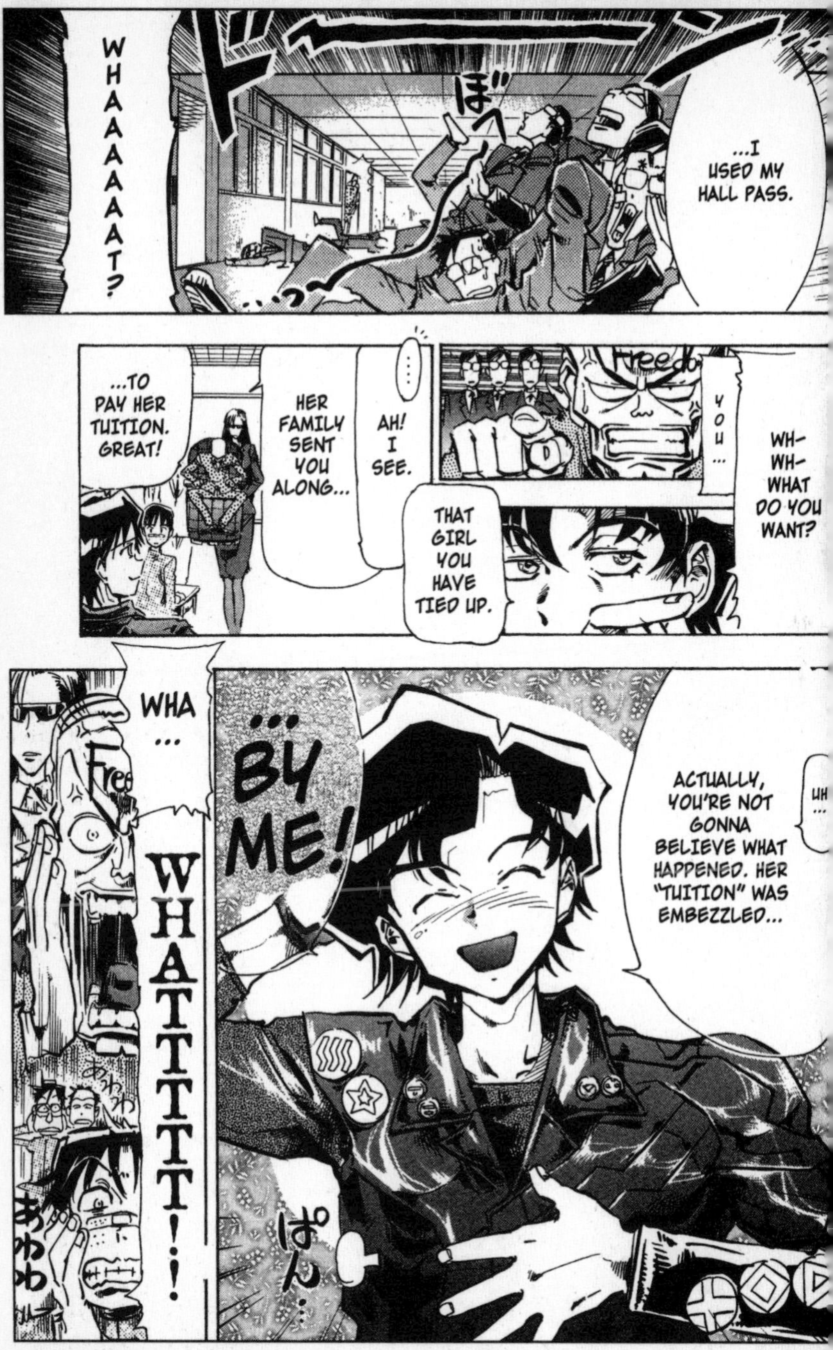

...I USED MY HALL PASS.
ドー
ぼ
WHAAAAAAAT?
WH-WH-WHAT DO YOU WANT?
YOU...
THAT GIRL YOU HAVE TIED UP.
...
AH! I SEE.
HER FAMILY SENT YOU ALONG...
...TO PAY HER TUITION. GREAT!
UH...
ACTUALLY, YOU'RE NOT GONNA BELIEVE WHAT HAPPENED. HER "TUITION" WAS EMBEZZLED...
...BY ME!
ぱん...
WHA...
WHATTTTT!!
あわわ
あわわ

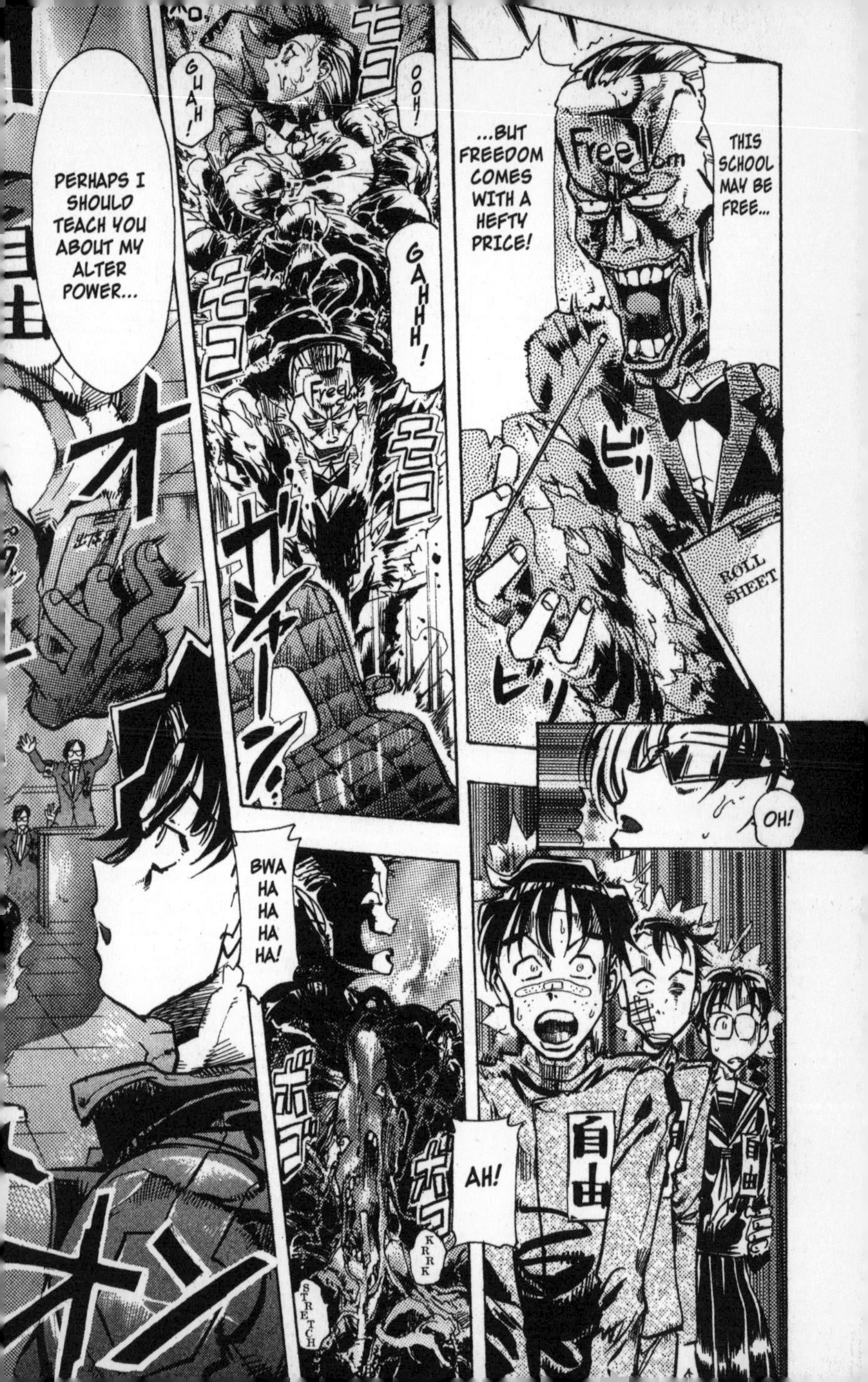
THIS SCHOOL MAY BE FREE...
...BUT FREEDOM COMES WITH A HEFTY PRICE!
ROLL SHEET
OOH!
GUAH!
GAHHHH!
OH!
AH!
BWA HA HA HA HA HA!
KRRK
STRETCH
PERHAPS I SHOULD TEACH YOU ABOUT MY ALTER POWER...

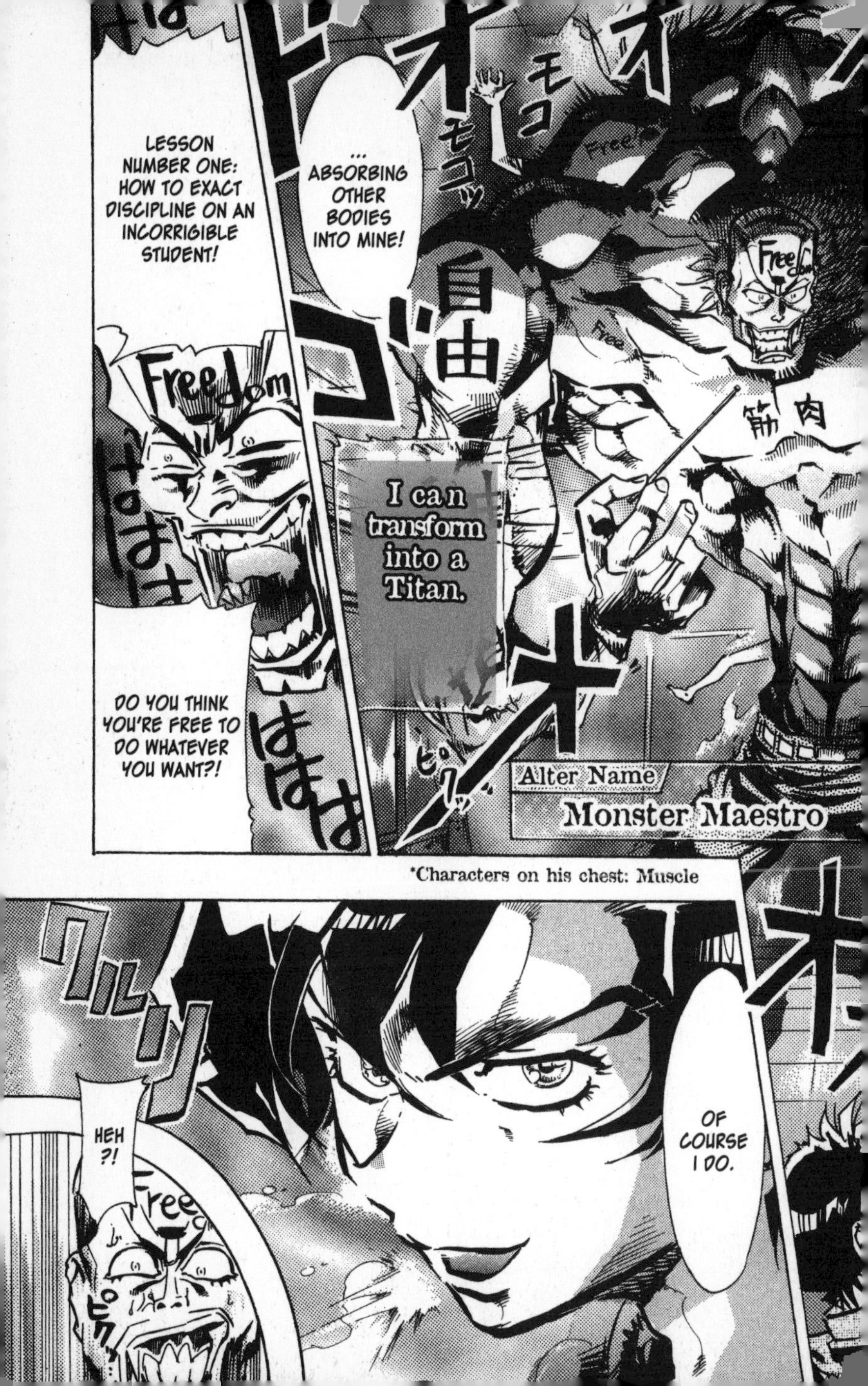
Free dom
筋肉
Alter Name
Monster Maestro
I can transform into a Titan.
自由
... ABSORBING OTHER BODIES INTO MINE!
LESSON NUMBER ONE: HOW TO EXACT DISCIPLINE ON AN INCORRIGIBLE STUDENT!
Free dom
DO YOU THINK YOU'RE FREE TO DO WHATEVER YOU WANT?!
OF COURSE I DO.
HEH ?!
Free
*Characters on his chest: Muscle

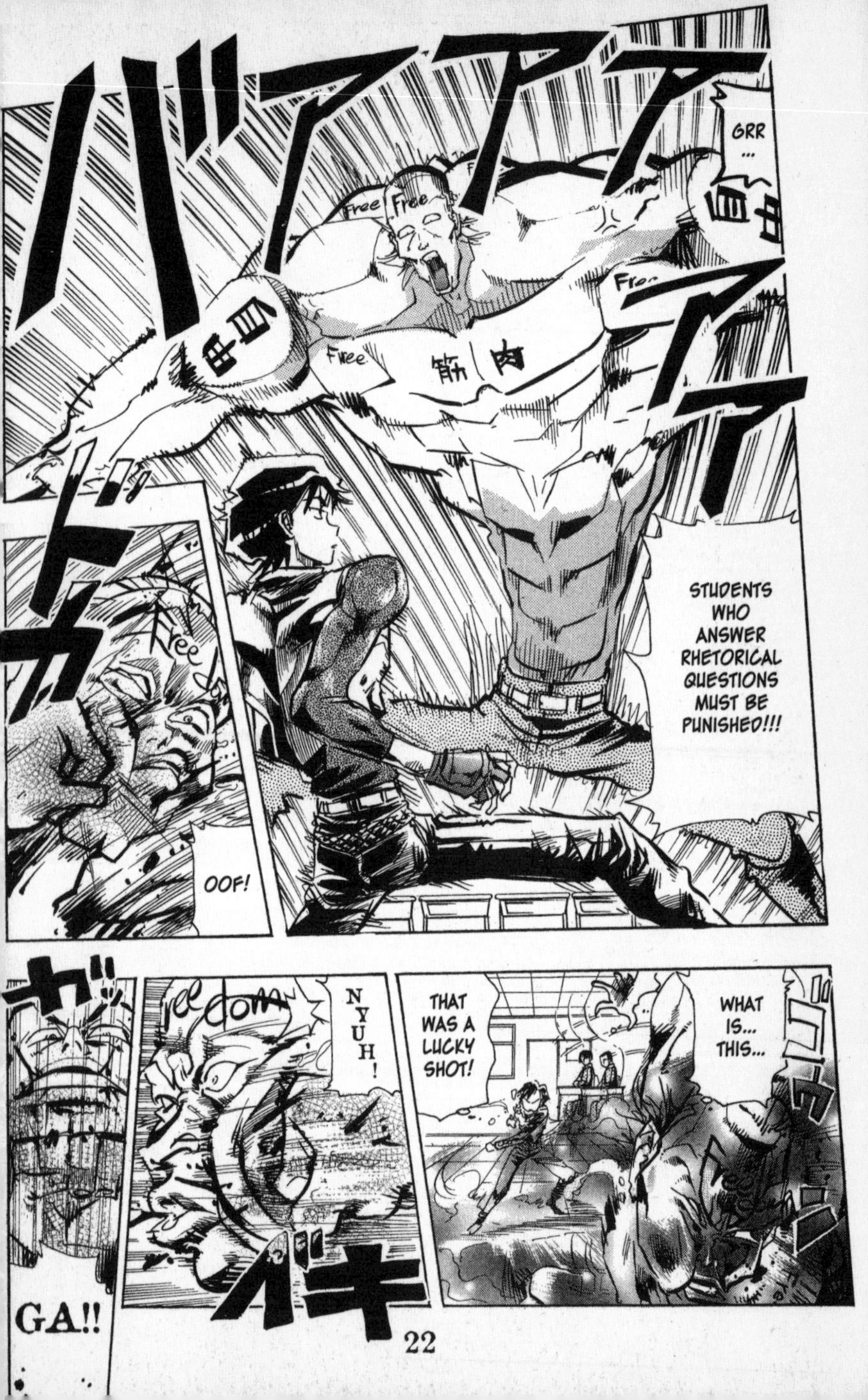
GRR ...
筋肉
STUDENTS WHO ANSWER RHETORICAL QUESTIONS MUST BE PUNISHED!!!
OOF!
WHAT IS... THIS...
THAT WAS A LUCKY SHOT!
NYUH!
GA!!

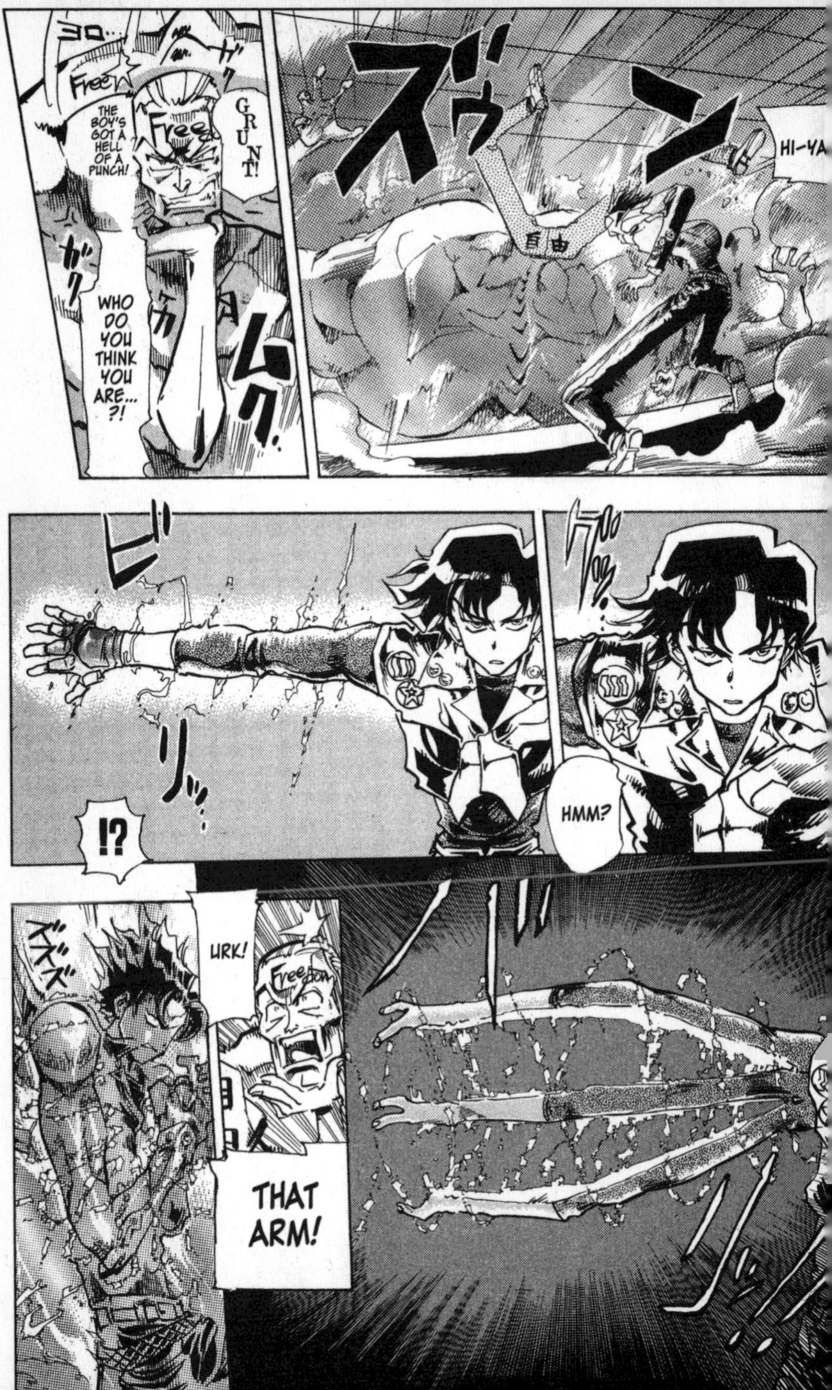
HI-YA
GRUNT!
THE BOY'S GOT A HELL OF A PUNCH!
WHO DO YOU THINK YOU ARE...?!
HMM?
!?
URK!
THAT ARM!

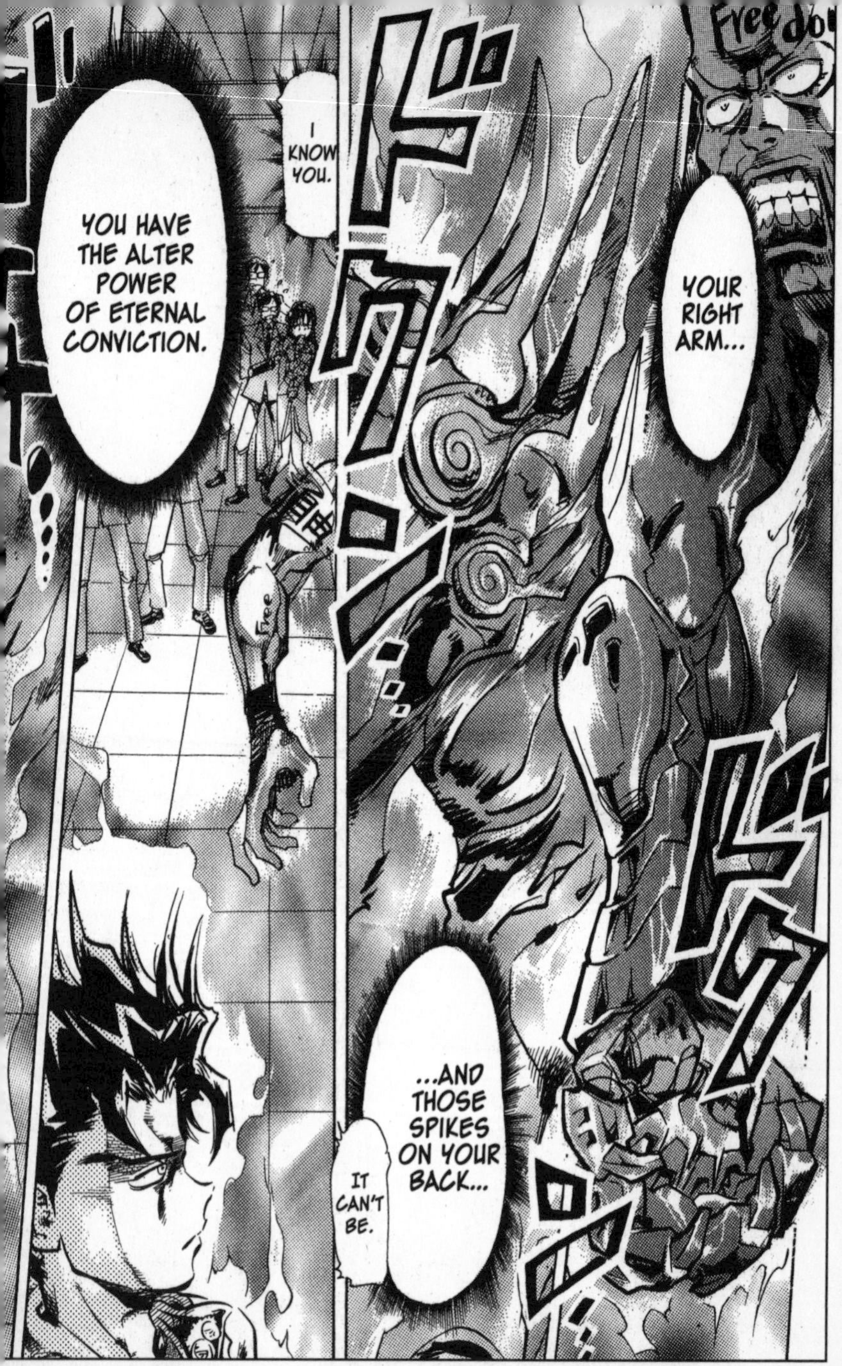
YOUR RIGHT ARM...
...AND THOSE SPIKES ON YOUR BACK...
IT CAN'T BE.
I KNOW YOU.
YOU HAVE THE ALTER POWER OF ETERNAL CONVICTION.

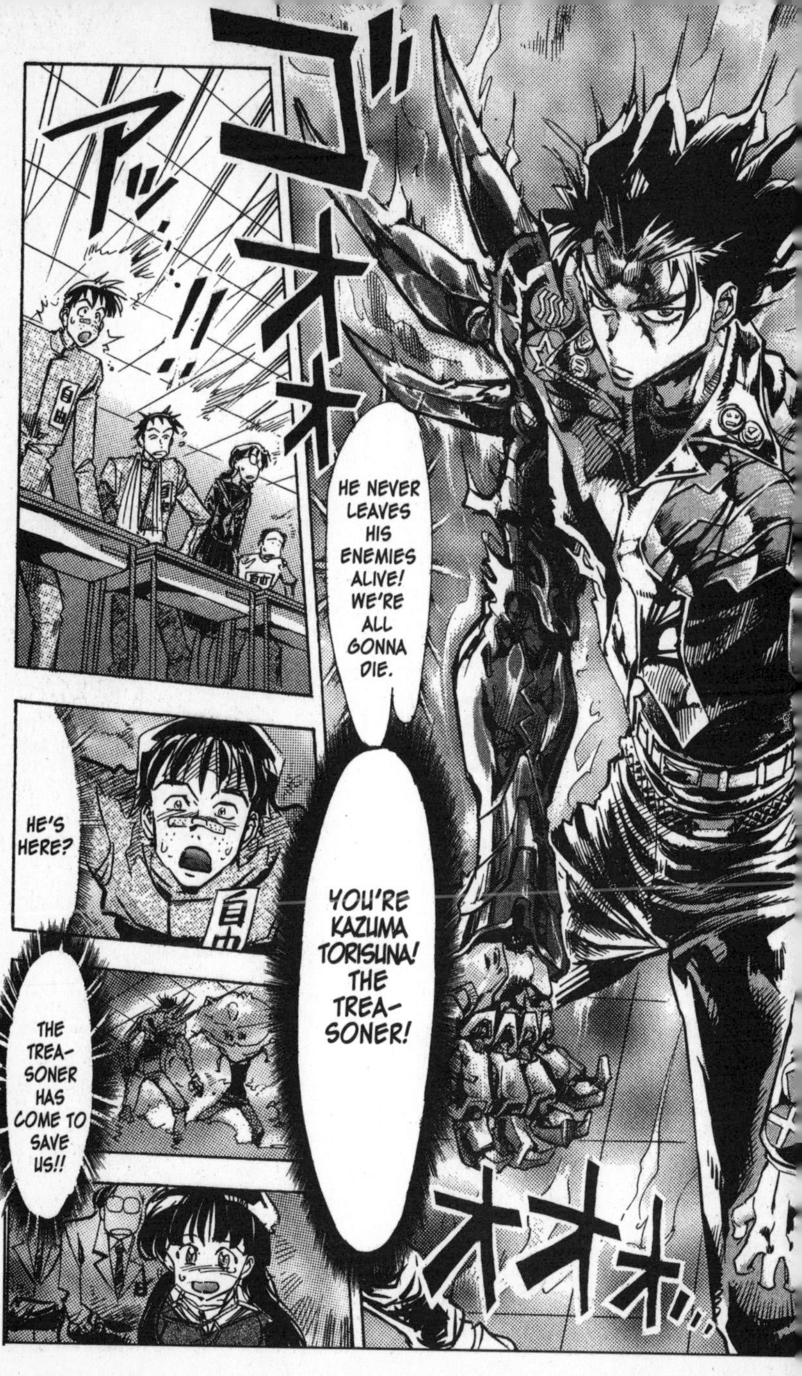

ゴオオ
HE NEVER LEAVES HIS ENEMIES ALIVE! WE'RE ALL GONNA DIE.
YOU'RE KAZUMA TORISUNA! THE TREA-SONER!
オオオ…
アッ…!!
HE'S HERE?
THE TREA-SONER HAS COME TO SAVE US!!

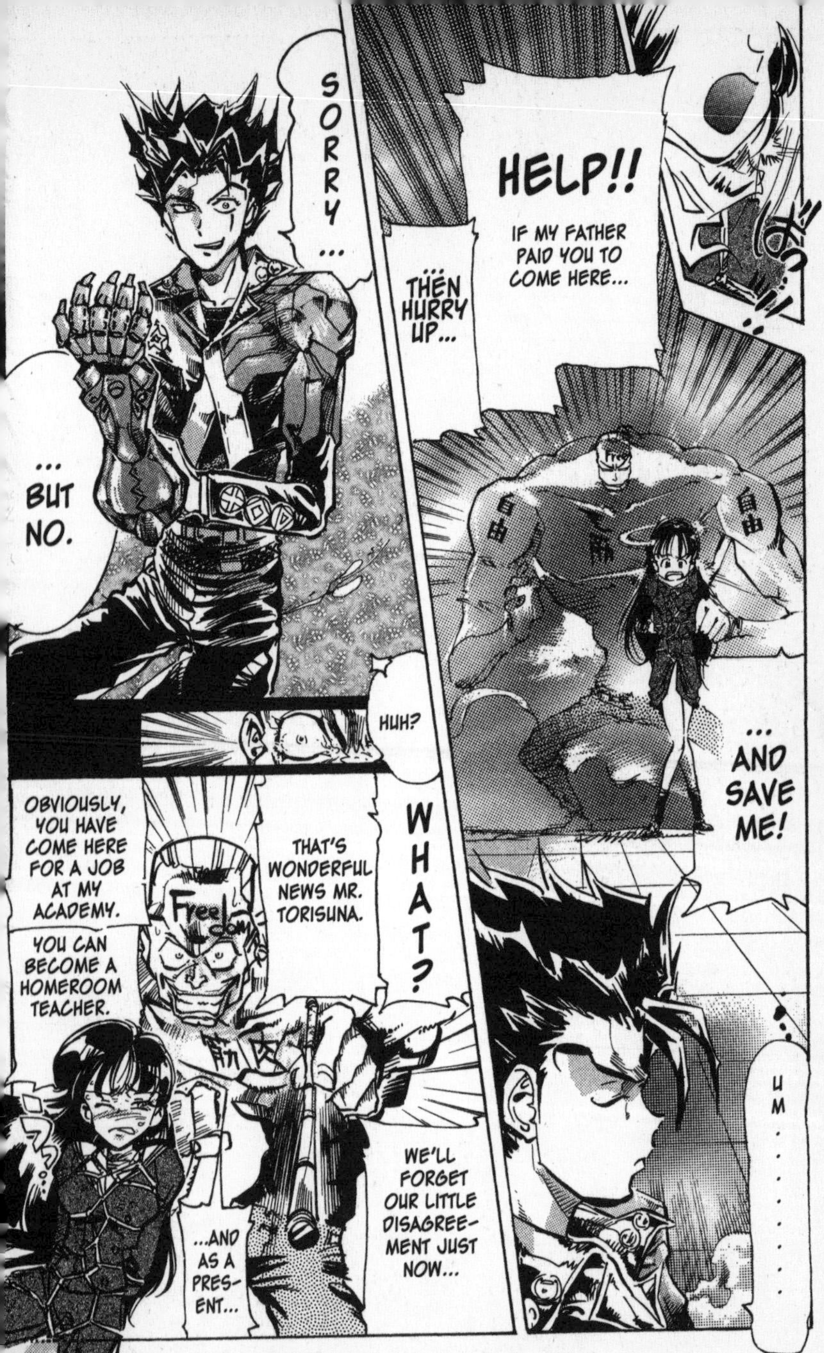
HELP!!
IF MY FATHER PAID YOU TO COME HERE...
THEN HURRY UP...
...AND SAVE ME!
...
UM.......
SORRY...
...BUT NO.
HUH?
WHAT?
THAT'S WONDERFUL NEWS MR. TORISUNA.
OBVIOUSLY, YOU HAVE COME HERE FOR A JOB AT MY ACADEMY.
YOU CAN BECOME A HOMEROOM TEACHER.
WE'LL FORGET OUR LITTLE DISAGREEMENT JUST NOW...
...AND AS A PRESENT...

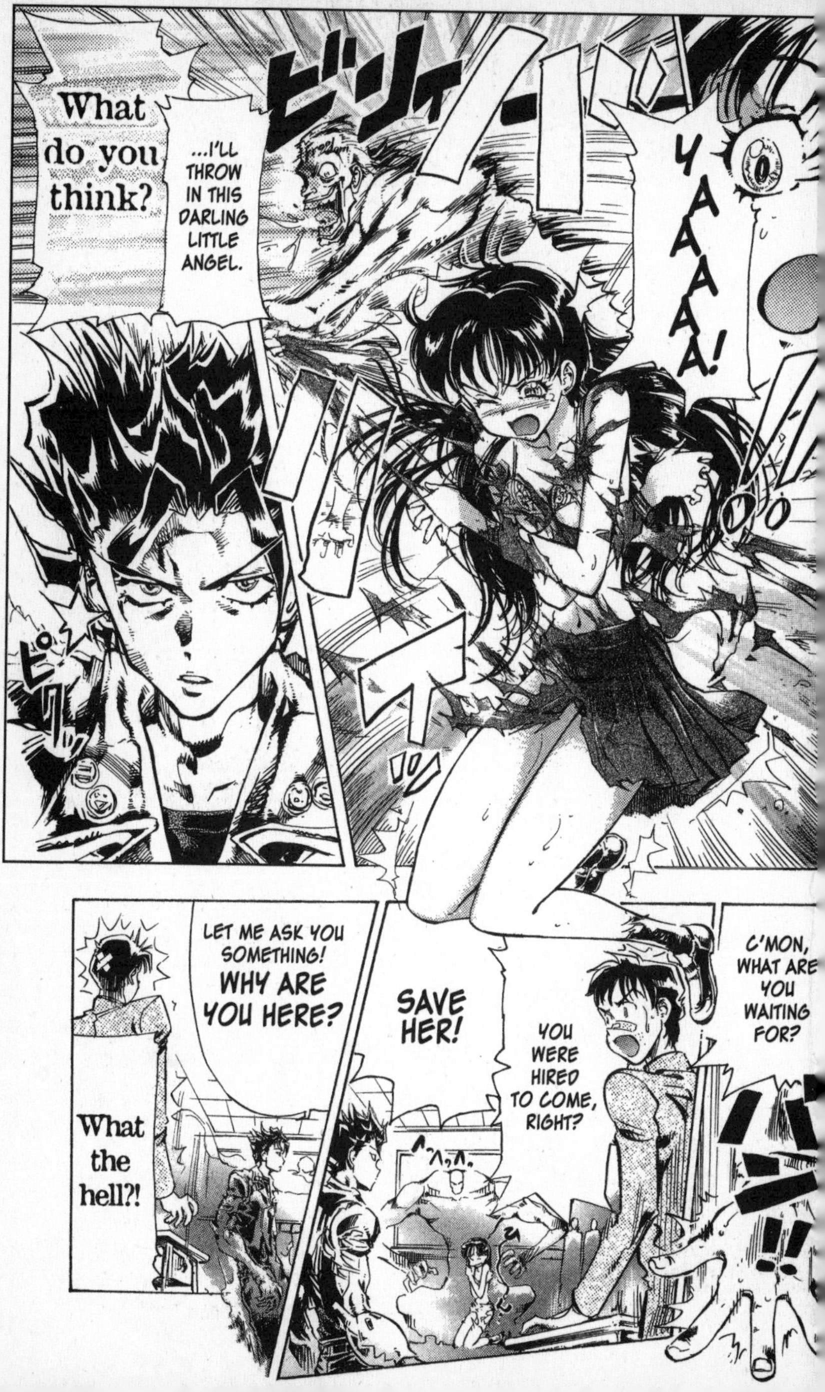
YAAAAA!
...I'LL THROW IN THIS DARLING LITTLE ANGEL.
What do you think?
C'MON, WHAT ARE YOU WAITING FOR?
YOU WERE HIRED TO COME, RIGHT?
SAVE HER!
LET ME ASK YOU SOMETHING! WHY ARE YOU HERE?
What the hell?!

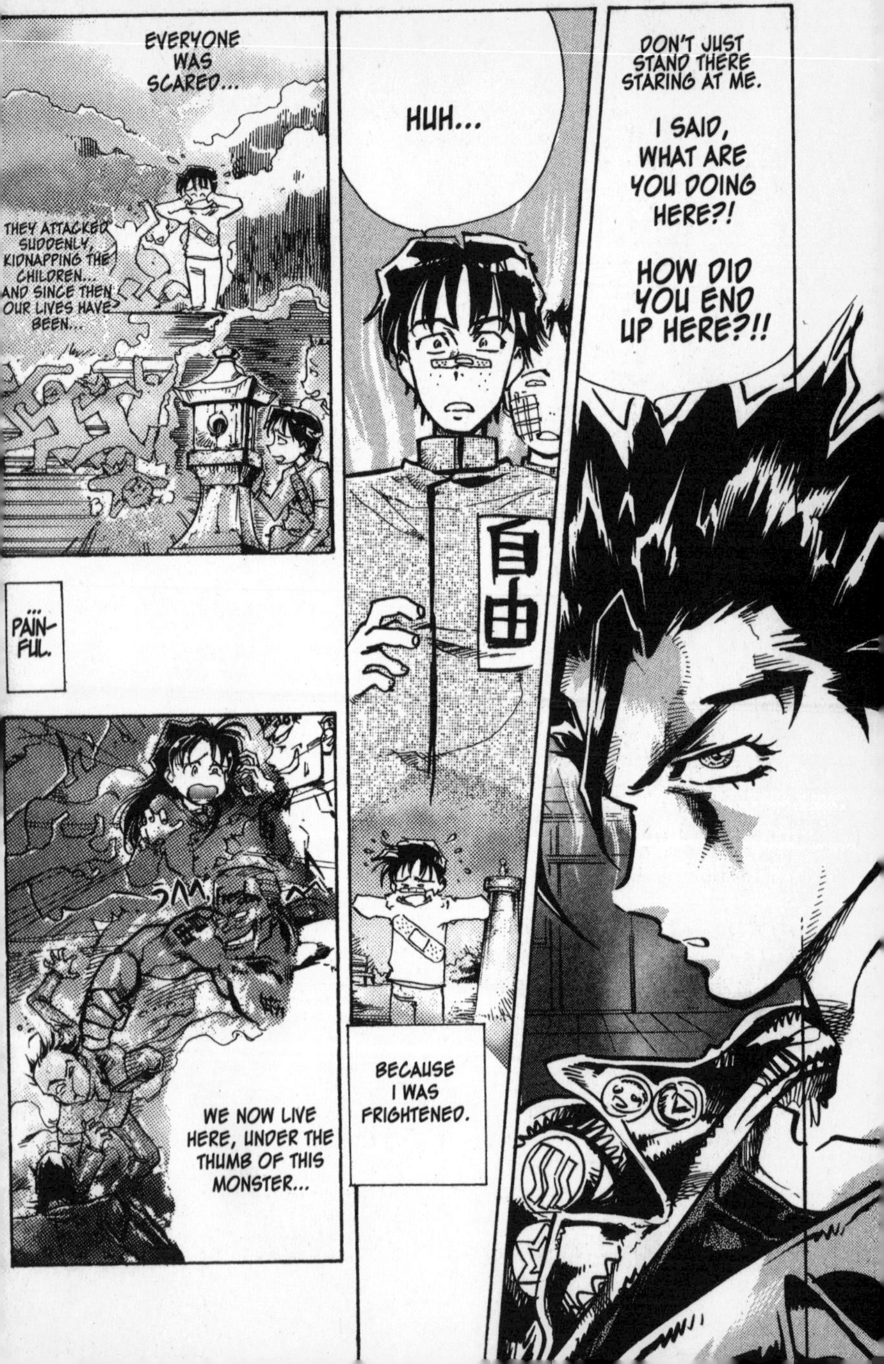
DON'T JUST STAND THERE STARING AT ME.
I SAID, WHAT ARE YOU DOING HERE?!
HOW DID YOU END UP HERE?!!
HUH...
BECAUSE I WAS FRIGHTENED.
EVERYONE WAS SCARED...
THEY ATTACKED SUDDENLY, KIDNAPPING THE CHILDREN... AND SINCE THEN OUR LIVES HAVE BEEN...
...PAIN-FUL.
WE NOW LIVE HERE, UNDER THE THUMB OF THIS MONSTER...

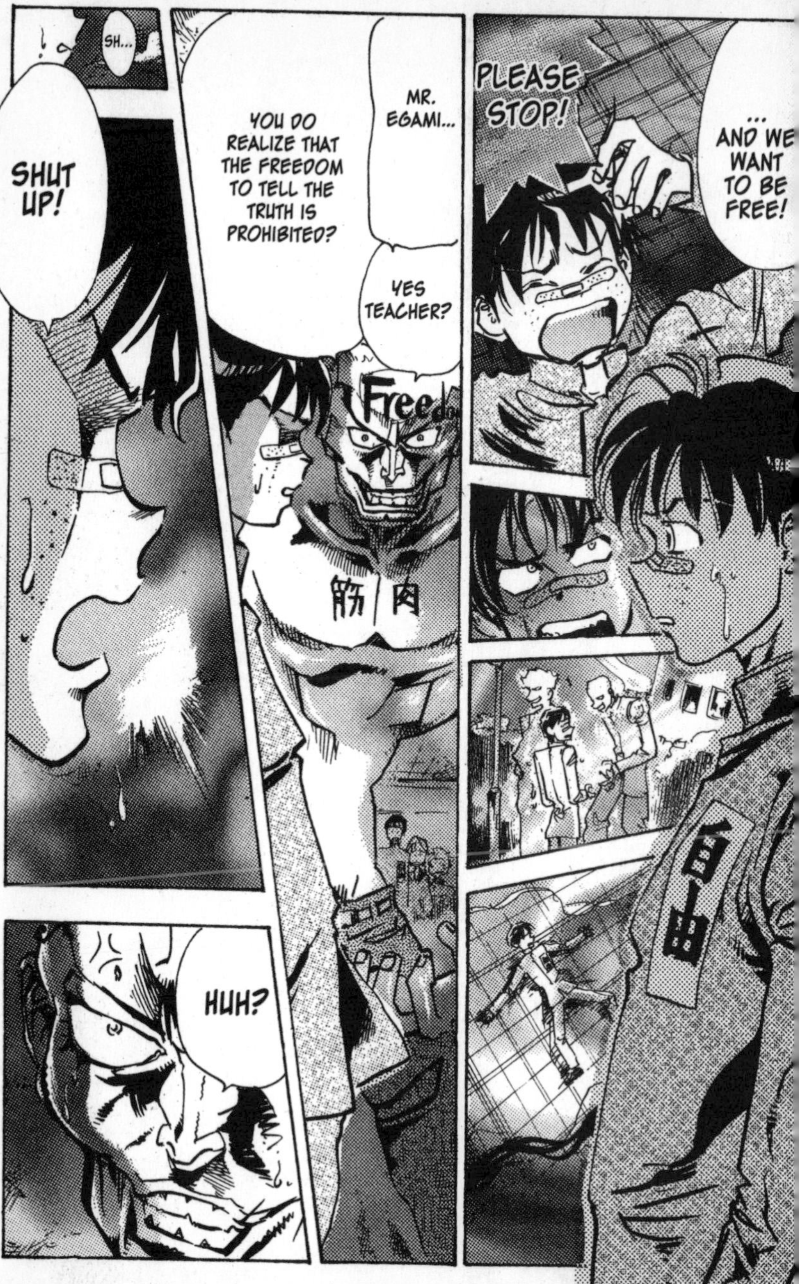

... AND WE WANT TO BE FREE!
PLEASE STOP!
自由
MR. EGAMI...
YOU DO REALIZE THAT THE FREEDOM TO TELL THE TRUTH IS PROHIBITED?
YES TEACHER?
筋肉
SH...
SHUT UP!
HUH?

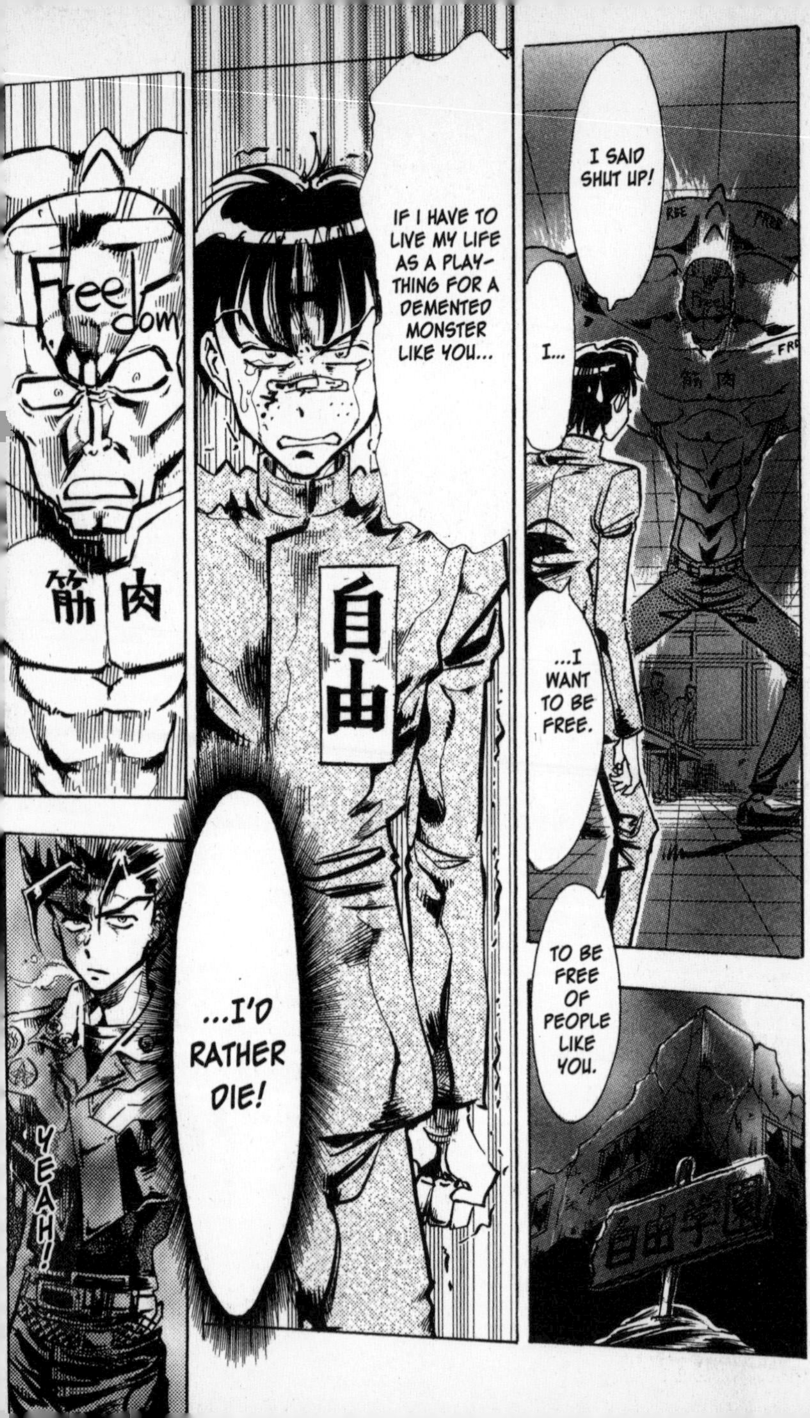
I SAID SHUT UP!
I...
...I WANT TO BE FREE.
筋肉
TO BE FREE OF PEOPLE LIKE YOU.
自由学園
IF I HAVE TO LIVE MY LIFE AS A PLAYTHING FOR A DEMENTED MONSTER LIKE YOU...
自由
...I'D RATHER DIE!
Freedom
筋肉
YEAH!

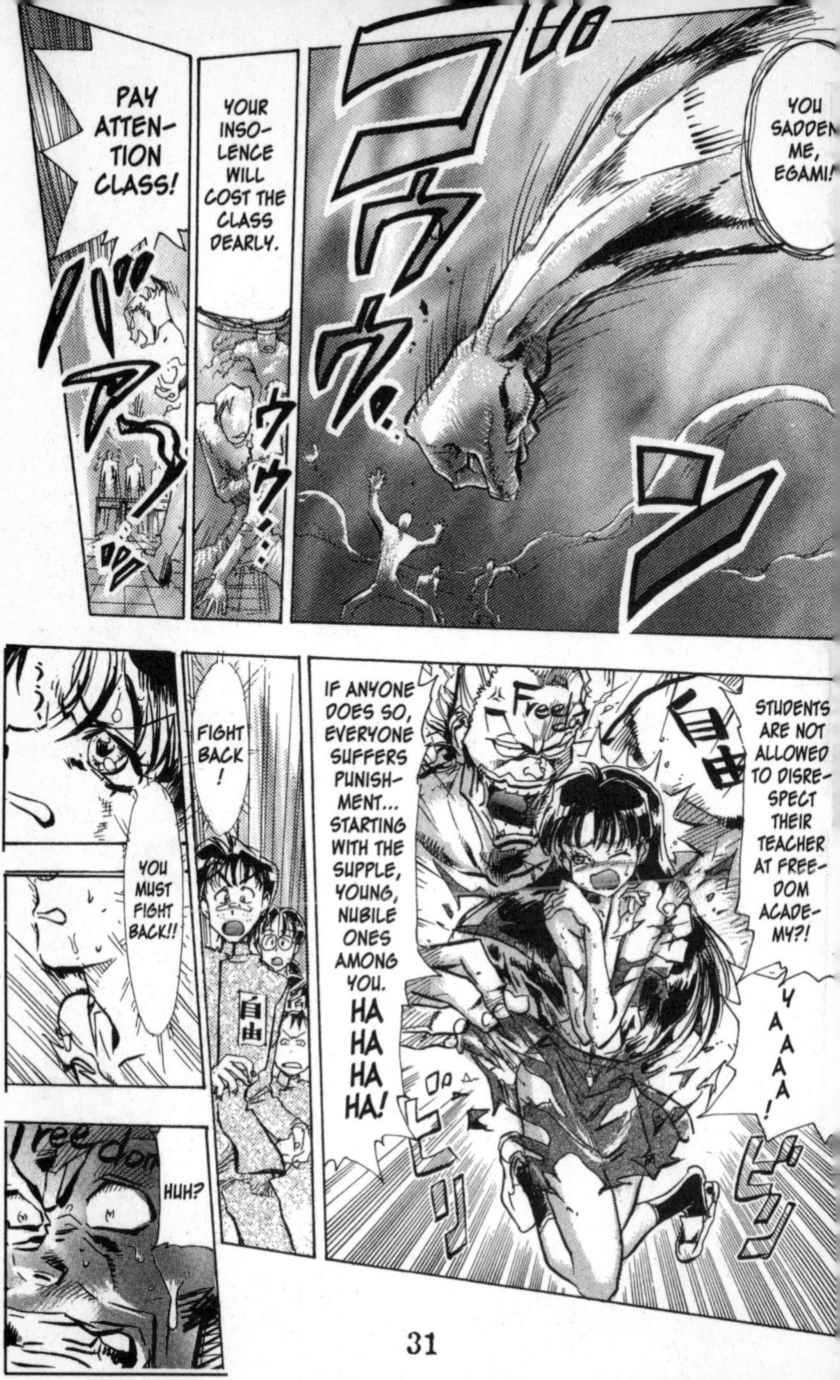
YOU SADDEN ME, EGAMI!
YOUR INSOLENCE WILL COST THE CLASS DEARLY.
PAY ATTENTION CLASS!
STUDENTS ARE NOT ALLOWED TO DISRESPECT THEIR TEACHER AT FREEDOM ACADEMY?!
IF ANYONE DOES SO, EVERYONE SUFFERS PUNISHMENT... STARTING WITH THE SUPPLE, YOUNG, NUBILE ONES AMONG YOU.
HA HA HA HA!
YAAAAA!
FIGHT BACK!
YOU MUST FIGHT BACK!!
HUH?

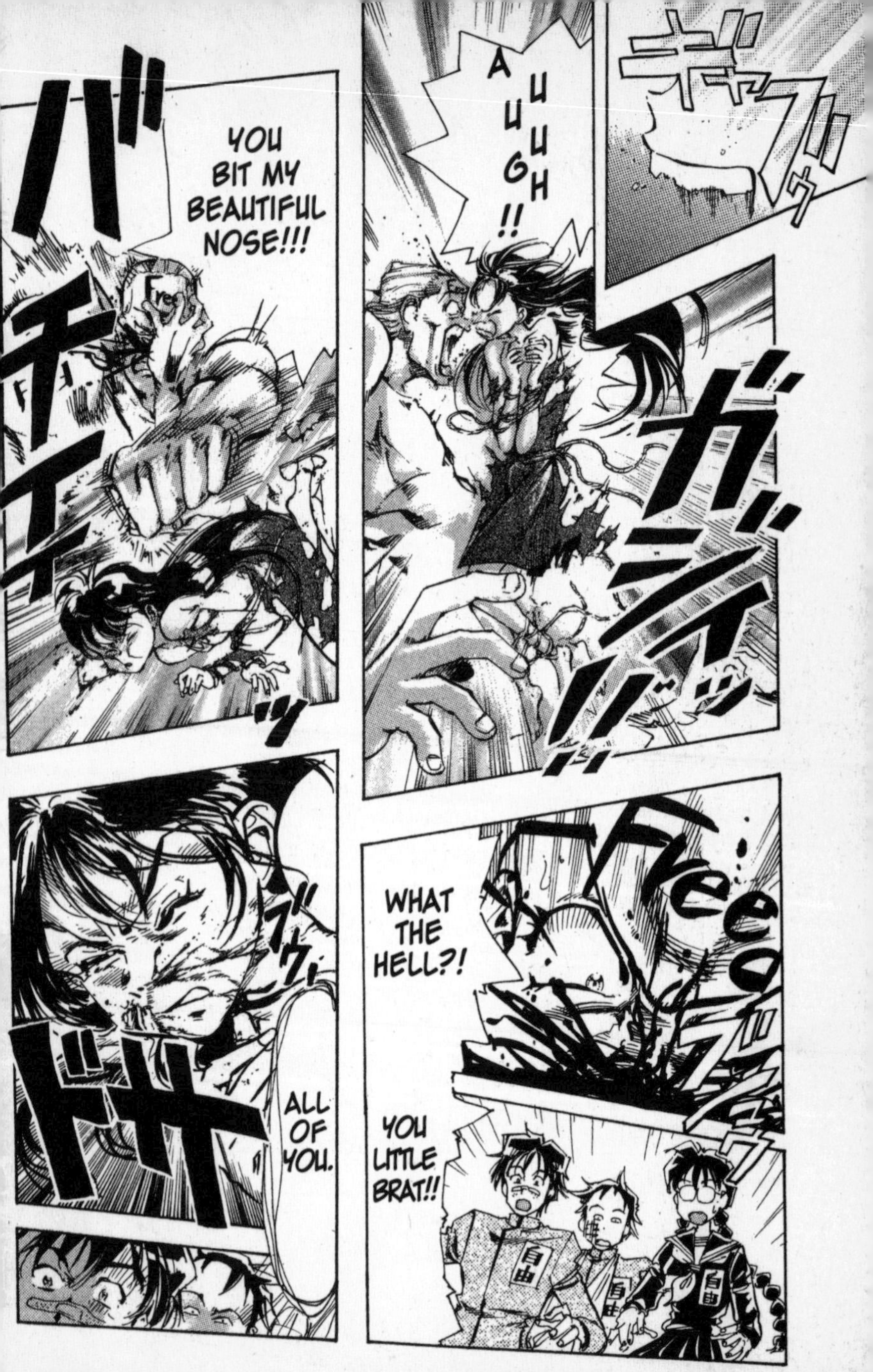
AUUUGH!!
YOU BIT MY BEAUTIFUL NOSE!!!
WHAT THE HELL?!
Free
YOU LITTLE BRAT!!
ALL OF YOU.

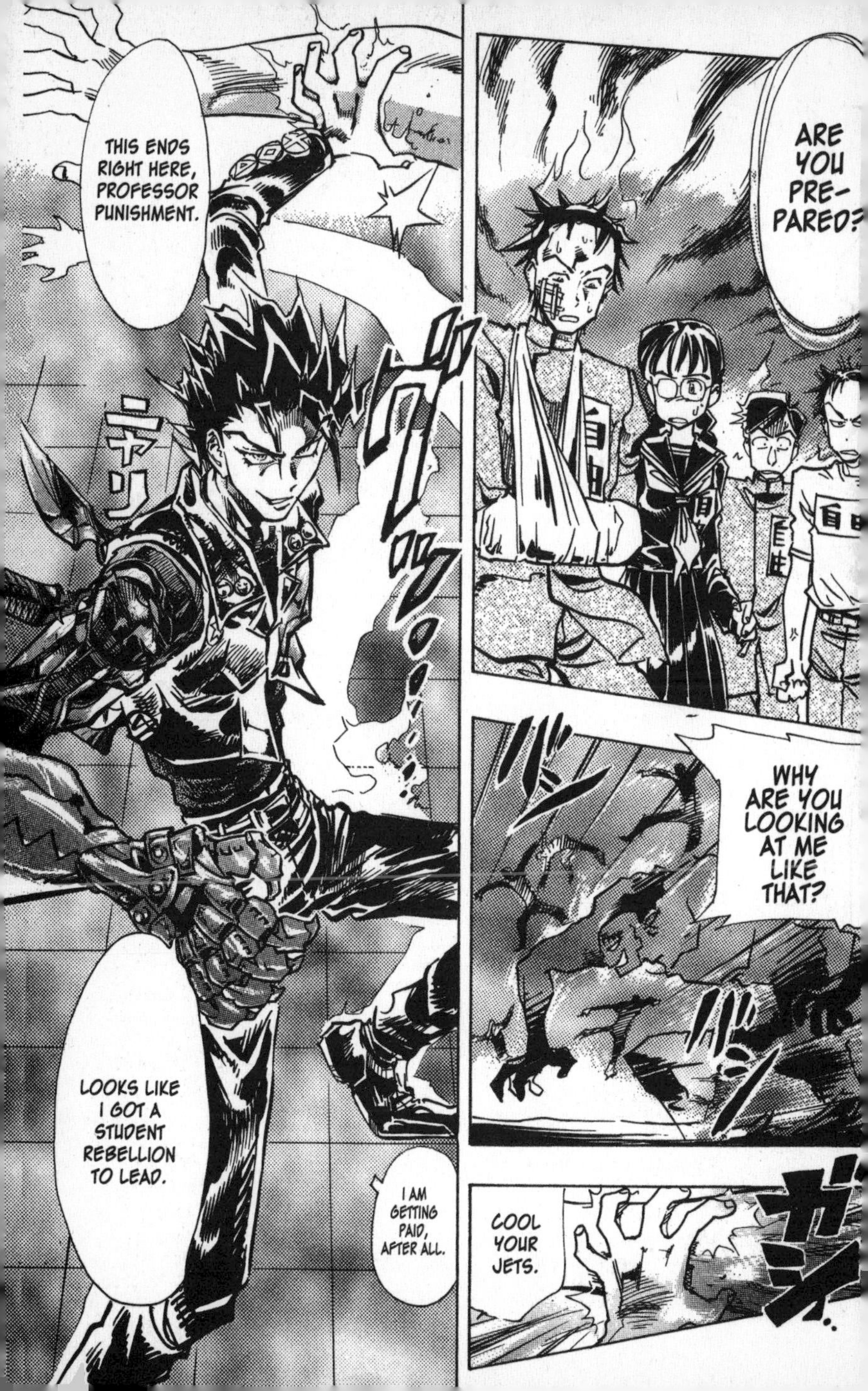
ARE YOU PRE-PARED?
WHY ARE YOU LOOKING AT ME LIKE THAT?
COOL YOUR JETS.
THIS ENDS RIGHT HERE, PROFESSOR PUNISHMENT.
ニヤリ
LOOKS LIKE I GOT A STUDENT REBELLION TO LEAD.
I AM GETTING PAID, AFTER ALL.

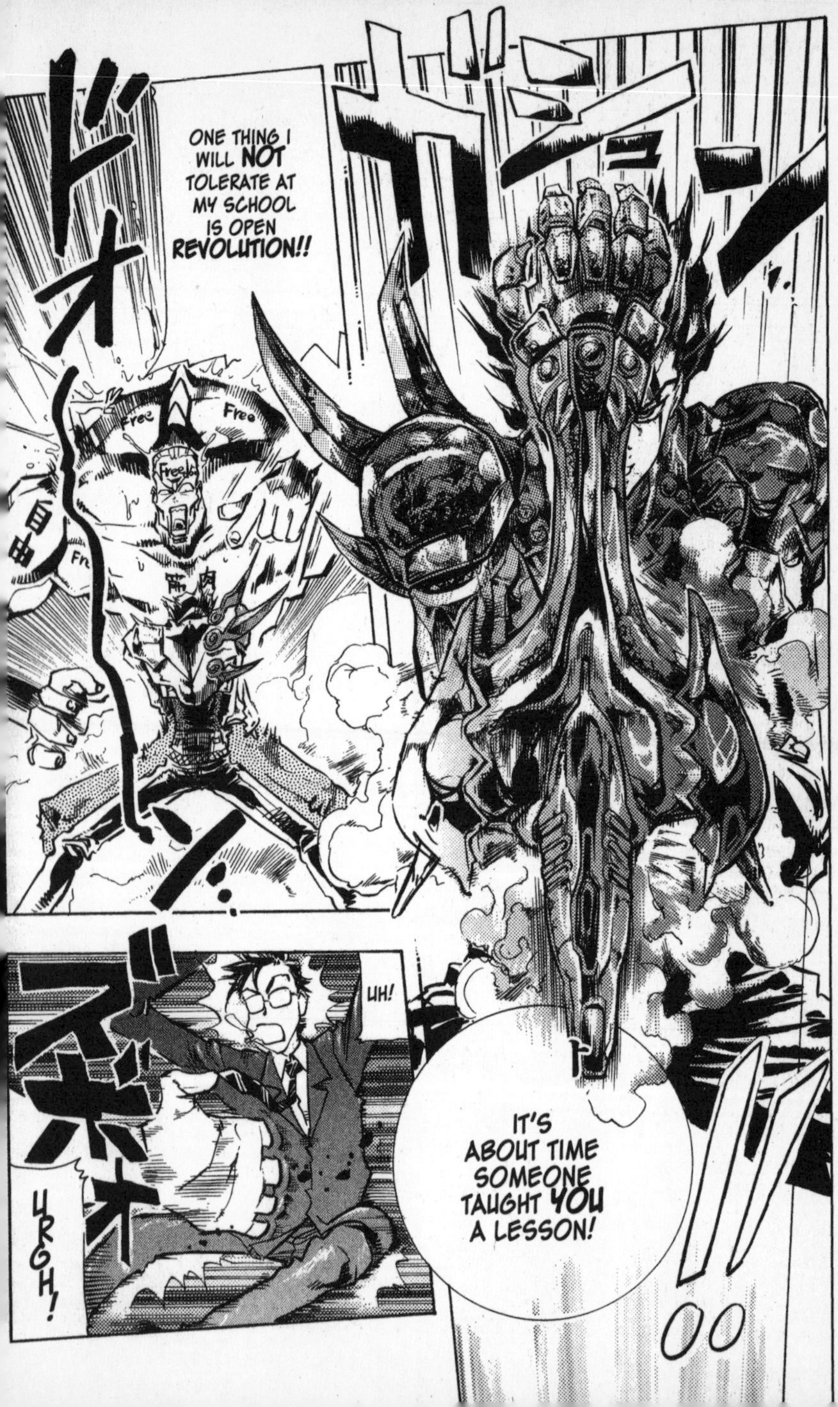
IT'S ABOUT TIME SOMEONE TAUGHT YOU A LESSON!
ONE THING I WILL NOT TOLERATE AT MY SCHOOL IS OPEN REVOLUTION!!
UH!
URGH!

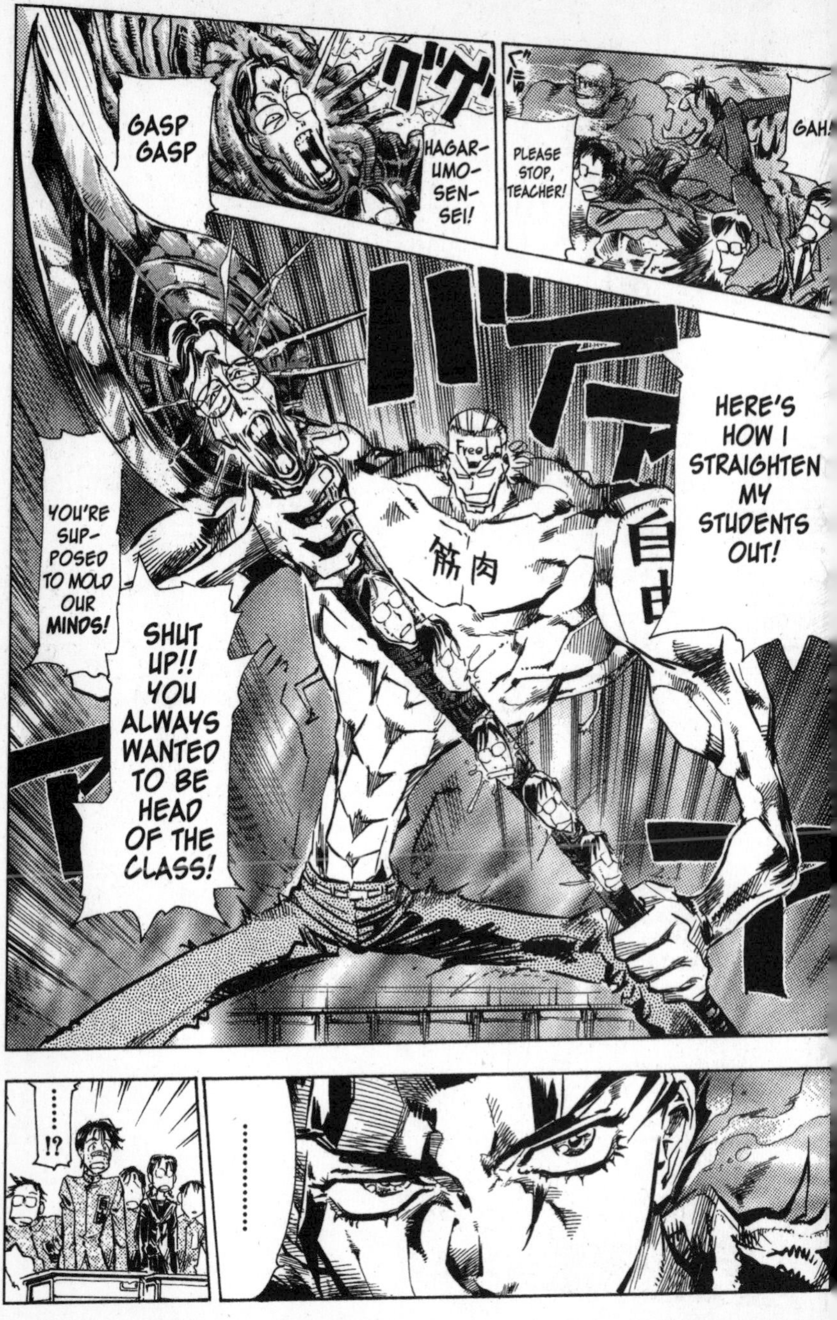

GAH!
PLEASE STOP, TEACHER!
HAGAR-UMO-SEN-SEI!
GASP GASP
HERE'S HOW I STRAIGHTEN MY STUDENTS OUT!
自由
筋肉
YOU'RE SUP-POSED TO MOLD OUR MINDS!
SHUT UP!! YOU ALWAYS WANTED TO BE HEAD OF THE CLASS!
......
......
!?

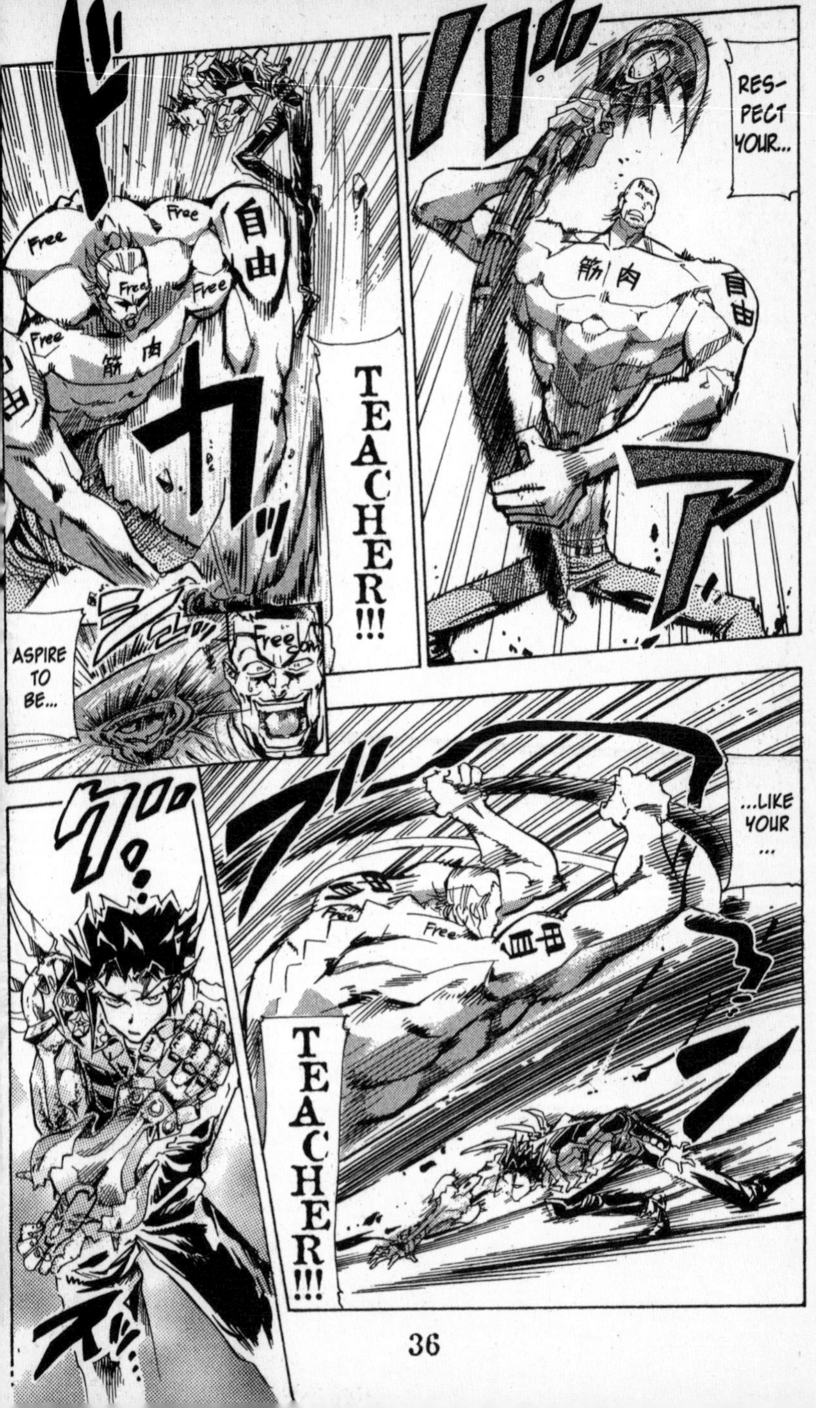
RES-PECT YOUR...
TEACHER!!!
ASPIRE TO BE...
...LIKE YOUR ...
TEACHER!!!

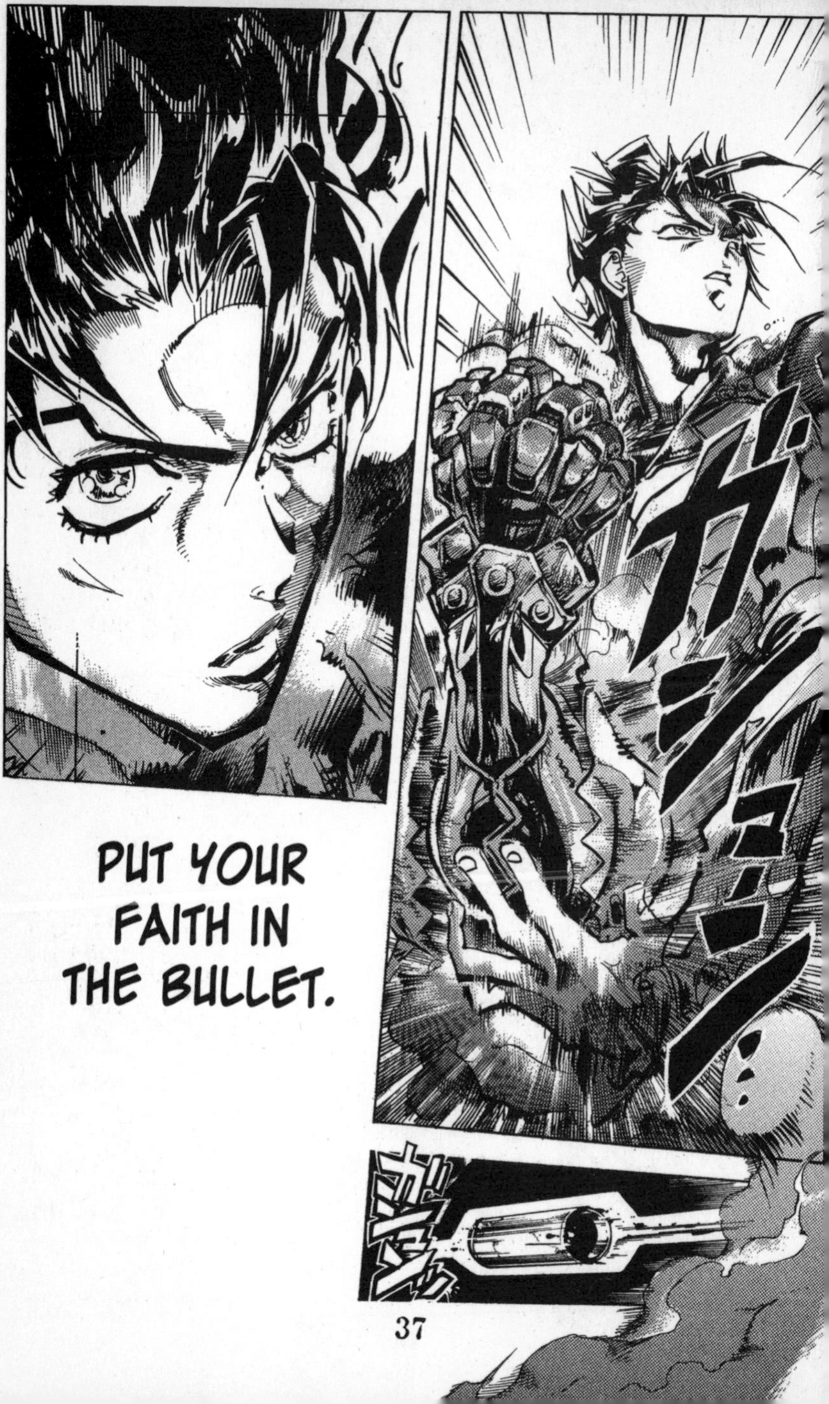
PUT YOUR FAITH IN THE BULLET.

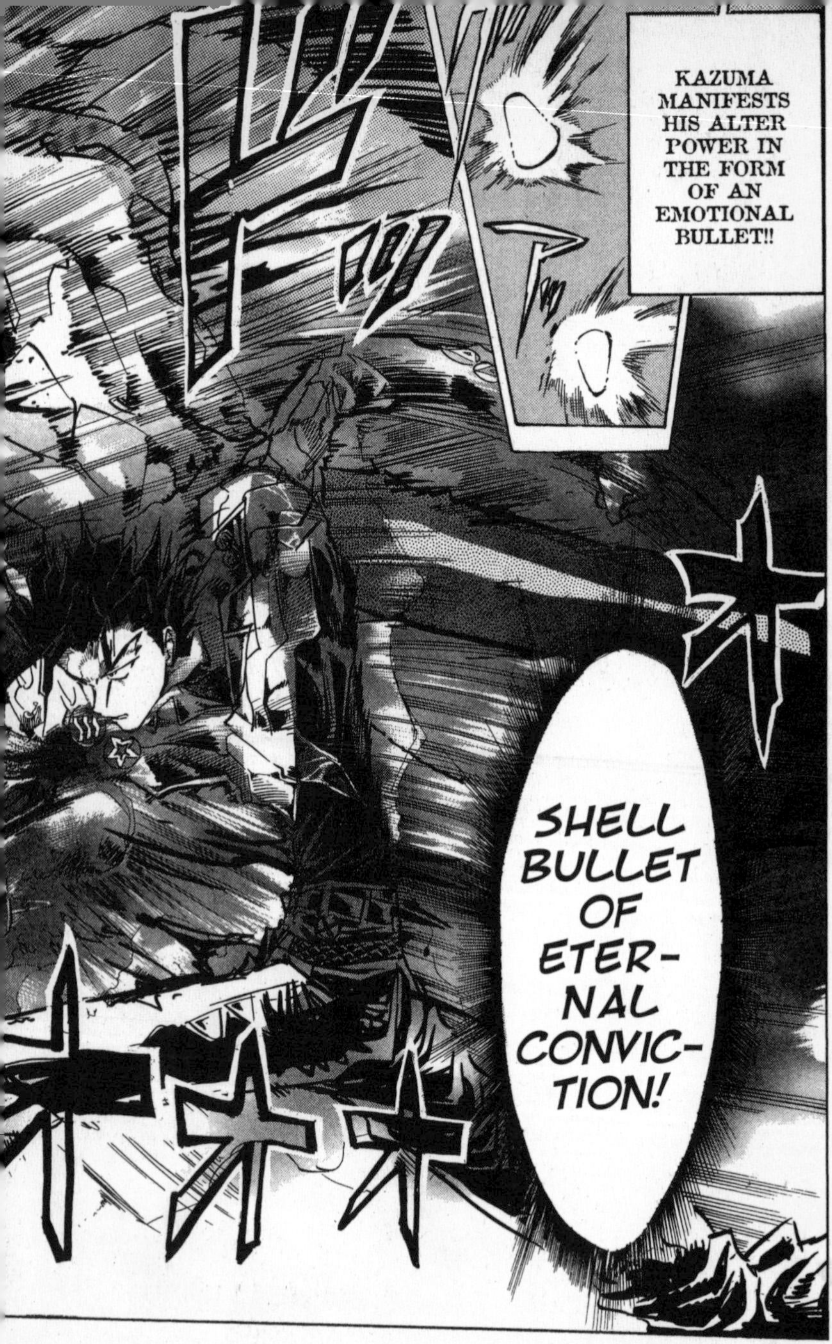
KAZUMA MANIFESTS HIS ALTER POWER IN THE FORM OF AN EMOTIONAL BULLET!!
SHELL BULLET OF ETER- NAL CONVIC- TION!

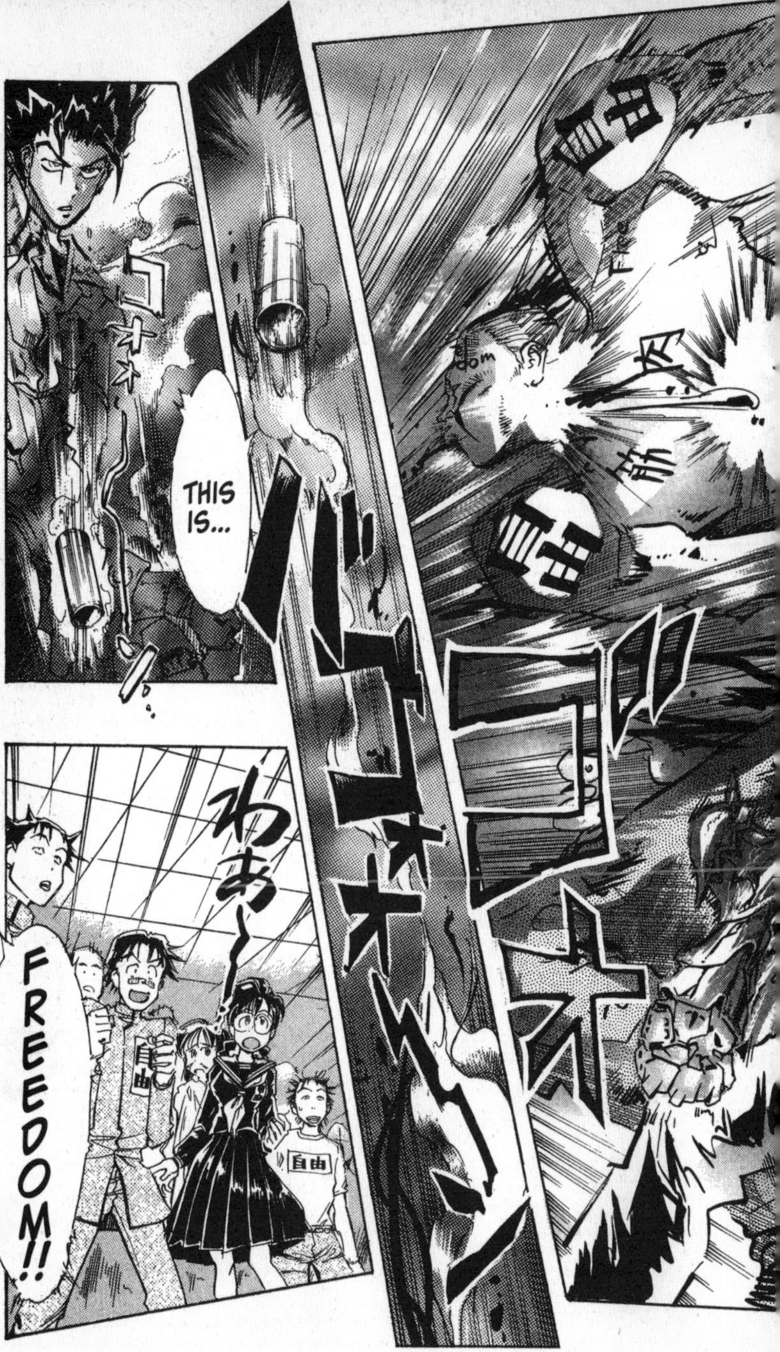
THIS IS...
わあ～
FREEDOM!!

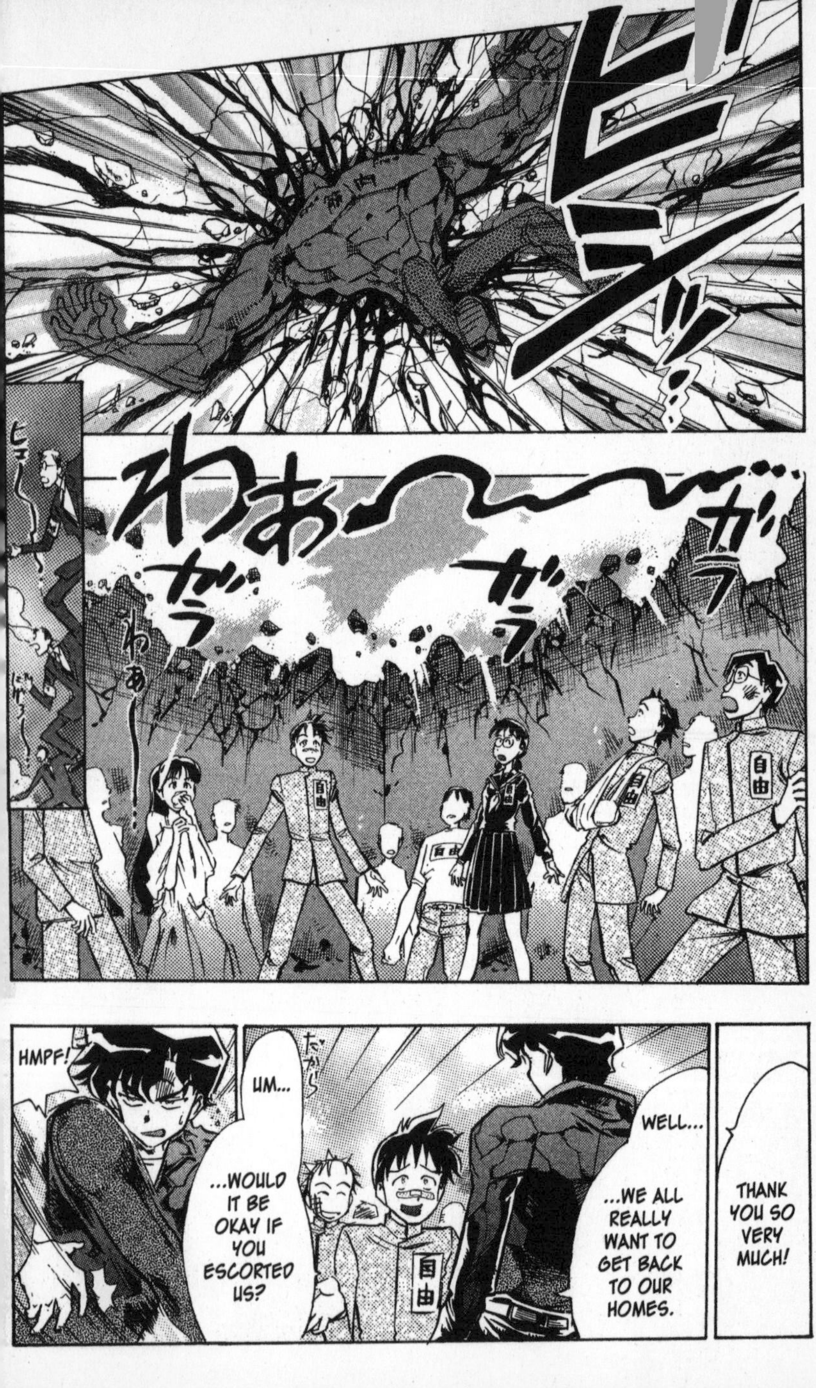
ビシッ!!
わあ〜〜〜
ガラ
ガラ
ガラ
わあ…
ヒェ〜〜…
にげろ〜…
THANK YOU SO VERY MUCH!
WELL...
...WE ALL REALLY WANT TO GET BACK TO OUR HOMES.
だから
UM...
...WOULD IT BE OKAY IF YOU ESCORTED US?
HMPF!

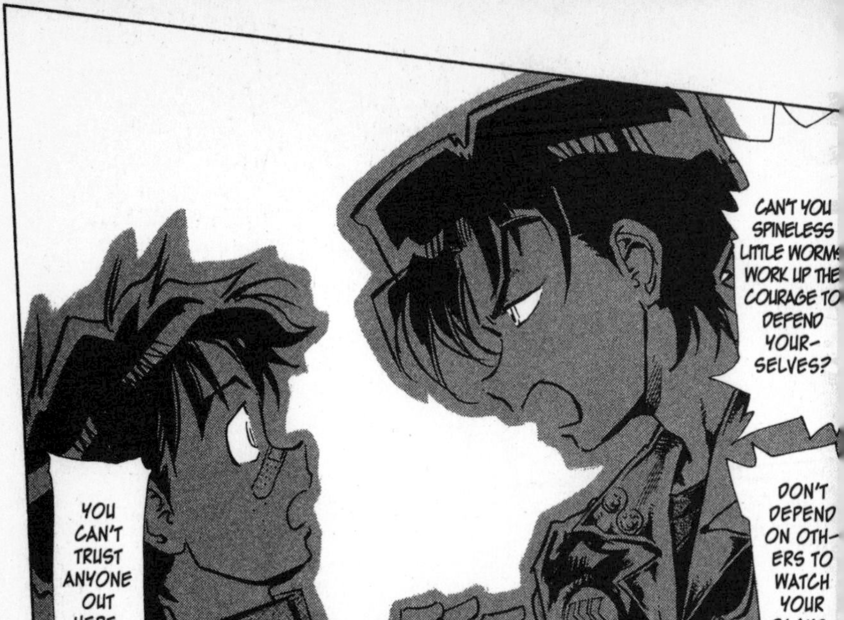
CAN'T YOU SPINELESS LITTLE WORMS WORK UP THE COURAGE TO DEFEND YOUR-SELVES?
DON'T DEPEND ON OTH-ERS TO WATCH YOUR BACKS, 'CAUSE THEY WON'T.
YOU CAN'T TRUST ANYONE OUT HERE.
THAT'S WHAT LANDED YOUR SORRY ASSES HERE TO BEGIN WITH!

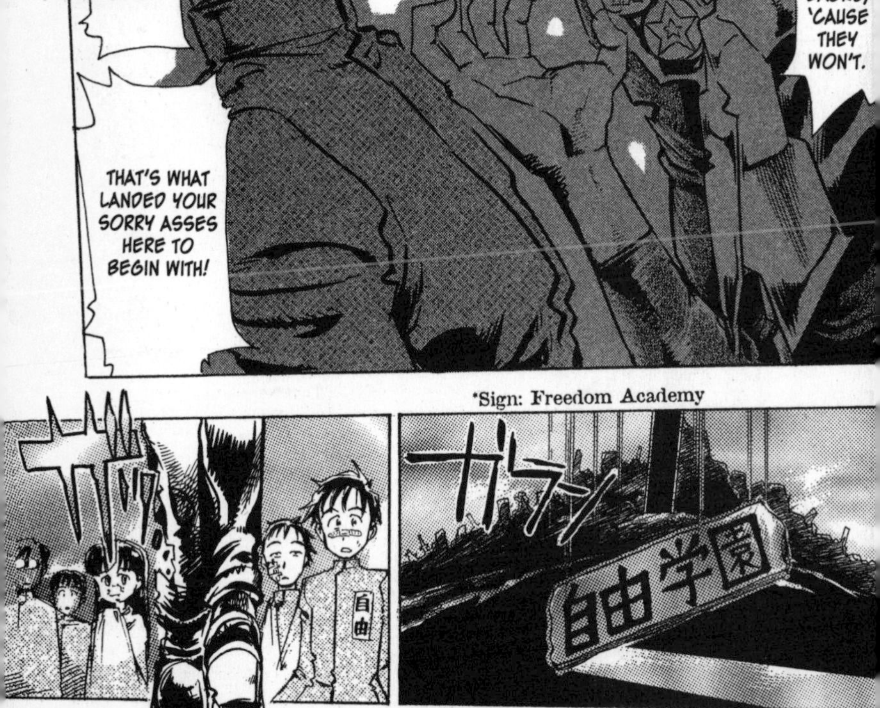
自由学園
自由

*Sign: Freedom Academy

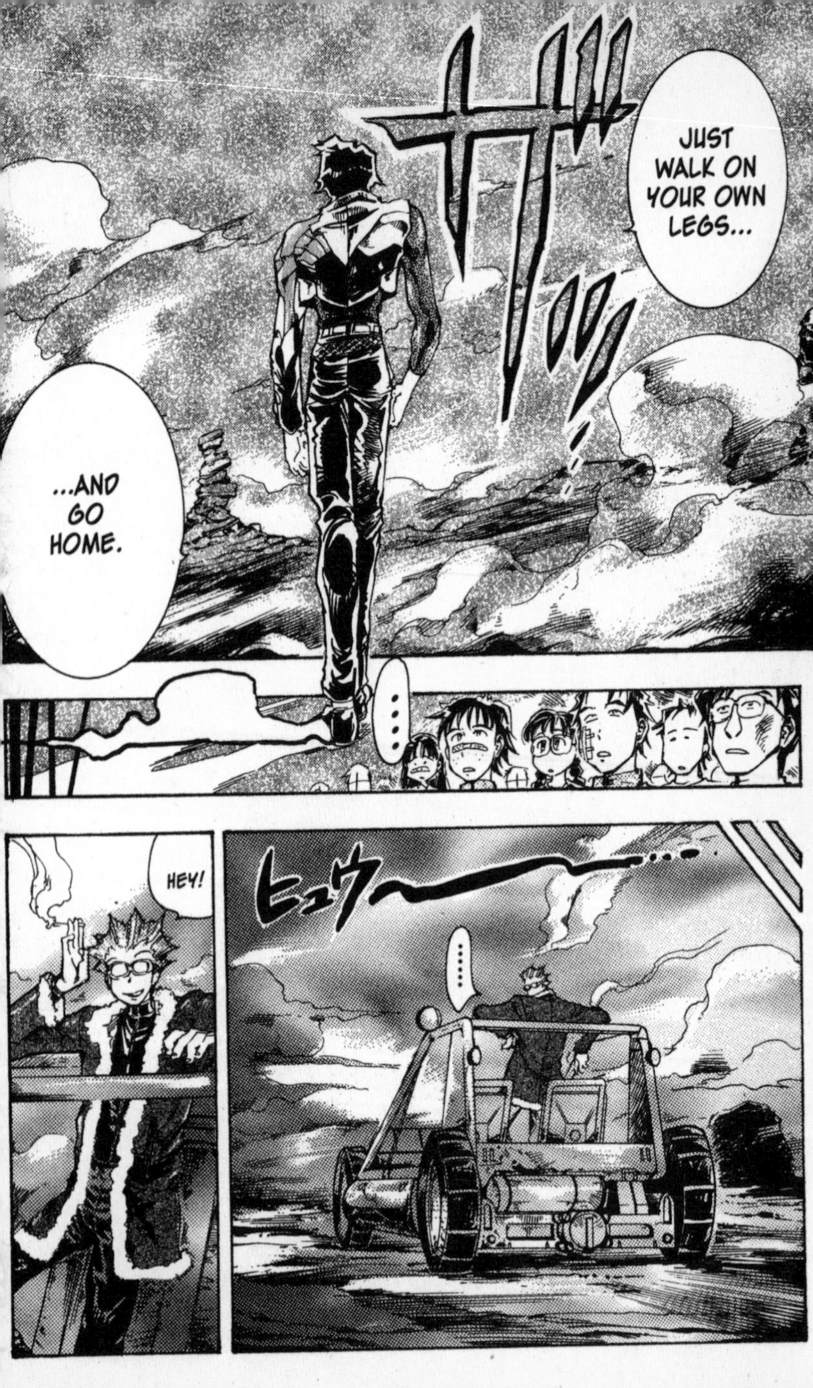
JUST WALK ON YOUR OWN LEGS...
ザッ
...AND GO HOME.
....
ヒュウ~
.....
HEY!

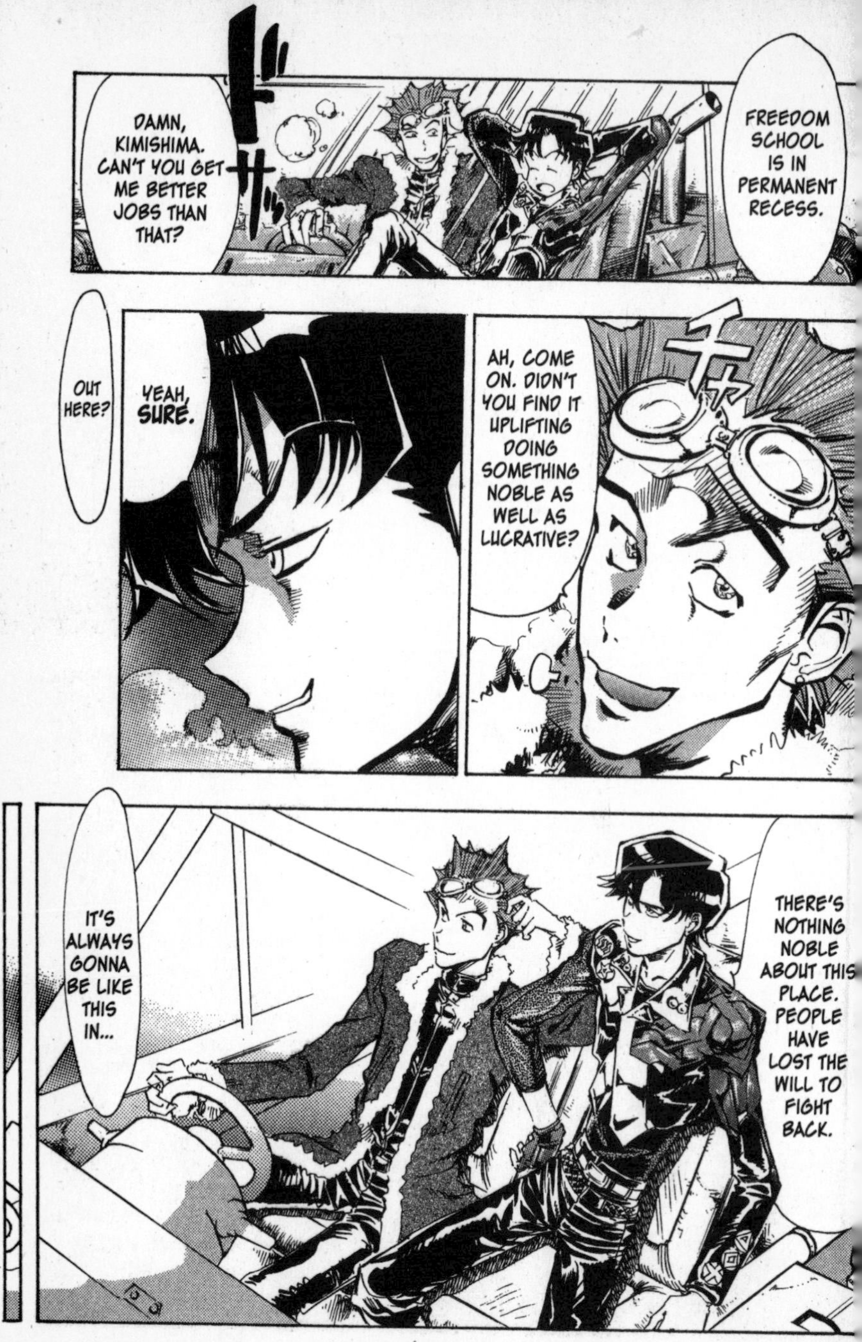
FREEDOM SCHOOL IS IN PERMANENT RECESS.
DAMN, KIMISHIMA. CAN'T YOU GET ME BETTER JOBS THAN THAT?
AH, COME ON. DIDN'T YOU FIND IT UPLIFTING DOING SOMETHING NOBLE AS WELL AS LUCRATIVE?
YEAH, SURE.
OUT HERE?
THERE'S NOTHING NOBLE ABOUT THIS PLACE. PEOPLE HAVE LOST THE WILL TO FIGHT BACK.
IT'S ALWAYS GONNA BE LIKE THIS IN...

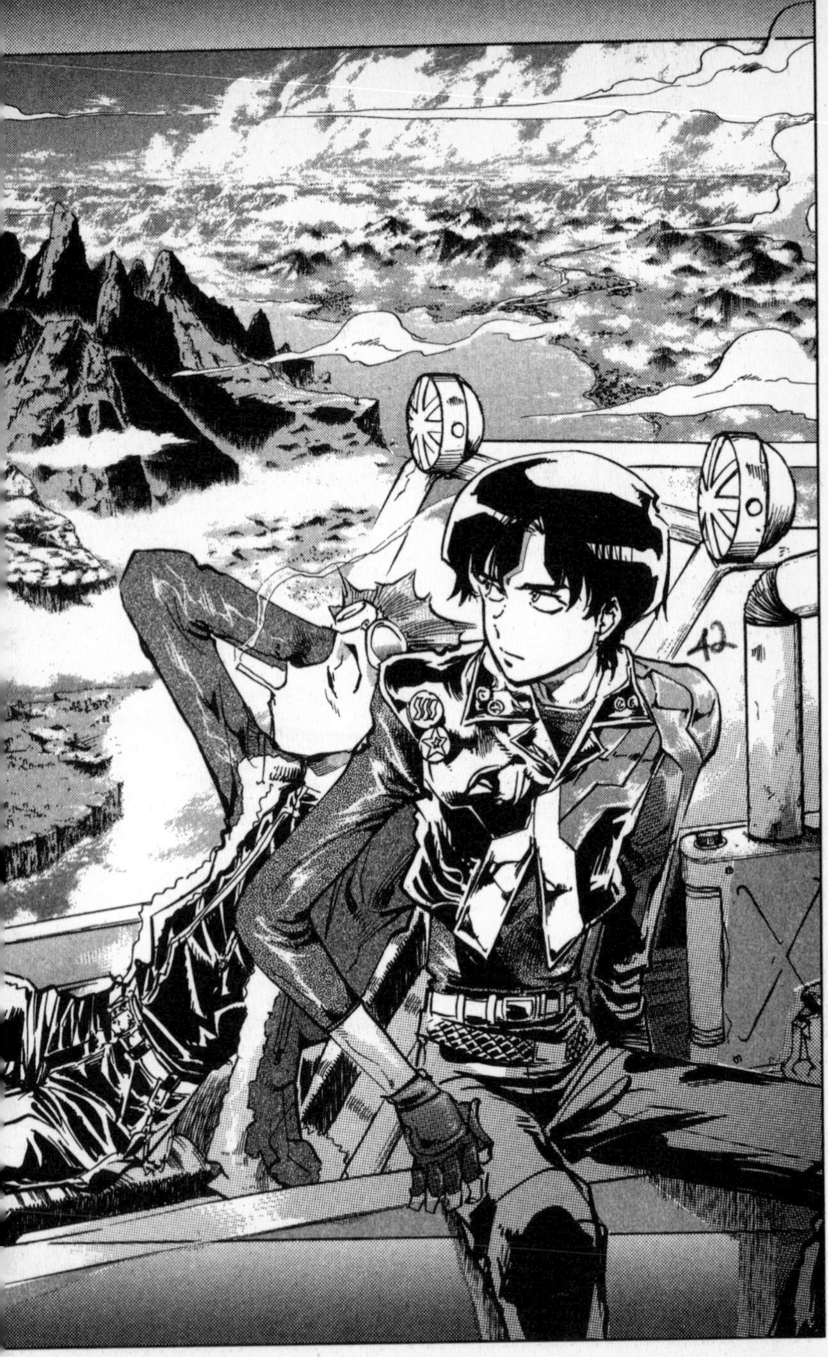
42

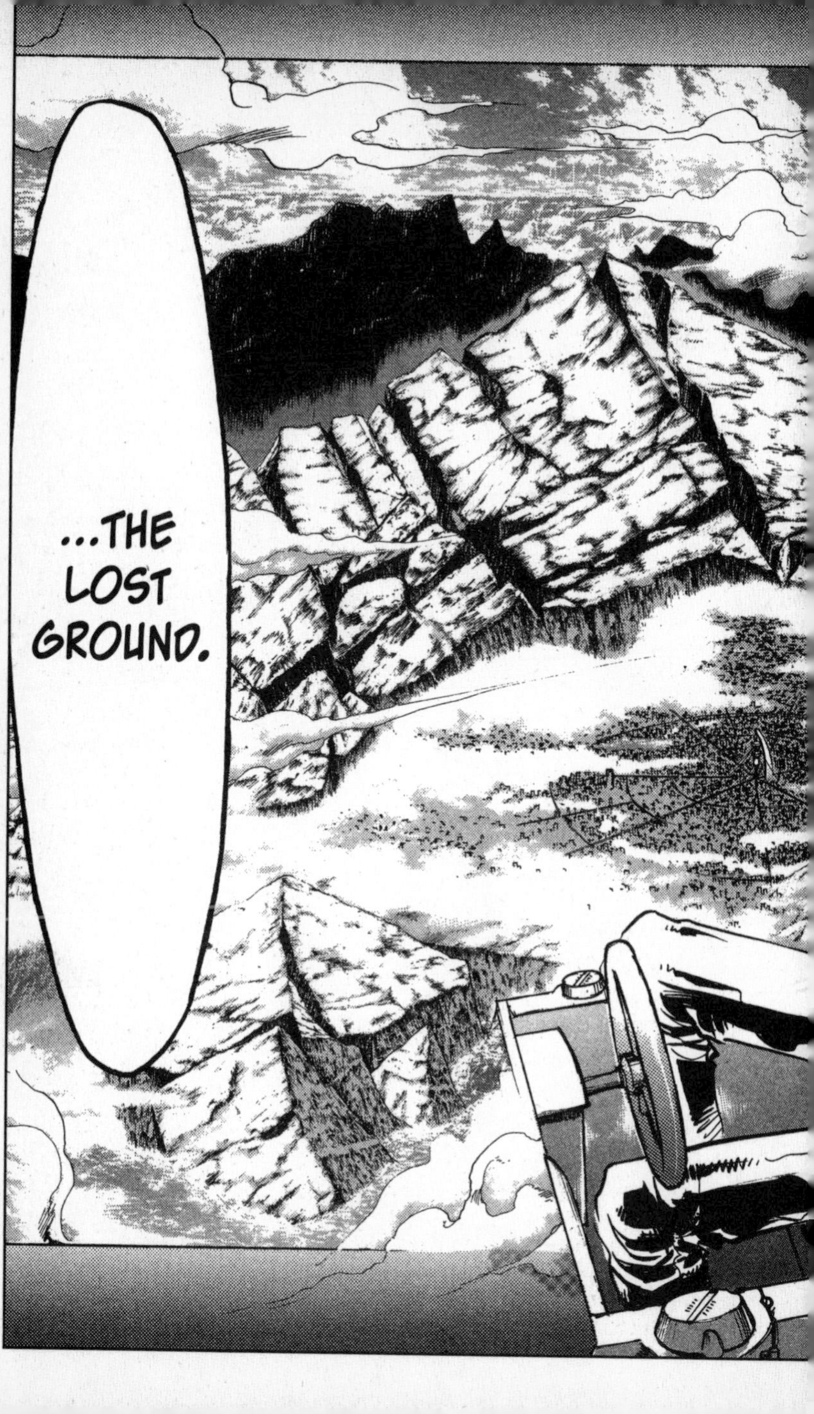
...THE LOST GROUND.

22 years ago, an unknown force caused a 30 km radius area around Yokohama to thrust into the sky, separating the metropolis and its suburbs geographically, politically and socially from the Japanese mainland. This area became known as the Lost Ground. Today, the seeds of a new civilization have sprouted through the ruins of the old. One tenth of the Lost Ground land mass has been developed into fledgling cities, the people there desperate to rekindle the way of life they lost decades ago. However, most of the Lost Ground remains a desolate wasteland, a chaotic dust bowl of poverty and crime. Kazuma and crew live in this wasteland.

Alter

Mysteriously, after the seismic phenomenon that created the Lost Ground, a fraction of the newly born children developed an inexplicable ability, the ability to alter matter at the atomic level - the ability to breakdown and reconstruct the physical substance of the universe at will - hence the term that came to signify this power: Alter. Those with the power came to be known as Alter Users. The way Alters manifest in Alter Users is directly related to the personality and desires of the possessor. Unfortunately, many Alter Users use their powers to pillage and destroy, preventing the complete restoration of the Lost Ground.

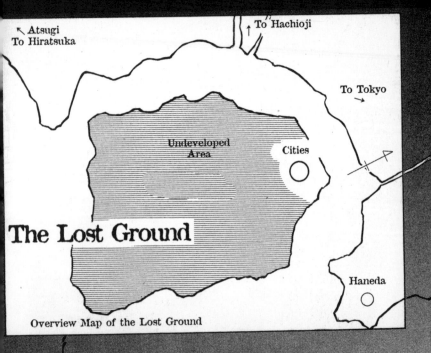

↖ Atsugi
To Hiratsuka

↑ To Hachioji

To Tokyo →

Undeveloped Area

Cities

The Lost Ground

Haneda

Overview Map of the Lost Ground

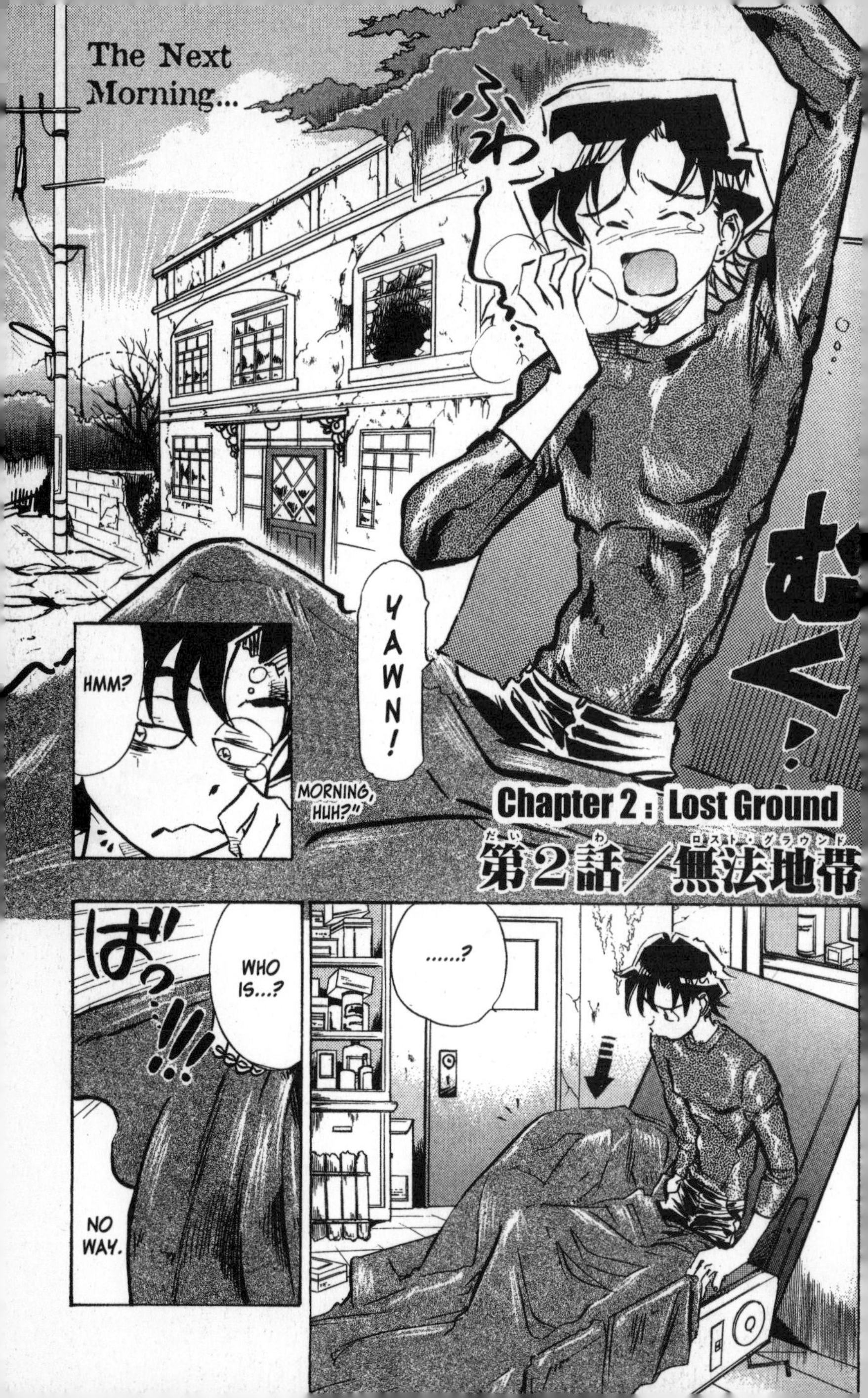
ふわ～…
むく！
The Next Morning...
YAWN!
Chapter 2 : Lost Ground
第2話／無法地帯
HMM?
MORNING, HUH?"
......?
ばっ!!!
WHO IS...?
NO WAY.

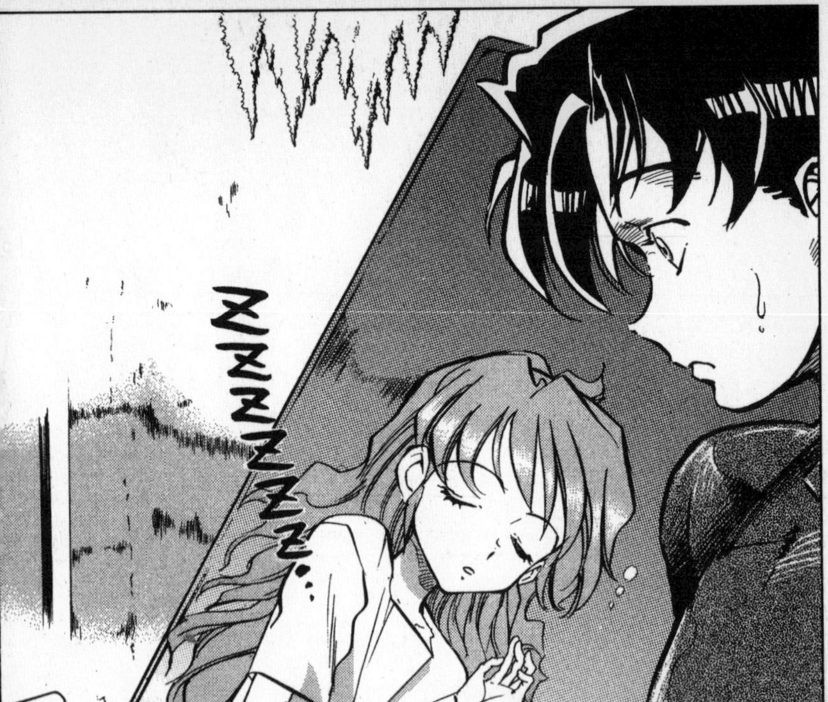
……
ZZZZZZZ
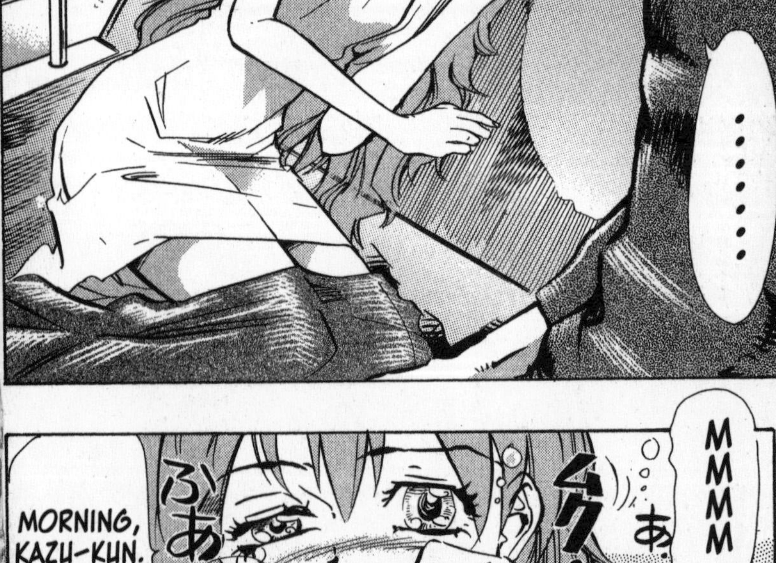
MMMM
ムク…
あ…
ふあ…
MORNING, KAZU-KUN.

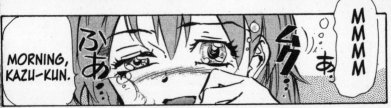

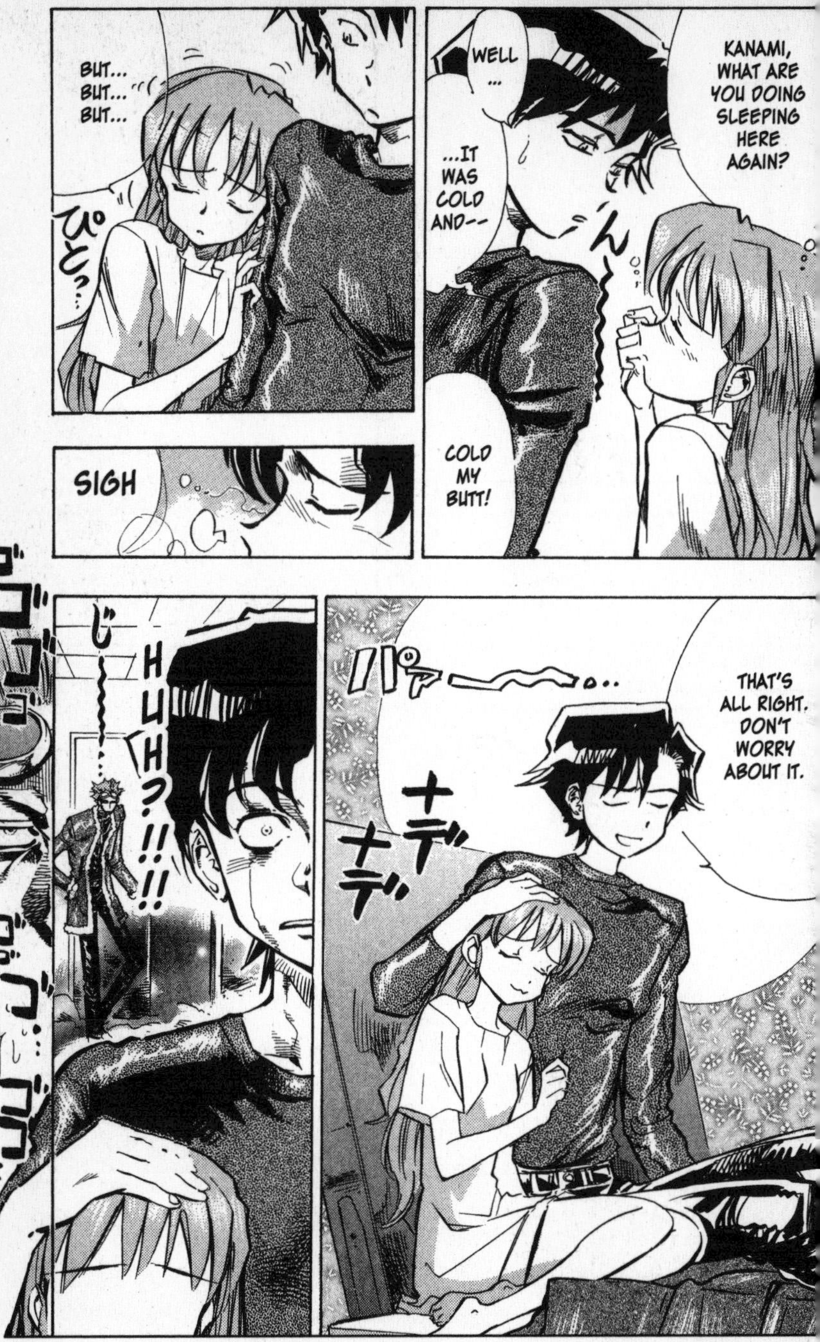
KANAMI, WHAT ARE YOU DOING SLEEPING HERE AGAIN?
WELL ...
...IT WAS COLD AND--
んー
COLD MY BUTT!
BUT... BUT... BUT...
ぴとっ...
SIGH
パァーーー..
THAT'S ALL RIGHT. DON'T WORRY ABOUT IT.
ナデ
ナデ
HUH?!!!!
じーーー...
ゴゴゴ

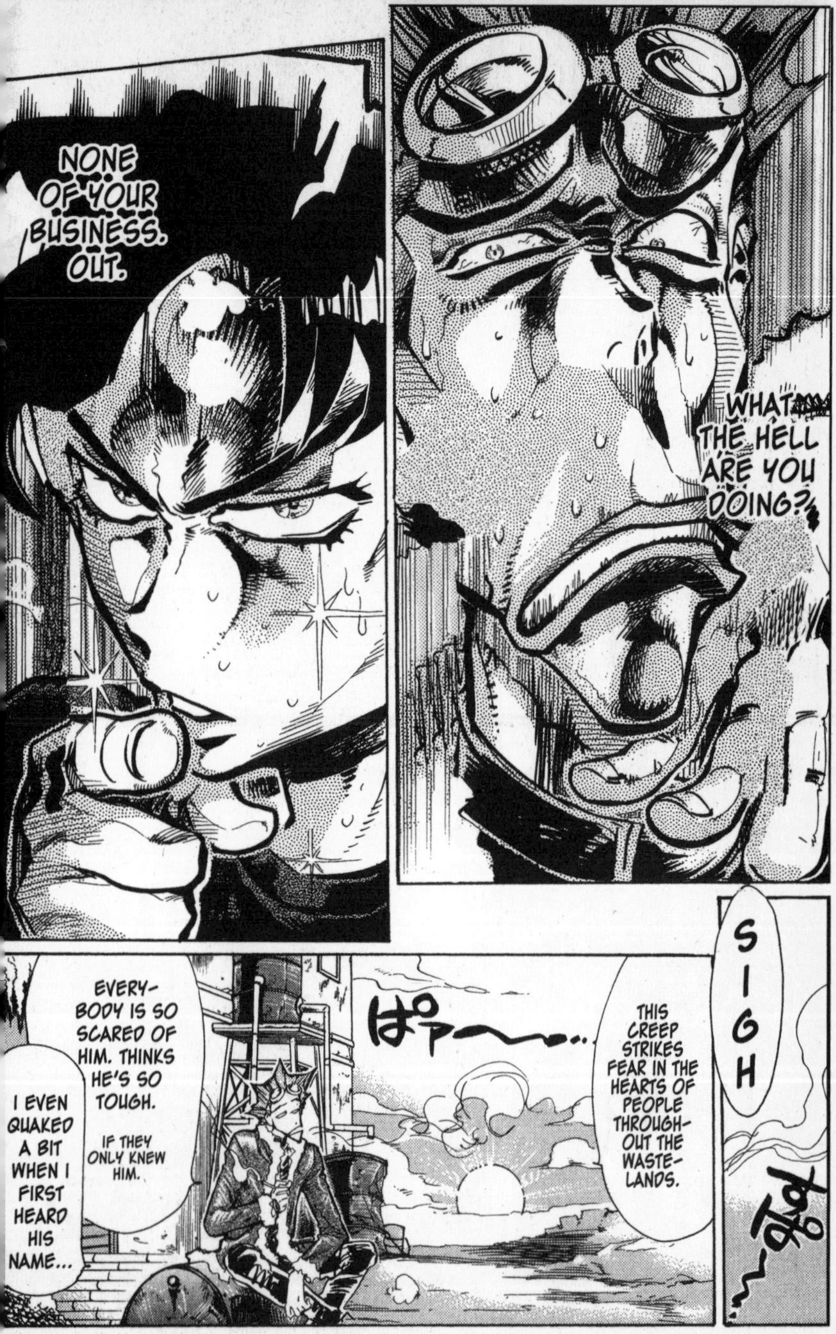
WHAT THE HELL ARE YOU DOING?
NONE OF YOUR BUSINESS. OUT.
SIGH
THIS CREEP STRIKES FEAR IN THE HEARTS OF PEOPLE THROUGHOUT THE WASTELANDS.
ぱァ〜〜...
EVERYBODY IS SO SCARED OF HIM. THINKS HE'S SO TOUGH.
IF THEY ONLY KNEW HIM.
I EVEN QUAKED A BIT WHEN I FIRST HEARD HIS NAME...

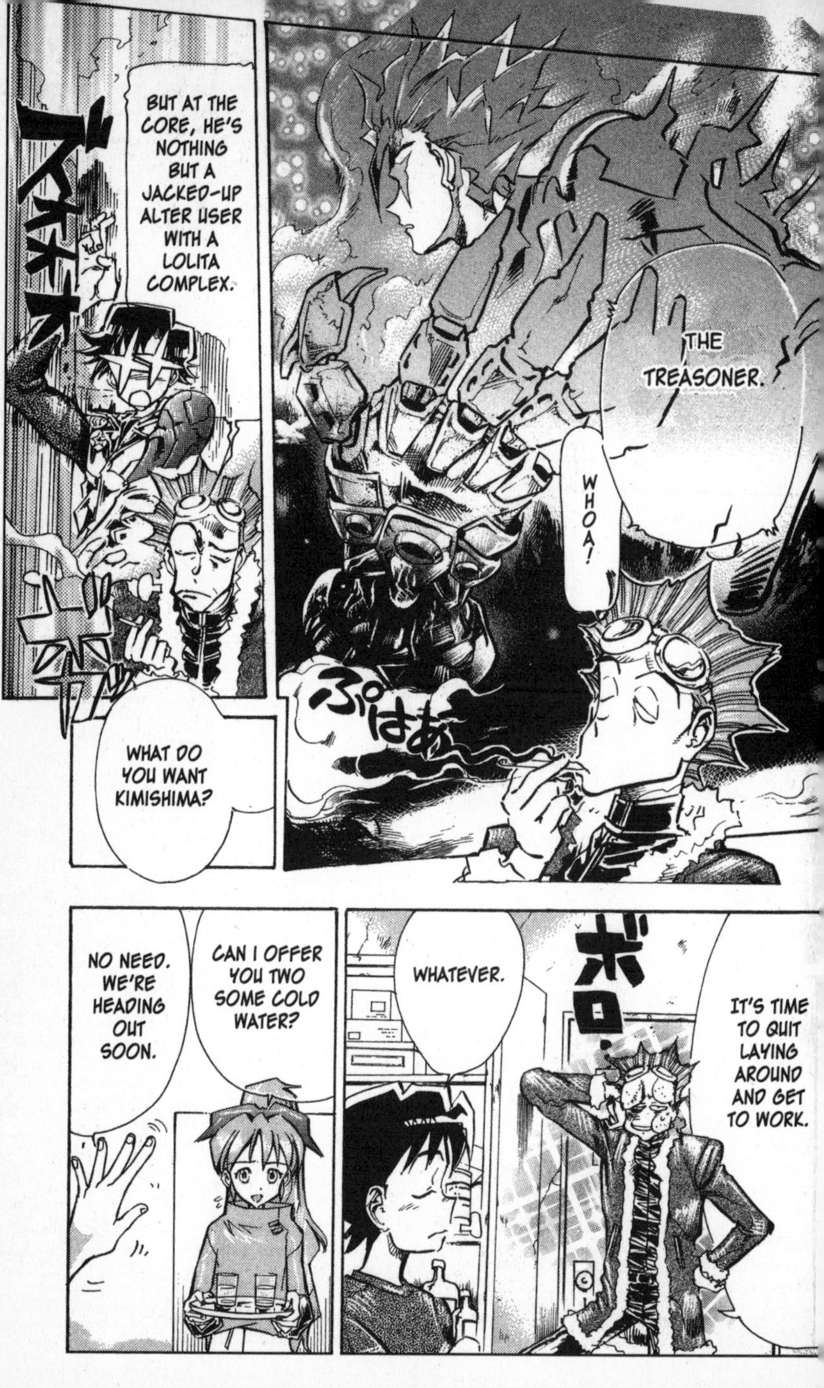
THE TREASONER.
WHOA!
ぷはあ
BUT AT THE CORE, HE'S NOTHING BUT A JACKED-UP ALTER USER WITH A LOLITA COMPLEX.
WHAT DO YOU WANT KIMISHIMA?
IT'S TIME TO QUIT LAYING AROUND AND GET TO WORK.
ボロ
WHATEVER.
CAN I OFFER YOU TWO SOME COLD WATER?
NO NEED. WE'RE HEADING OUT SOON.

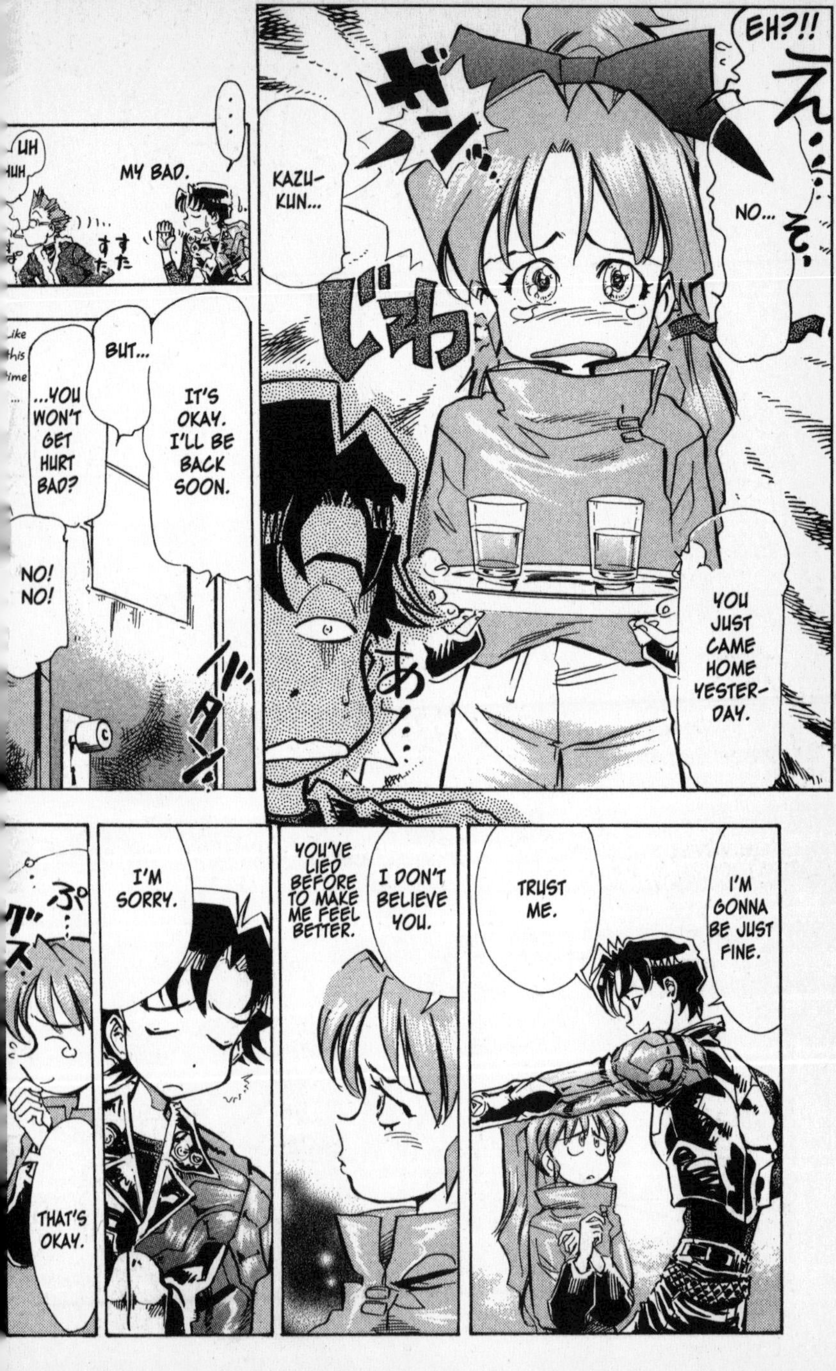
EH?!!
NO...
KAZU-KUN...
じわ
YOU JUST CAME HOME YESTERDAY.
あ...
...
MY BAD.
UH HUH
すたすた
IT'S OKAY. I'LL BE BACK SOON.
BUT...
...YOU WON'T GET HURT BAD?
NO! NO!
Like this time...
I'M GONNA BE JUST FINE.
TRUST ME.
I DON'T BELIEVE YOU.
YOU'VE LIED BEFORE TO MAKE ME FEEL BETTER.
I'M SORRY.
ぷ...
THAT'S OKAY.

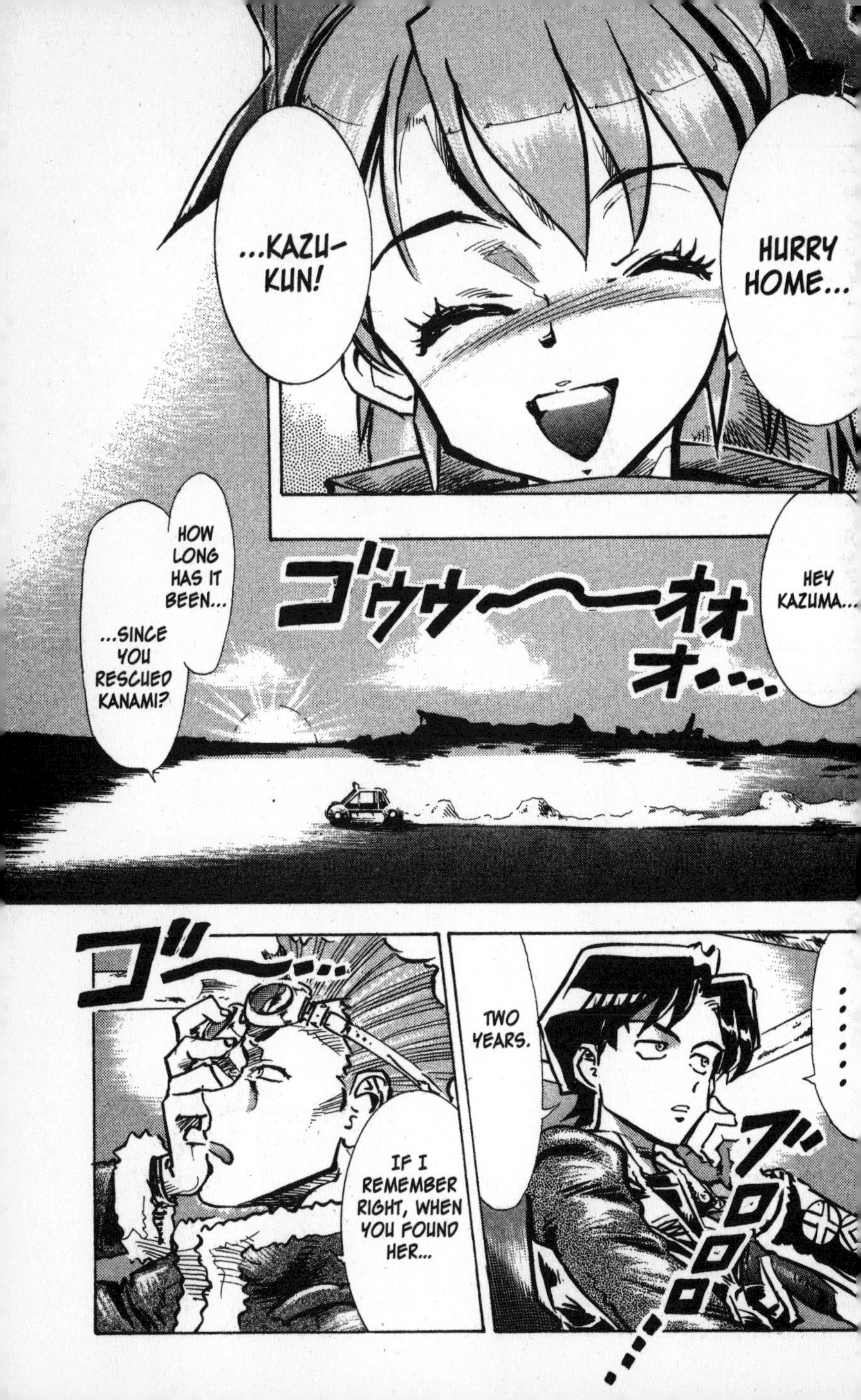
HURRY HOME...
...KAZU-KUN!
HEY KAZUMA...
ゴウウ〜〜オオオー…
HOW LONG HAS IT BEEN...
...SINCE YOU RESCUED KANAMI?
......
TWO YEARS.
ブロロロロ…
ゴー…
IF I REMEMBER RIGHT, WHEN YOU FOUND HER...

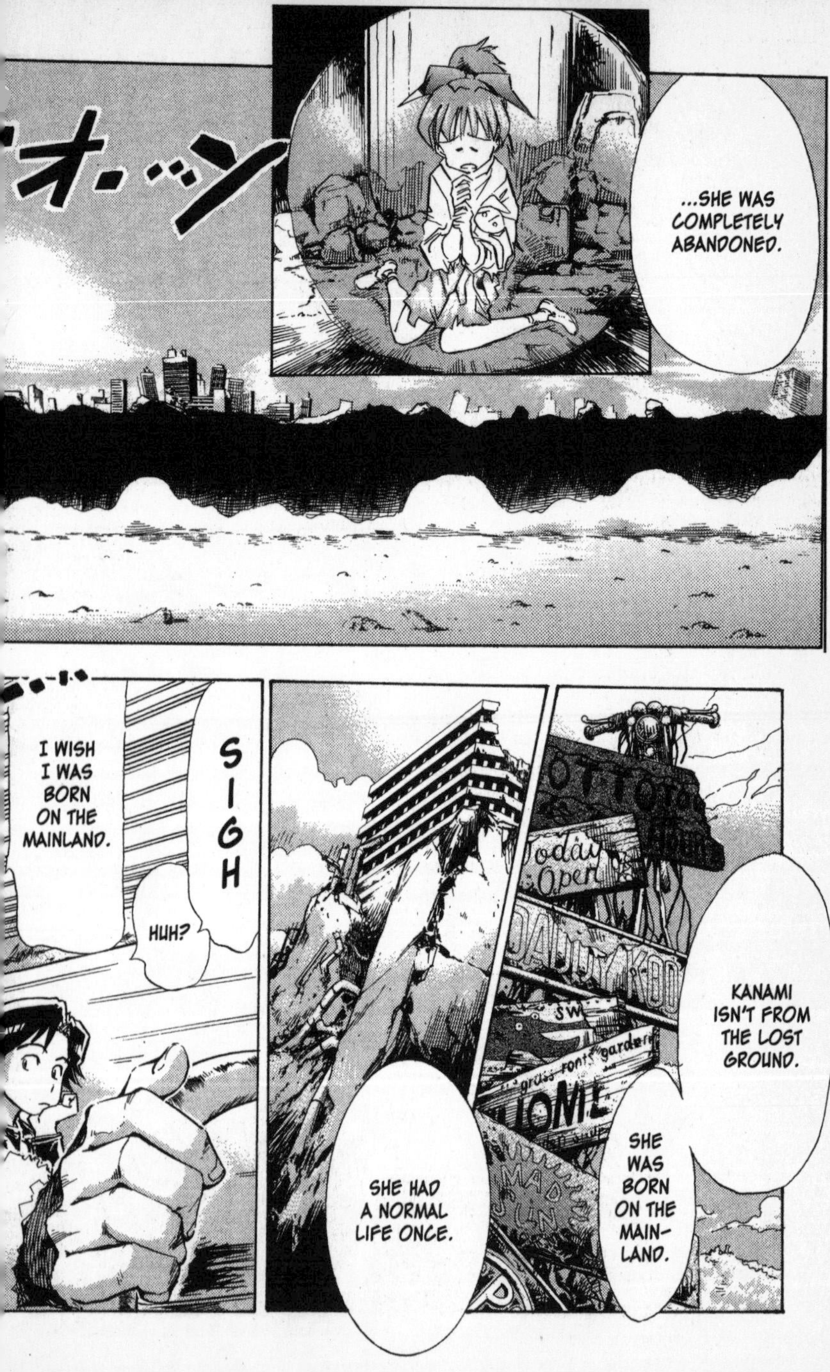
...SHE WAS COMPLETELY ABANDONED.
KANAMI ISN'T FROM THE LOST GROUND.
SHE WAS BORN ON THE MAIN-LAND.
SHE HAD A NORMAL LIFE ONCE.
SIGH
I WISH I WAS BORN ON THE MAINLAND.
HUH?

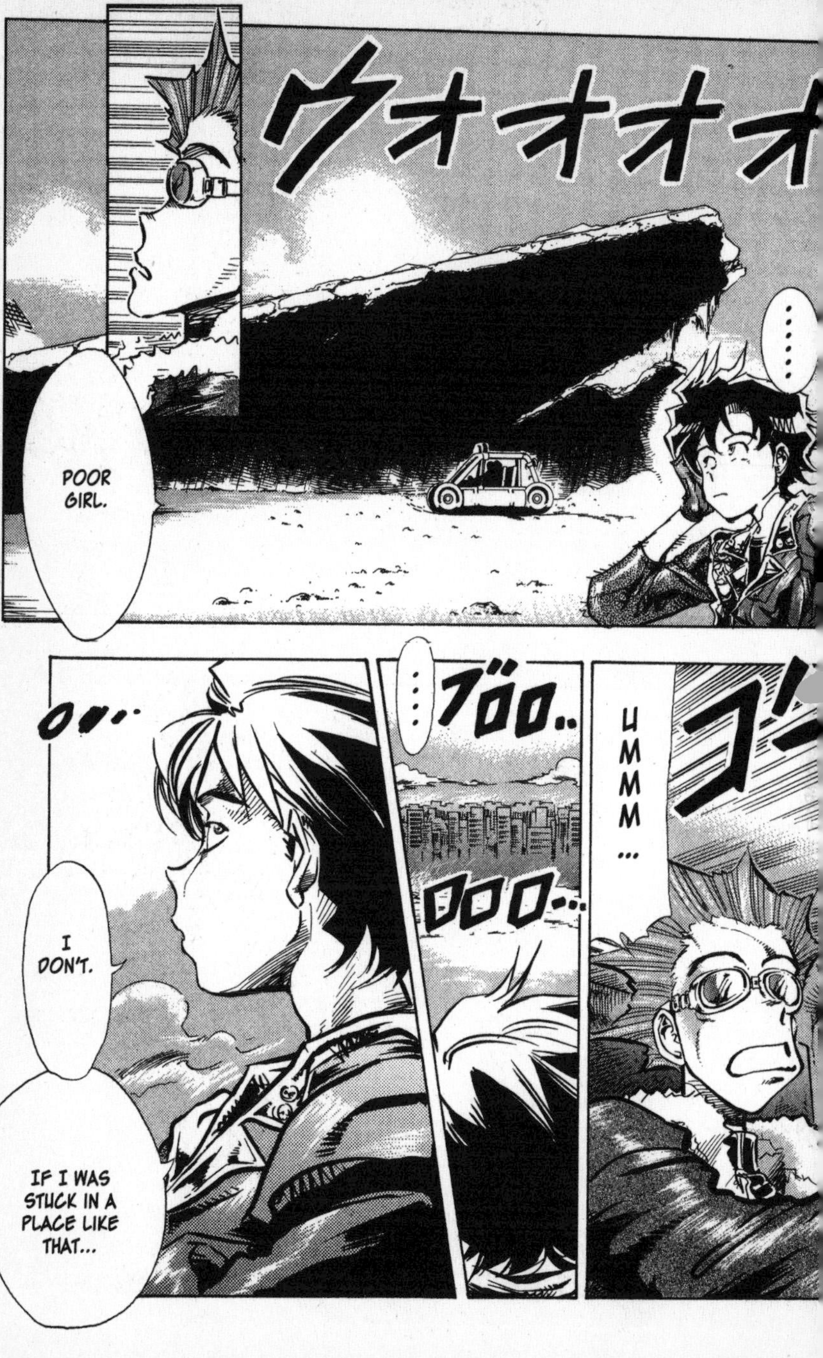
ウオオオオ
……
POOR GIRL.
コ
UMMMM...
……
ブOO..
OOO...
O...
I DON'T.
IF I WAS STUCK IN A PLACE LIKE THAT...

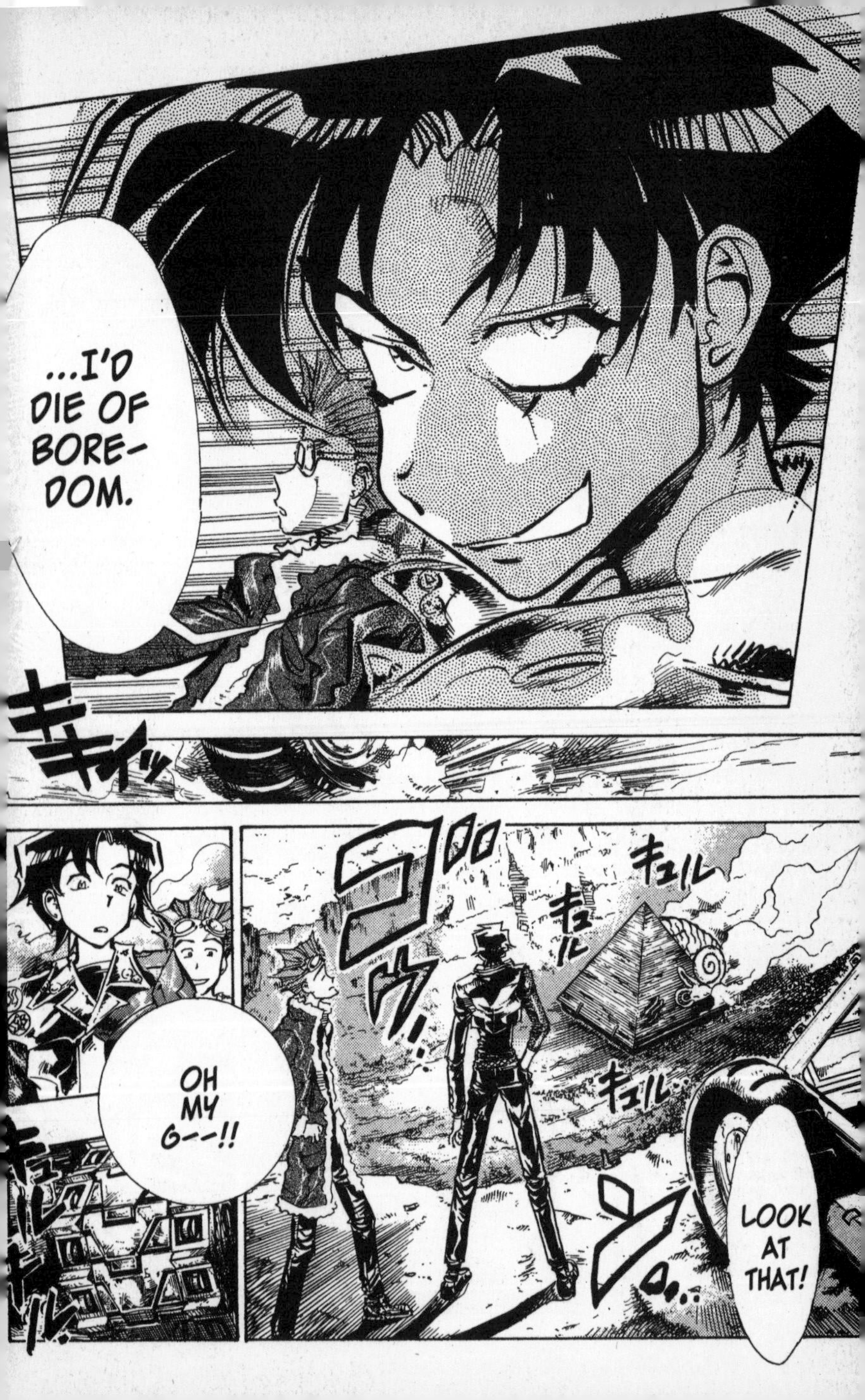
...I'D DIE OF BORE- DOM.
キキィッ
LOOK AT THAT!
キュル
キュル
キュル...
OH MY G--!!

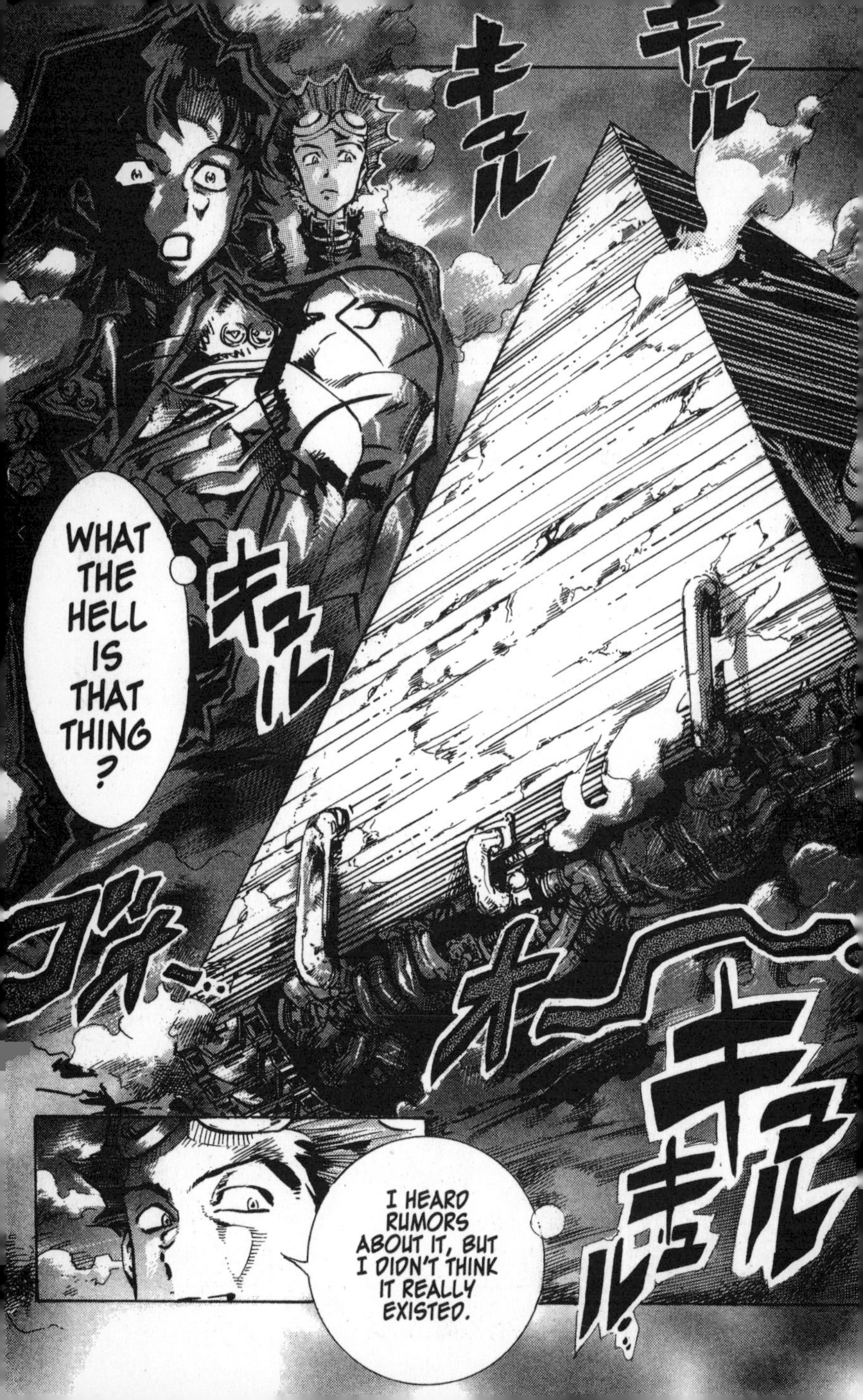
WHAT THE HELL IS THAT THING?
I HEARD RUMORS ABOUT IT, BUT I DIDN'T THINK IT REALLY EXISTED.

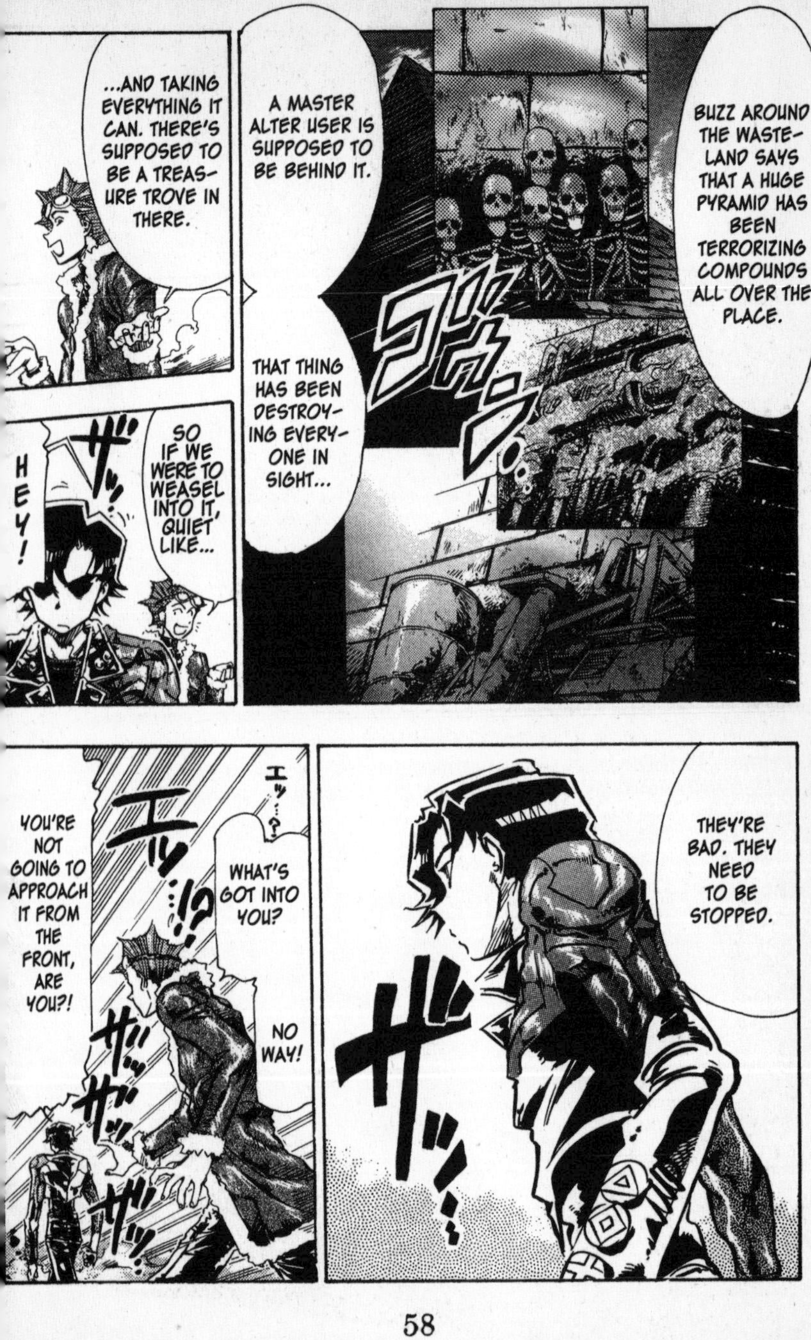
BUZZ AROUND THE WASTE-LAND SAYS THAT A HUGE PYRAMID HAS BEEN TERRORIZING COMPOUNDS ALL OVER THE PLACE.
A MASTER ALTER USER IS SUPPOSED TO BE BEHIND IT.
THAT THING HAS BEEN DESTROYING-ING EVERY-ONE IN SIGHT...
...AND TAKING EVERYTHING IT CAN. THERE'S SUPPOSED TO BE A TREAS-URE TROVE IN THERE.
SO IF WE WERE TO WEASEL INTO IT, QUIET LIKE...
HEY!
THEY'RE BAD. THEY NEED TO BE STOPPED.
WHAT'S GOT INTO YOU?
YOU'RE NOT GOING TO APPROACH IT FROM THE FRONT, ARE YOU?!
NO WAY!

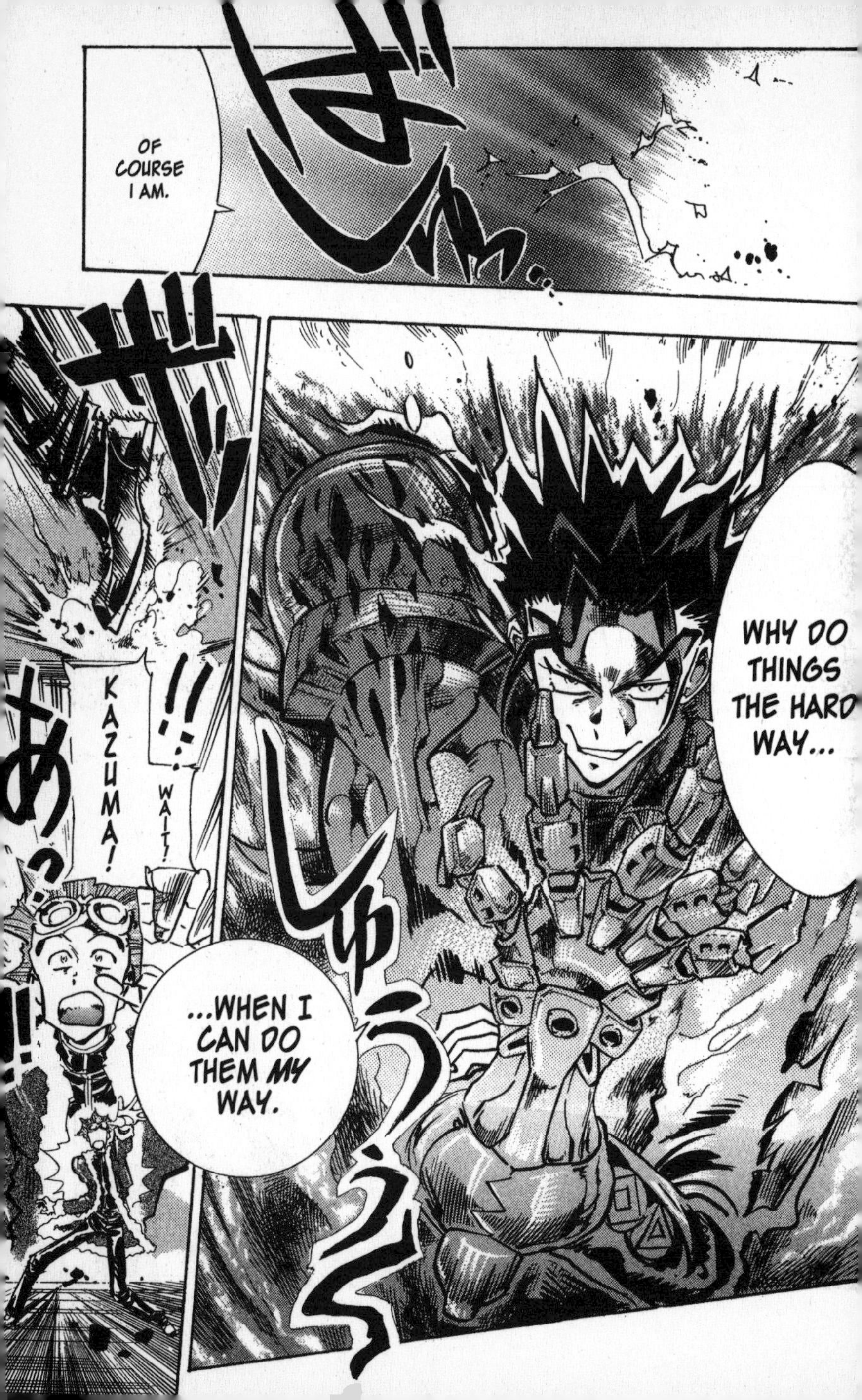
OF COURSE I AM.
WHY DO THINGS THE HARD WAY...
...WHEN I CAN DO THEM MY WAY.
KAZUMA!
WAIT!

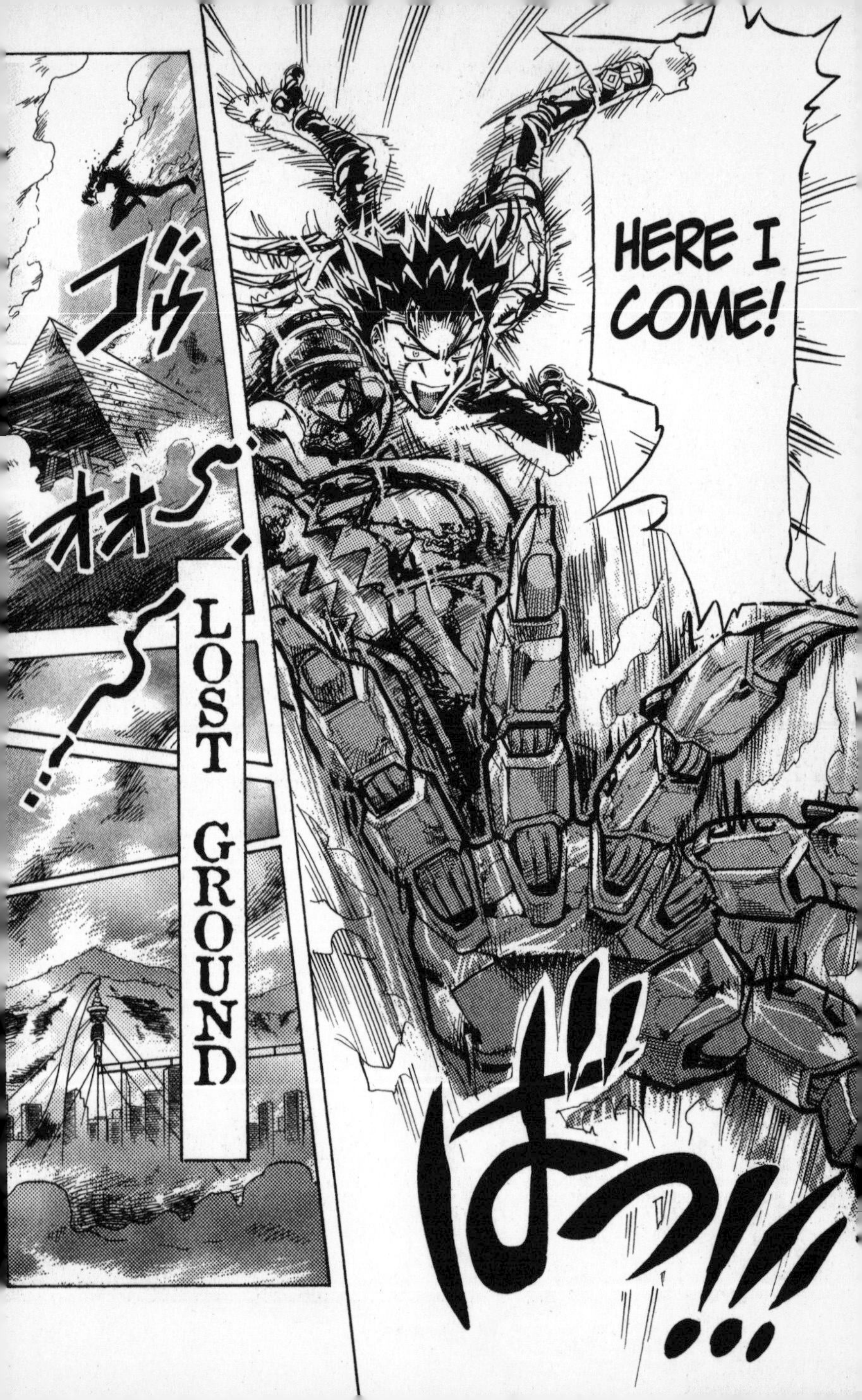
HERE I COME!
はっ!!
ゴゥ
オオ〜ン
LOST GROUND

22 years ago, when the great tectonic phenomenon occurred...

...an area 30 km in all directions around Yokohama was ripped from Japanese government control.

The people found themselves alone against chaos.

Then...

...the children of chaos were born...

Civilization split asunder. morals were abandoned.

ALTERS

61

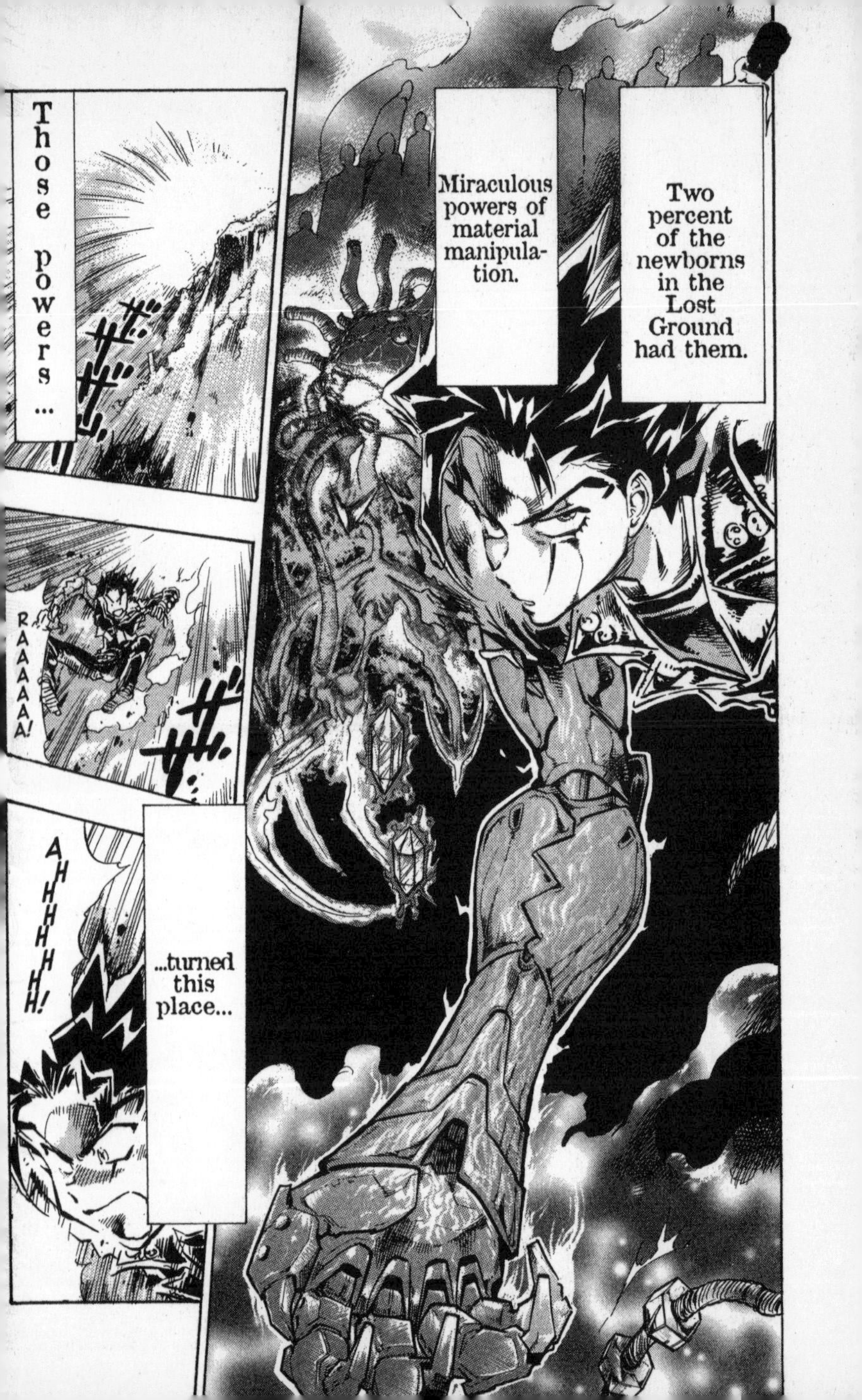
Two percent of the newborns in the Lost Ground had them.
Miraculous powers of material manipulation.
Those powers...
RAAAAAAA!
...turned this place...
AHHHHHH!

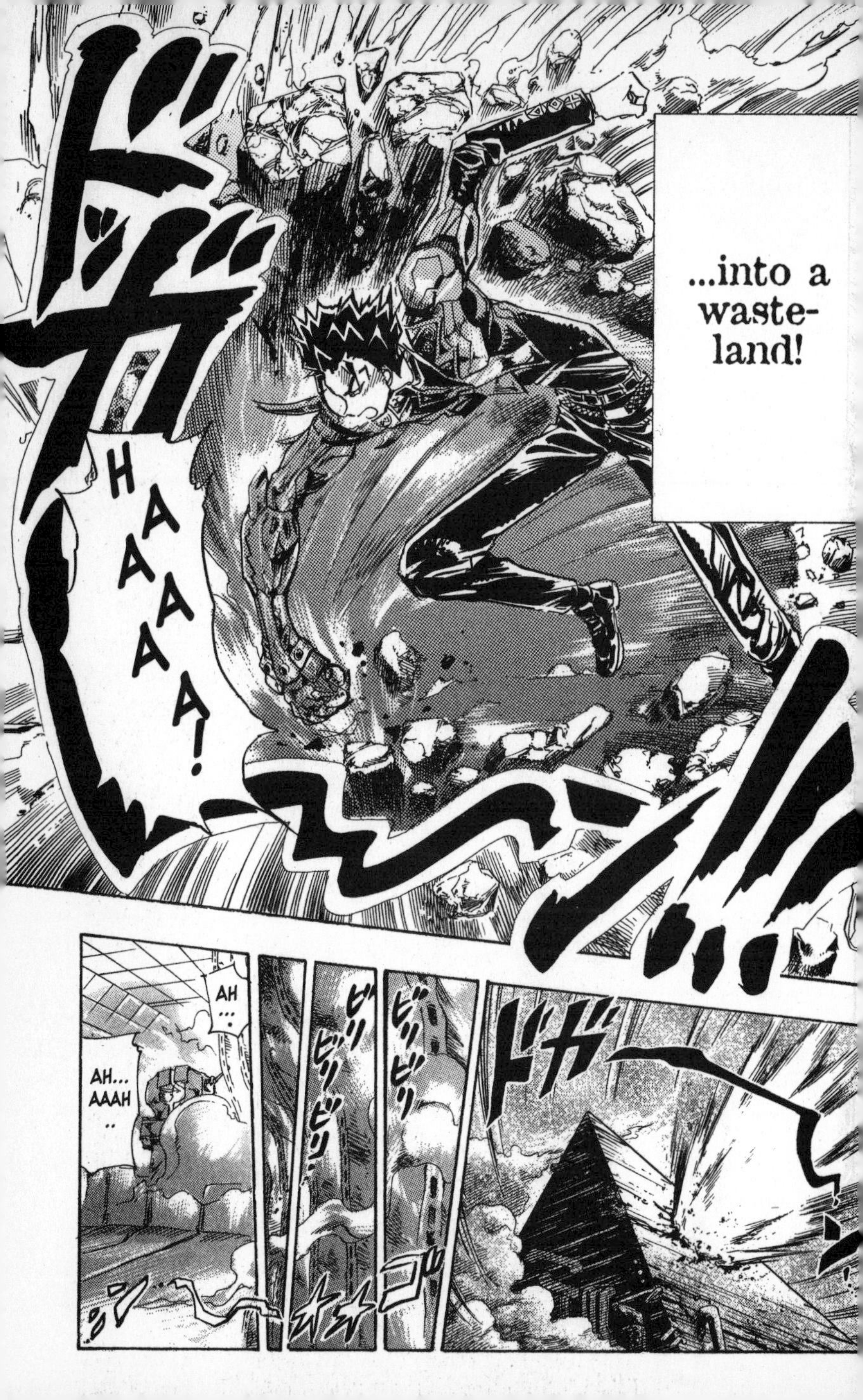
...into a waste-land!
HAAAAA!
ドガ
ビリビリ
ビリビリ
AH...
AH... AAAH..

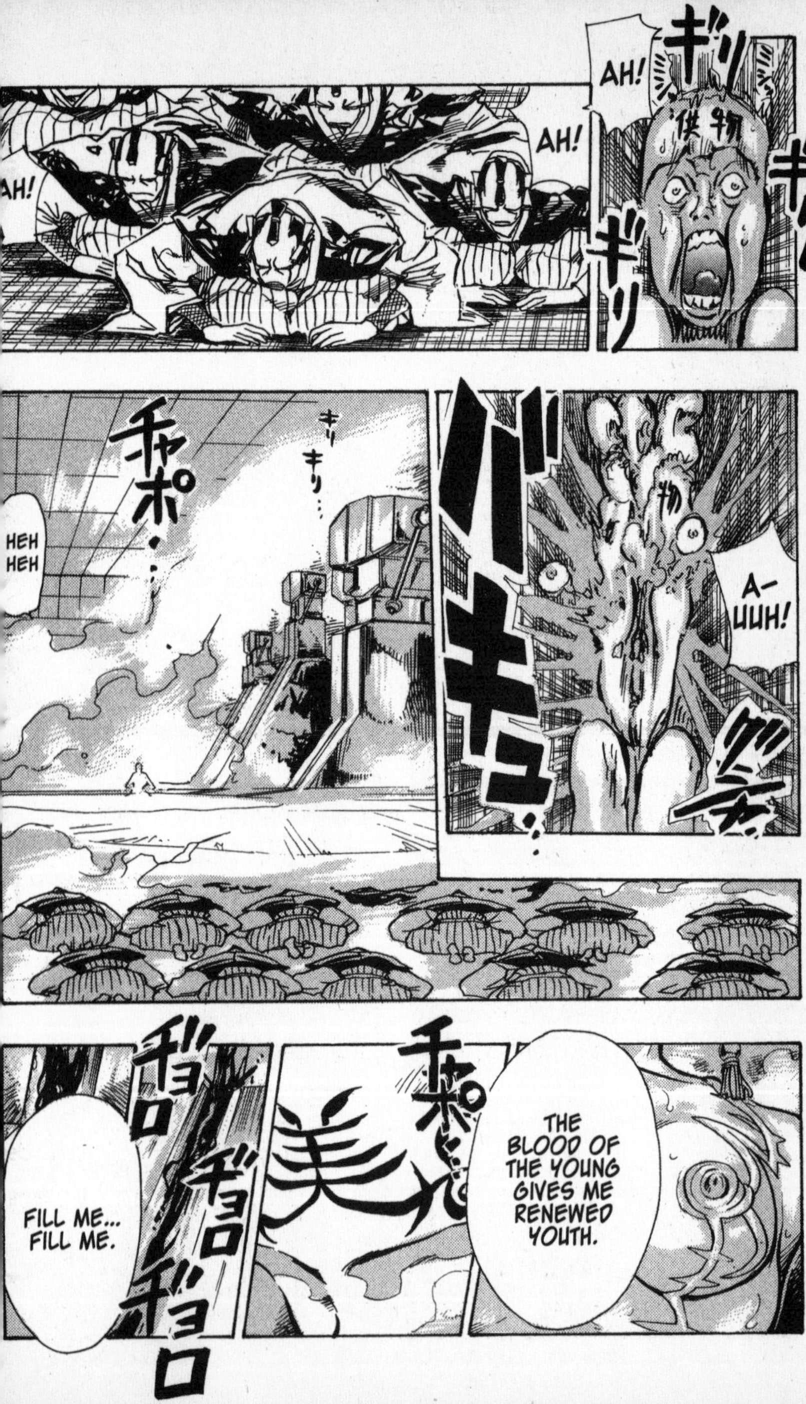

ギリ
ギリ
ギリ
AH!
AH!
AH!
バキュ…
A-UUH!
キリ キリ…
チャポ…
HEH HEH
THE BLOOD OF THE YOUNG GIVES ME RENEWED YOUTH.
チャポン…
ギョロ
ギョロ
ギョロ
FILL ME... FILL ME.

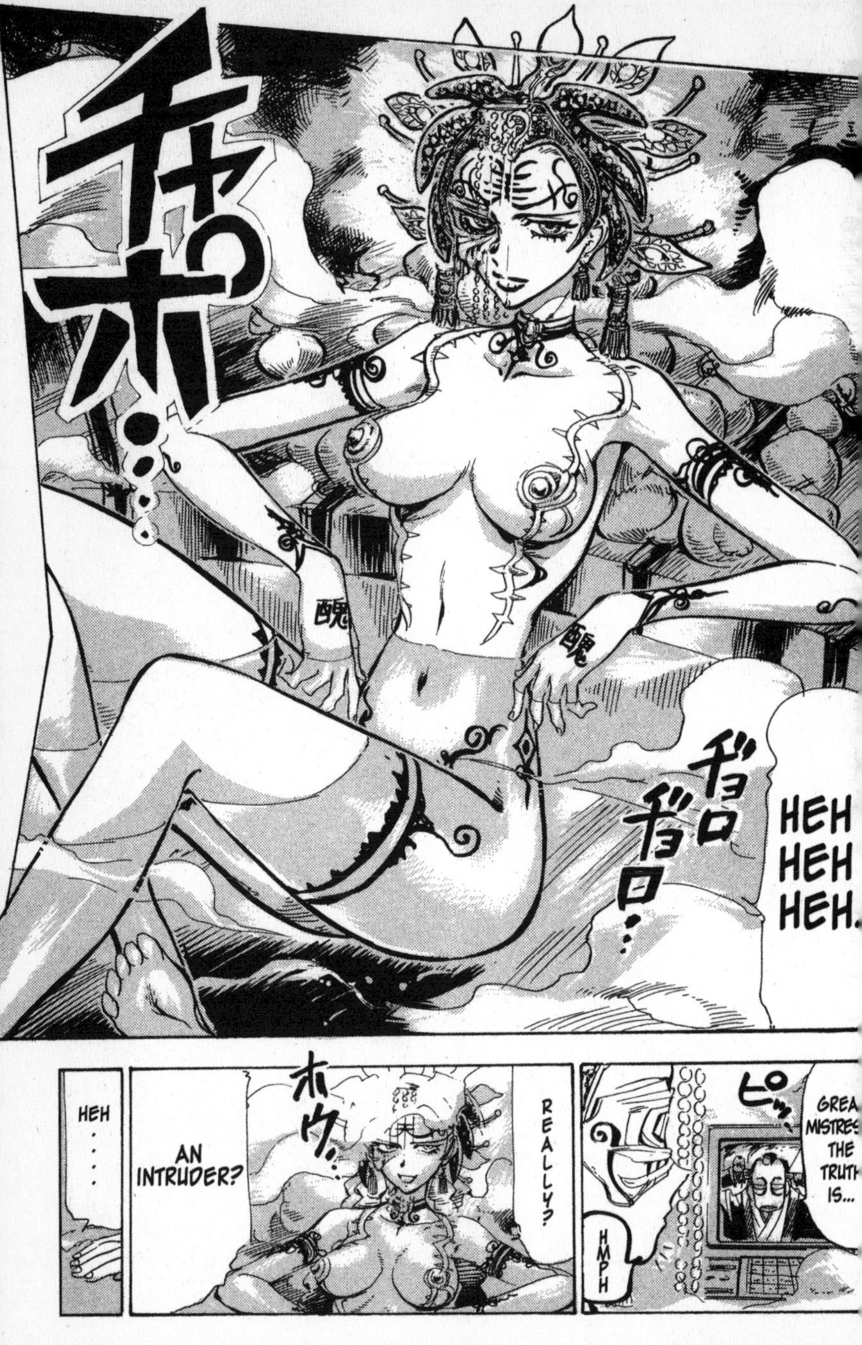

チャポ…
ギョロギョロ…
HEH HEH HEH.
ピッ…
GREA MISTRES THE TRUT IS...
HMPH
ホウ…
REALLY?
AN INTRUDER?
HEH....

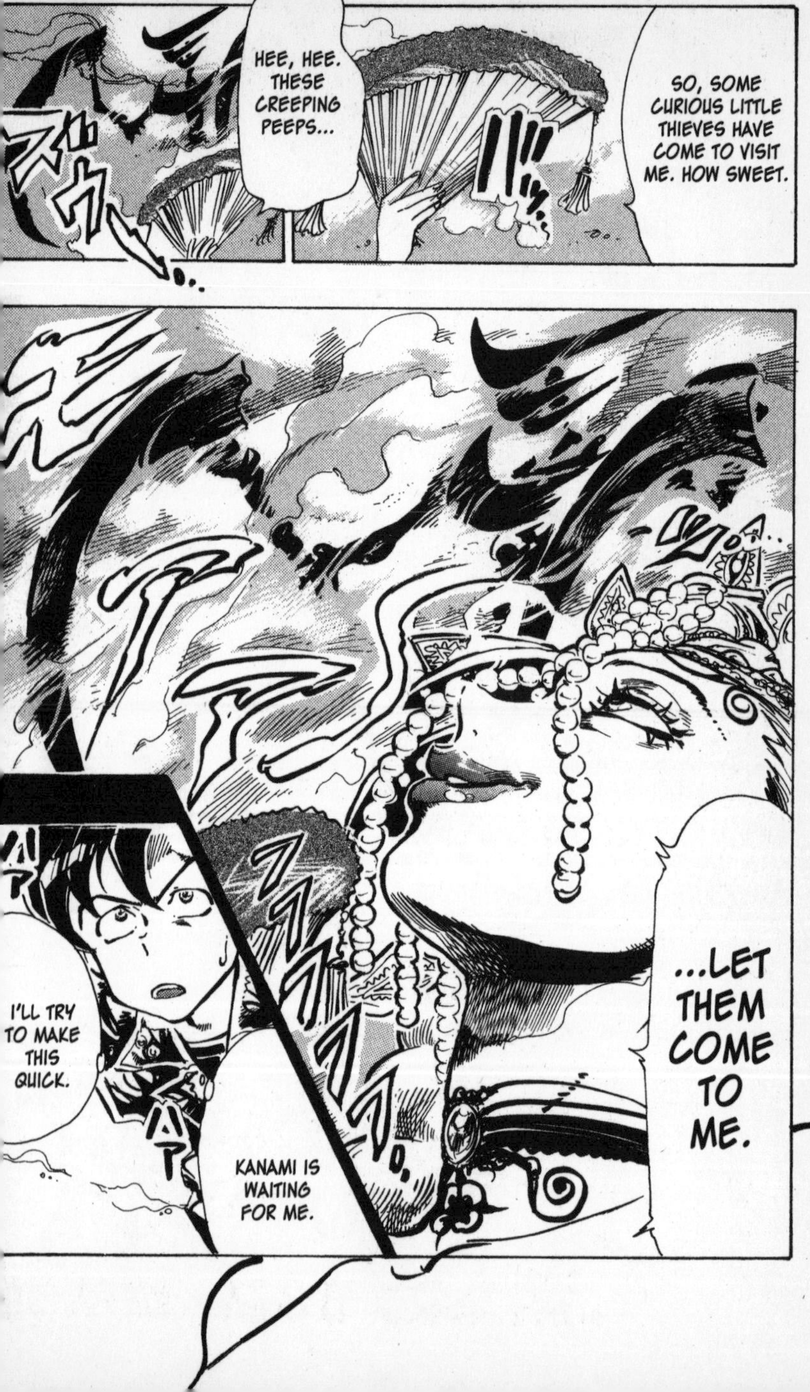
SO, SOME CURIOUS LITTLE THIEVES HAVE COME TO VISIT ME. HOW SWEET.
HEE, HEE. THESE CREEPING PEEPS...
...LET THEM COME TO ME.
KANAMI IS WAITING FOR ME.
I'LL TRY TO MAKE THIS QUICK.

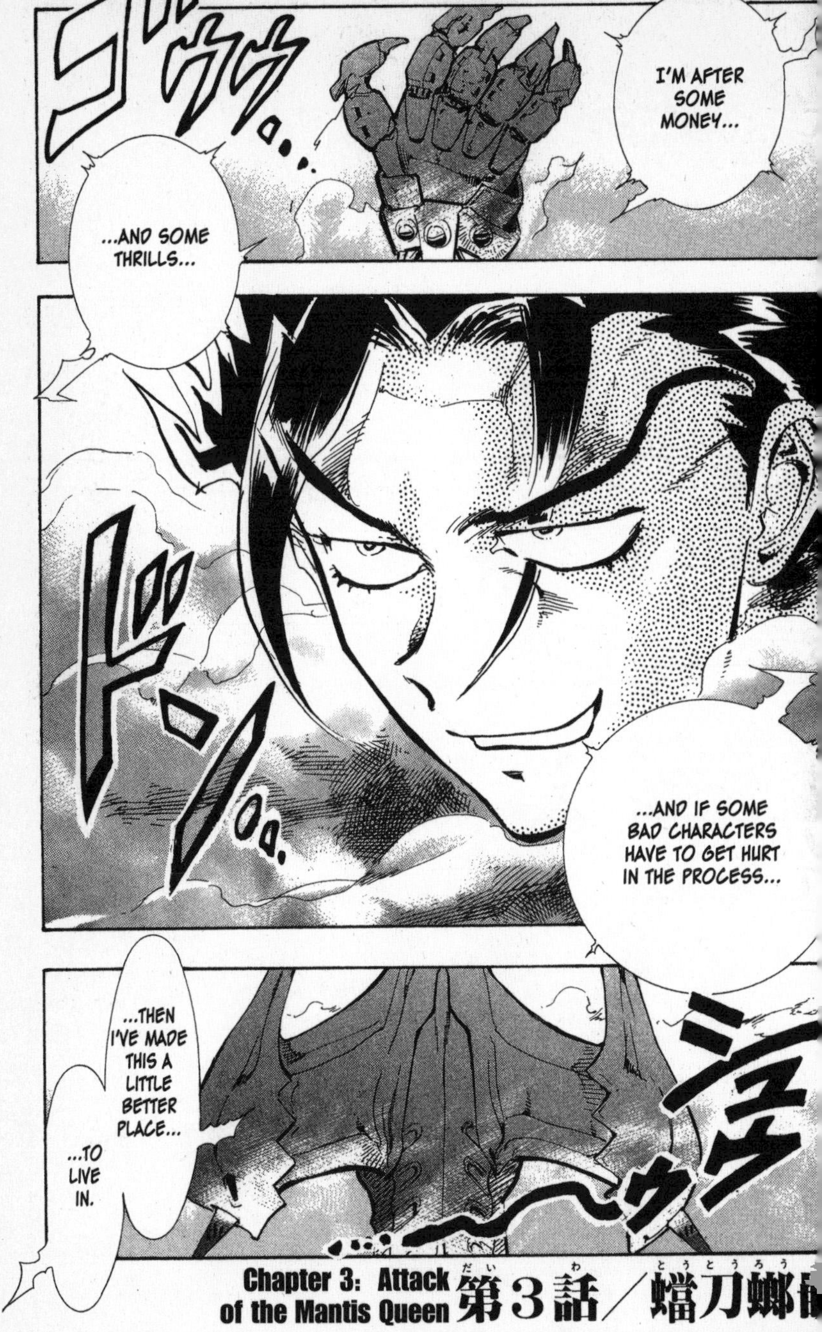
I'M AFTER SOME MONEY...
...AND SOME THRILLS...
...AND IF SOME BAD CHARACTERS HAVE TO GET HURT IN THE PROCESS...
...THEN I'VE MADE THIS A LITTLE BETTER PLACE...
...TO LIVE IN.

Chapter 3: Attack of the Mantis Queen 第3話／蟷刀螂

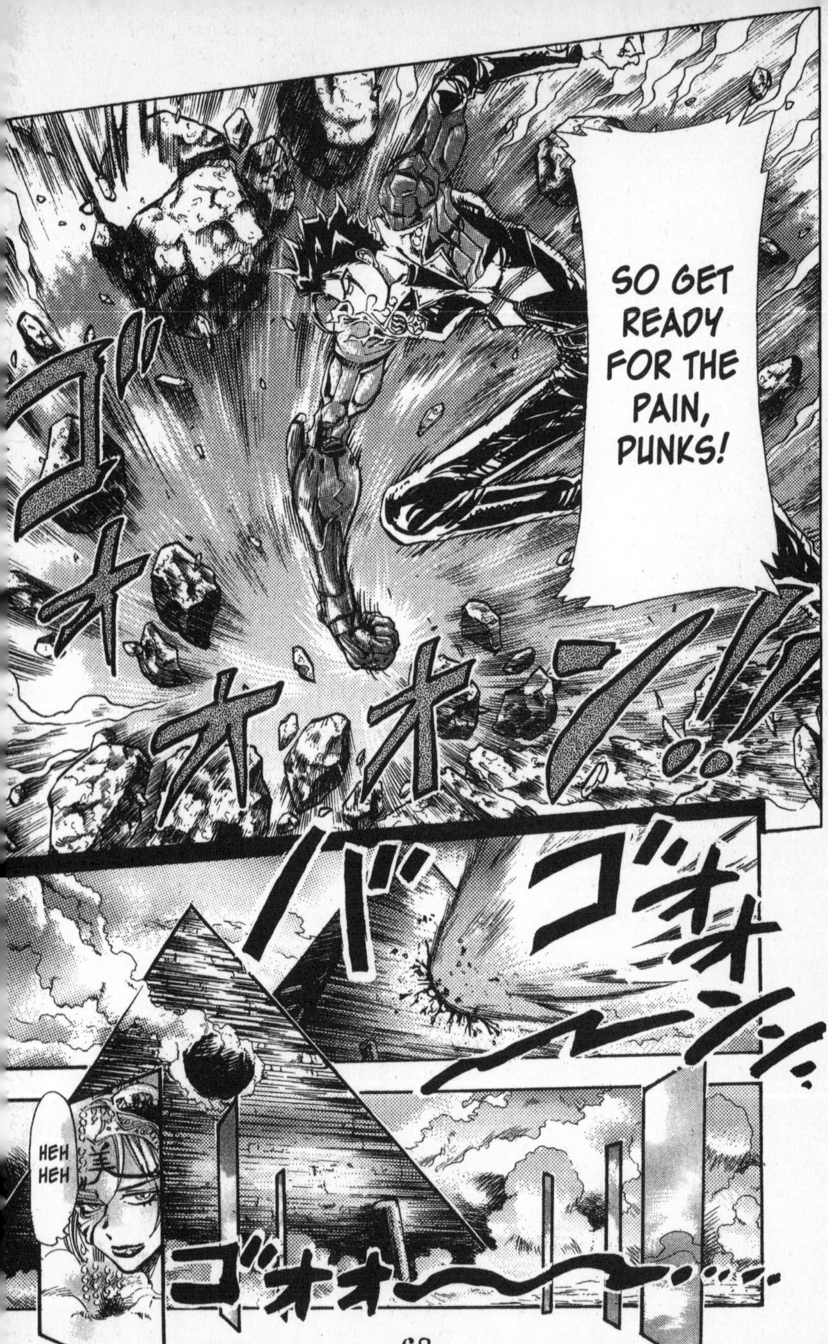
SO GET READY FOR THE PAIN, PUNKS!
ゴオオオン!!
ドゴオーン!!
HEH HEH
ゴオオ〜〜〜……

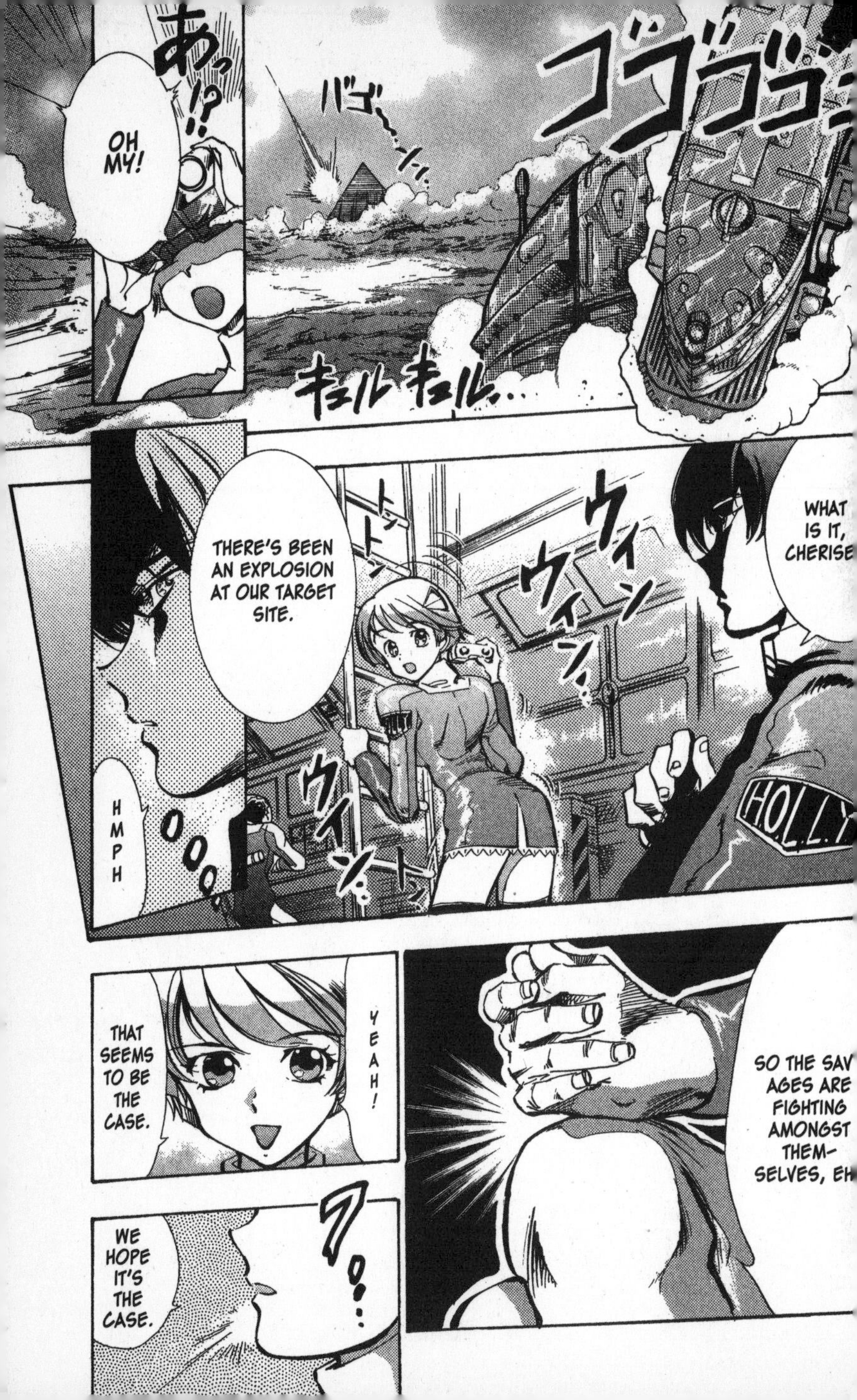
ゴゴゴゴ
バゴ~ン
キュルキュル...
あっ!?!!
OH MY!
WHAT IS IT, CHERISE
ウィンウィン
トントン
THERE'S BEEN AN EXPLOSION AT OUR TARGET SITE.
ウィン
H.O.L.L.Y.
HMPH
SO THE SAV AGES ARE FIGHTING AMONGST THEM- SELVES, EH
YEAH!
THAT SEEMS TO BE THE CASE.
フ...
WE HOPE IT'S THE CASE.

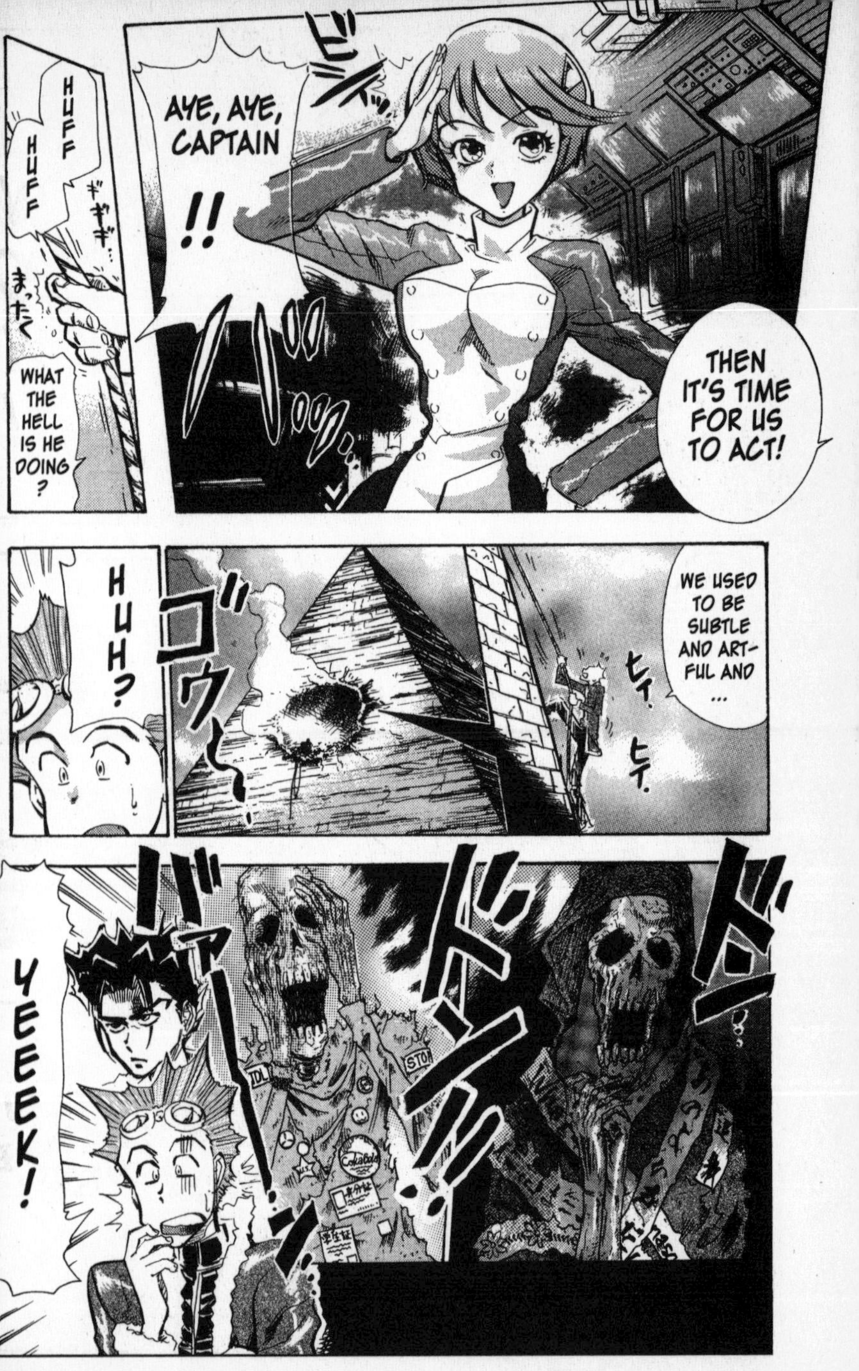
ビシィッ
THEN IT'S TIME FOR US TO ACT!
AYE, AYE, CAPTAIN !!
HUFF HUFF
ぎぎぎ…
まったく
WHAT THE HELL IS HE DOING?
WE USED TO BE SUBTLE AND ARTFUL AND ...
ヒィ. ヒィ.
ゴウ〜
HUH?
ドーン
バァー
YEEEEK!

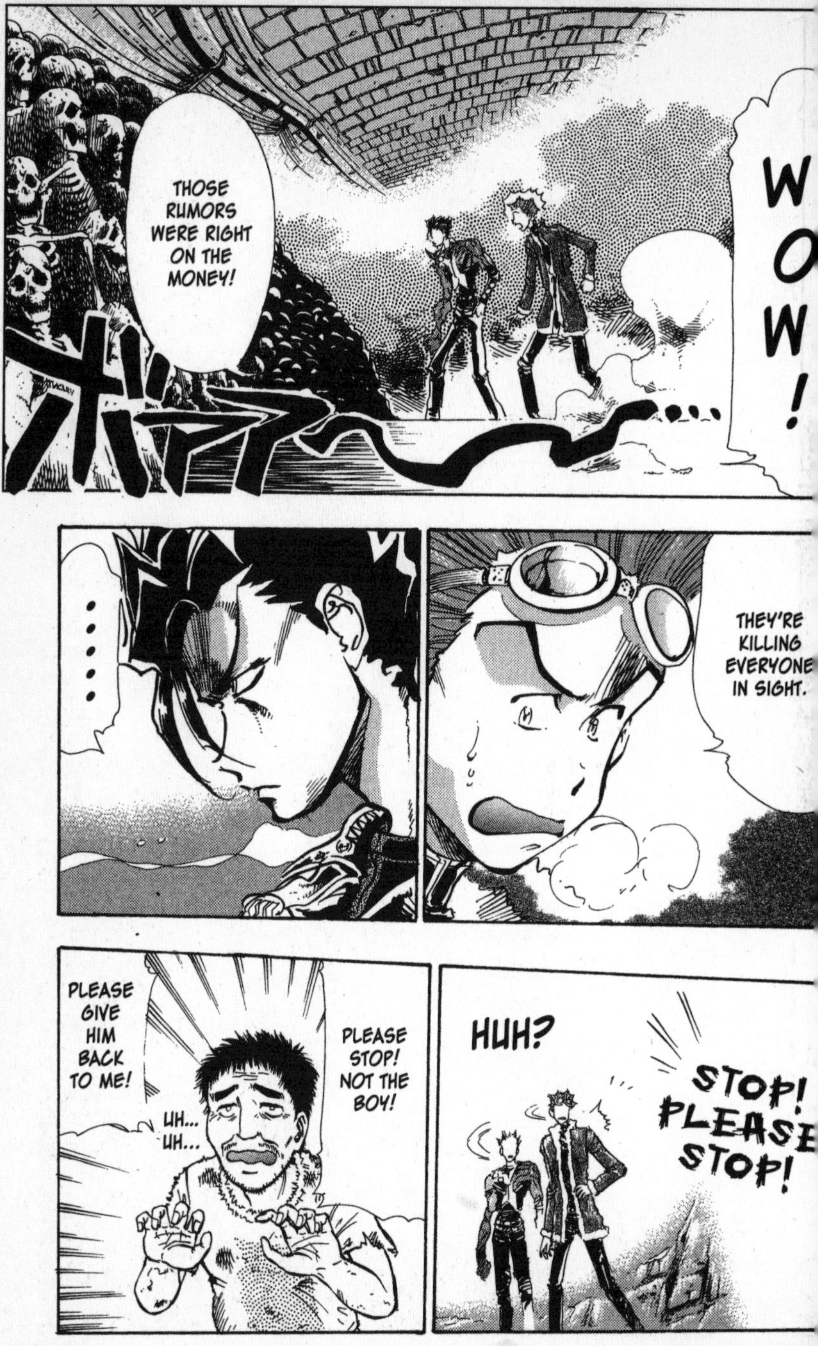
WOW!
THOSE RUMORS WERE RIGHT ON THE MONEY!
THEY'RE KILLING EVERYONE IN SIGHT.
......
STOP! PLEASE STOP!
HUH?
PLEASE STOP! NOT THE BOY!
PLEASE GIVE HIM BACK TO ME!
UH... UH...

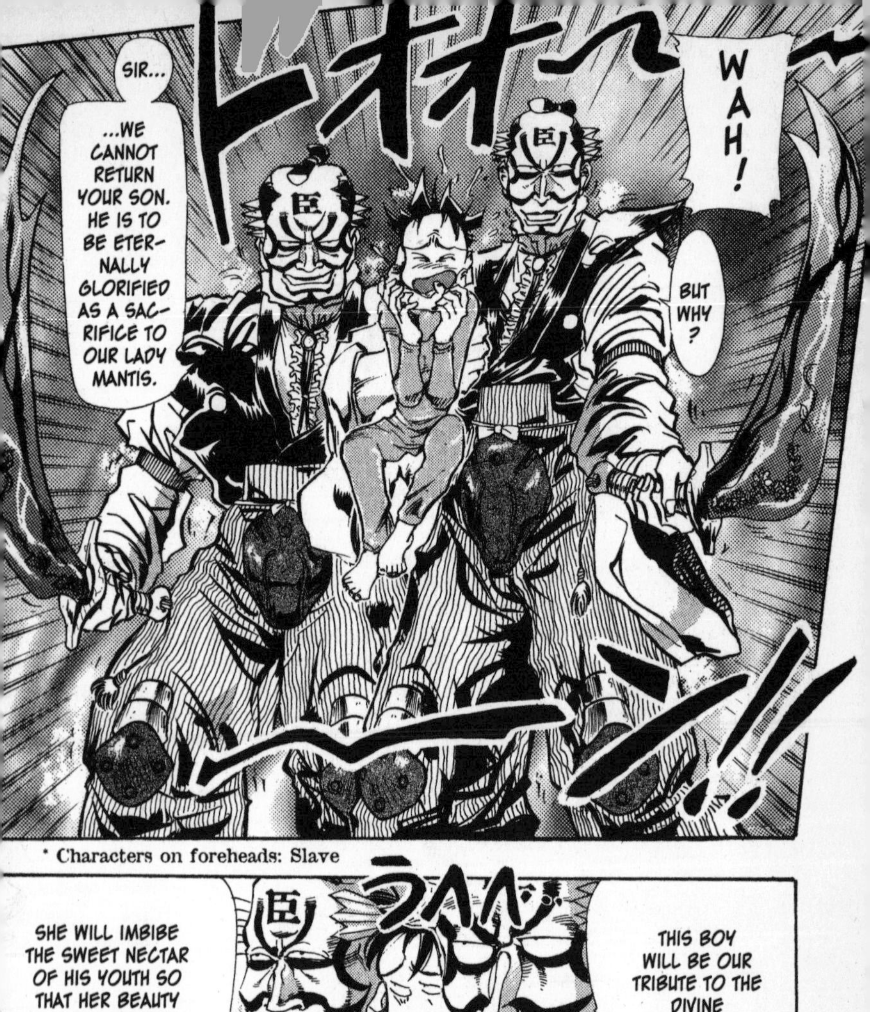
WAH!
BUT WHY?
SIR...
...WE CANNOT RETURN YOUR SON. HE IS TO BE ETERNALLY GLORIFIED AS A SACRIFICE TO OUR LADY MANTIS.

* Characters on foreheads: Slave

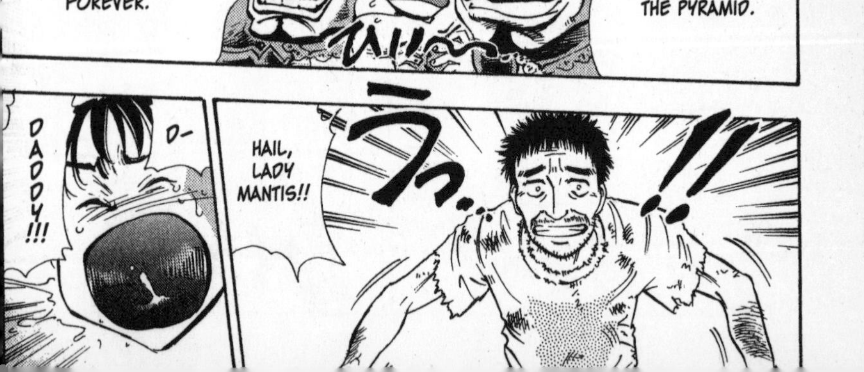
THIS BOY WILL BE OUR TRIBUTE TO THE DIVINE MISTRESS OF THE PYRAMID.
SHE WILL IMBIBE THE SWEET NECTAR OF HIS YOUTH SO THAT HER BEAUTY MAY BE PRESERVED FOREVER.
HAIL, LADY MANTIS!!
D-
DADDY!!!

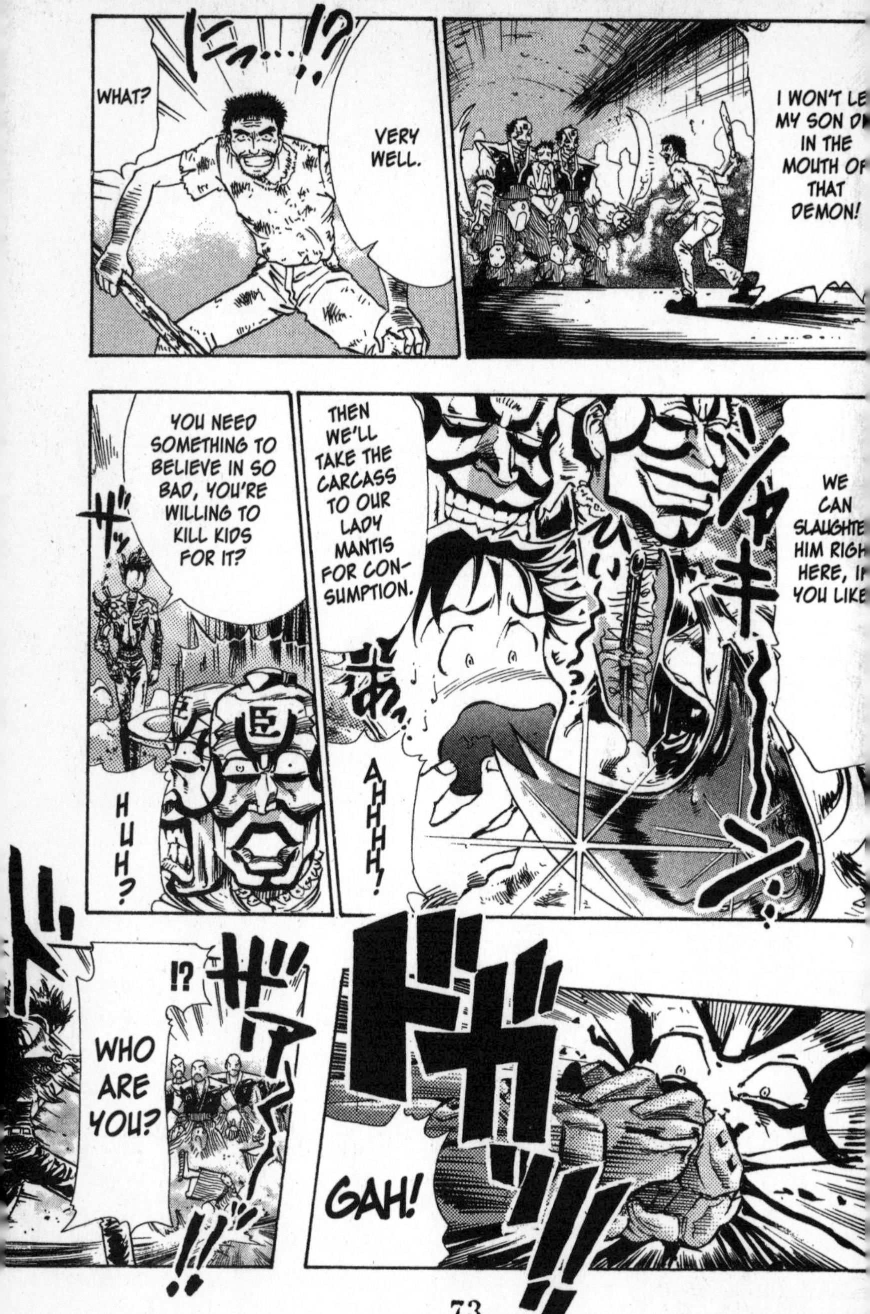
I WON'T LE
MY SON D
IN THE
MOUTH OF
THAT
DEMON!
VERY WELL.
WHAT?
WE CAN SLAUGHTE HIM RIGH HERE, I YOU LIKE
THEN WE'LL TAKE THE CARCASS TO OUR LADY MANTIS FOR CON-SUMPTION.
AHHHH!
YOU NEED SOMETHING TO BELIEVE IN SO BAD, YOU'RE WILLING TO KILL KIDS FOR IT?
HUH?
GAH!
!?
WHO ARE YOU?

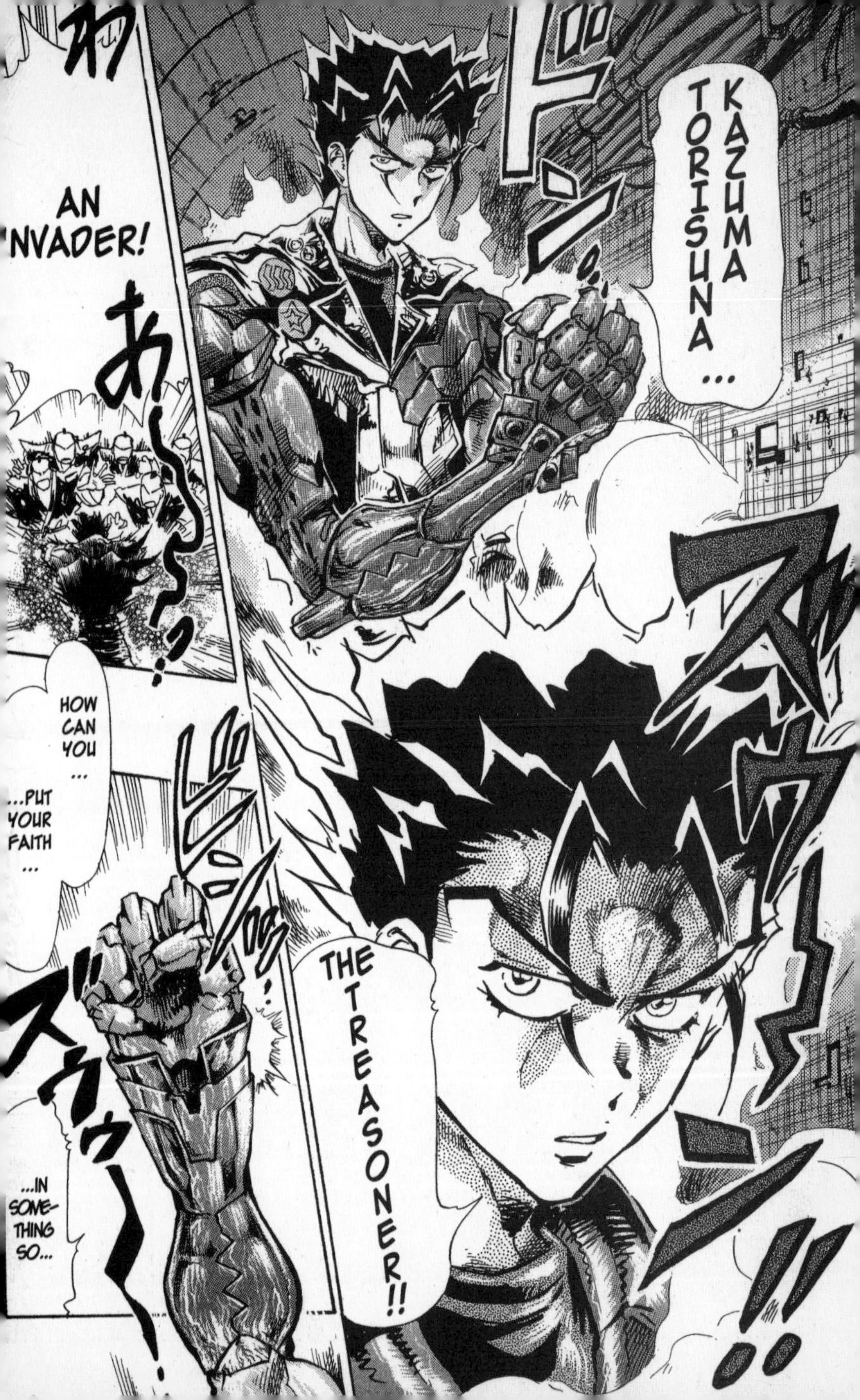
KAZUMA TORISUNA...
THE TREASONER!!
AN NVADER!
HOW CAN YOU...
...PUT YOUR FAITH...
...IN SOME-THING SO...

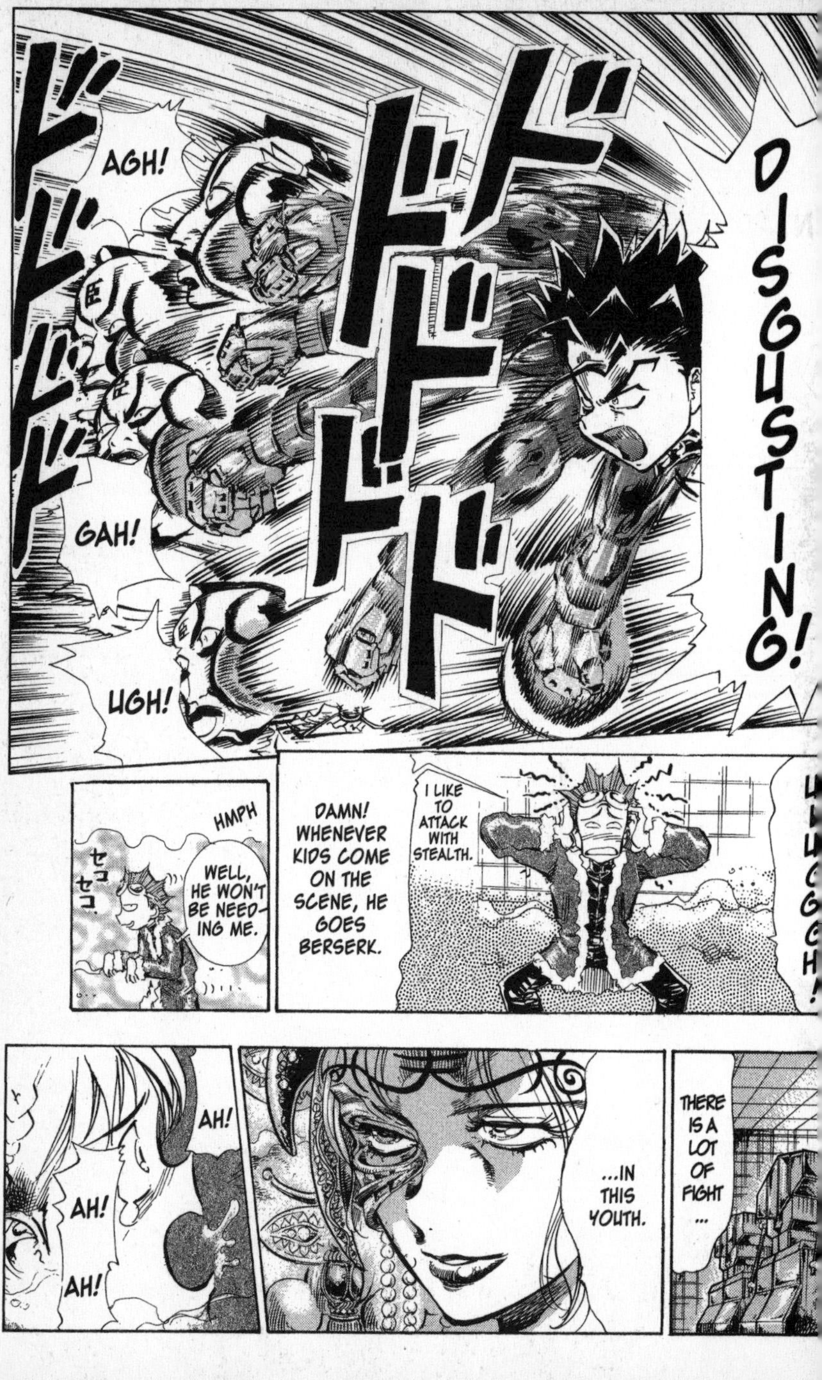
DISGUSTING!
ドドドド
ドドドド
AGH!
GAH!
UGH!
ドドドドド
I LIKE TO ATTACK WITH STEALTH.
DAMN! WHENEVER KIDS COME ON THE SCENE, HE GOES BERSERK.
HMPH
WELL, HE WON'T BE NEEDING ME.
セコセコ
THERE IS A LOT OF FIGHT ...
...IN THIS YOUTH.
AH!
AH!
AH!

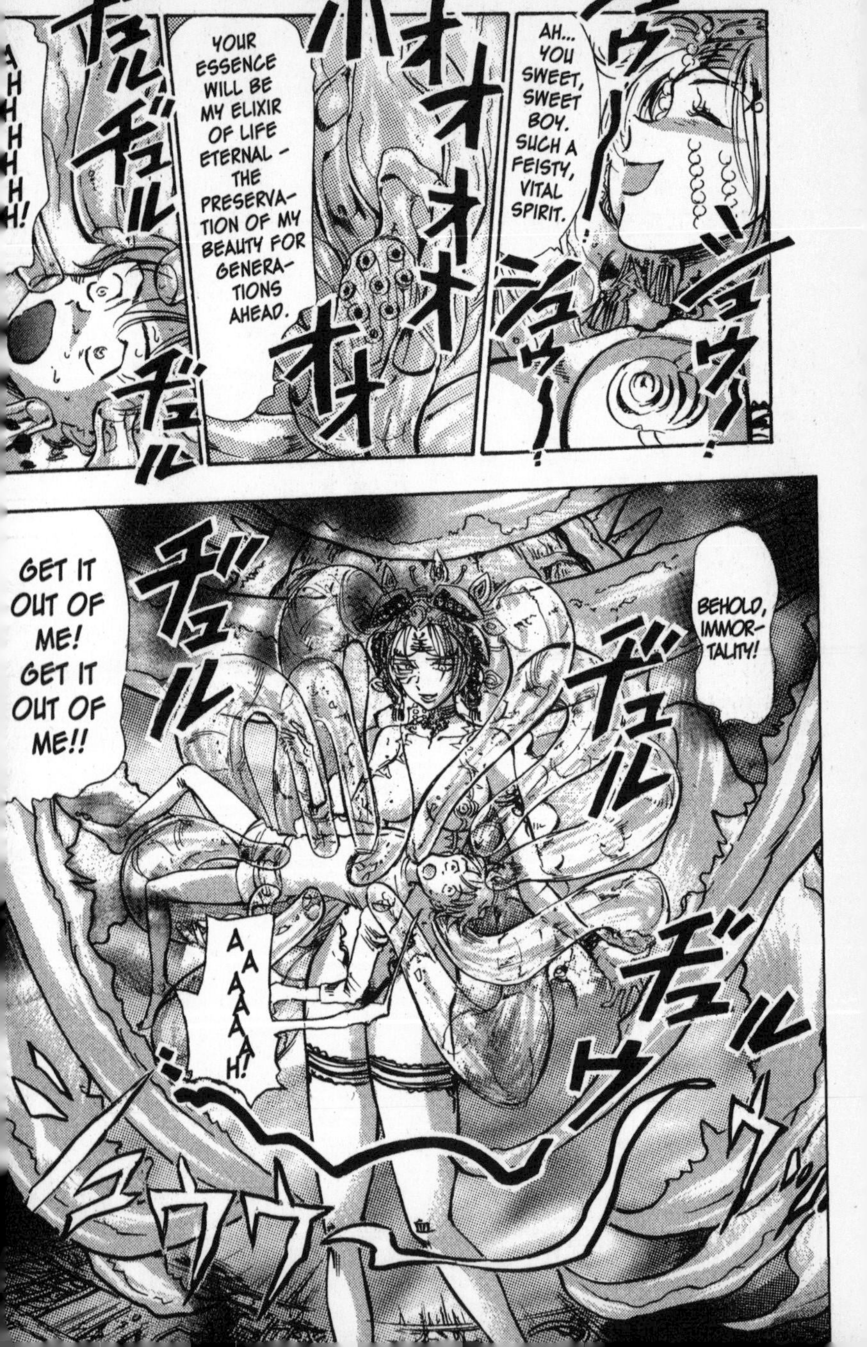

AH... YOU SWEET, SWEET BOY. SUCH A FEISTY, VITAL SPIRIT.
ボオオオオ
YOUR ESSENCE WILL BE MY ELIXIR OF LIFE ETERNAL - THE PRESERVATION OF MY BEAUTY FOR GENERATIONS AHEAD.
ヂュルヂュル
AHHHHHHH!
BEHOLD, IMMORTALITY!
GET IT OUT OF ME! GET IT OUT OF ME!!
AAAAAAH!

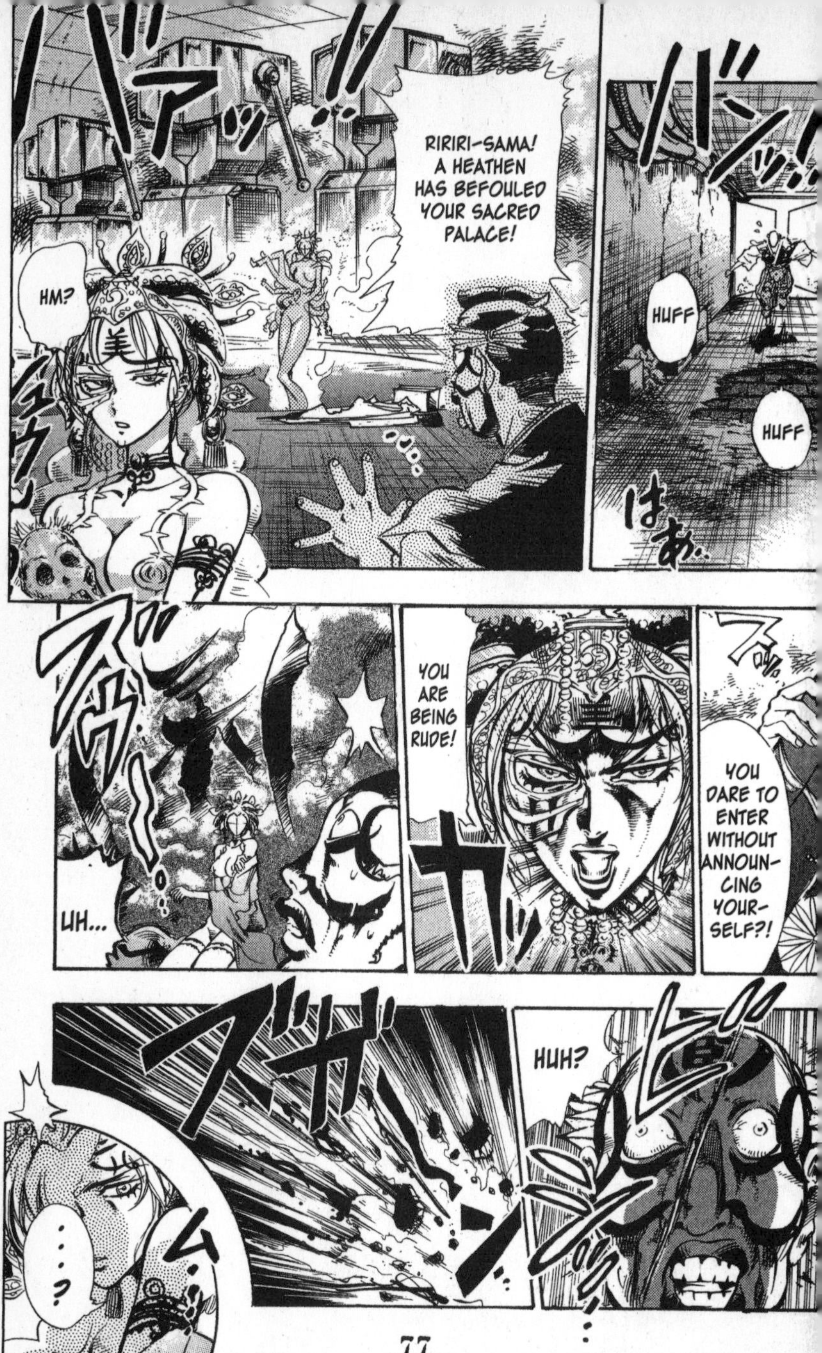
HUFF
HUFF
はあ…
RIRIRI-SAMA! A HEATHEN HAS BEFOULED YOUR SACRED PALACE!
HM?
YOU DARE TO ENTER WITHOUT ANNOUN-CING YOUR-SELF?!
YOU ARE BEING RUDE!
UH...
HUH?
...?

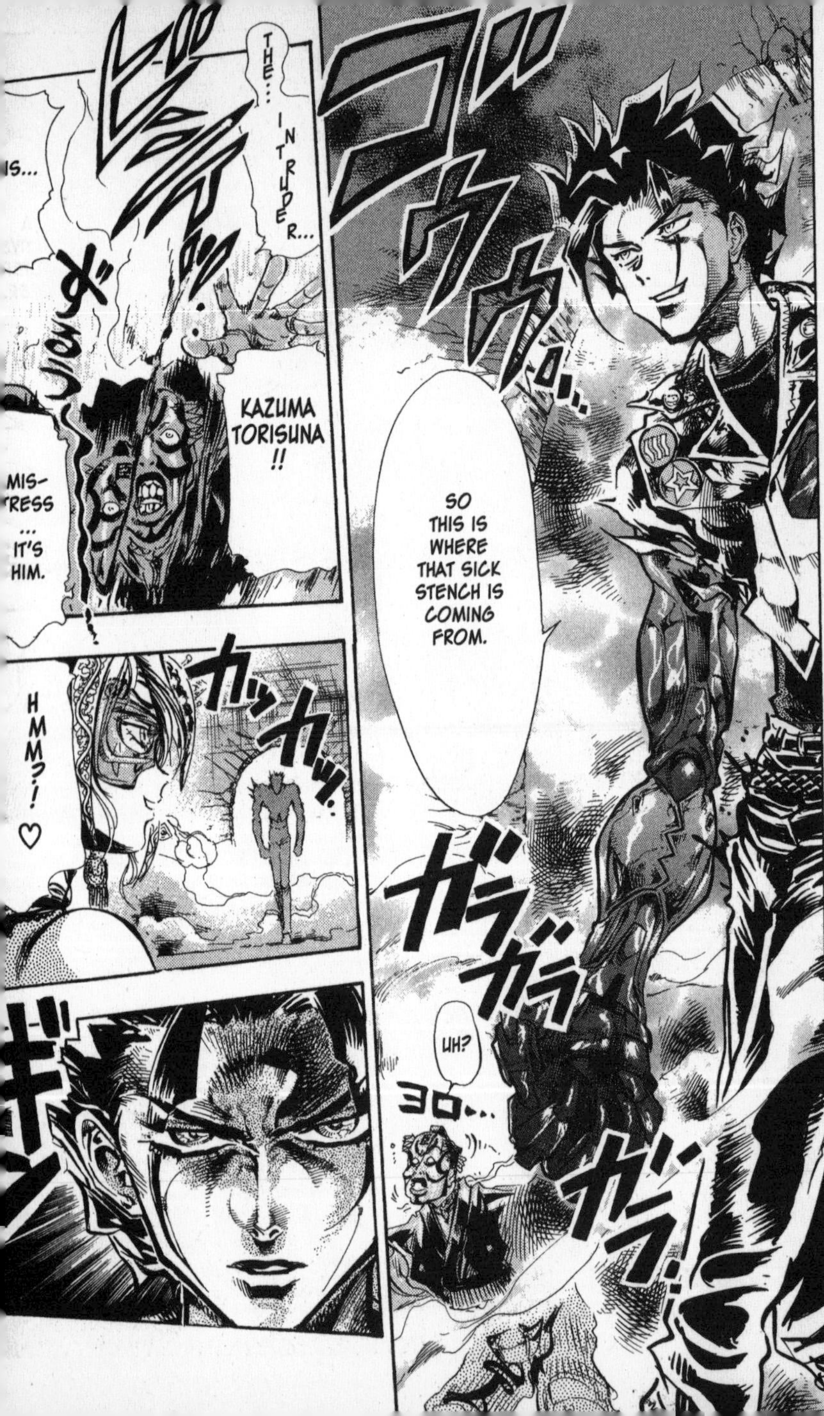
SO THIS IS WHERE THAT SICK STENCH IS COMING FROM.
UH?
ヨロ...
THE... INTRUDER...
IS...
KAZUMA TORISUNA!!
MISTRESS... IT'S HIM.
HMM?! ♡

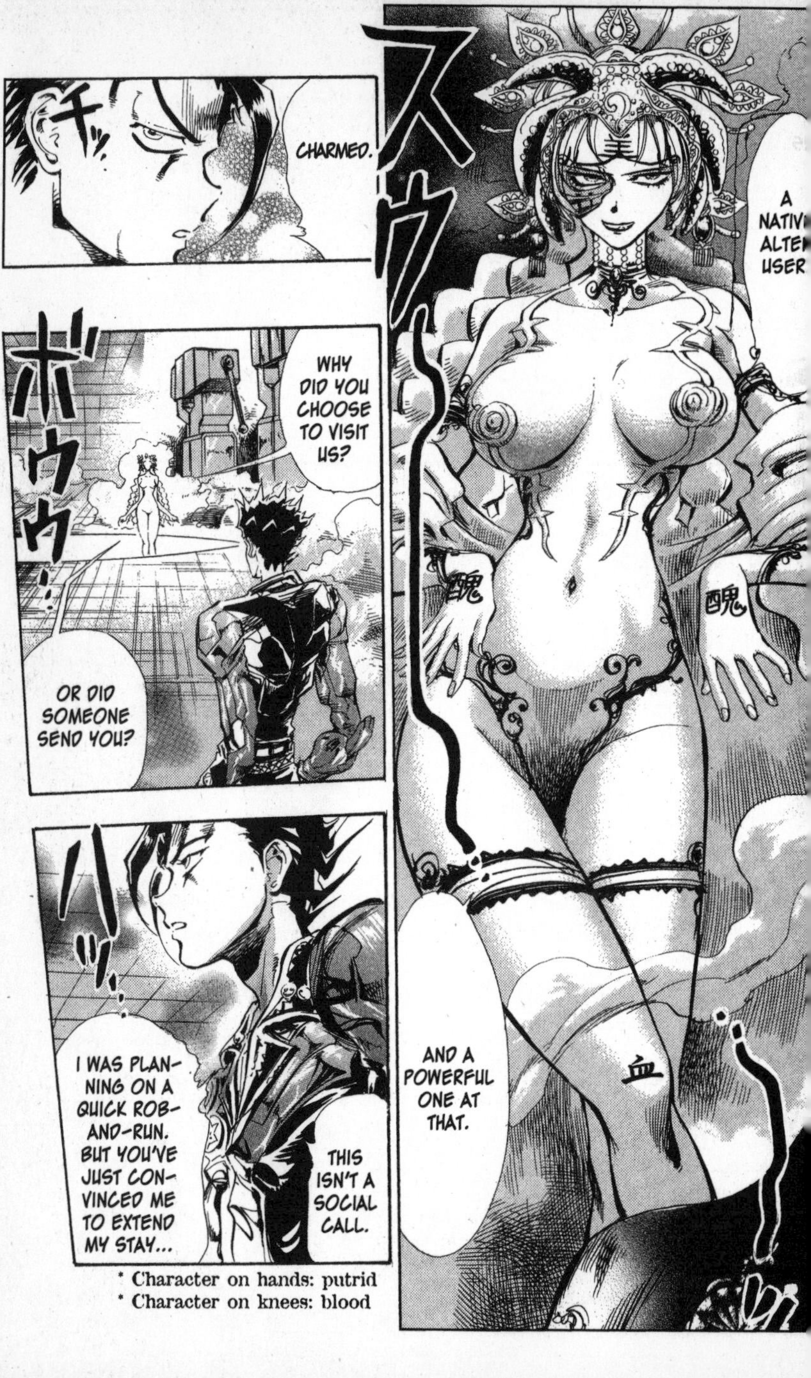
A
NATIV
ALTE
USER
AND A POWERFUL ONE AT THAT.
CHARMED.
WHY DID YOU CHOOSE TO VISIT US?
OR DID SOMEONE SEND YOU?
THIS ISN'T A SOCIAL CALL.
I WAS PLANNING ON A QUICK ROB-AND-RUN. BUT YOU'VE JUST CONVINCED ME TO EXTEND MY STAY...

* Character on hands: putrid
* Character on knees: blood

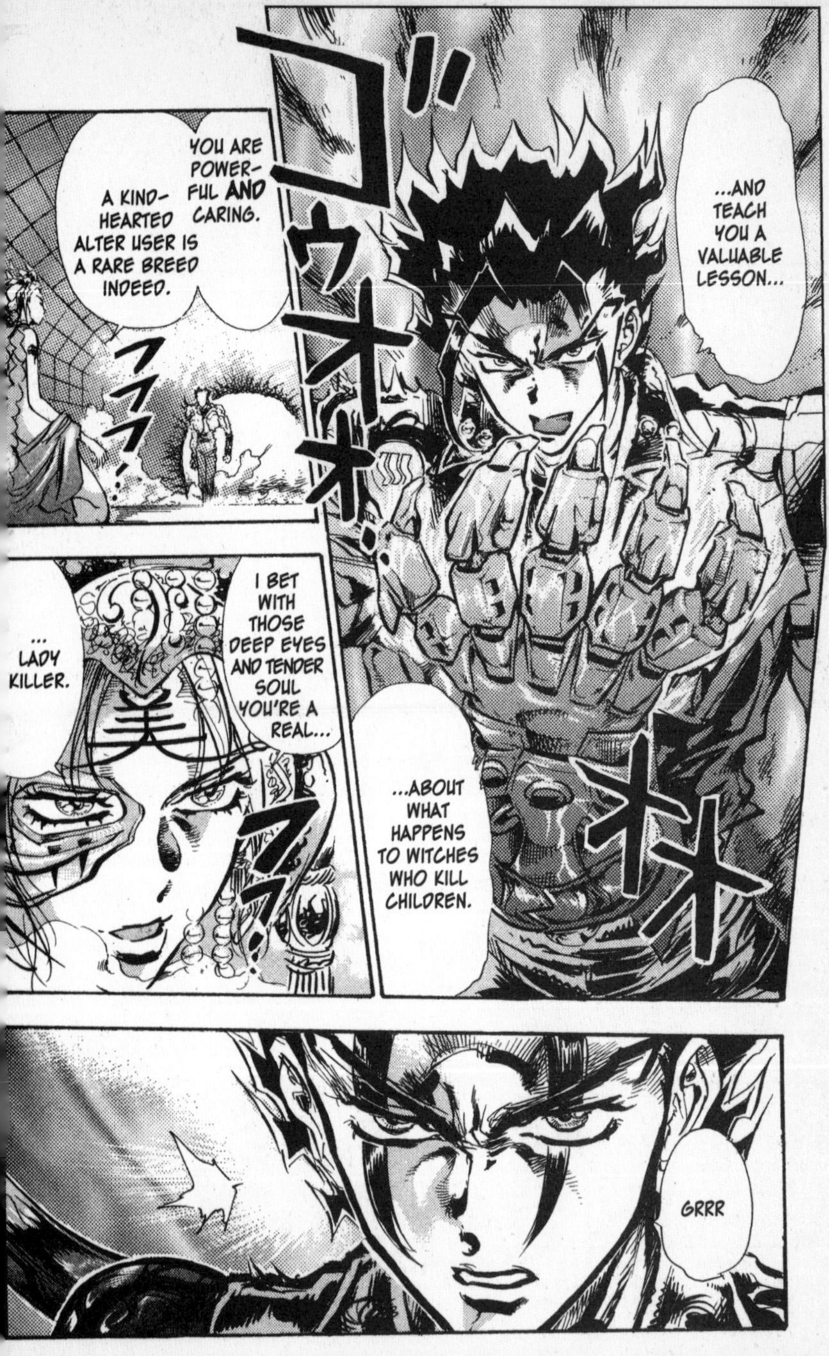
ゴウオオ
...AND TEACH YOU A VALUABLE LESSON...
...ABOUT WHAT HAPPENS TO WITCHES WHO KILL CHILDREN.
オオ
YOU ARE POWER-FUL AND CARING.
A KIND-HEARTED ALTER USER IS A RARE BREED INDEED.
フフフ
I BET WITH THOSE DEEP EYES AND TENDER SOUL YOU'RE A REAL...
...LADY KILLER.
フフ
GRRR

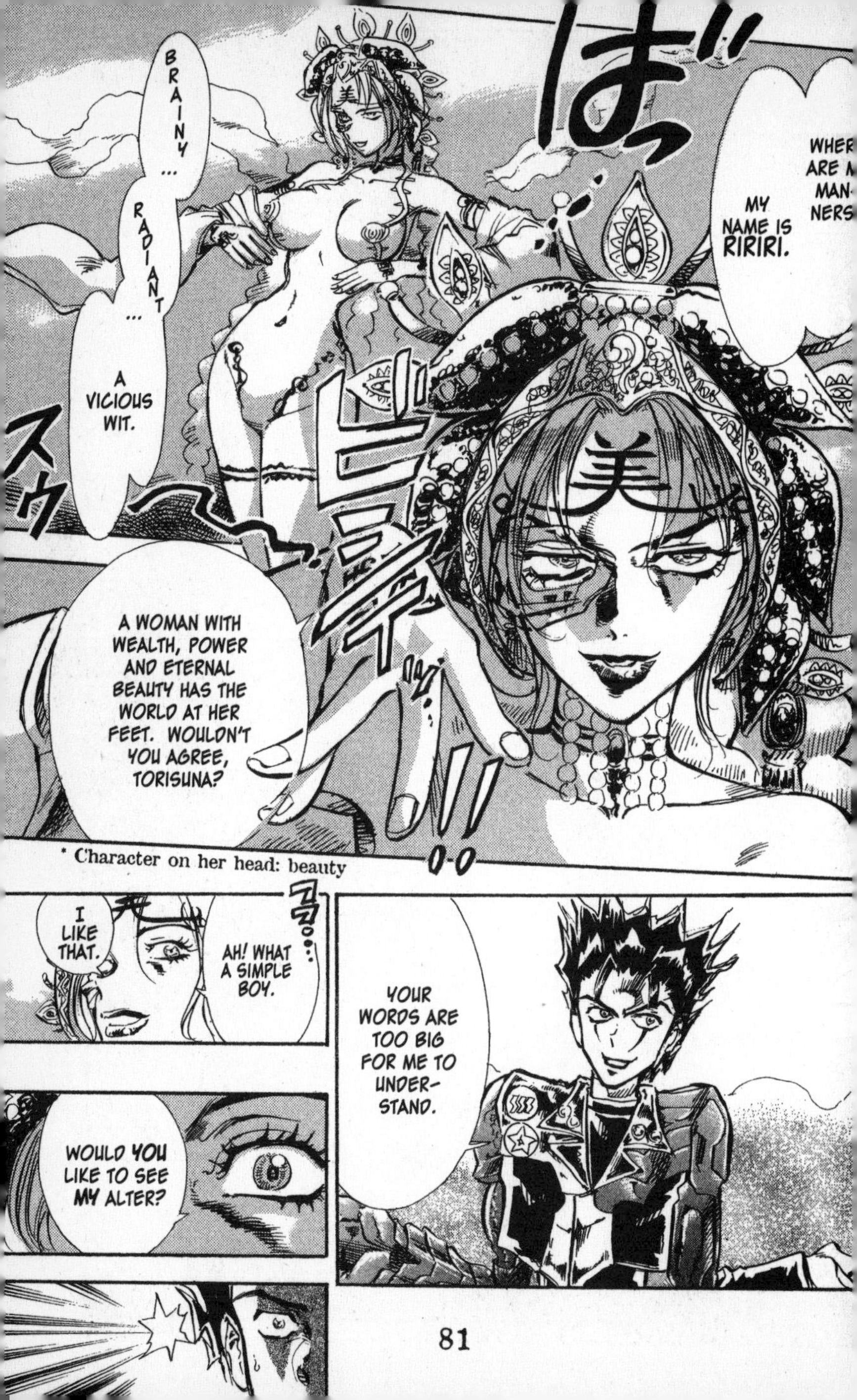
ばっ
WHER ARE M MAN-NERS
MY NAME IS RIRIRI.
BRAINY... RADIANT... A VICIOUS WIT.
スゥ
ビラァ
A WOMAN WITH WEALTH, POWER AND ETERNAL BEAUTY HAS THE WORLD AT HER FEET. WOULDN'T YOU AGREE, TORISUNA?
YOUR WORDS ARE TOO BIG FOR ME TO UNDER-STAND.
AH! WHAT A SIMPLE BOY.
I LIKE THAT.
WOULD YOU LIKE TO SEE MY ALTER?

* Character on her head: beauty

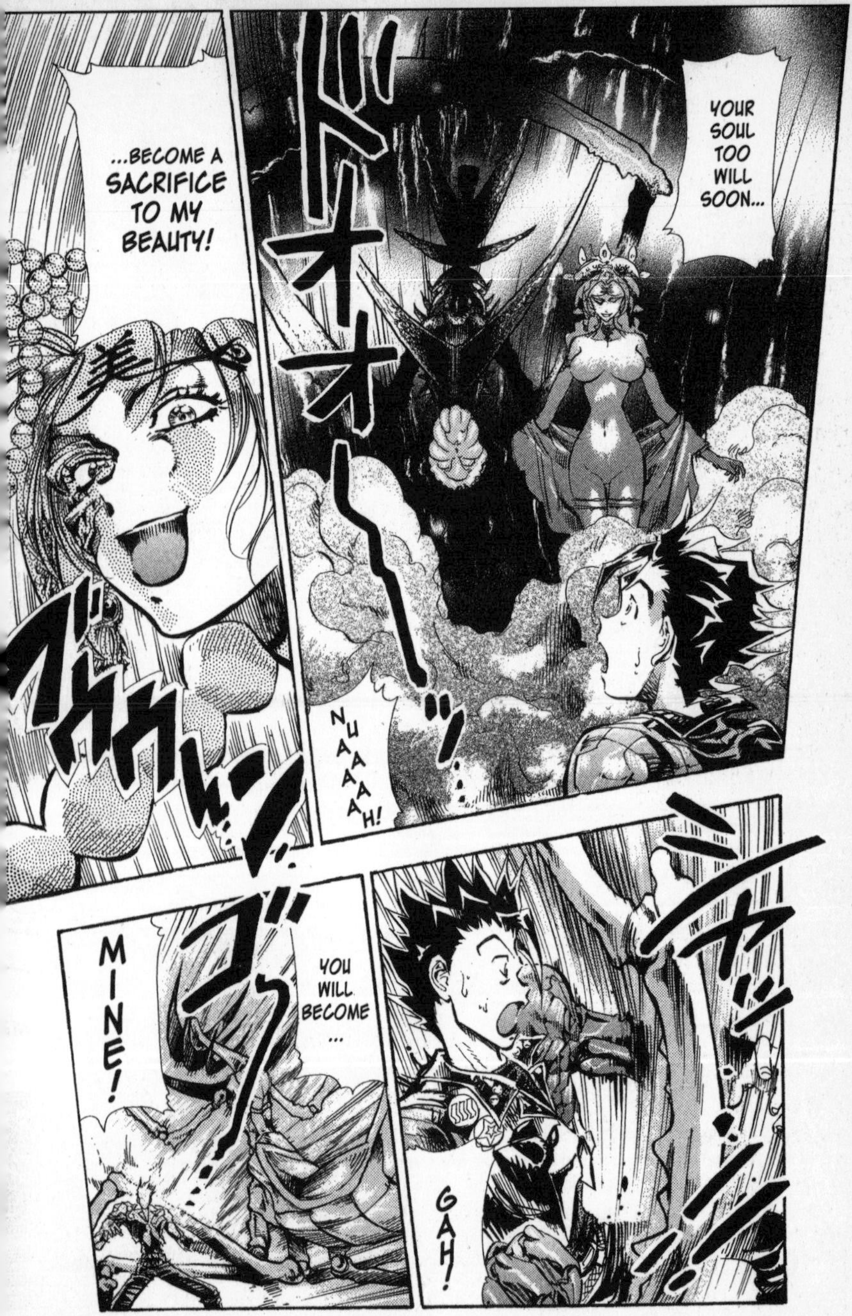
YOUR SOUL TOO WILL SOON...
NUAAAAAH!
...BECOME A SACRIFICE TO MY BEAUTY!
GAH!
YOU WILL BECOME ...
MINE!

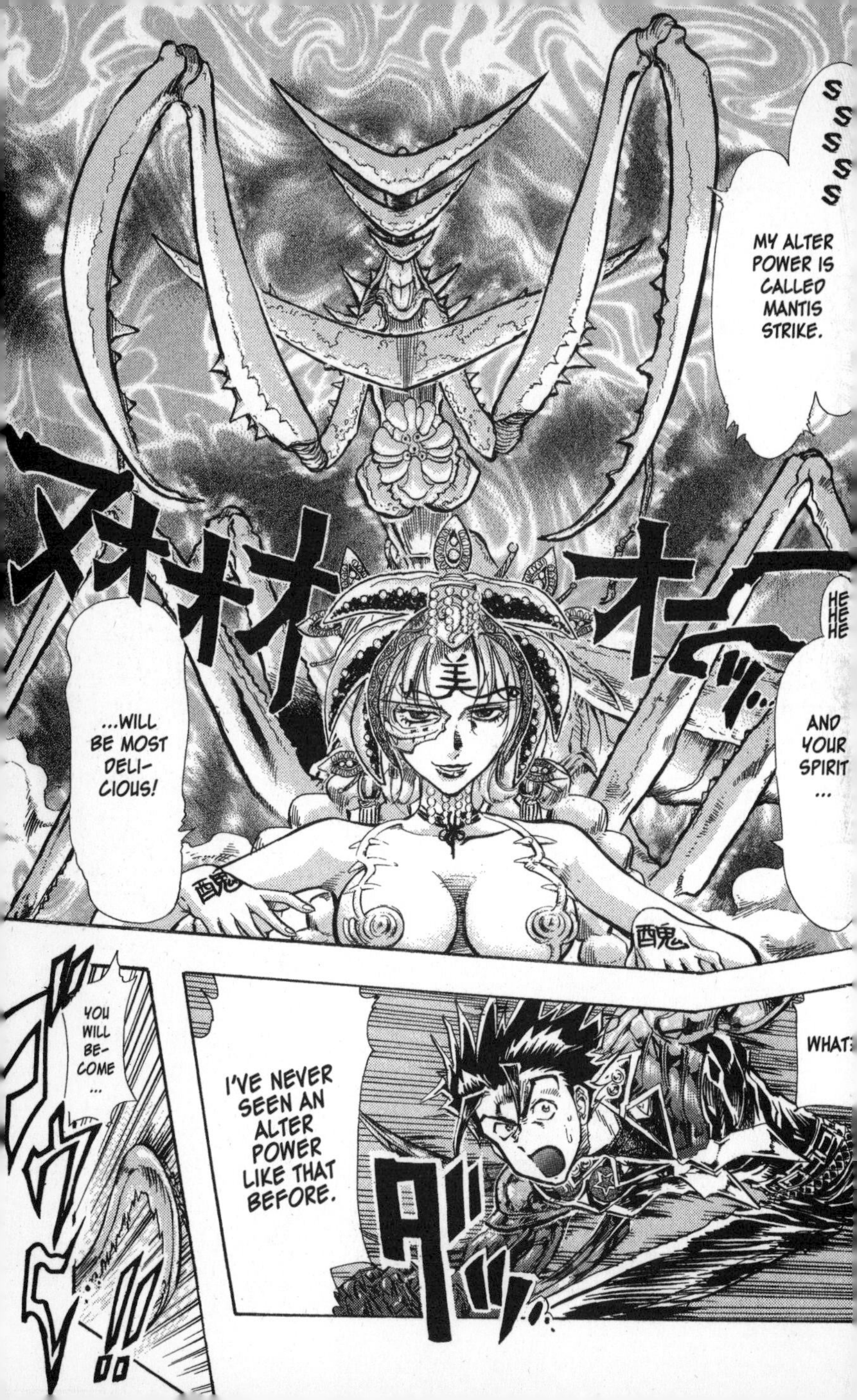
SSSSS
MY ALTER POWER IS CALLED MANTIS STRIKE.
HEHEHE
AND YOUR SPIRIT ...
...WILL BE MOST DELI-CIOUS!
WHAT
I'VE NEVER SEEN AN ALTER POWER LIKE THAT BEFORE.
YOU WILL BE-COME ...

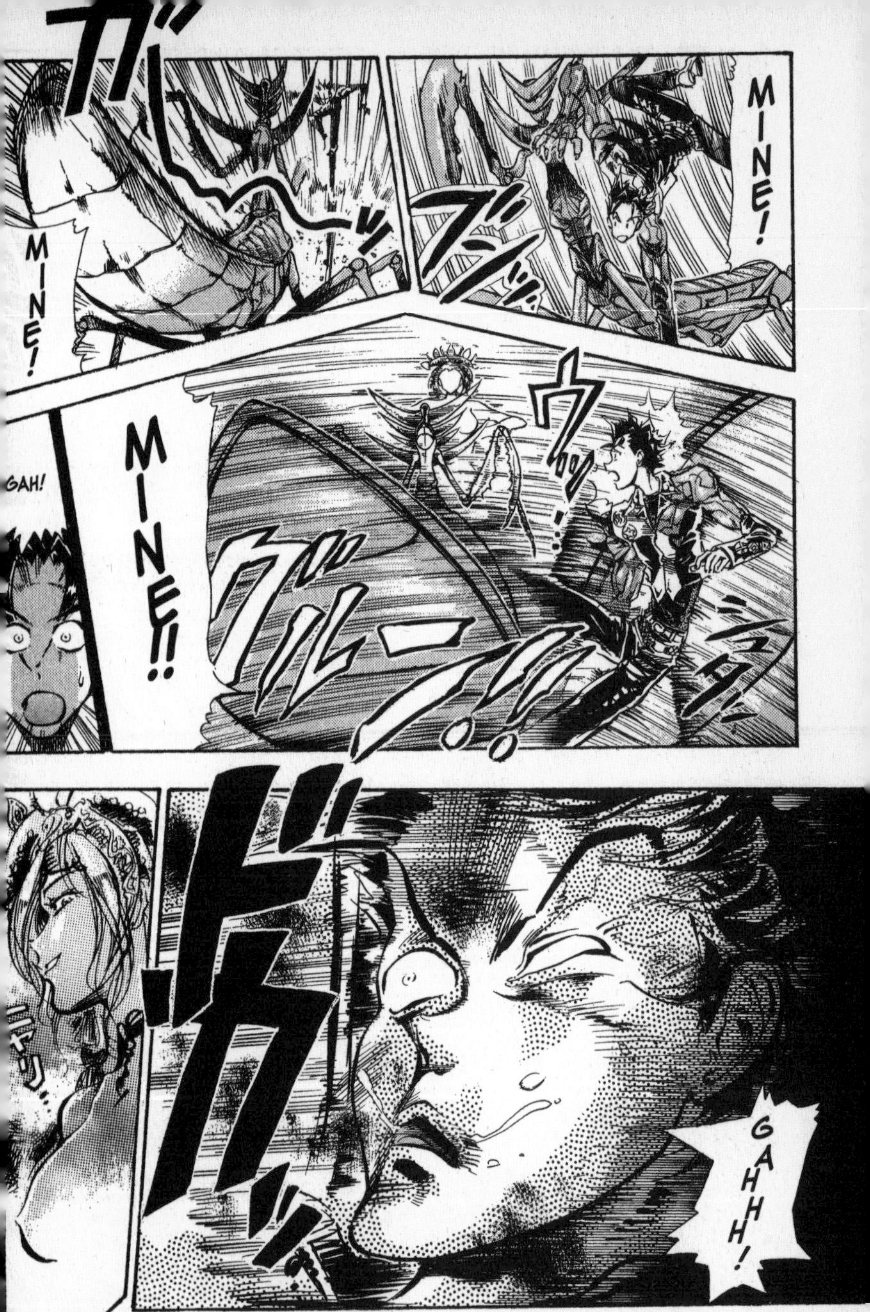
MINE!
MINE!
MINE MINE!!
GAH!
GAHHH!

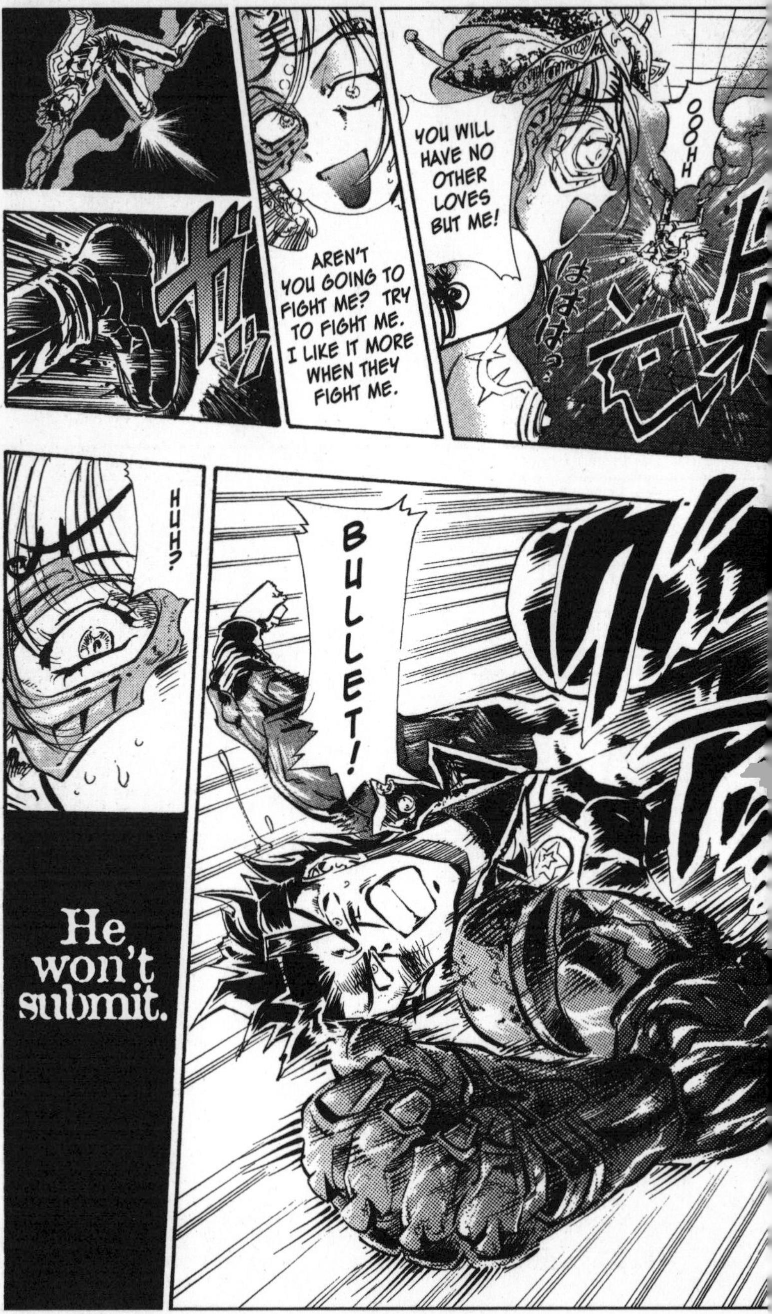
OOOHH
YOU WILL HAVE NO OTHER LOVES BUT ME!
はははっ
AREN'T YOU GOING TO FIGHT ME? TRY TO FIGHT ME. I LIKE IT MORE WHEN THEY FIGHT ME.
ガ!!
BULLET!
HUH?
He won't submit.

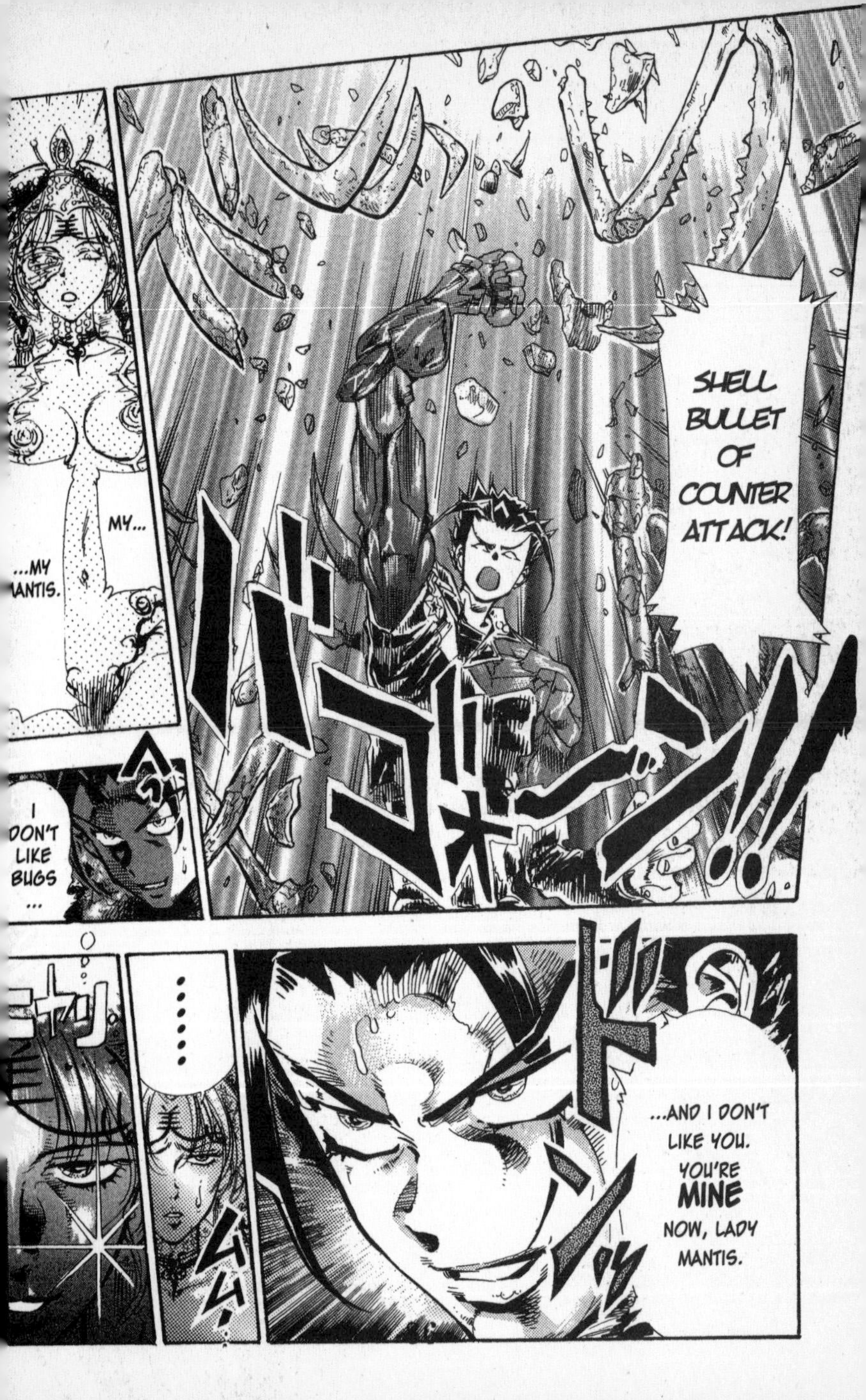
SHELL BULLET OF COUNTER ATTACK!
バゴーン!!
MY...
...MY MANTIS.
I DON'T LIKE BUGS...
...AND I DON'T LIKE YOU. YOU'RE MINE NOW, LADY MANTIS.
......

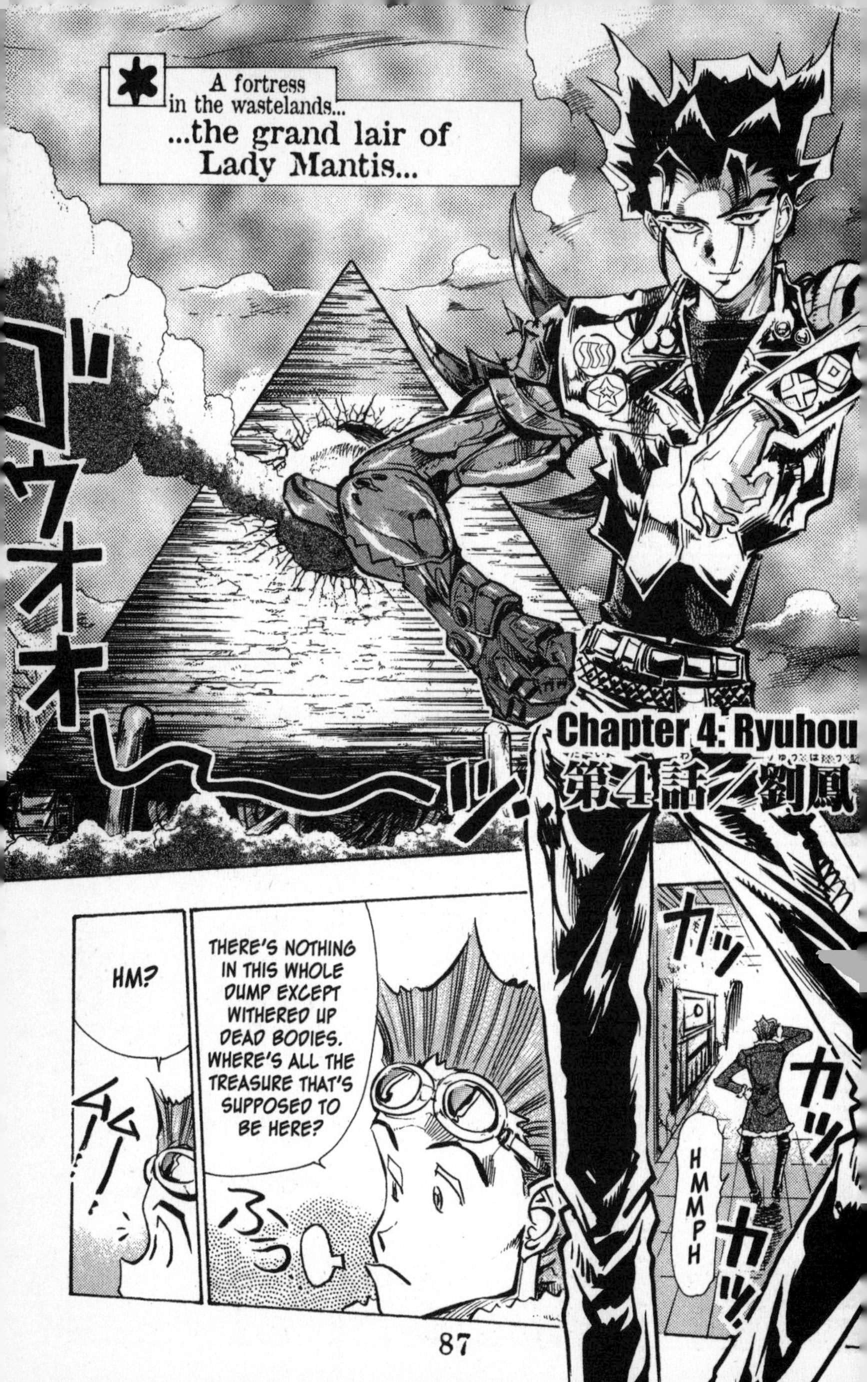
A fortress in the wastelands...
...the grand lair of Lady Mantis...
ゴウオオ〜〜〜ン
Chapter 4: Ryuhou
第4話／劉鳳
カッ
カッ
カッ
HMMPH
THERE'S NOTHING IN THIS WHOLE DUMP EXCEPT WITHERED UP DEAD BODIES. WHERE'S ALL THE TREASURE THAT'S SUPPOSED TO BE HERE?
ふっ
HM?
ムー！

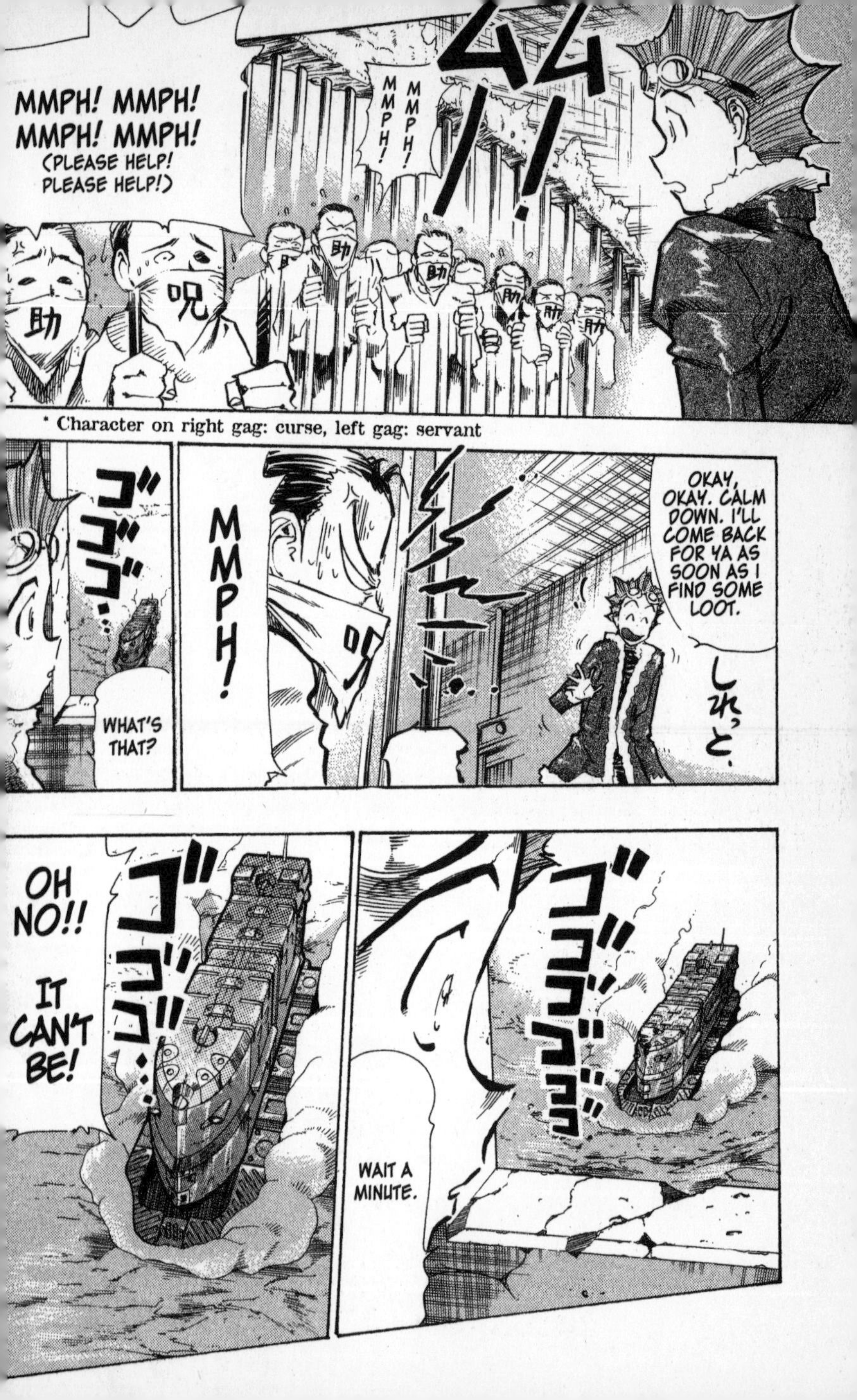
MMPH! MMPH!
MMPH! MMPH! MMPH! MMPH! (PLEASE HELP! PLEASE HELP!)
呪
助
OKAY, OKAY. CALM DOWN. I'LL COME BACK FOR YA AS SOON AS I FIND SOME LOOT.
しれっと.
MMPH!
WHAT'S THAT?
WAIT A MINUTE.
OH NO!! IT CAN'T BE!

* Character on right gag: curse, left gag: servant

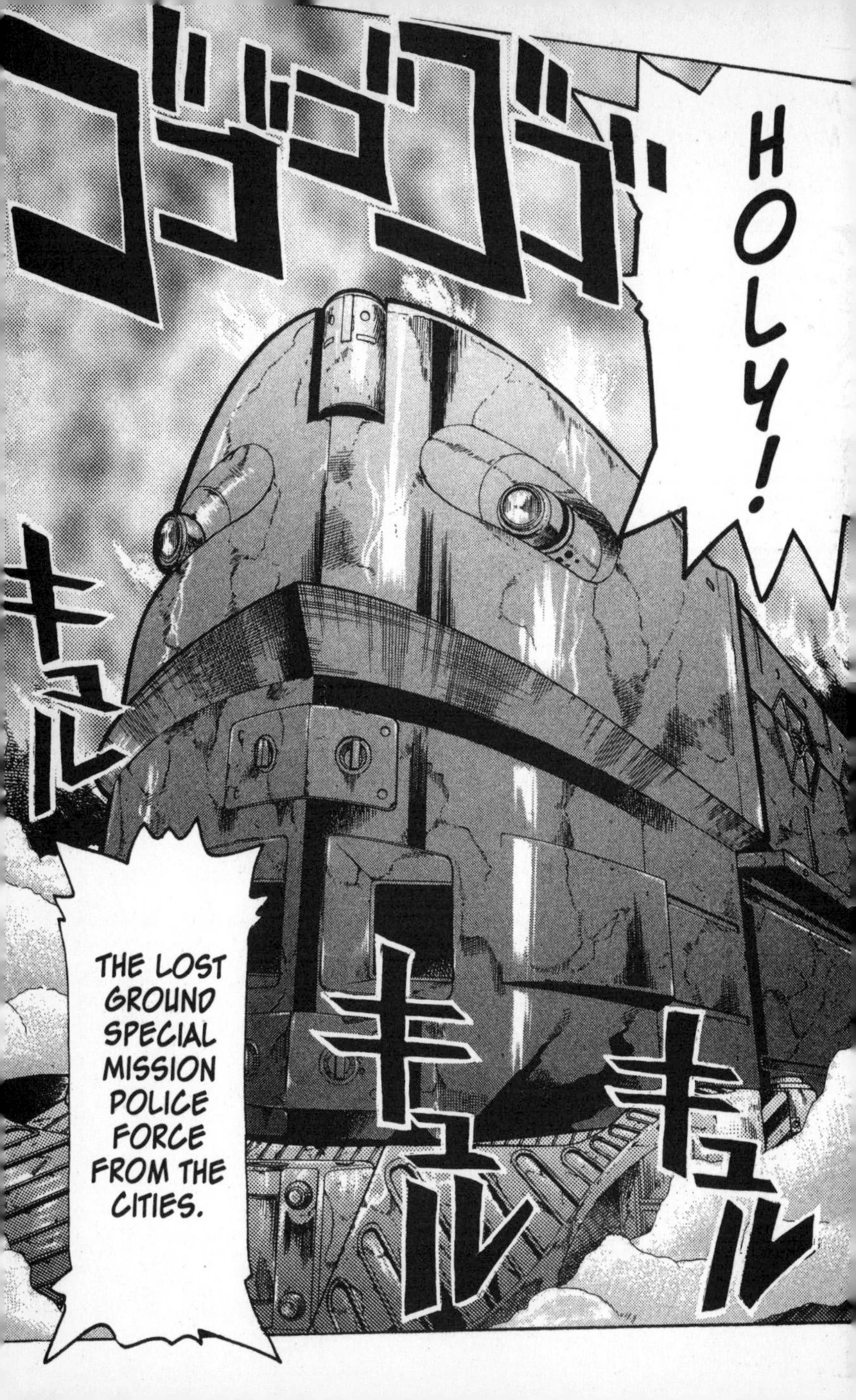
ゴゴゴゴ
HOLY!!
キュル
キュル
THE LOST GROUND SPECIAL MISSION POLICE FORCE FROM THE CITIES.
キュル

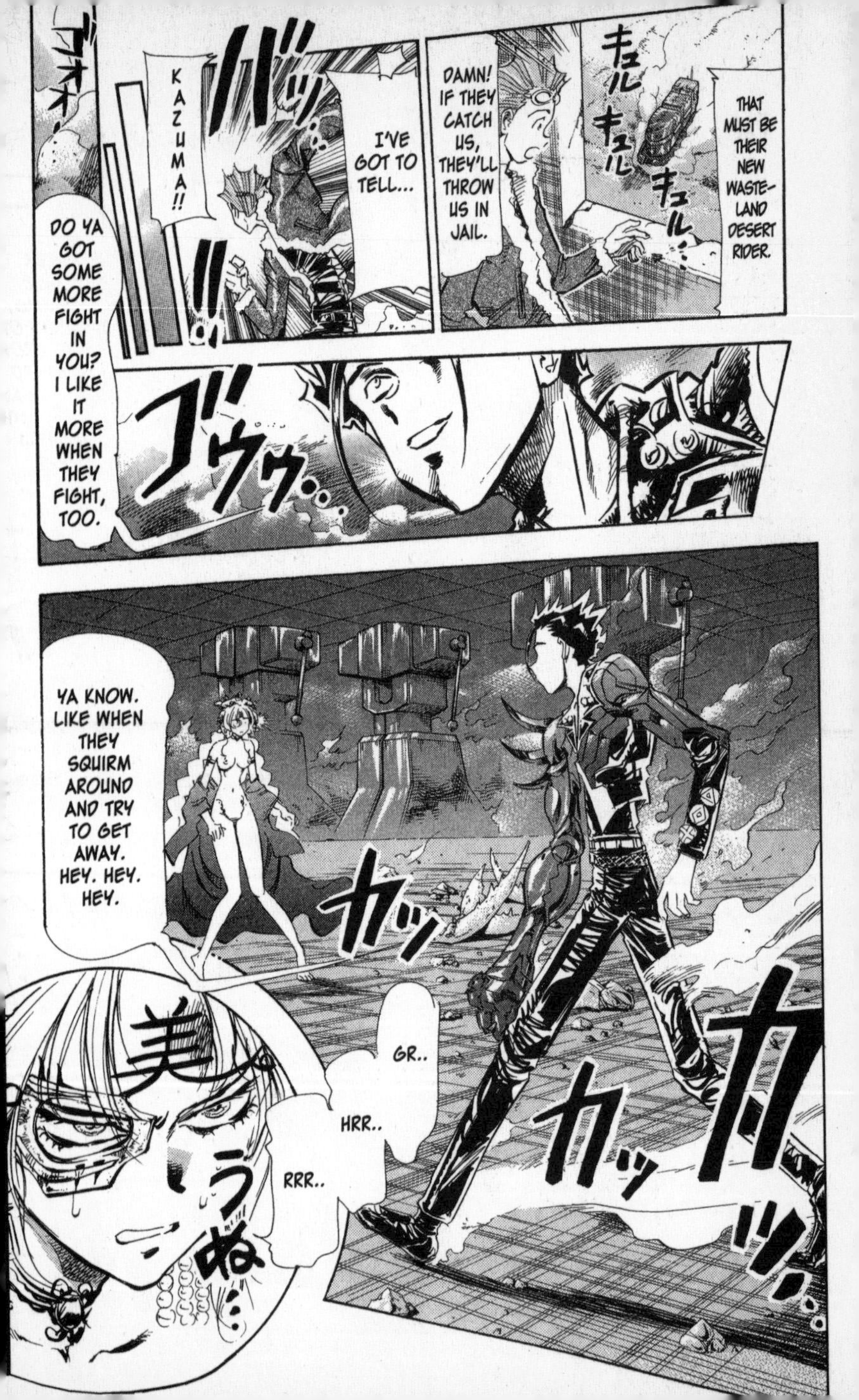
THAT MUST BE THEIR NEW WASTE-LAND DESERT RIDER.
キュルキュルキュル
DAMN! IF THEY CATCH US, THEY'LL THROW US IN JAIL.
I'VE GOT TO TELL...
バッ
KAZUMA!!
ゴオオ
DO YA GOT SOME MORE FIGHT IN YOU? I LIKE IT MORE WHEN THEY FIGHT, TOO.
ゴウウ...
YA KNOW. LIKE WHEN THEY SQUIRM AROUND AND TRY TO GET AWAY. HEY. HEY. HEY.
カッ
カッ
カツ
GR..
HRR..
RRR..
美
うぬ

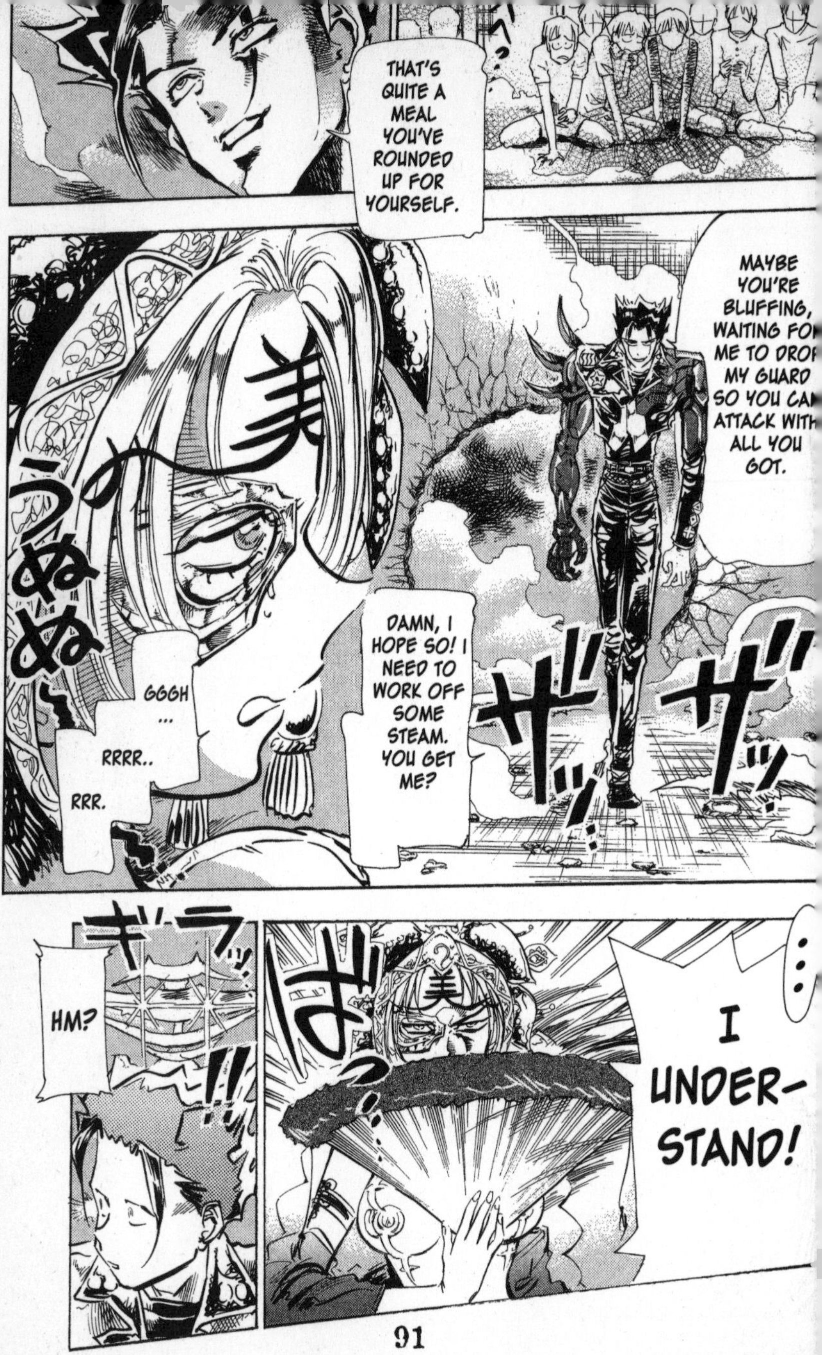

THAT'S QUITE A MEAL YOU'VE ROUNDED UP FOR YOURSELF.
MAYBE YOU'RE BLUFFING, WAITING FO ME TO DRO MY GUARD SO YOU CA ATTACK WITH ALL YOU GOT.
ザッ ザッ
DAMN, I HOPE SO! I NEED TO WORK OFF SOME STEAM. YOU GET ME?
GGGH ... RRRR.. RRR.
うぬぬぬ
...
I UNDER-STAND!
ばっ
HM?
ギラッ
!!

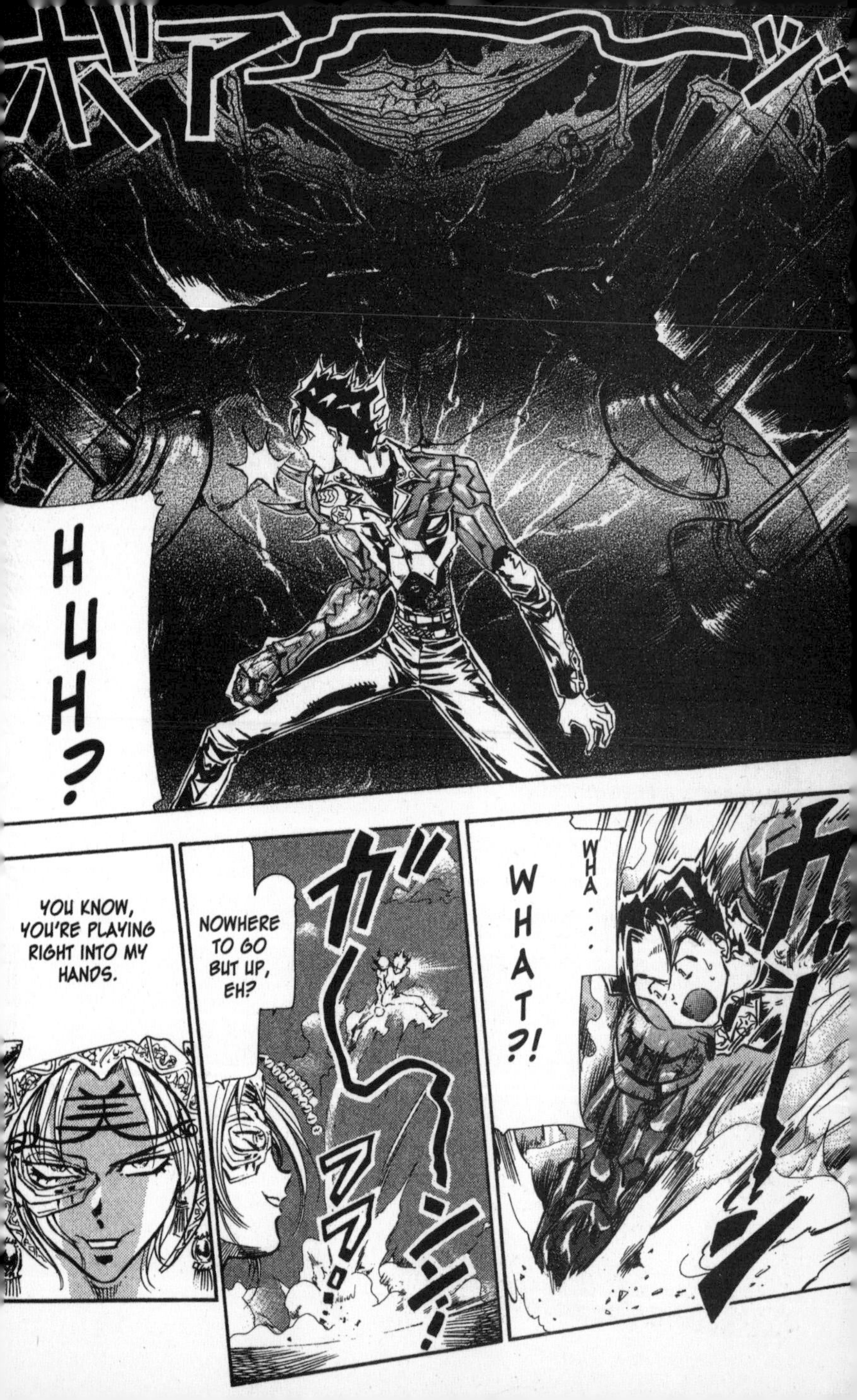
HUH?
WHA...
WHAT?!
NOWHERE TO GO BUT UP, EH?
YOU KNOW, YOU'RE PLAYING RIGHT INTO MY HANDS.

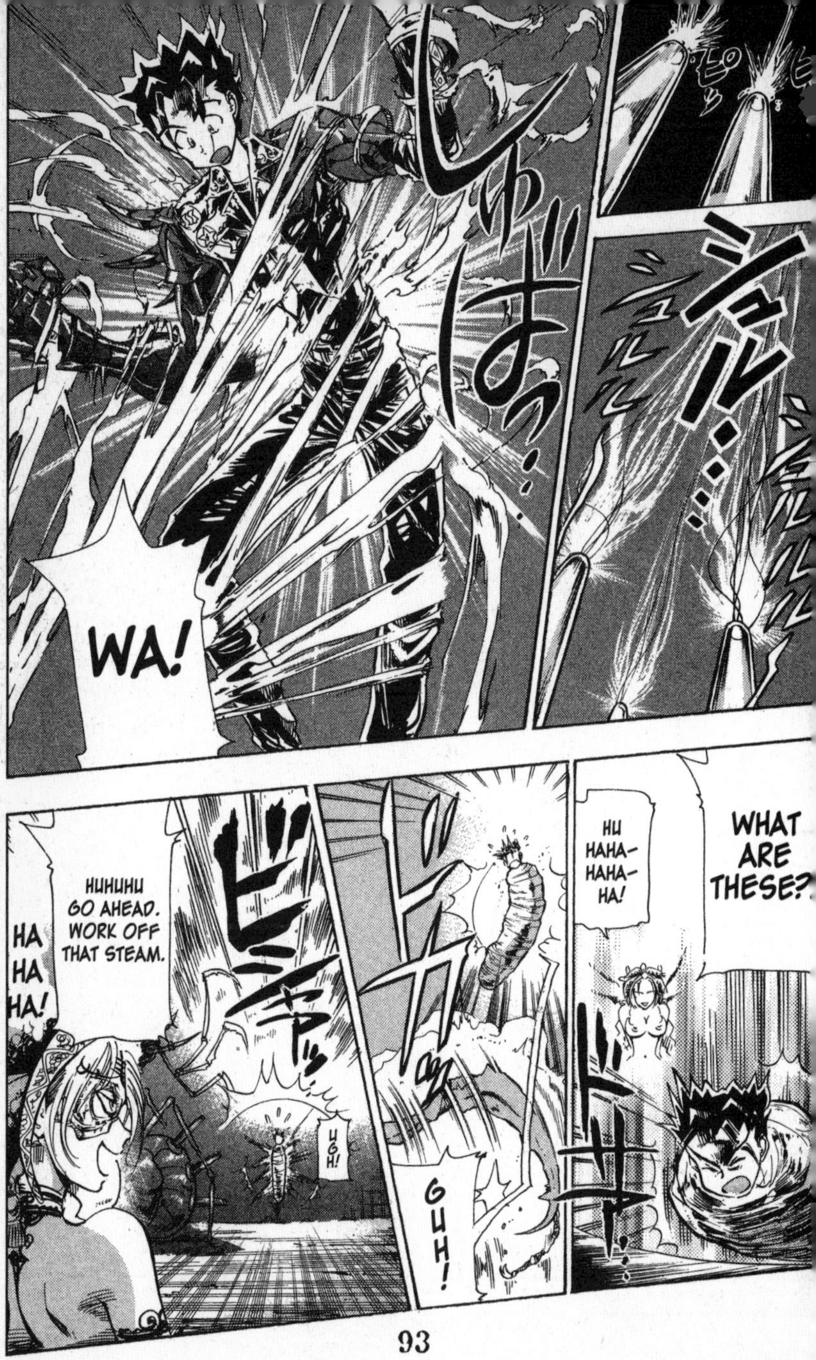
WA!
WHAT ARE THESE?!
HU HAHA-HAHAHA!
GUH!
HUHUHU GO AHEAD. WORK OFF THAT STEAM.
HA HA HA!
UGH!

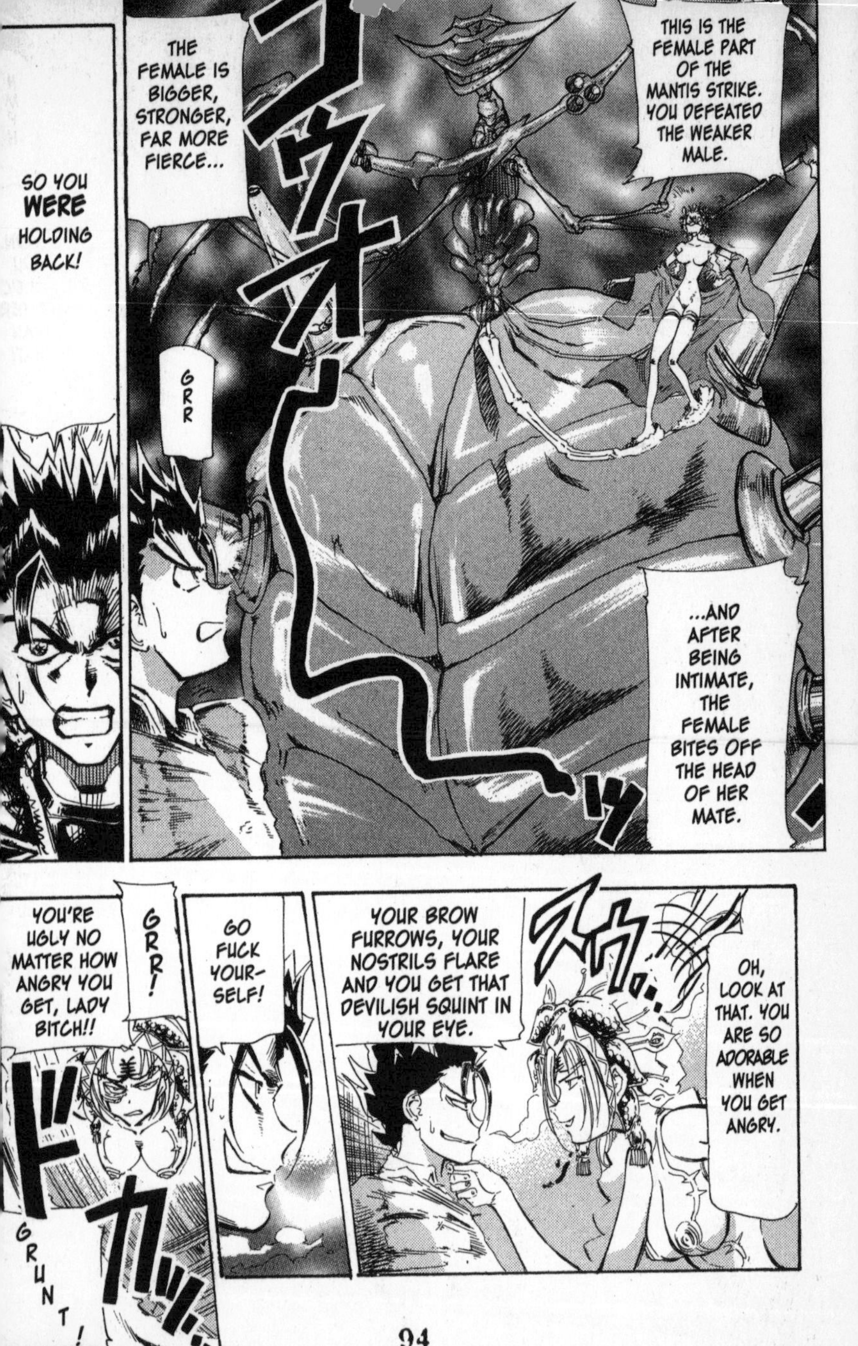
THIS IS THE FEMALE PART OF THE MANTIS STRIKE. YOU DEFEATED THE WEAKER MALE.
THE FEMALE IS BIGGER, STRONGER, FAR MORE FIERCE...
GRR
...AND AFTER BEING INTIMATE, THE FEMALE BITES OFF THE HEAD OF HER MATE.
SO YOU **WERE** HOLDING BACK!
OH, LOOK AT THAT. YOU ARE SO ADORABLE WHEN YOU GET ANGRY.
YOUR BROW FURROWS, YOUR NOSTRILS FLARE AND YOU GET THAT DEVILISH SQUINT IN YOUR EYE.
GO FUCK YOURSELF!
GRR!
YOU'RE UGLY NO MATTER HOW ANGRY YOU GET, LADY BITCH!!
GRUNT!

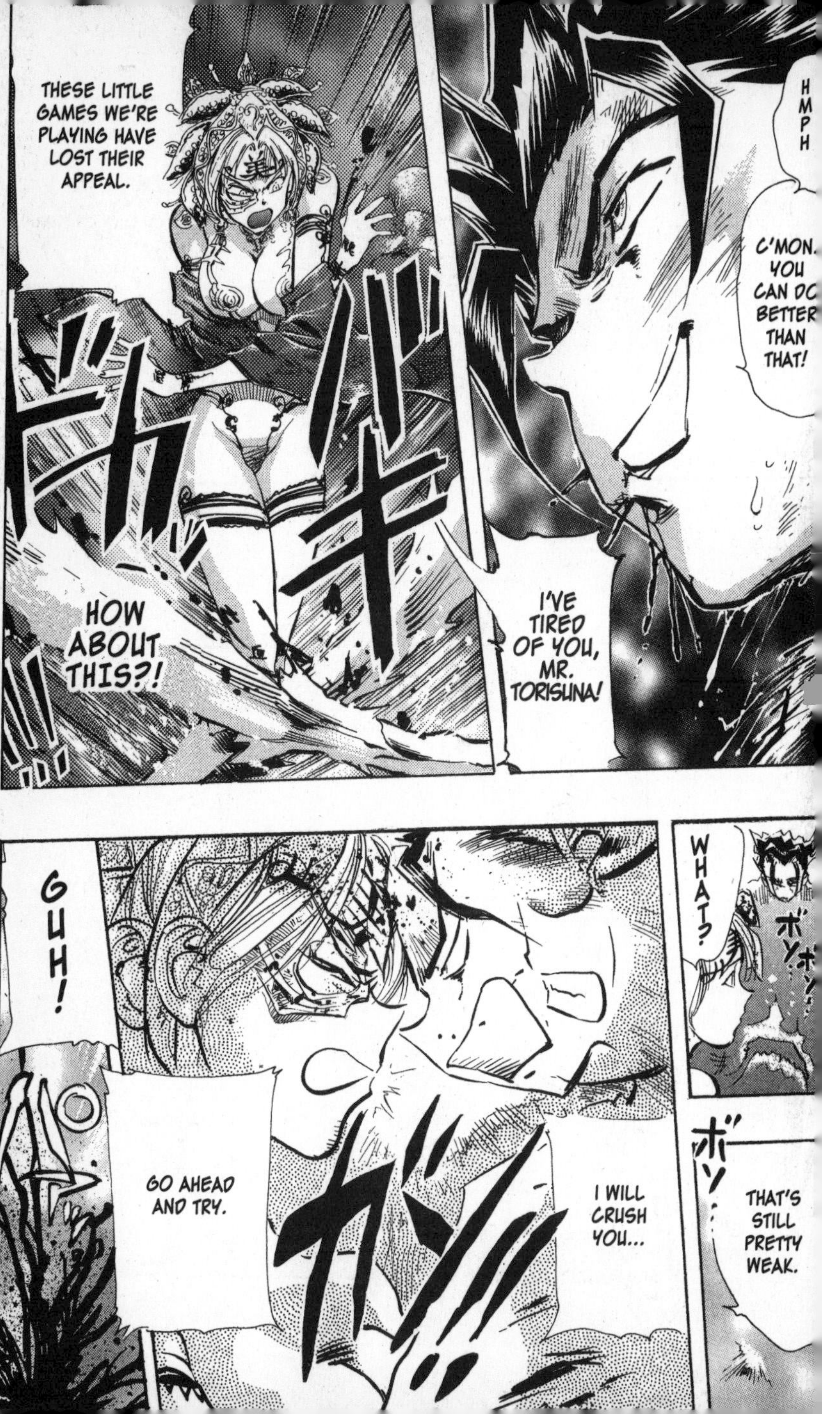
HMPH
C'MON. YOU CAN DO BETTER THAN THAT!
I'VE TIRED OF YOU, MR. TORISUNA!
THESE LITTLE GAMES WE'RE PLAYING HAVE LOST THEIR APPEAL.
HOW ABOUT THIS?!
WHAT?!
THAT'S STILL PRETTY WEAK.
I WILL CRUSH YOU...
GO AHEAD AND TRY.
GUH!

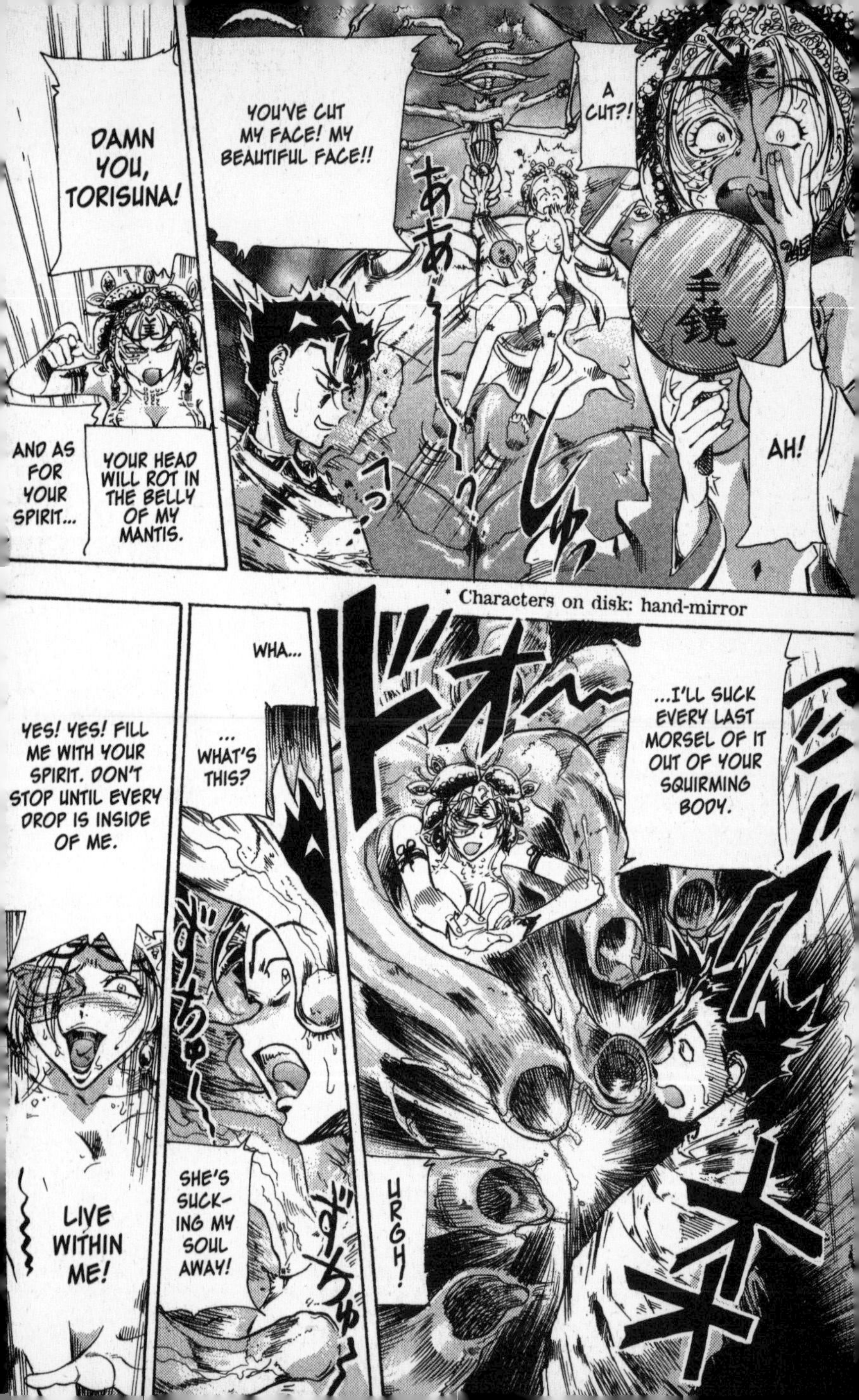
A CUT?!
AH!
YOU'VE CUT MY FACE! MY BEAUTIFUL FACE!!
DAMN YOU, TORISUNA!
YOUR HEAD WILL ROT IN THE BELLY OF MY MANTIS.
AND AS FOR YOUR SPIRIT...
* Characters on disk: hand-mirror
...I'LL SUCK EVERY LAST MORSEL OF IT OUT OF YOUR SQUIRMING BODY.
WHA...
...WHAT'S THIS?
URGH!
SHE'S SUCK-ING MY SOUL AWAY!
YES! YES! FILL ME WITH YOUR SPIRIT. DON'T STOP UNTIL EVERY DROP IS INSIDE OF ME.
LIVE WITHIN ME!

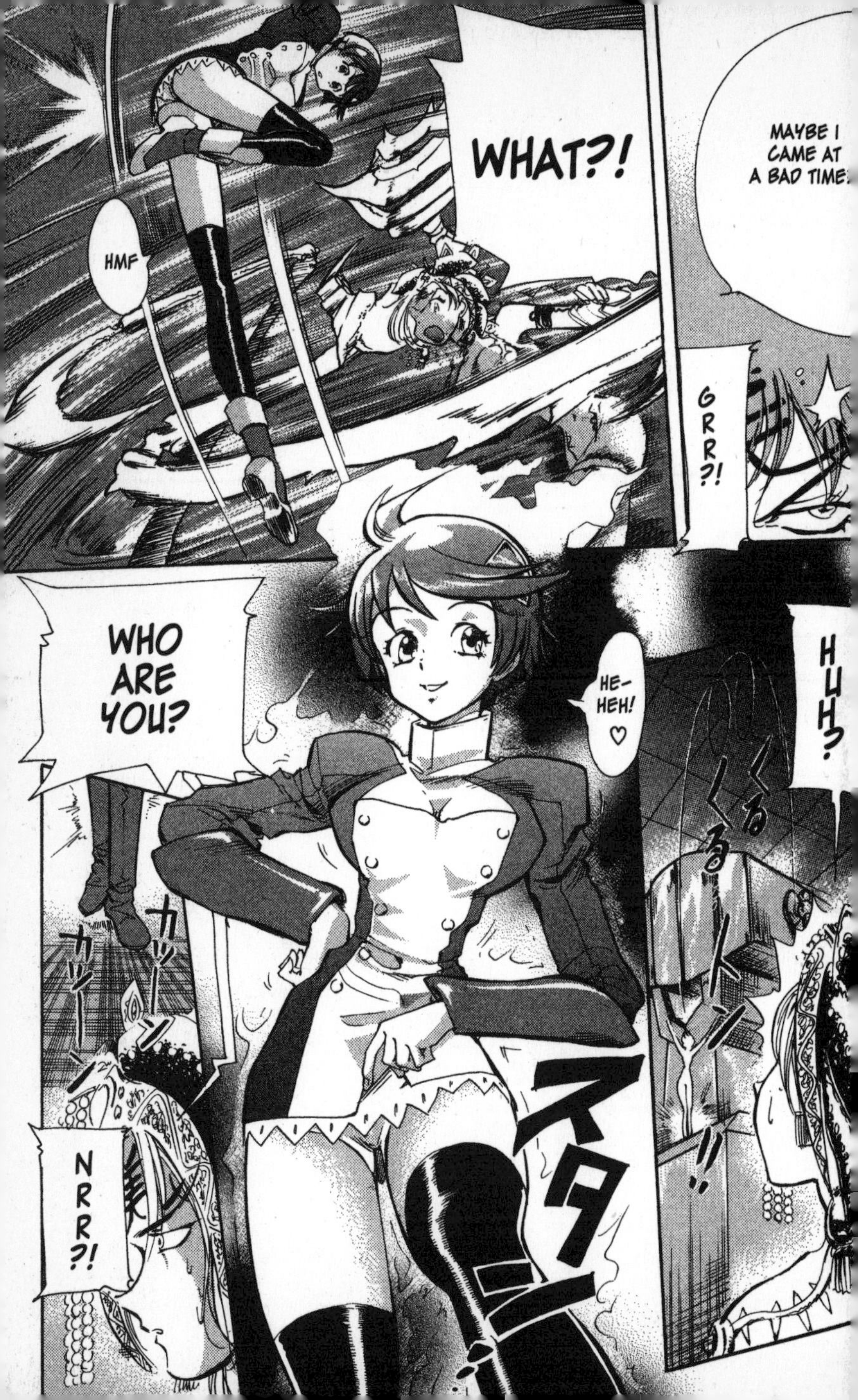
MAYBE I CAME AT A BAD TIME...
GRR?!
WHAT?!
HMF
HUH?
くるくるストン!!
HE-HEH! ♥
WHO ARE YOU?
スタ
カツーン カツーン
NRR?!

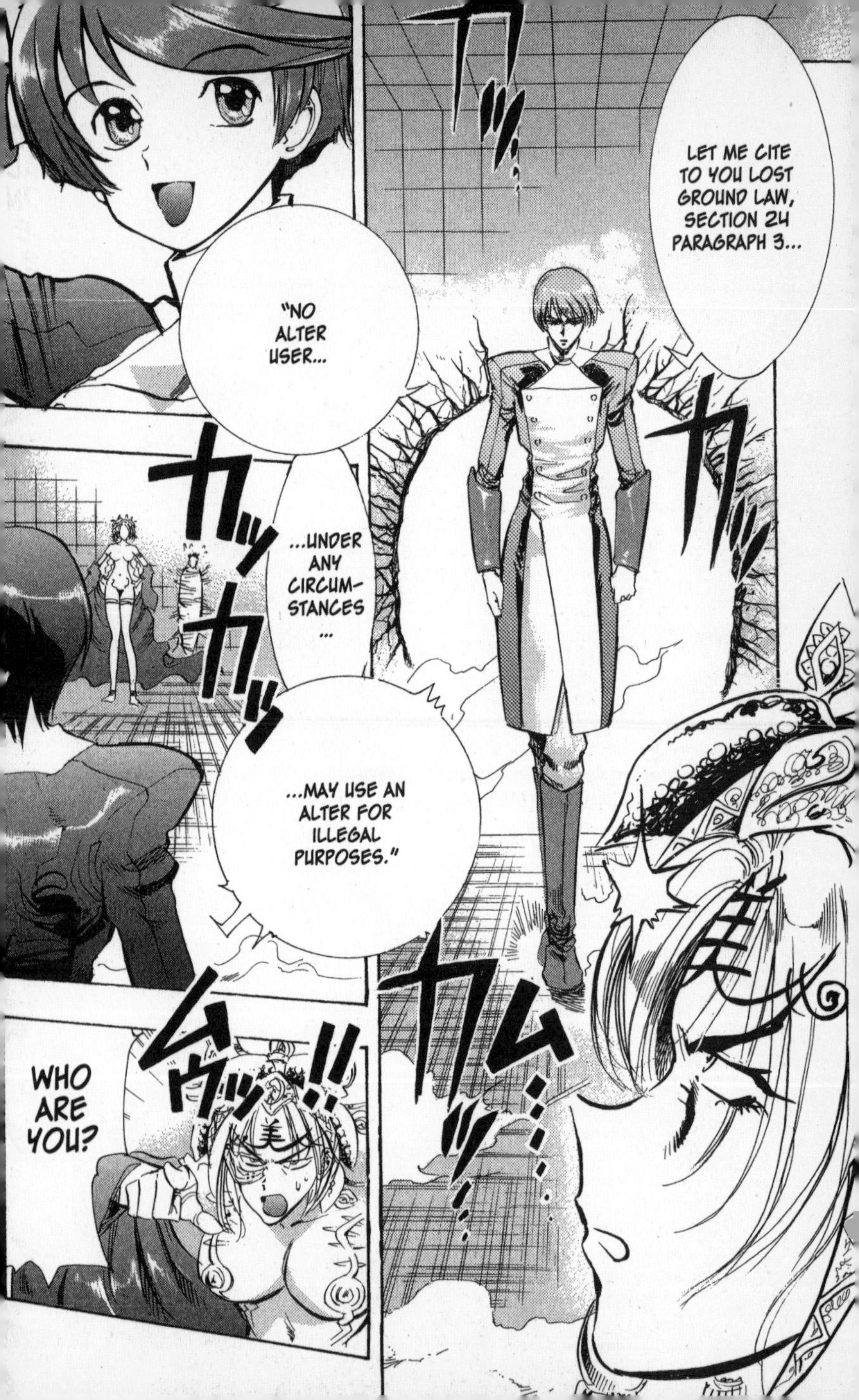
LET ME CITE TO YOU LOST GROUND LAW, SECTION 24 PARAGRAPH 3...
"NO ALTER USER...
...UNDER ANY CIRCUM-STANCES...
...MAY USE AN ALTER FOR ILLEGAL PURPOSES."
WHO ARE YOU?

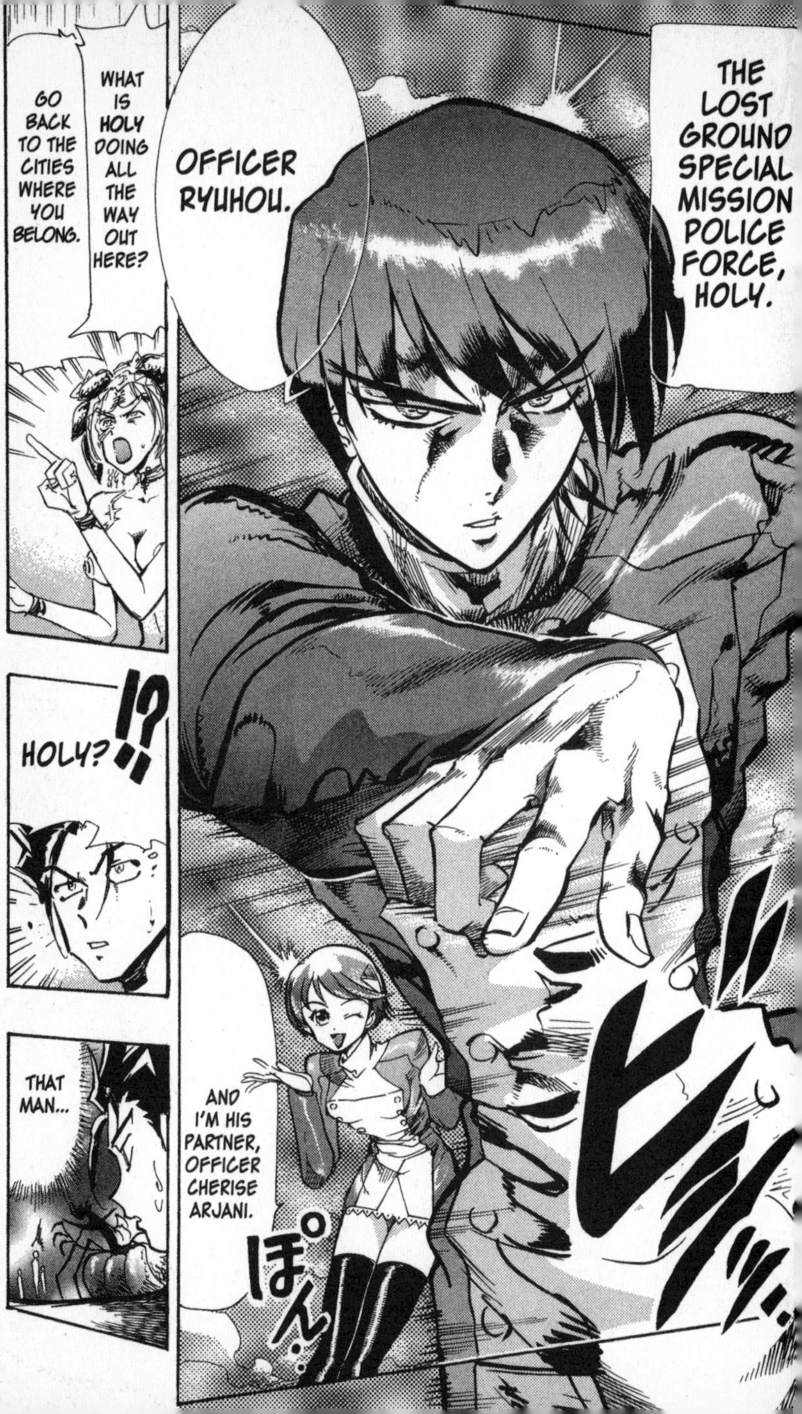
THE LOST GROUND SPECIAL MISSION POLICE FORCE, HOLY.
OFFICER RYUHOU.
AND I'M HIS PARTNER, OFFICER CHERISE ARJANI.
ぽん..
WHAT IS HOLY DOING ALL THE WAY OUT HERE?
GO BACK TO THE CITIES WHERE YOU BELONG.
HOLY?!!?
THAT MAN...

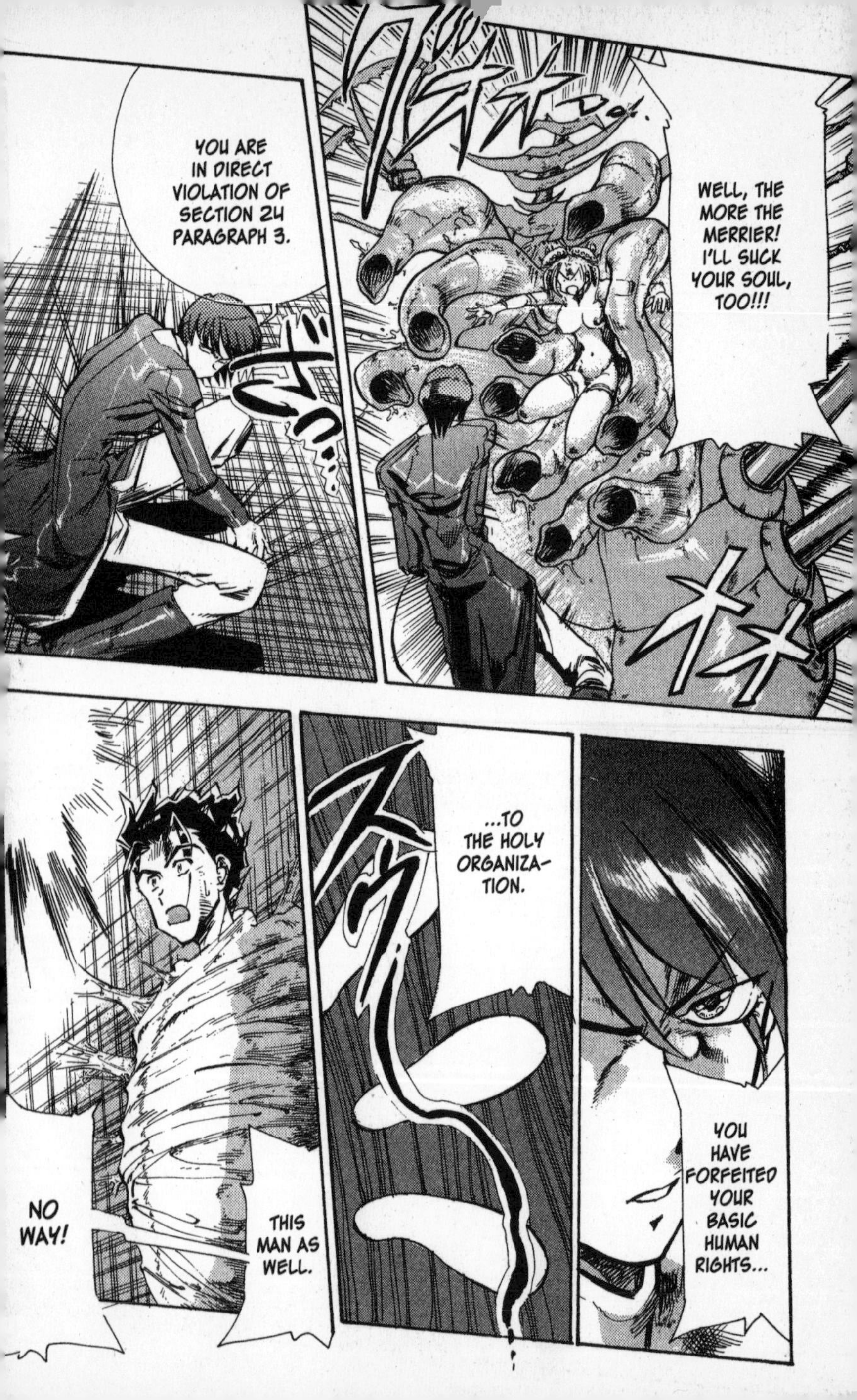
WELL, THE MORE THE MERRIER! I'LL SUCK YOUR SOUL, TOO!!!
YOU ARE IN DIRECT VIOLATION OF SECTION 24 PARAGRAPH 3.
YOU HAVE FORFEITED YOUR BASIC HUMAN RIGHTS...
...TO THE HOLY ORGANIZATION.
THIS MAN AS WELL.
NO WAY!

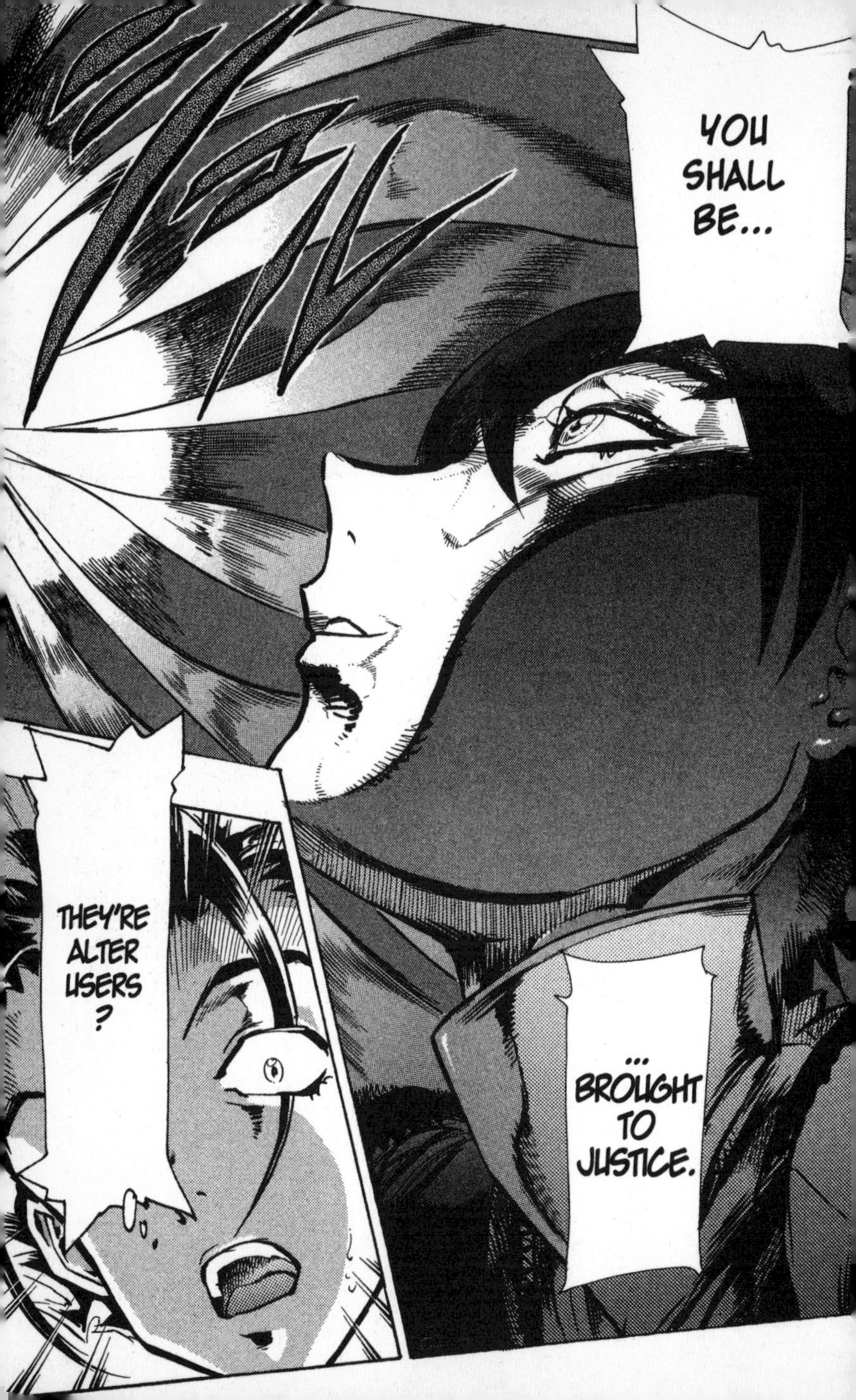
YOU SHALL BE...
THEY'RE ALTER USERS?
...BROUGHT TO JUSTICE.

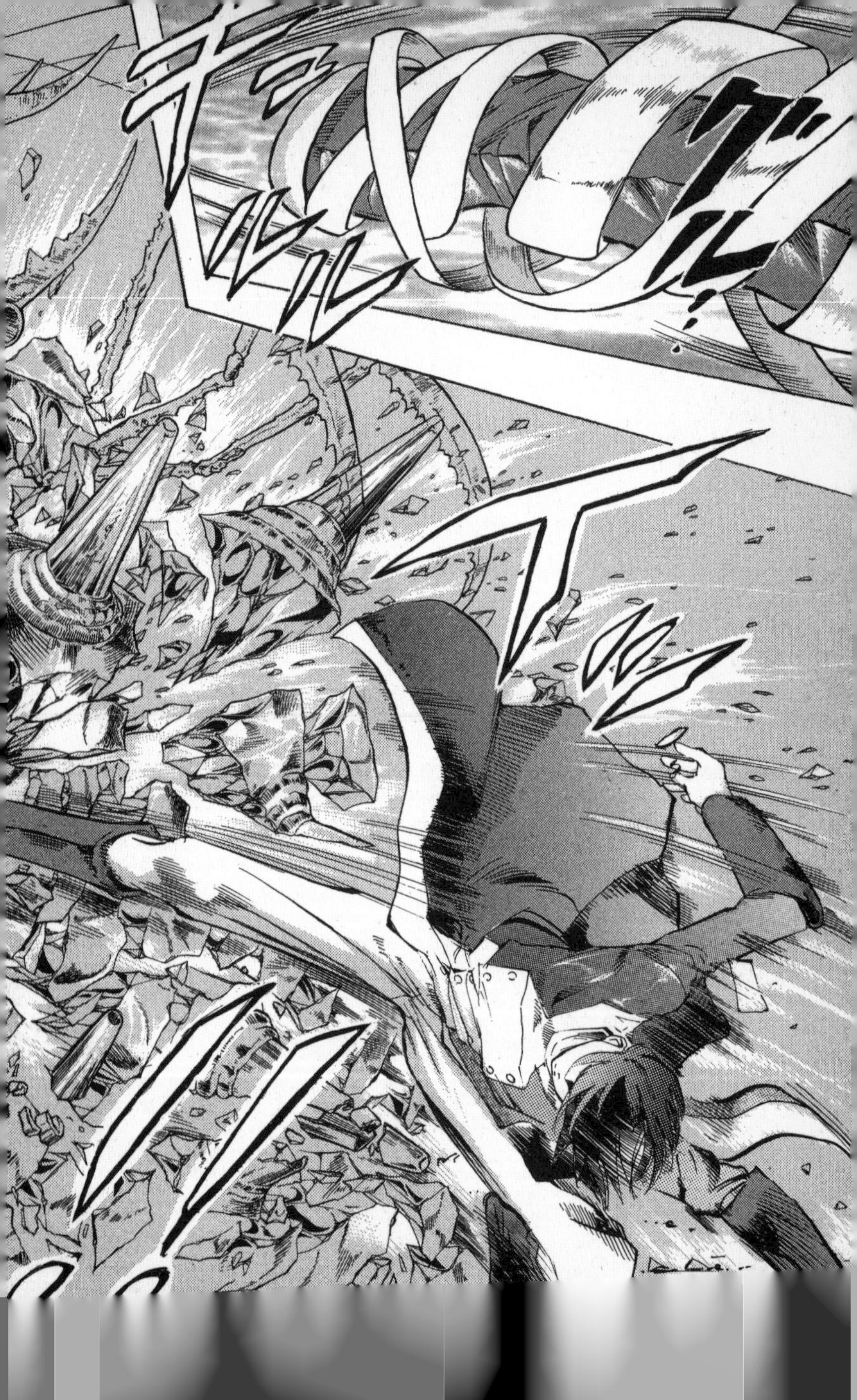
ギュルルル

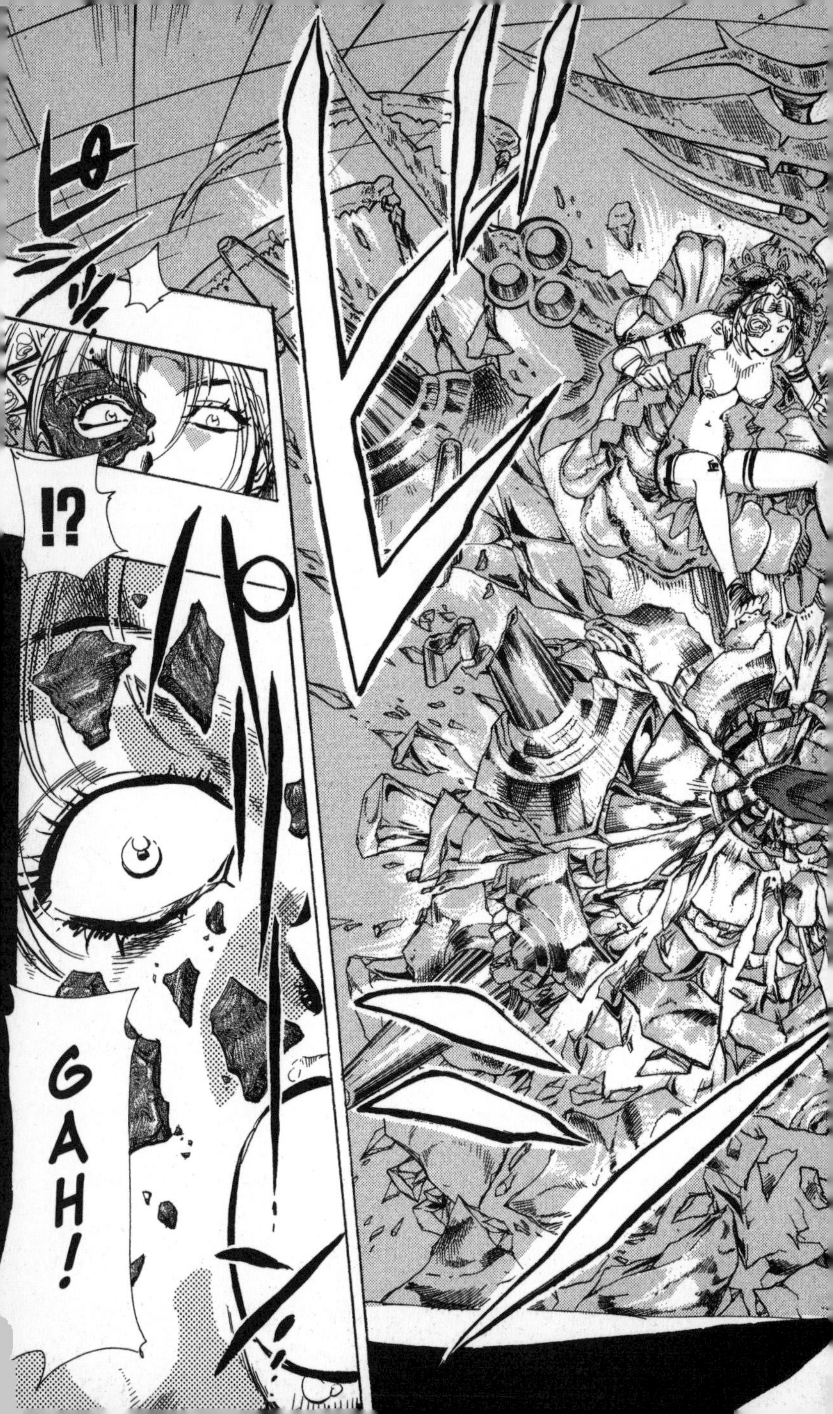
!?
GAH!

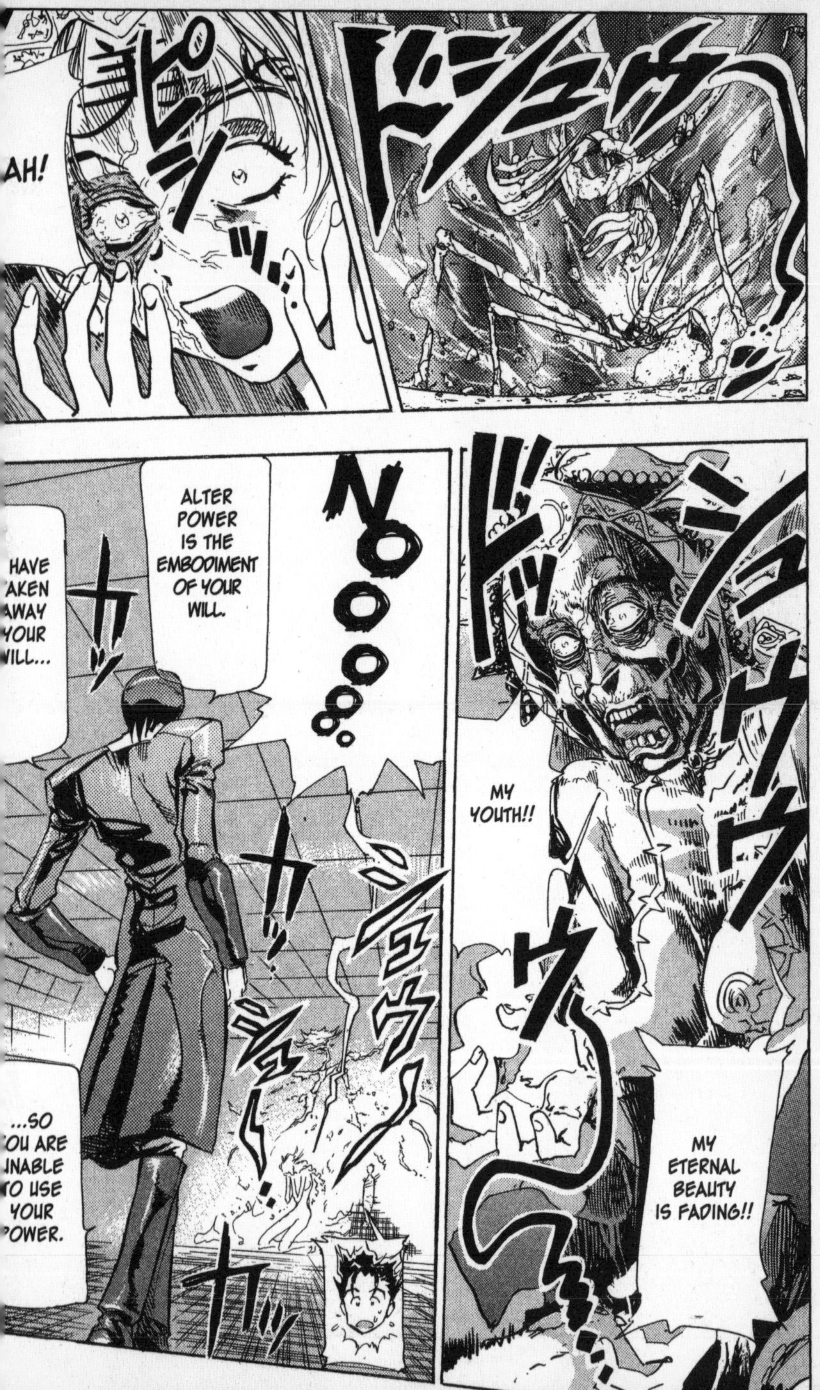
AH!
NOOOOOO
ALTER POWER IS THE EMBODIMENT OF YOUR WILL.
HAVE AKEN AWAY YOUR WILL...
...SO OU ARE NABLE O USE YOUR POWER.
MY YOUTH!!
MY ETERNAL BEAUTY IS FADING!!

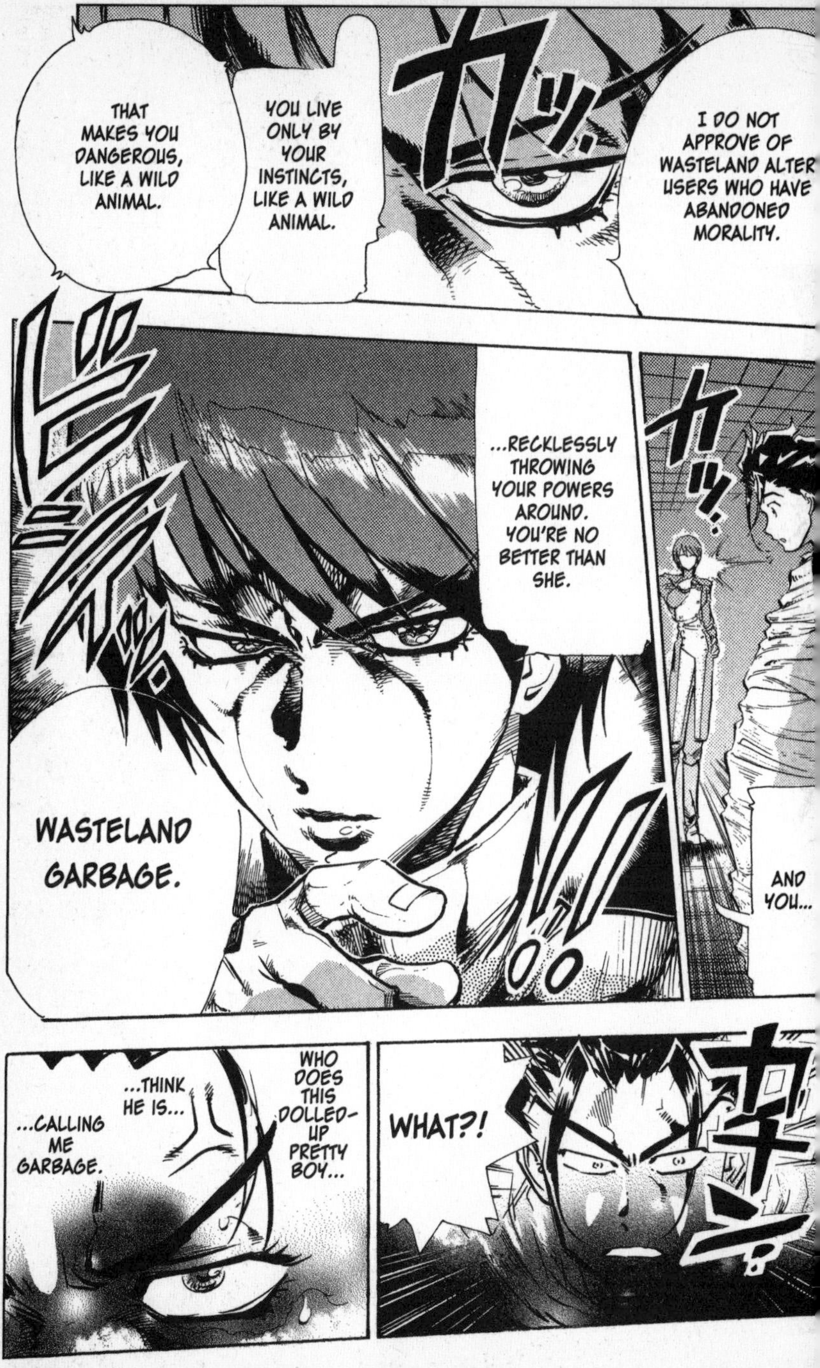
I DO NOT APPROVE OF WASTELAND ALTER USERS WHO HAVE ABANDONED MORALITY.
YOU LIVE ONLY BY YOUR INSTINCTS, LIKE A WILD ANIMAL.
THAT MAKES YOU DANGEROUS, LIKE A WILD ANIMAL.
AND YOU...
...RECKLESSLY THROWING YOUR POWERS AROUND. YOU'RE NO BETTER THAN SHE.
WASTELAND GARBAGE.
WHAT?!
WHO DOES THIS DOLLED-UP PRETTY BOY...
...THINK HE IS...
...CALLING ME GARBAGE.

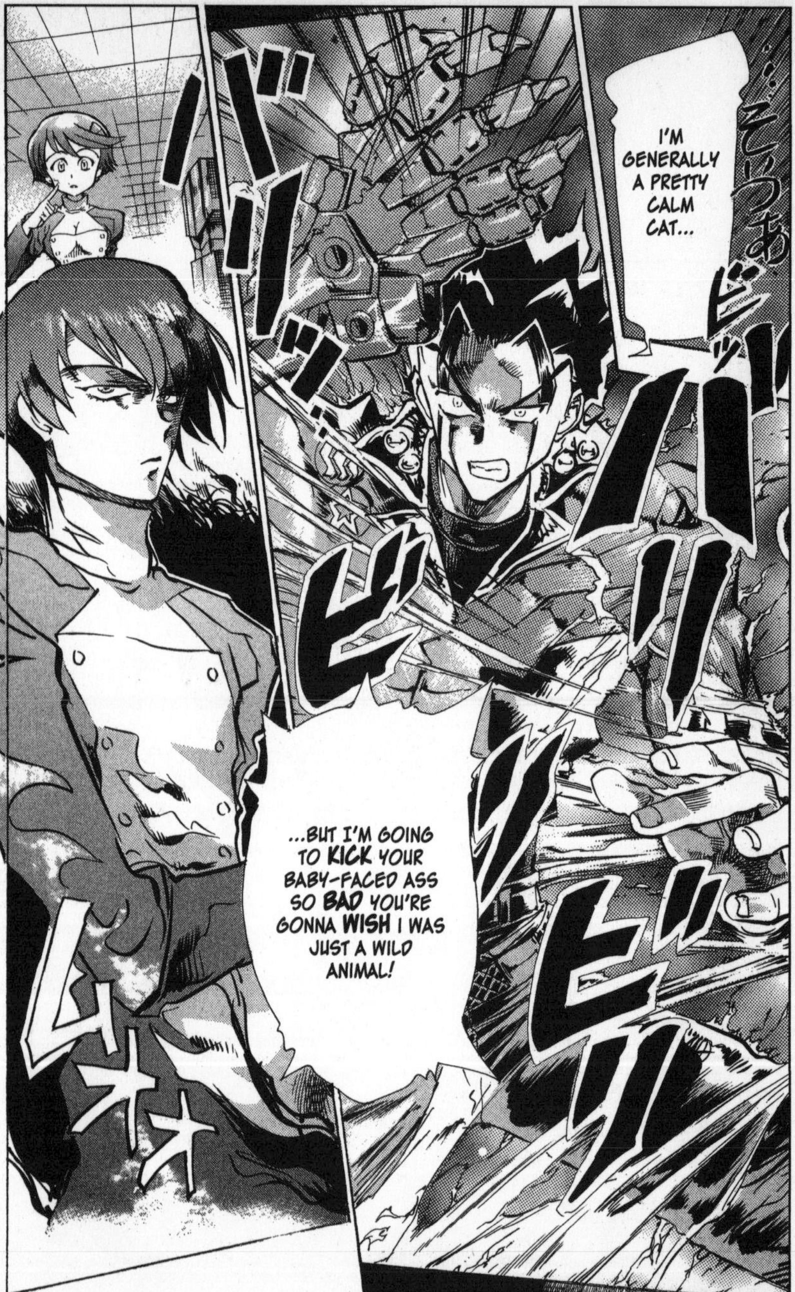
I'M GENERALLY A PRETTY CALM CAT...
...BUT I'M GOING TO KICK YOUR BABY-FACED ASS SO BAD YOU'RE GONNA WISH I WAS JUST A WILD ANIMAL!

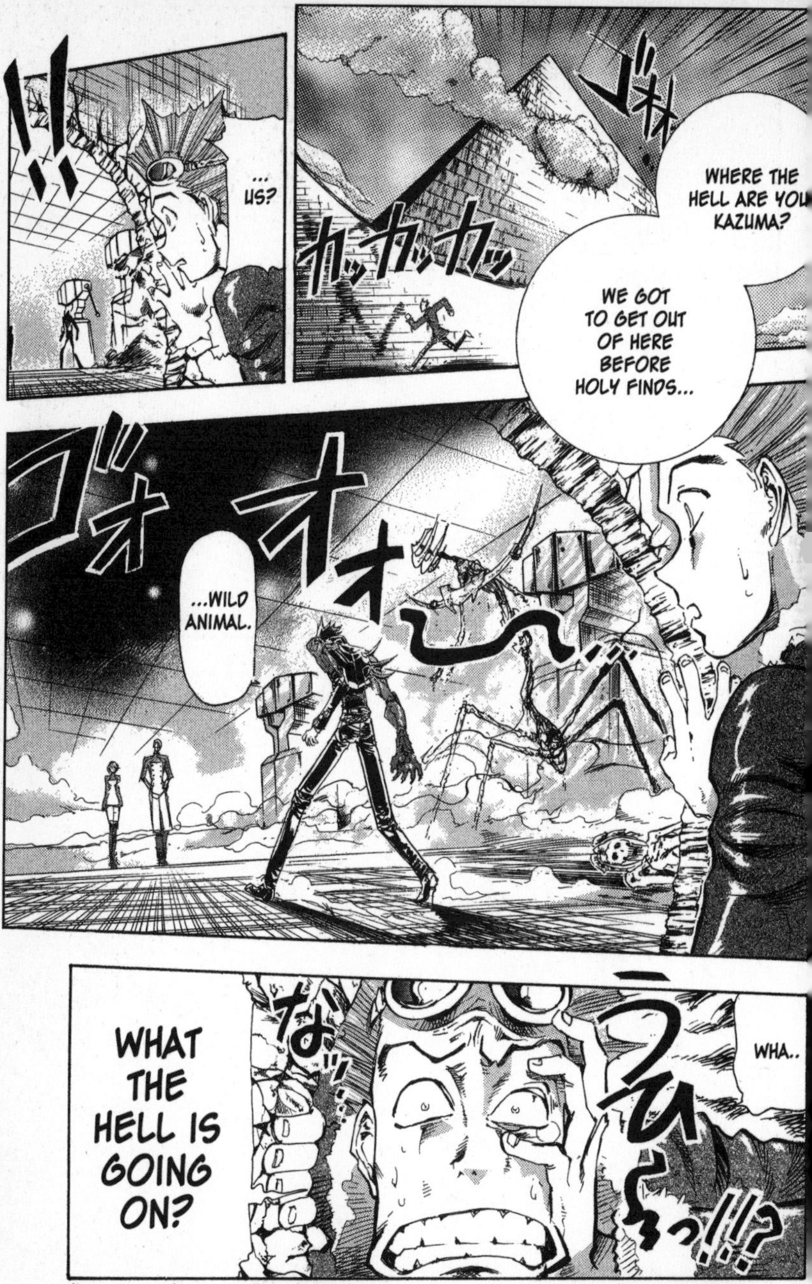
WHERE THE HELL ARE YOU KAZUMA?
WE GOT TO GET OUT OF HERE BEFORE HOLY FINDS...
カッカッカッ
... US?
!!
ゴォオオ
...WILD ANIMAL.
WHA..
うひょっ!!?
なっ
WHAT THE HELL IS GOING ON?

第5話／絶影 **Chapter 5: Final Shadow**

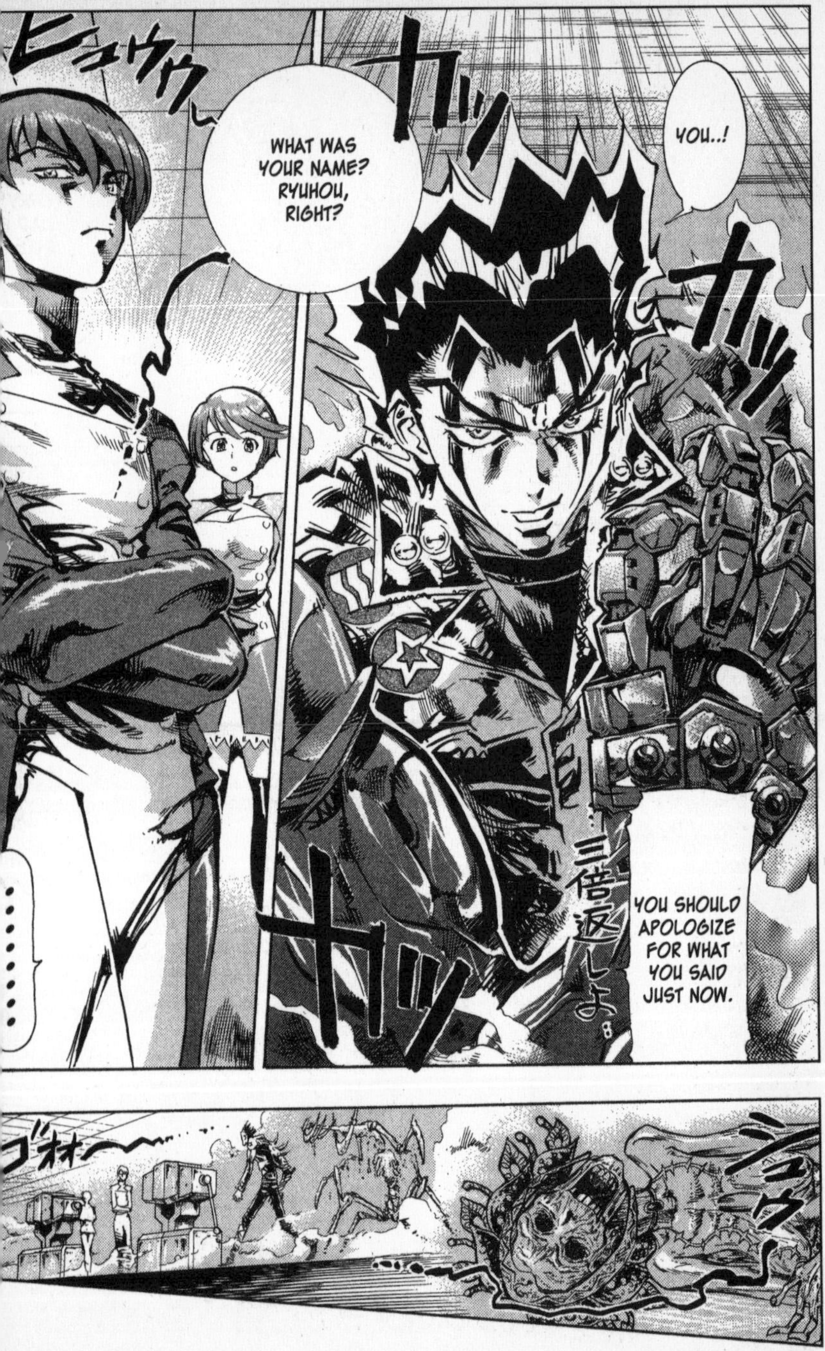

YOU..!
カッ
カッ
三倍返しよ
YOU SHOULD APOLOGIZE FOR WHAT YOU SAID JUST NOW.
ザッ
WHAT WAS YOUR NAME? RYUHOU, RIGHT?
......

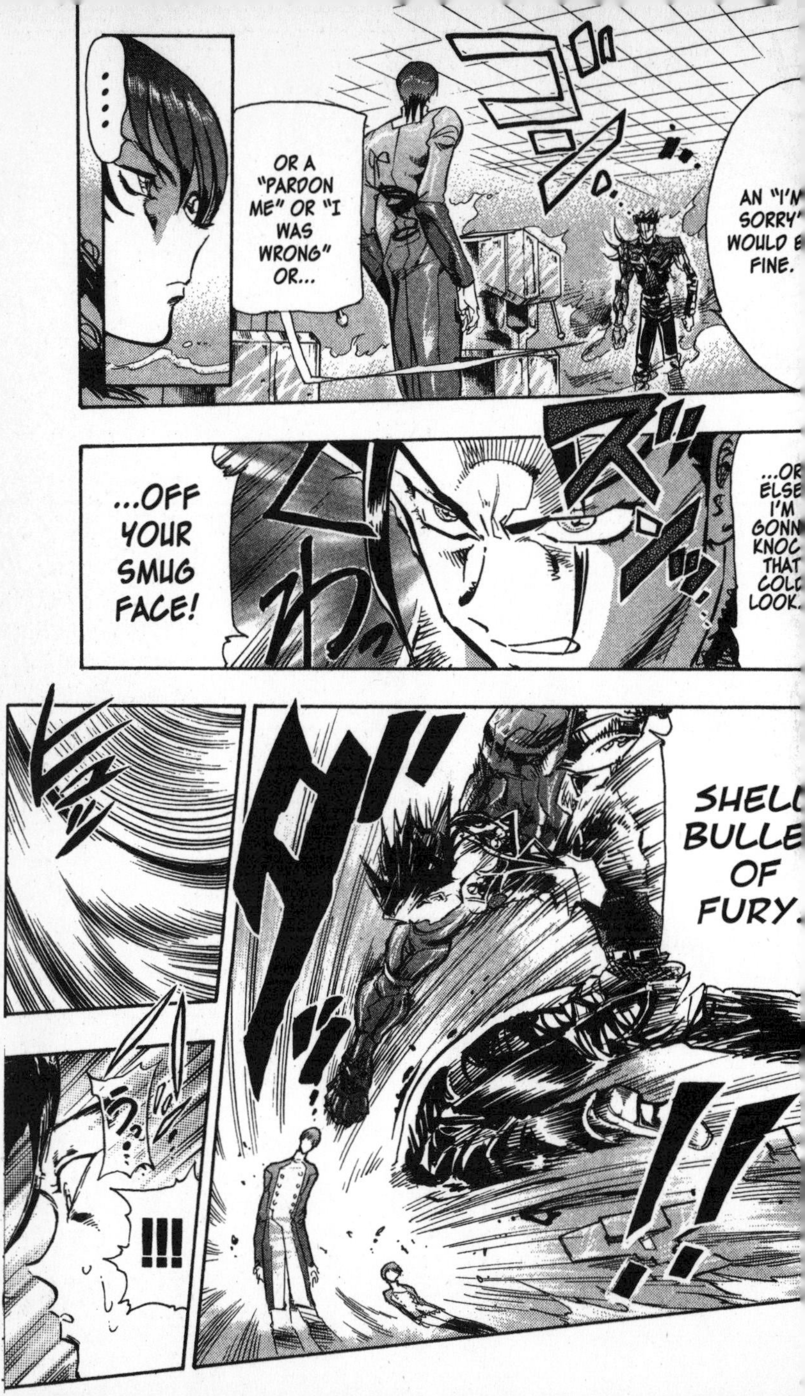
AN "I'M SORRY" WOULD B FINE.
OR A "PARDON ME" OR "I WAS WRONG" OR...
....
...OR ELSE I'M GONN KNOC THAT COLD LOOK...
...OFF YOUR SMUG FACE!
SHELL BULLE OF FURY.
!!!

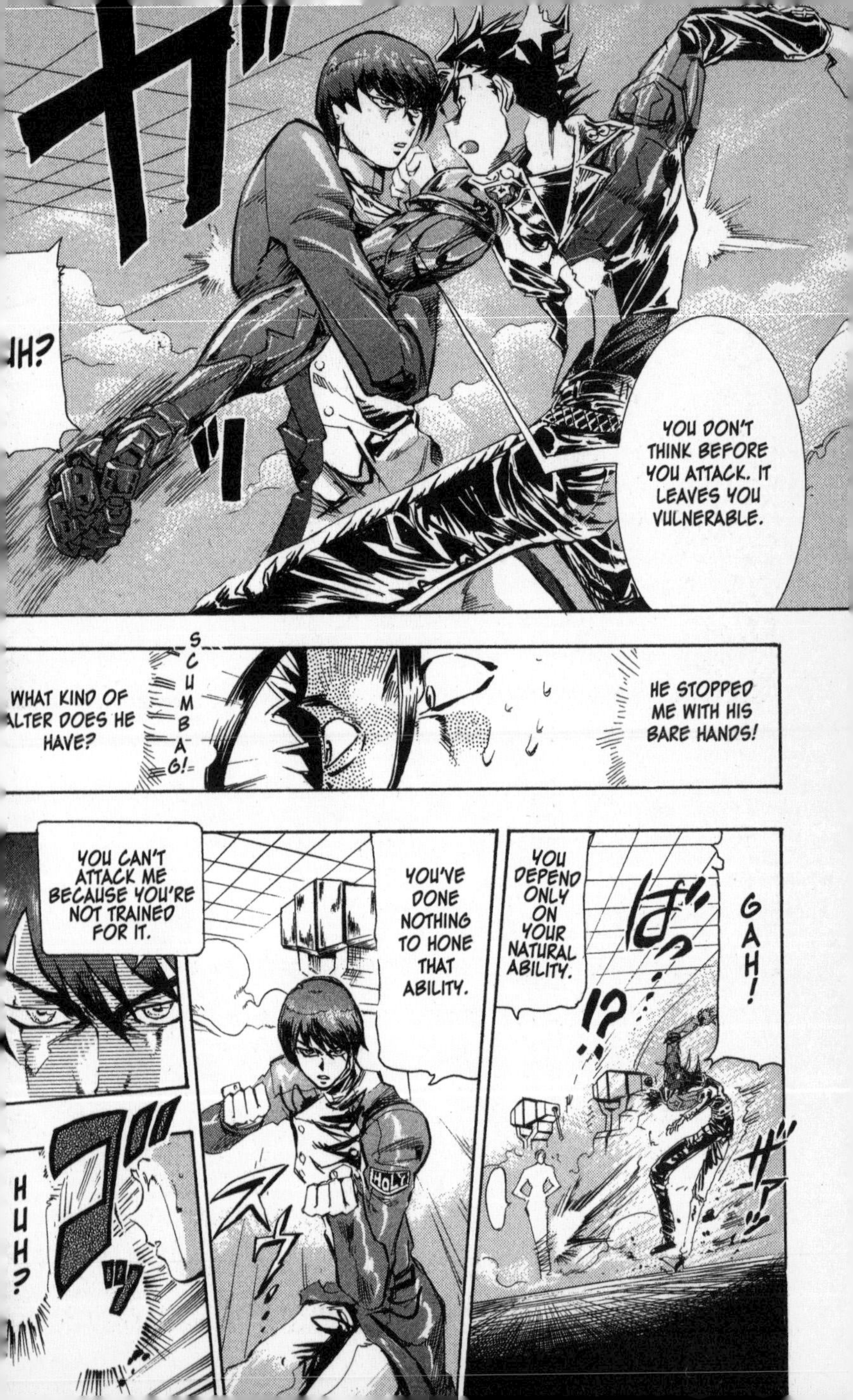
YOU DON'T THINK BEFORE YOU ATTACK. IT LEAVES YOU VULNERABLE.
H?
HE STOPPED ME WITH HIS BARE HANDS!
SCUMBAG!
WHAT KIND OF ALTER DOES HE HAVE?
GAH!
!?
YOU DEPEND ONLY ON YOUR NATURAL ABILITY.
YOU'VE DONE NOTHING TO HONE THAT ABILITY.
YOU CAN'T ATTACK ME BECAUSE YOU'RE NOT TRAINED FOR IT.
HUH?

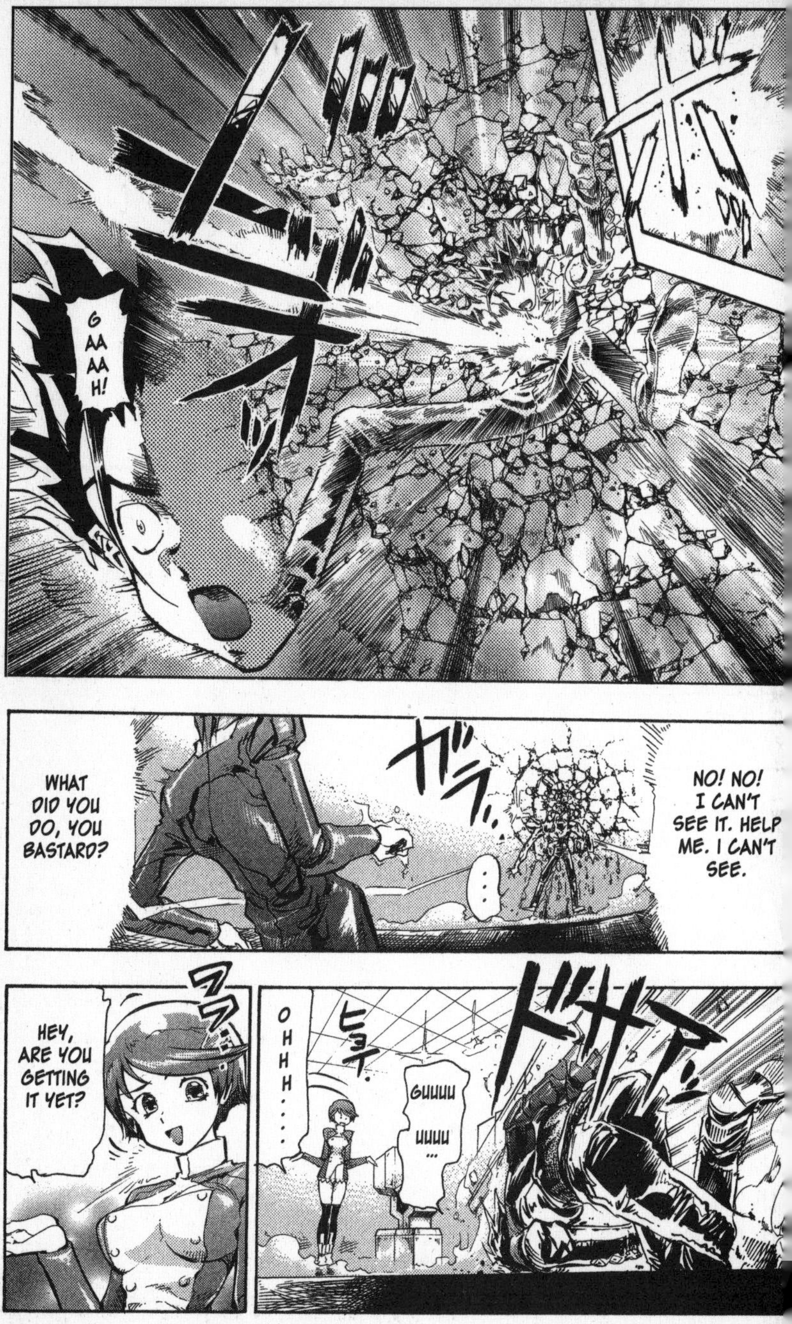
GAAAAH!
NO! NO! I CAN'T SEE IT. HELP ME. I CAN'T SEE.
...
WHAT DID YOU DO, YOU BASTARD?
GUUUU UUUU...
OHHH......
HEY, ARE YOU GETTING IT YET?

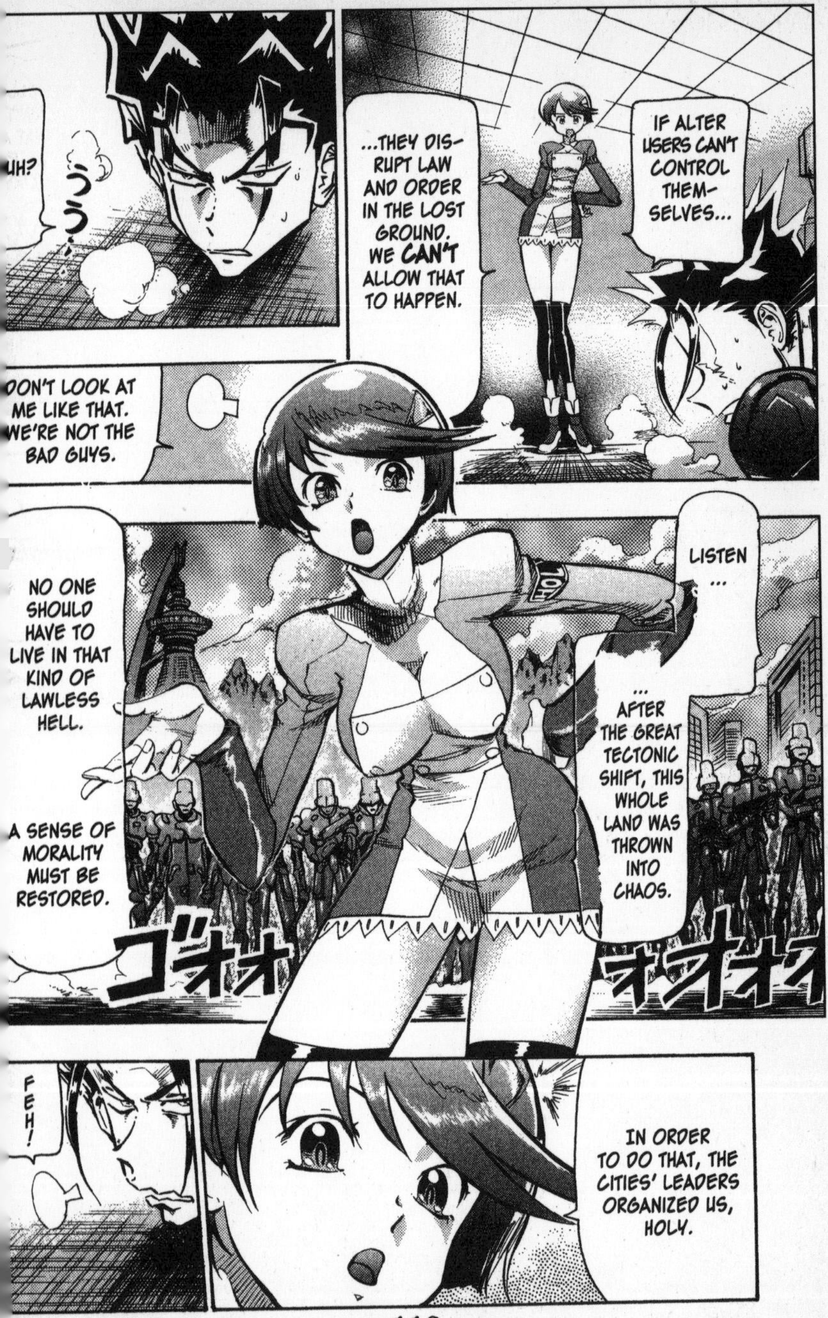
IF ALTER USERS CAN'T CONTROL THEM-SELVES...
...THEY DIS-RUPT LAW AND ORDER IN THE LOST GROUND. WE **CAN'T** ALLOW THAT TO HAPPEN.
UH?
うう…
DON'T LOOK AT ME LIKE THAT. WE'RE NOT THE BAD GUYS.
LISTEN...
...AFTER THE GREAT TECTONIC SHIFT, THIS WHOLE LAND WAS THROWN INTO CHAOS.
NO ONE SHOULD HAVE TO LIVE IN THAT KIND OF LAWLESS HELL.
A SENSE OF MORALITY MUST BE RESTORED.
ゴオオ
オオオオ
IN ORDER TO DO THAT, THE CITIES' LEADERS ORGANIZED US, HOLY.
FEH!

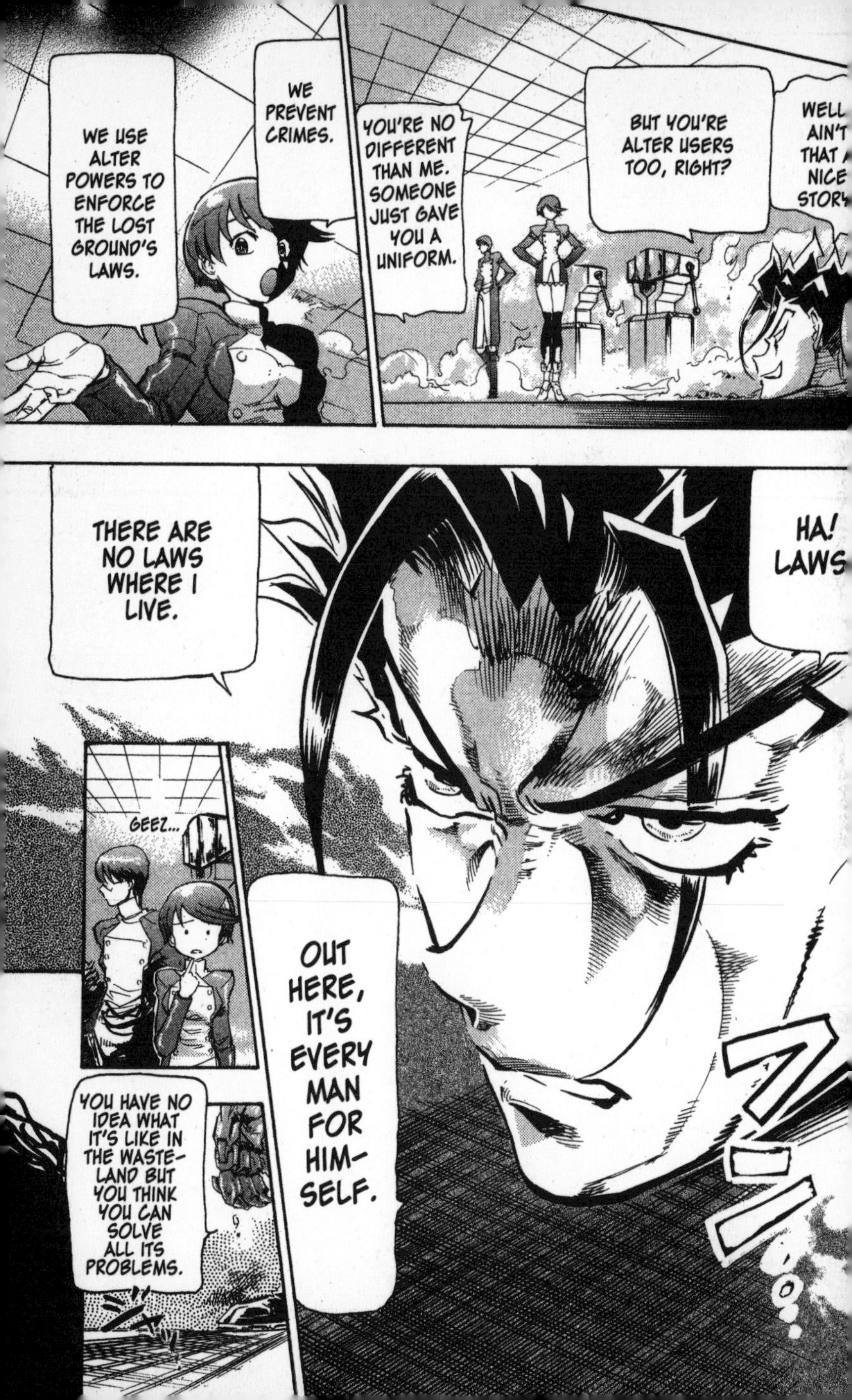
WELL AIN'T THAT A NICE STORY
BUT YOU'RE ALTER USERS TOO, RIGHT?
YOU'RE NO DIFFERENT THAN ME. SOMEONE JUST GAVE YOU A UNIFORM.
WE PREVENT CRIMES.
WE USE ALTER POWERS TO ENFORCE THE LOST GROUND'S LAWS.
HA! LAWS
THERE ARE NO LAWS WHERE I LIVE.
OUT HERE, IT'S EVERY MAN FOR HIMSELF.
GEEZ...
YOU HAVE NO IDEA WHAT IT'S LIKE IN THE WASTELAND BUT YOU THINK YOU CAN SOLVE ALL ITS PROBLEMS.

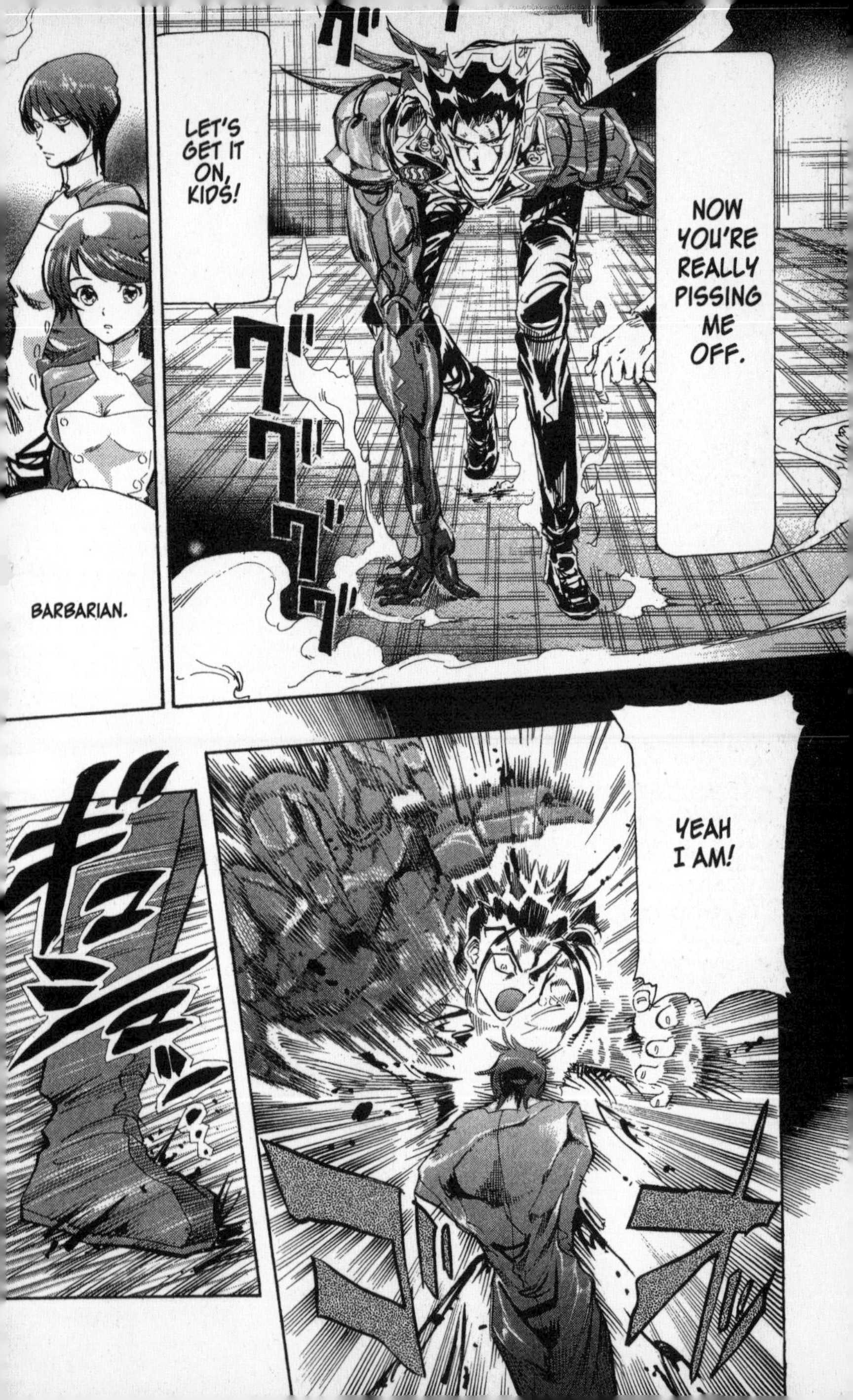
NOW YOU'RE REALLY PISSING ME OFF.
LET'S GET IT ON, KIDS!
BARBARIAN.
YEAH I AM!

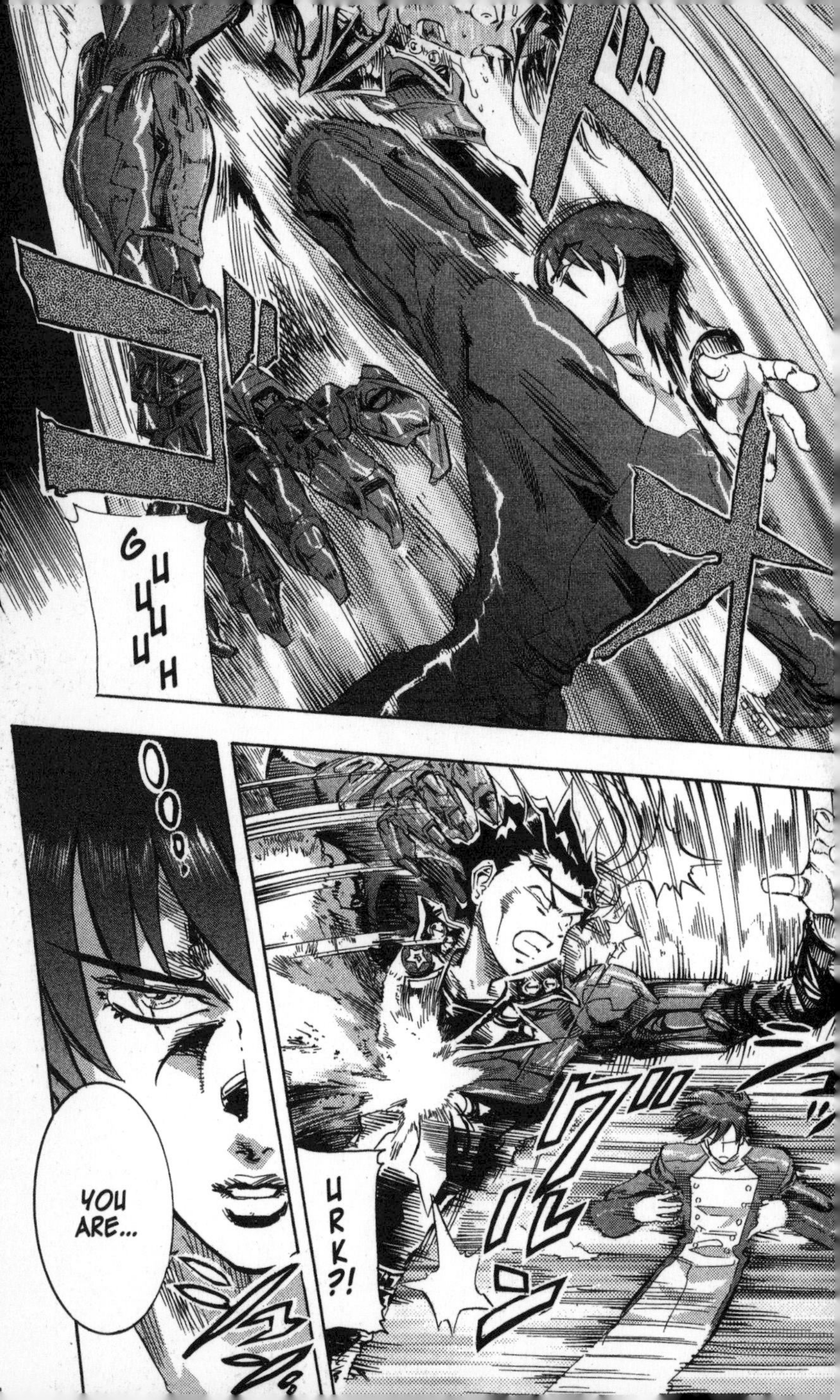
GUUUUUH
URK?!
YOU ARE...

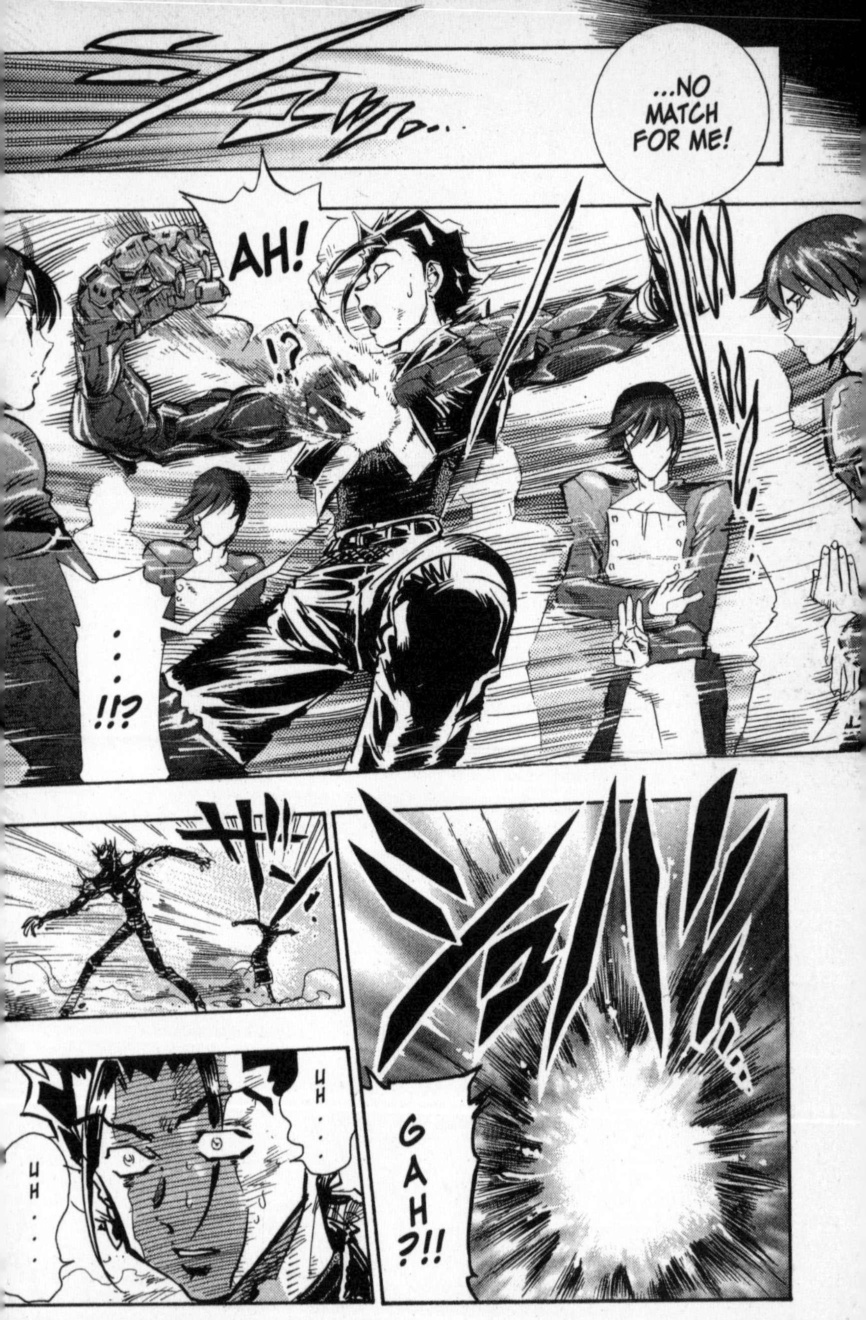
...NO MATCH FOR ME!
AH!
!?
...!!?
GAH?!!
UH...
UH...

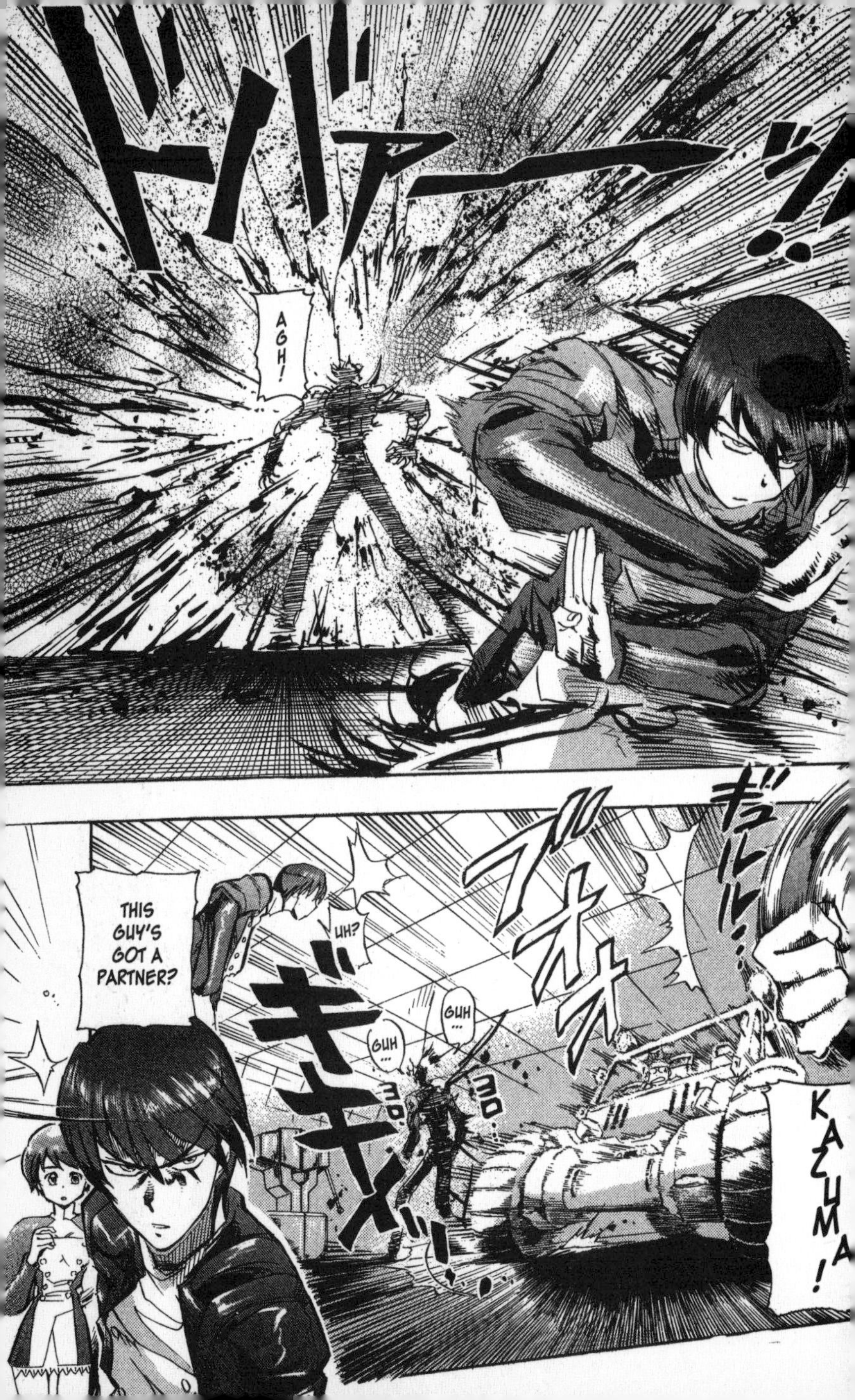
AGH!
KAZUMA!
GUH...
GUH...
UH?
THIS GUY'S GOT A PARTNER?

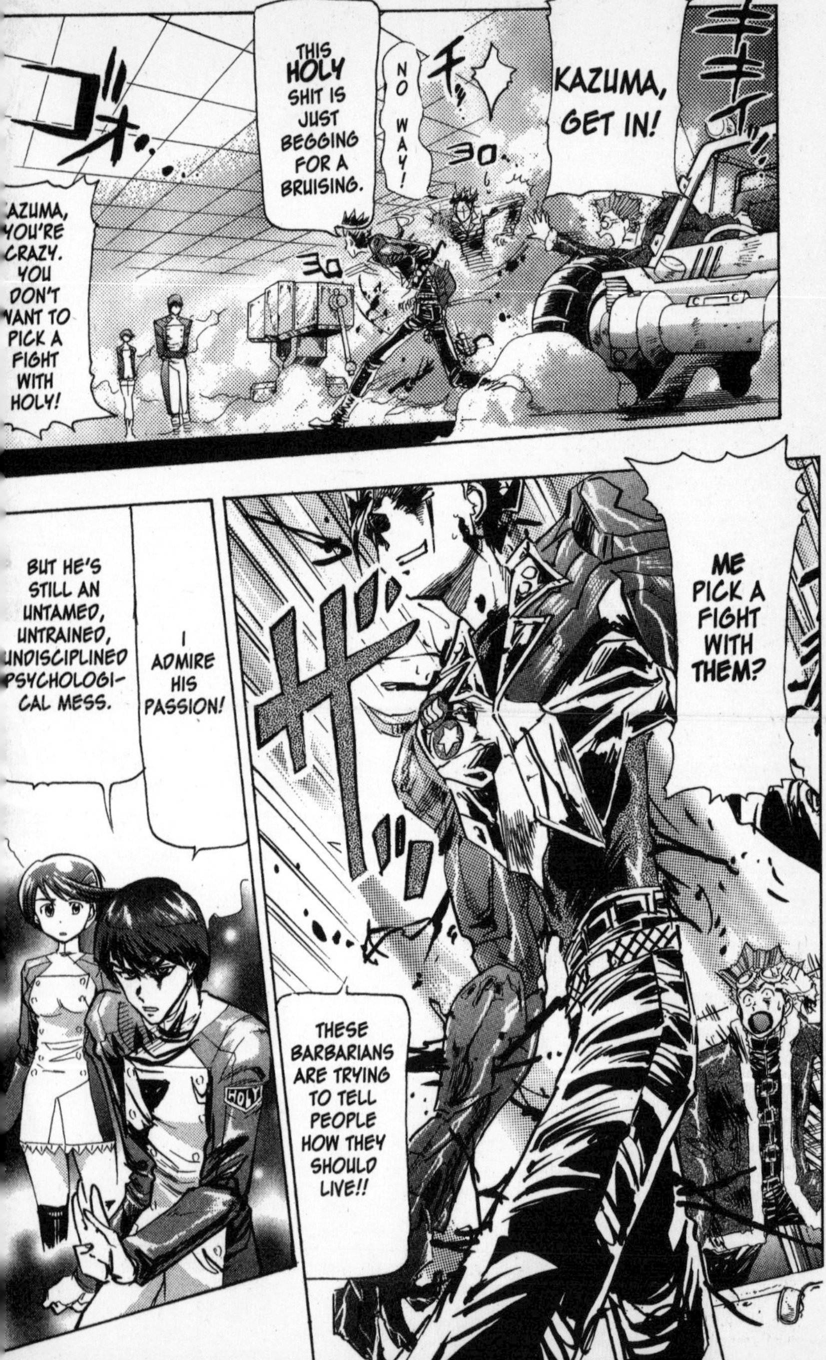
KAZUMA, GET IN!
NO WAY!
THIS HOLY SHIT IS JUST BEGGING FOR A BRUISING.
KAZUMA, YOU'RE CRAZY. YOU DON'T WANT TO PICK A FIGHT WITH HOLY!
ME PICK A FIGHT WITH THEM?
THESE BARBARIANS ARE TRYING TO TELL PEOPLE HOW THEY SHOULD LIVE!!
I ADMIRE HIS PASSION!
BUT HE'S STILL AN UNTAMED, UNTRAINED, UNDISCIPLINED PSYCHOLOGICAL MESS.

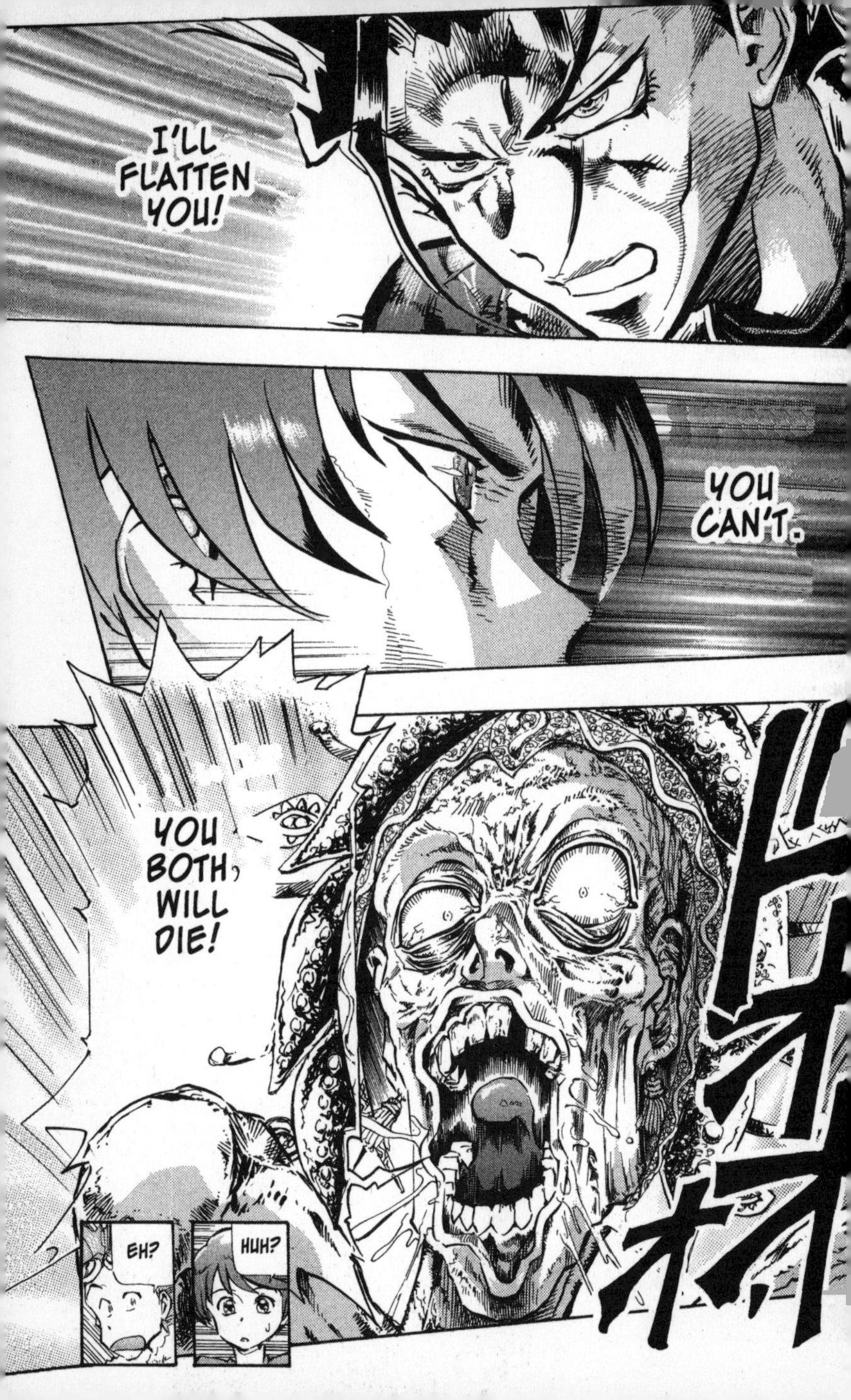
I'LL FLATTEN YOU!
YOU CAN'T.
YOU BOTH WILL DIE!
HUH?
EH?

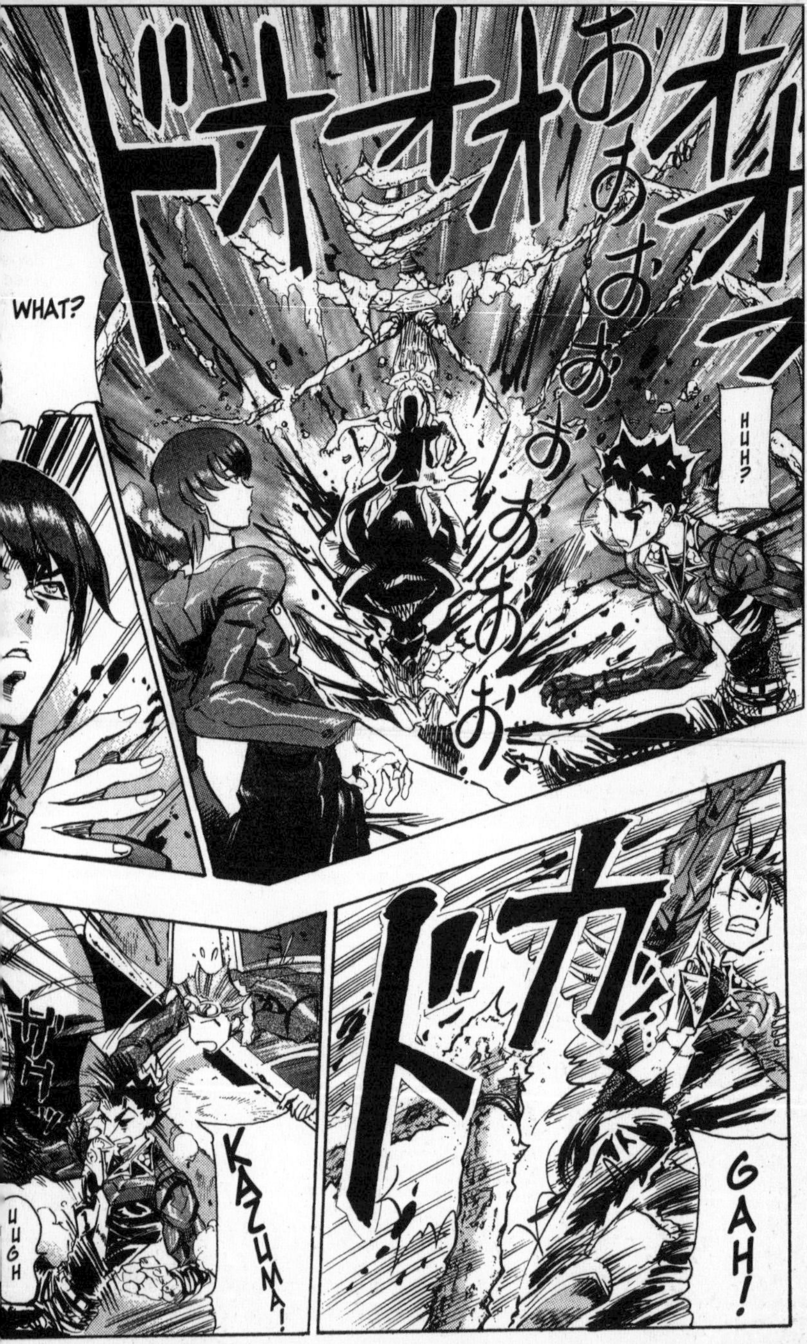
HUH?
WHAT?
GAH!
KAZUMA!
UGH

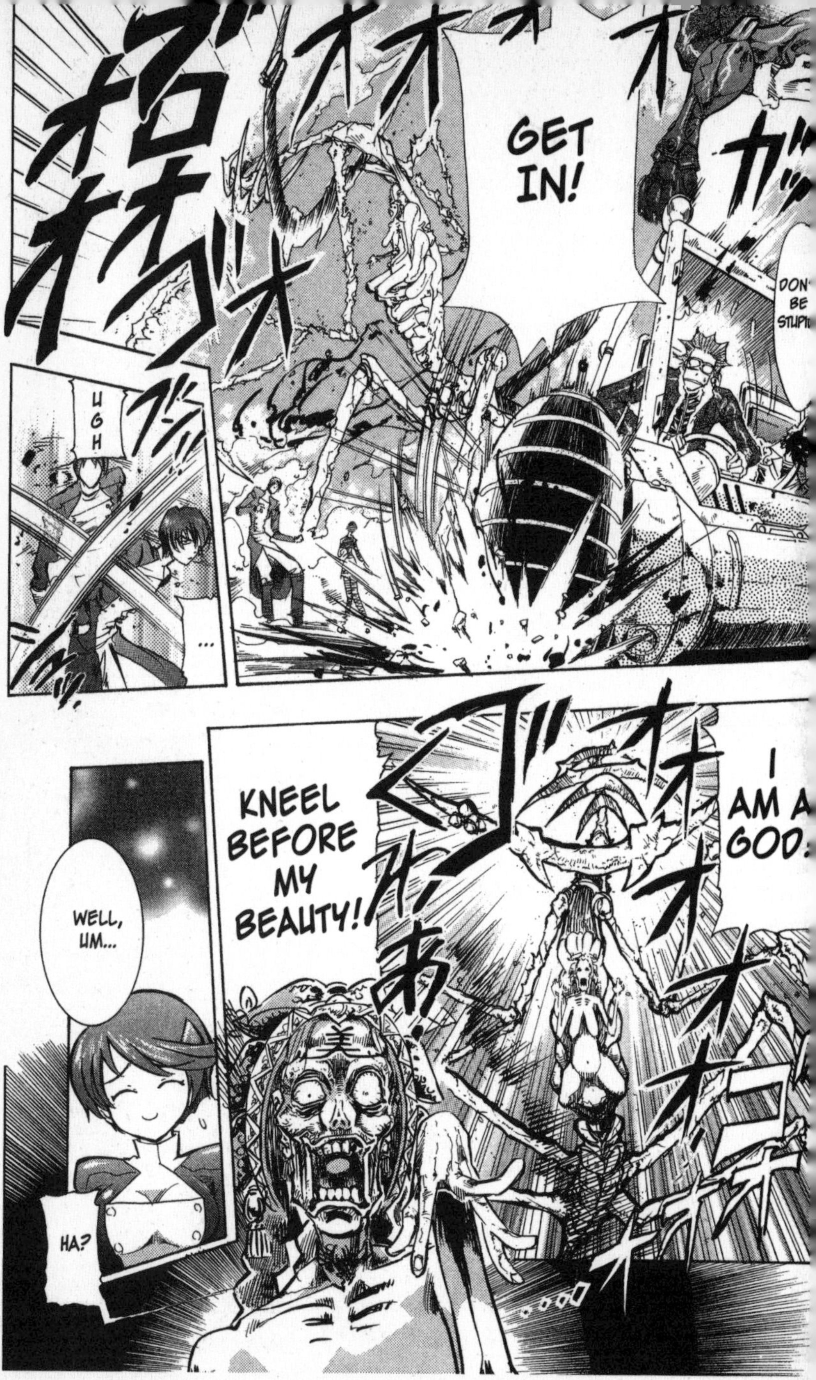
DON'T BE STUPI
GET IN!
UGH
...
I AM A GOD
KNEEL BEFORE MY BEAUTY!
WELL, UM...
HA?

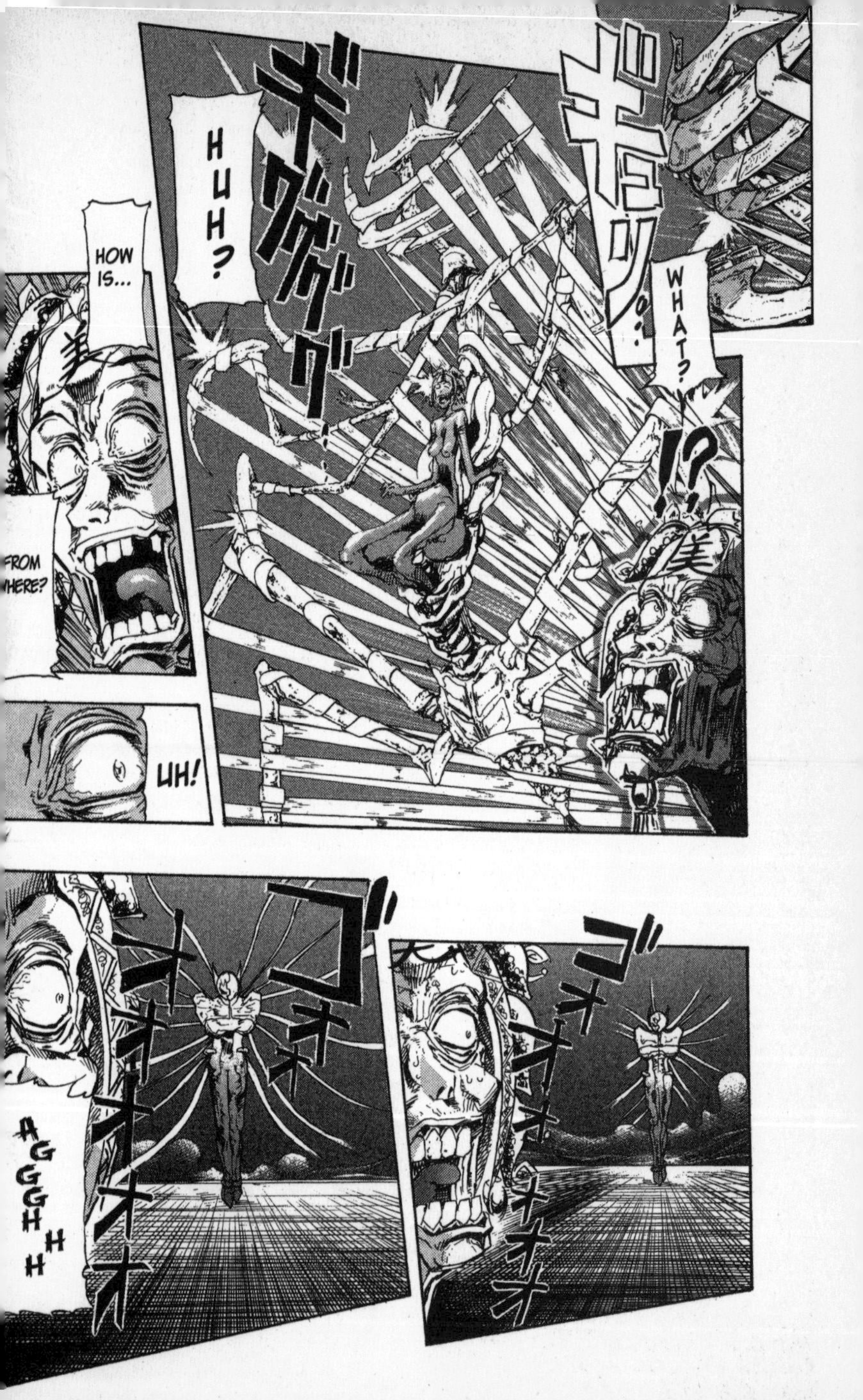

WHAT?!
!?
HUH?
HOW IS... FROM WHERE?
UH!
AGGGHHH

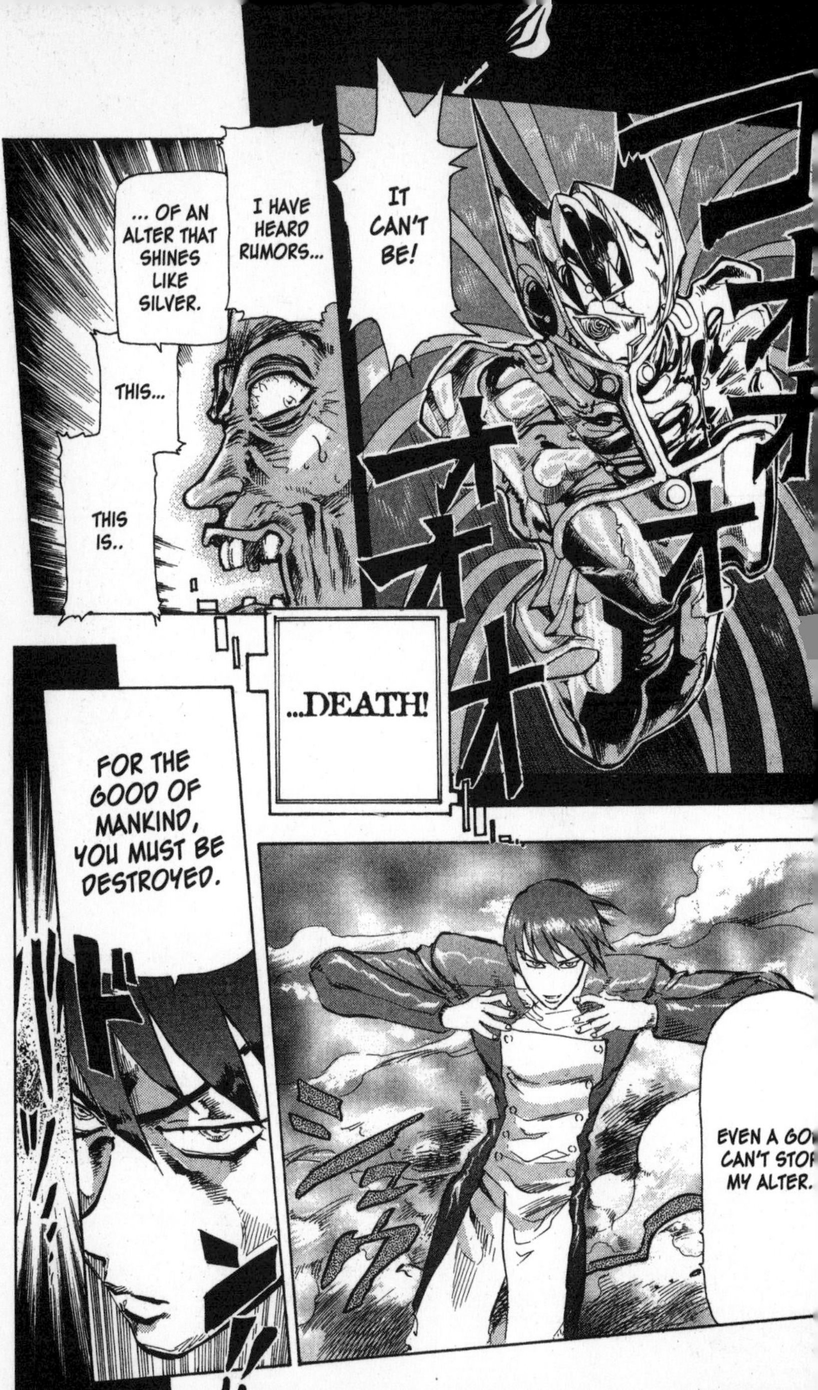
IT CAN'T BE!
I HAVE HEARD RUMORS...
... OF AN ALTER THAT SHINES LIKE SILVER.
THIS...
THIS IS..
...DEATH!
EVEN A GO CAN'T STO MY ALTER.
FOR THE GOOD OF MANKIND, YOU MUST BE DESTROYED.

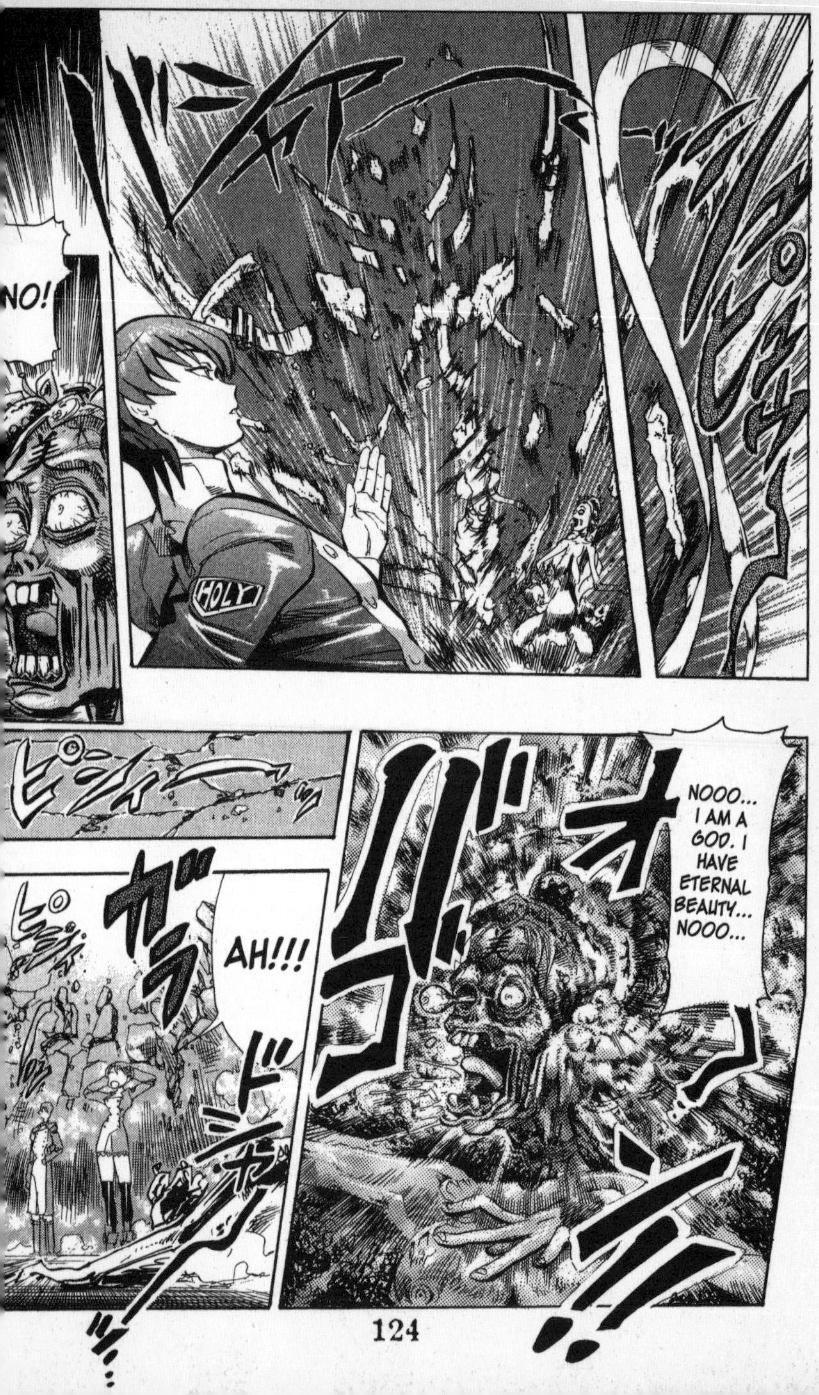
NO!
NOOO... I AM A GOD. I HAVE ETERNAL BEAUTY... NOOO...
AH!!!

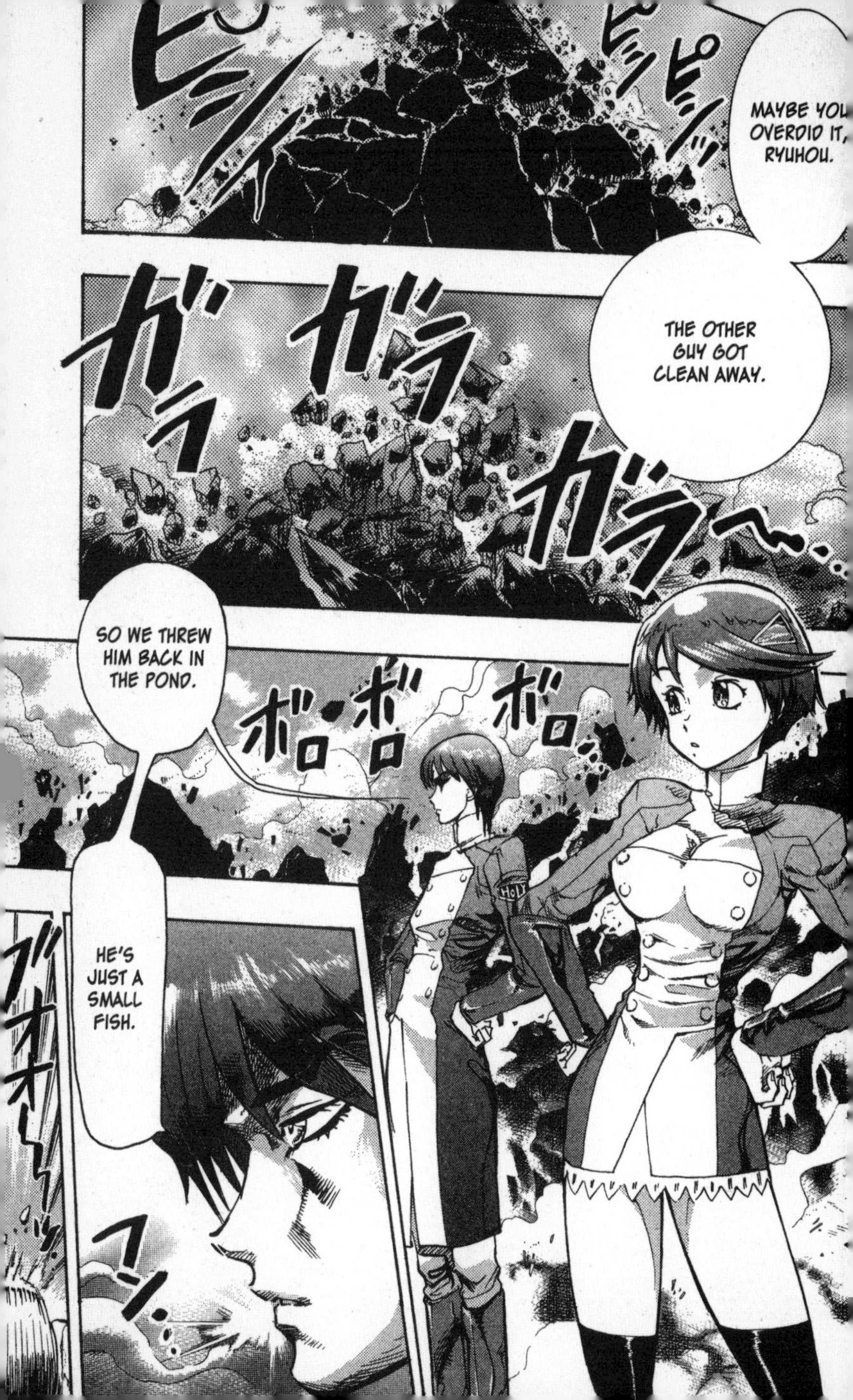
ピシピシッ
ピシ
MAYBE YOU OVERDID IT, RYUHOU.
THE OTHER GUY GOT CLEAN AWAY.
ガラ ガラ ガラへ…
ボロ ボロ ボロ
SO WE THREW HIM BACK IN THE POND.
HE'S JUST A SMALL FISH.
ブオーーッ
フン…

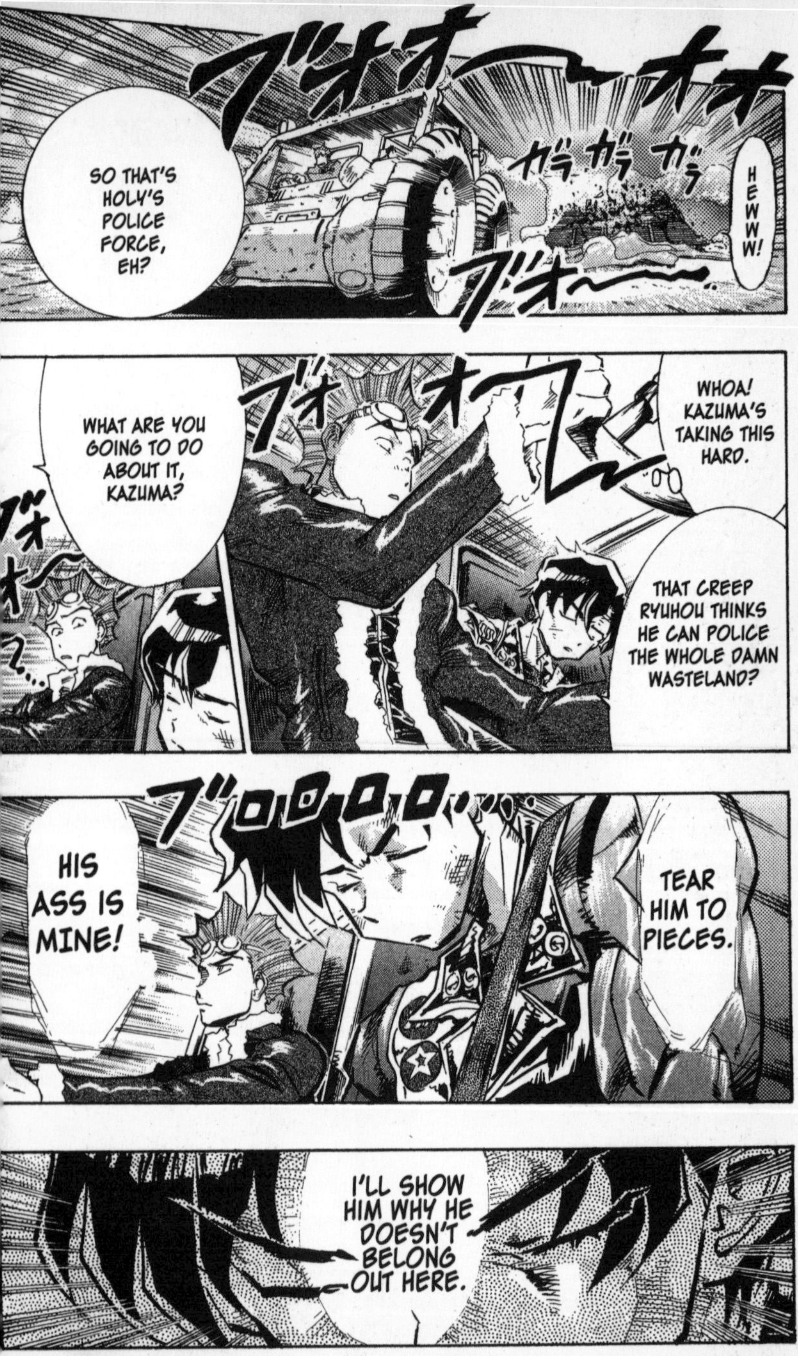
HEWWW!
SO THAT'S HOLY'S POLICE FORCE, EH?
WHOA! KAZUMA'S TAKING THIS HARD.
THAT CREEP RYUHOU THINKS HE CAN POLICE THE WHOLE DAMN WASTELAND?
WHAT ARE YOU GOING TO DO ABOUT IT, KAZUMA?
TEAR HIM TO PIECES.
HIS ASS IS MINE!
I'LL SHOW HIM WHY HE DOESN'T BELONG OUT HERE.

Chapter 6: Excessive Justice

第6話／越権正義

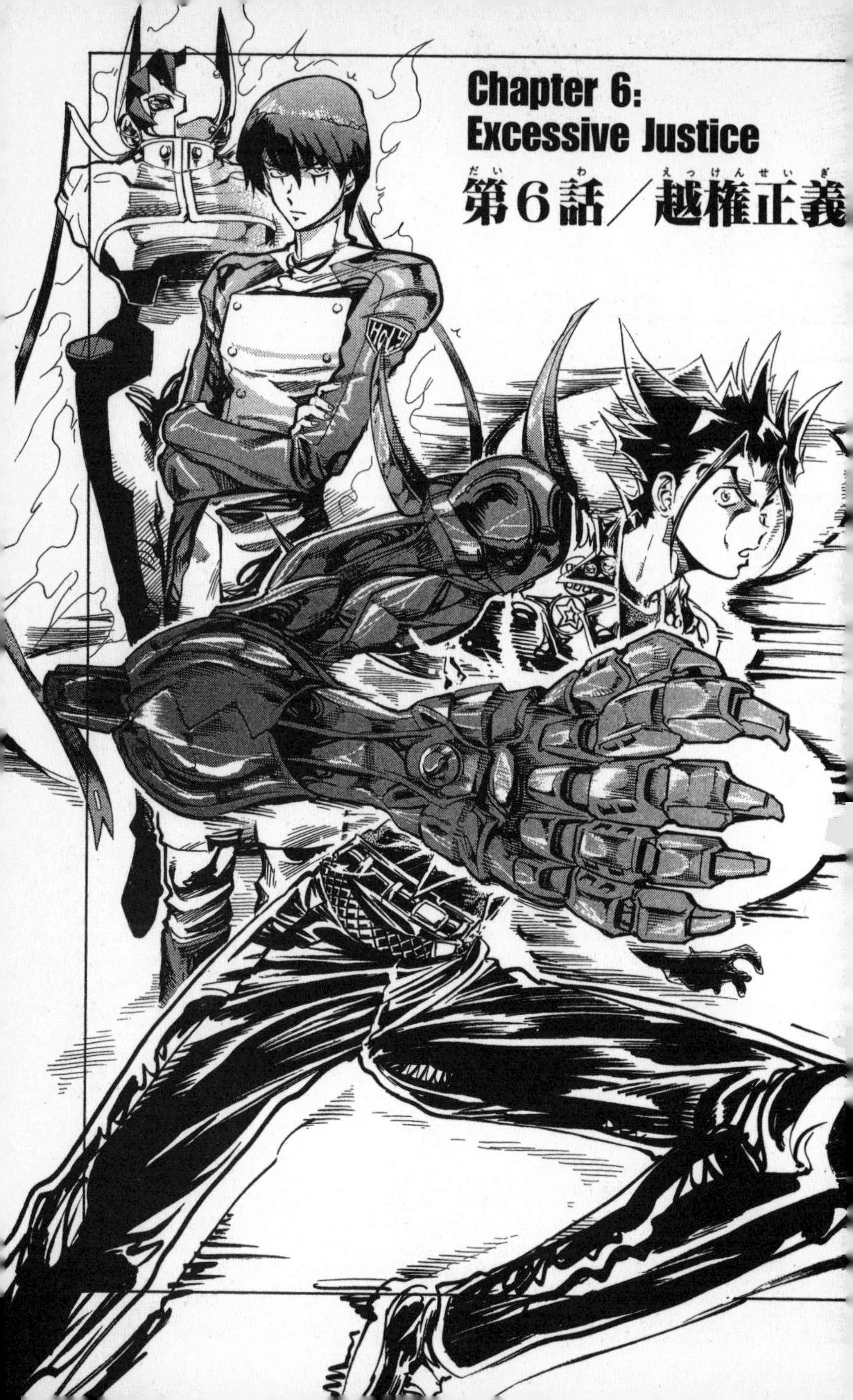

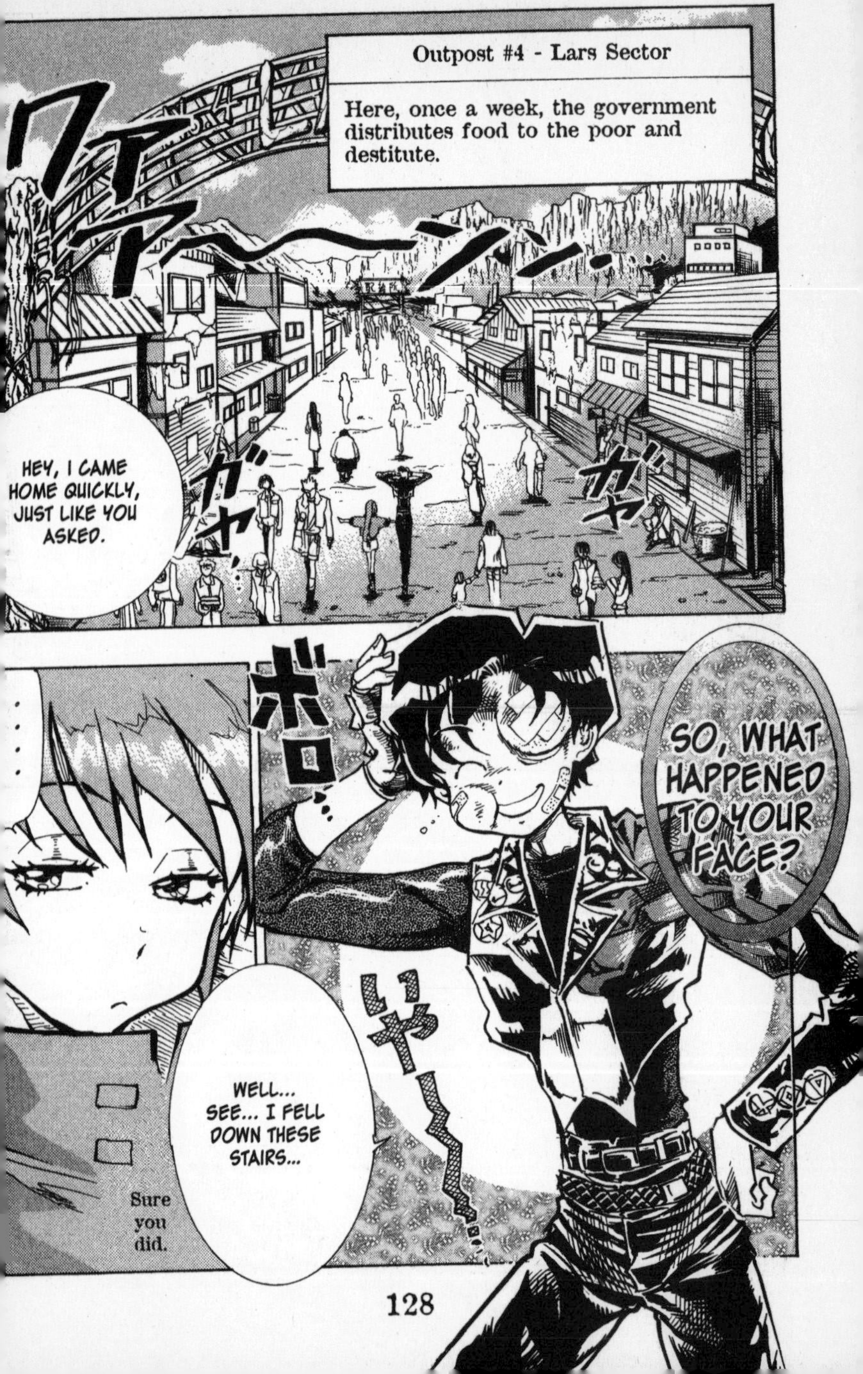
Outpost #4 - Lars Sector
Here, once a week, the government distributes food to the poor and destitute.
HEY, I CAME HOME QUICKLY, JUST LIKE YOU ASKED.
SO, WHAT HAPPENED TO YOUR FACE?
WELL... SEE... I FELL DOWN THESE STAIRS...
Sure you did.

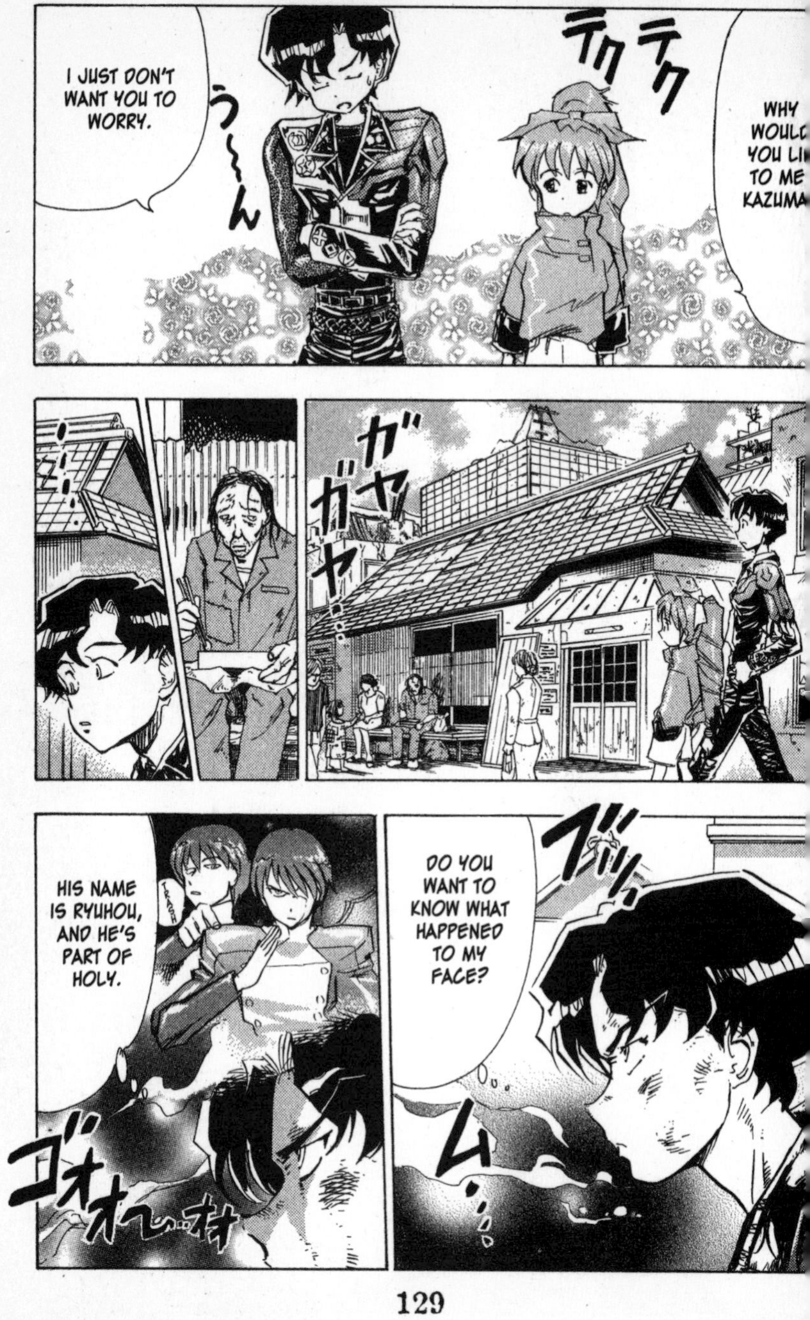
WHY WOUL YOU LI TO ME KAZUMA
テクテク
う〜ん
I JUST DON'T WANT YOU TO WORRY.
ガヤガヤ…
DO YOU WANT TO KNOW WHAT HAPPENED TO MY FACE?
ム…
HIS NAME IS RYUHOU, AND HE'S PART OF HOLY.
TRASH

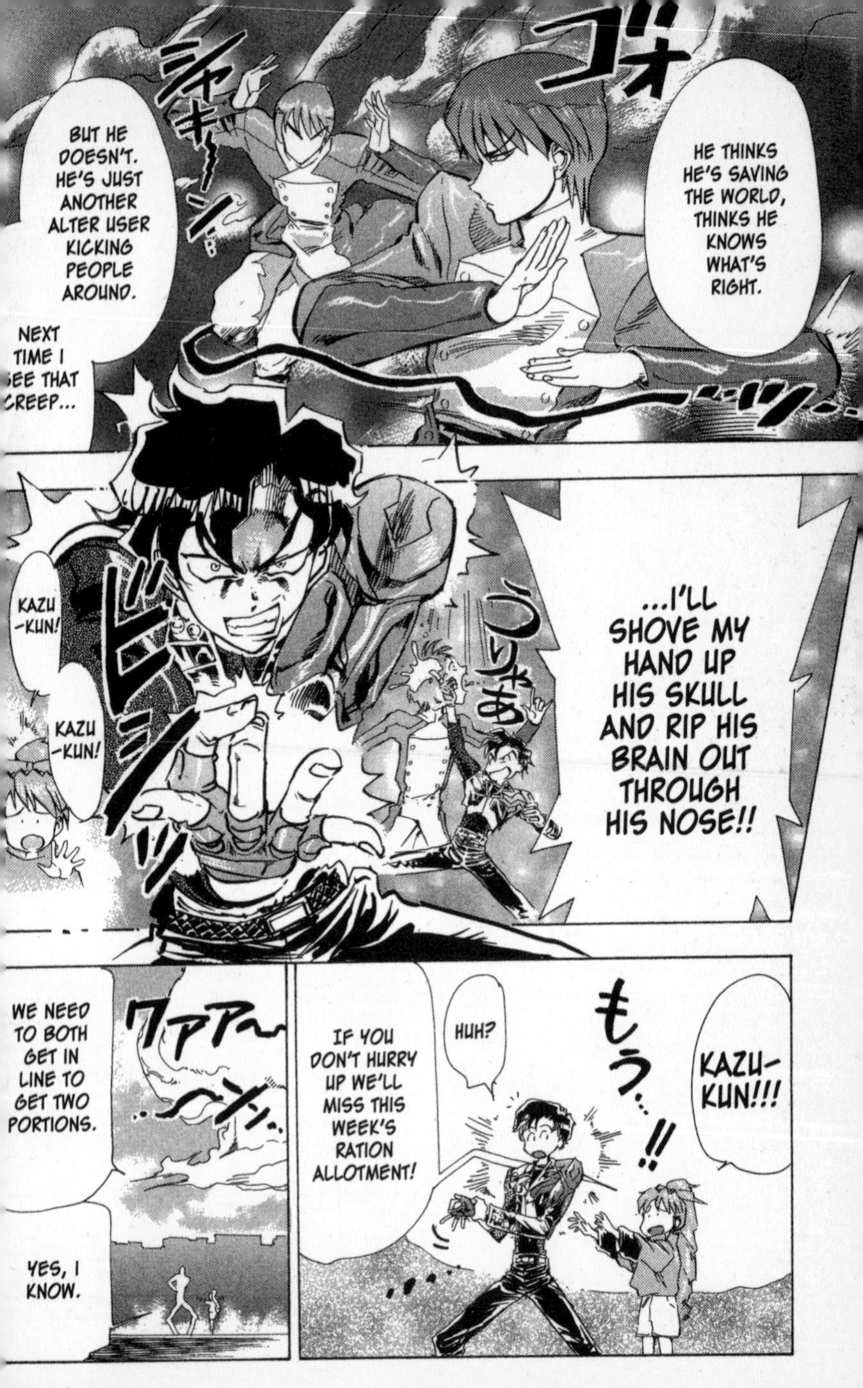
ゴオ
HE THINKS HE'S SAVING THE WORLD, THINKS HE KNOWS WHAT'S RIGHT.
シャキーン
BUT HE DOESN'T. HE'S JUST ANOTHER ALTER USER KICKING PEOPLE AROUND.
NEXT TIME I SEE THAT CREEP...
...I'LL SHOVE MY HAND UP HIS SKULL AND RIP HIS BRAIN OUT THROUGH HIS NOSE!!
うりゃあ
ビシッ
KAZU-KUN!
KAZU-KUN!
KAZU-KUN!!!
もう...!!
HUH?
IF YOU DON'T HURRY UP WE'LL MISS THIS WEEK'S RATION ALLOTMENT!
ワァァ〜ン
WE NEED TO BOTH GET IN LINE TO GET TWO PORTIONS.
YES, I KNOW.

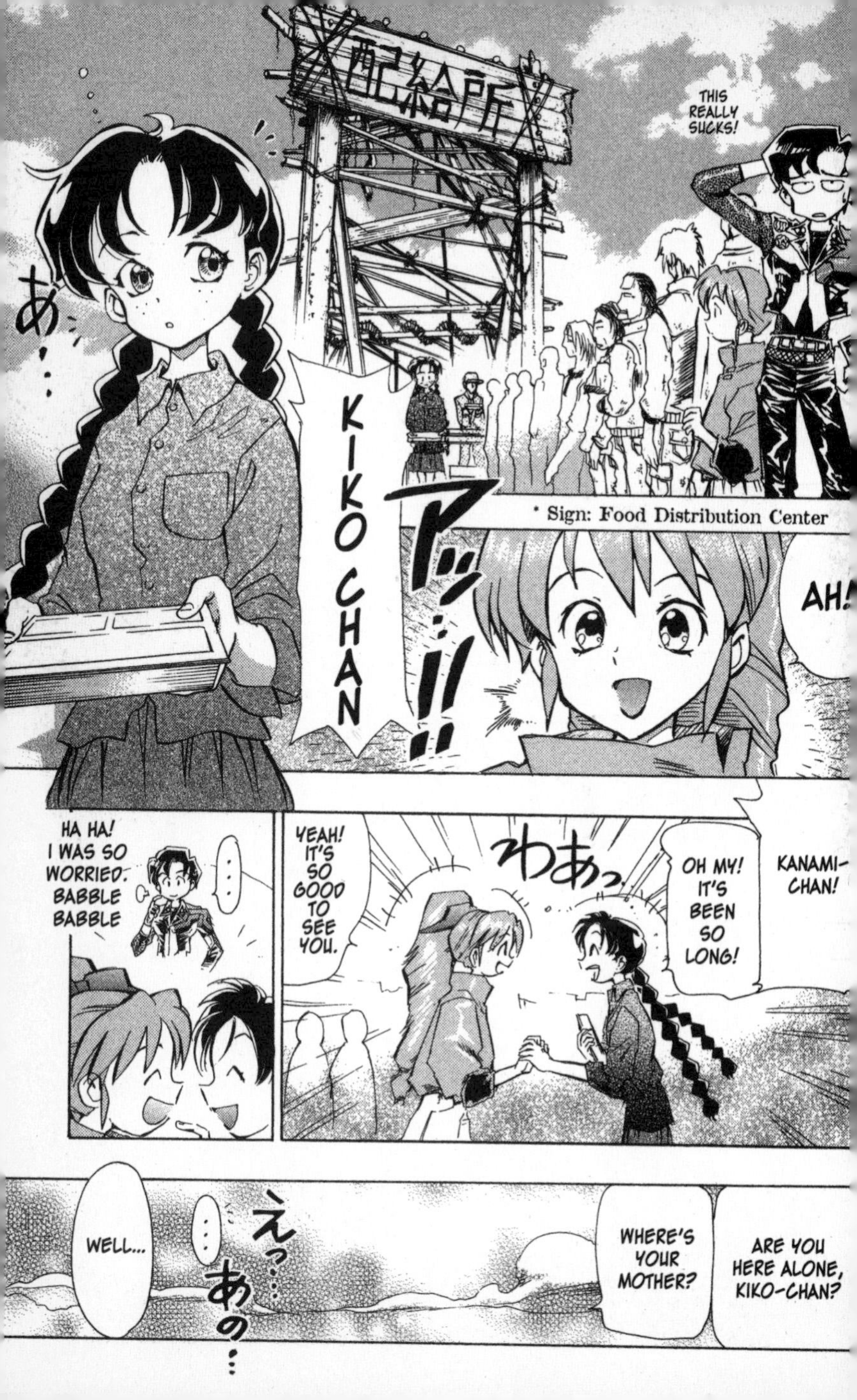
配給所
THIS REALLY SUCKS!
* Sign: Food Distribution Center
AH!
KIKO CHAN
アッ!!
あ…
KANAMI-CHAN!
OH MY! IT'S BEEN SO LONG!
わあっ
YEAH! IT'S SO GOOD TO SEE YOU.
…
HA HA! I WAS SO WORRIED. BABBLE BABBLE
ARE YOU HERE ALONE, KIKO-CHAN?
WHERE'S YOUR MOTHER?
えっ…あの…
…
WELL…

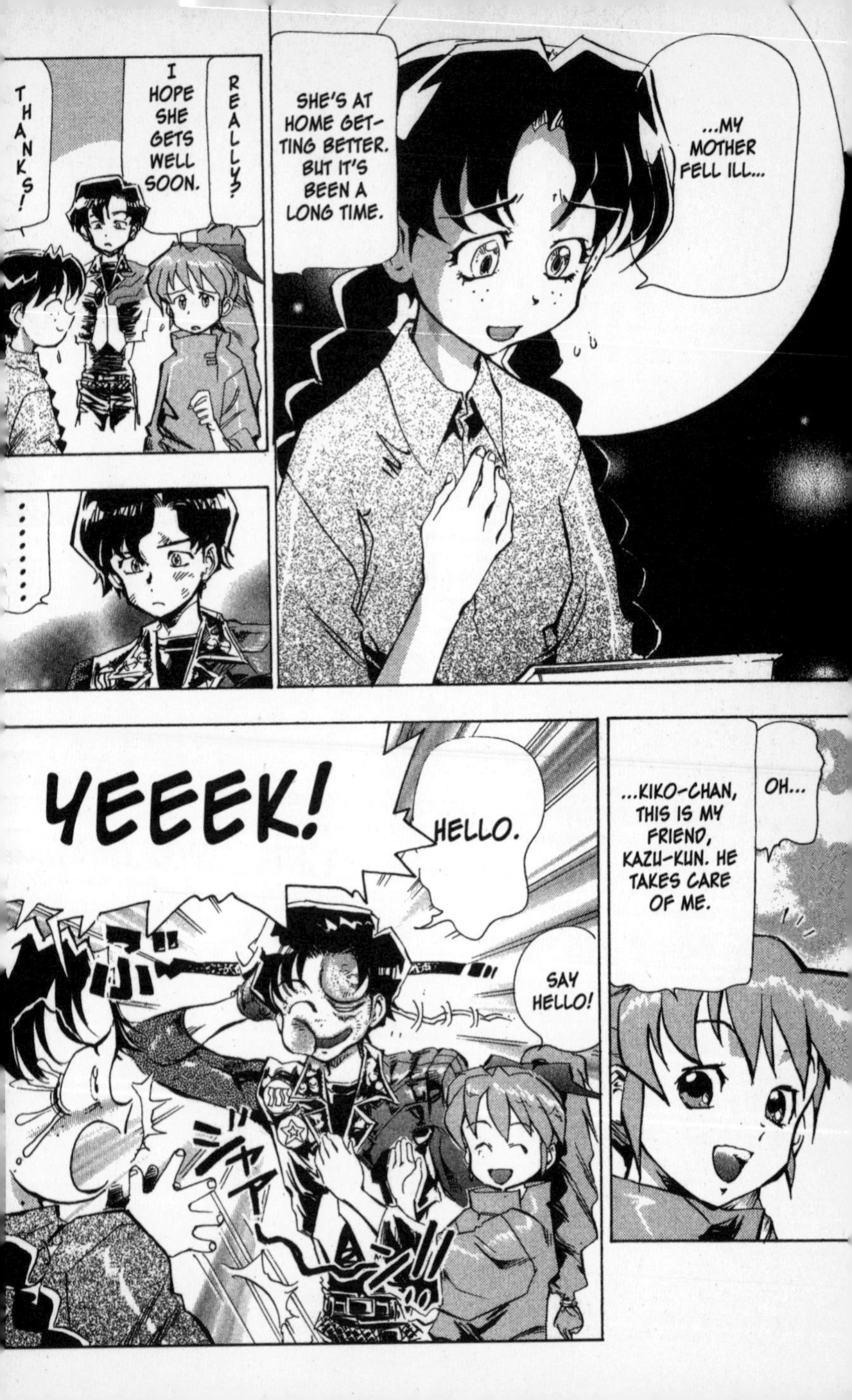
...MY MOTHER FELL ILL...
SHE'S AT HOME GETTING BETTER. BUT IT'S BEEN A LONG TIME.
REALLY?
I HOPE SHE GETS WELL SOON.
THANKS!
......
OH...
...KIKO-CHAN, THIS IS MY FRIEND, KAZU-KUN. HE TAKES CARE OF ME.
SAY HELLO!
HELLO.
YEEEK!

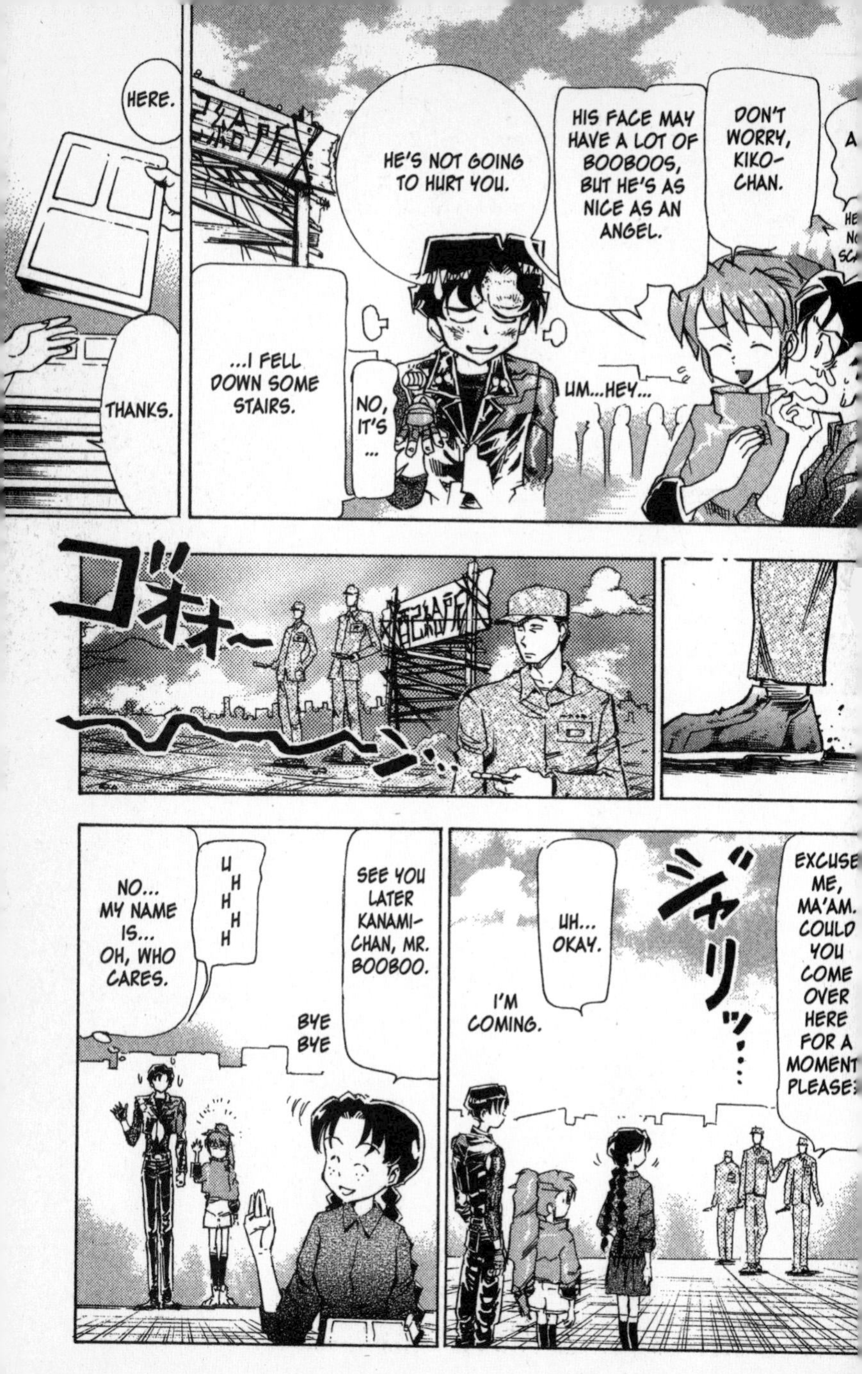
DON'T WORRY, KIKO-CHAN.
HIS FACE MAY HAVE A LOT OF BOOBOOS, BUT HE'S AS NICE AS AN ANGEL.
HE'S NOT GOING TO HURT YOU.
UM...HEY...
NO, IT'S ...
...I FELL DOWN SOME STAIRS.
HERE.
THANKS.
ゴオォー
EXCUSE ME, MA'AM. COULD YOU COME OVER HERE FOR A MOMENT PLEASE?
ジャリッ…
UH... OKAY.
I'M COMING.
SEE YOU LATER KANAMI-CHAN, MR. BOOBOO.
BYE BYE
UHHHH
NO... MY NAME IS... OH, WHO CARES.

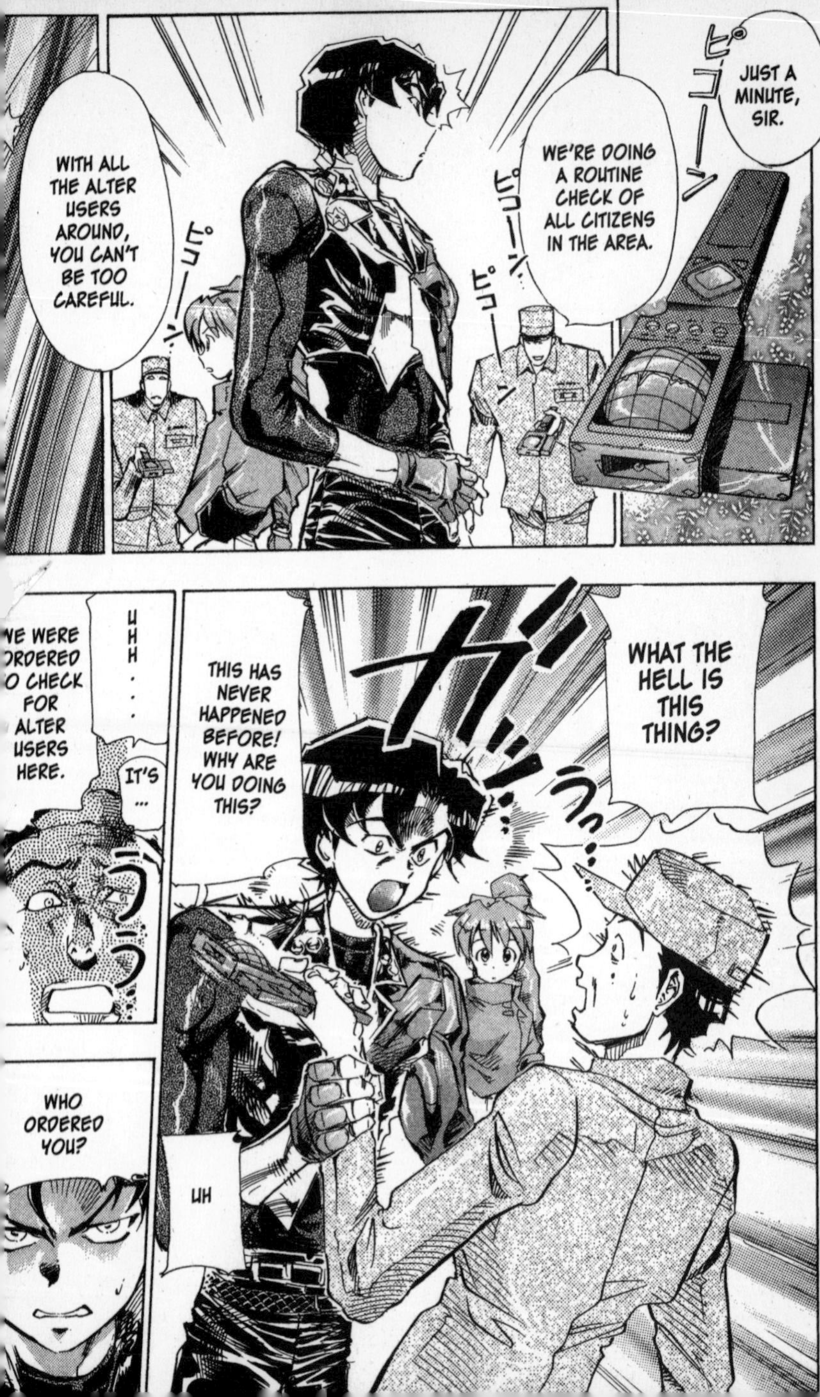
ピコーン
JUST A MINUTE, SIR.
WE'RE DOING A ROUTINE CHECK OF ALL CITIZENS IN THE AREA.
ピコーン
ピコーン
ピコーン
WITH ALL THE ALTER USERS AROUND, YOU CAN'T BE TOO CAREFUL.
WHAT THE HELL IS THIS THING?
うっ
THIS HAS NEVER HAPPENED BEFORE! WHY ARE YOU DOING THIS?
UH
UHH . . .
WE WERE ORDERED TO CHECK FOR ALTER USERS HERE.
IT'S ...
うう
WHO ORDERED YOU?

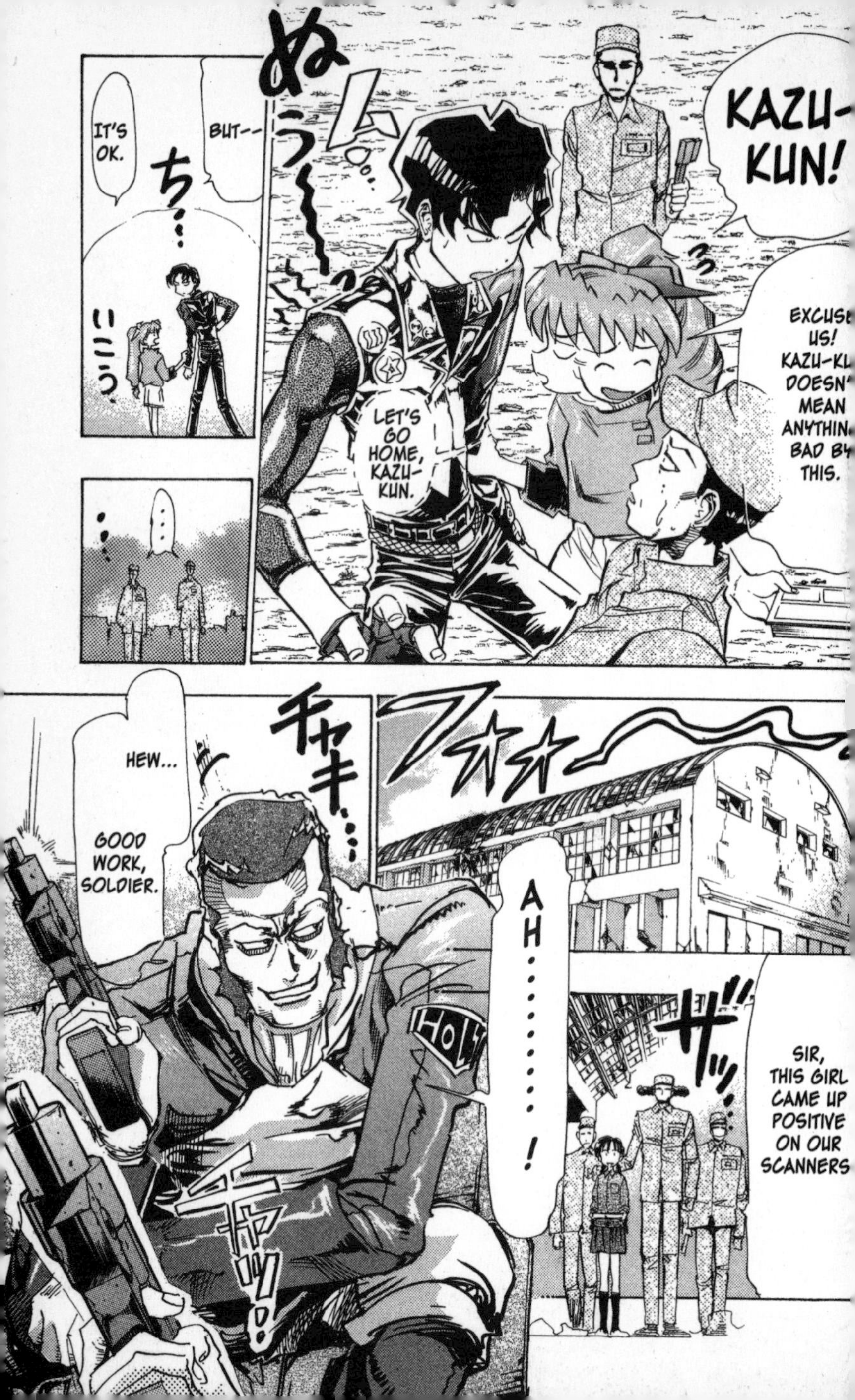

KAZU-KUN!
ぬう~~っ
ムっ
EXCUSE US! KAZU-KU DOESN' MEAN ANYTHIN BAD BY THIS.
LET'S GO HOME, KAZU-KUN.
BUT--
IT'S OK.
ち…
いこう
...
...
フォォォ~~
SIR, THIS GIRL CAME UP POSITIVE ON OUR SCANNERS
ザッ
チャキ…
HEW...
GOOD WORK, SOLDIER.
AH..........!
ガチャリ

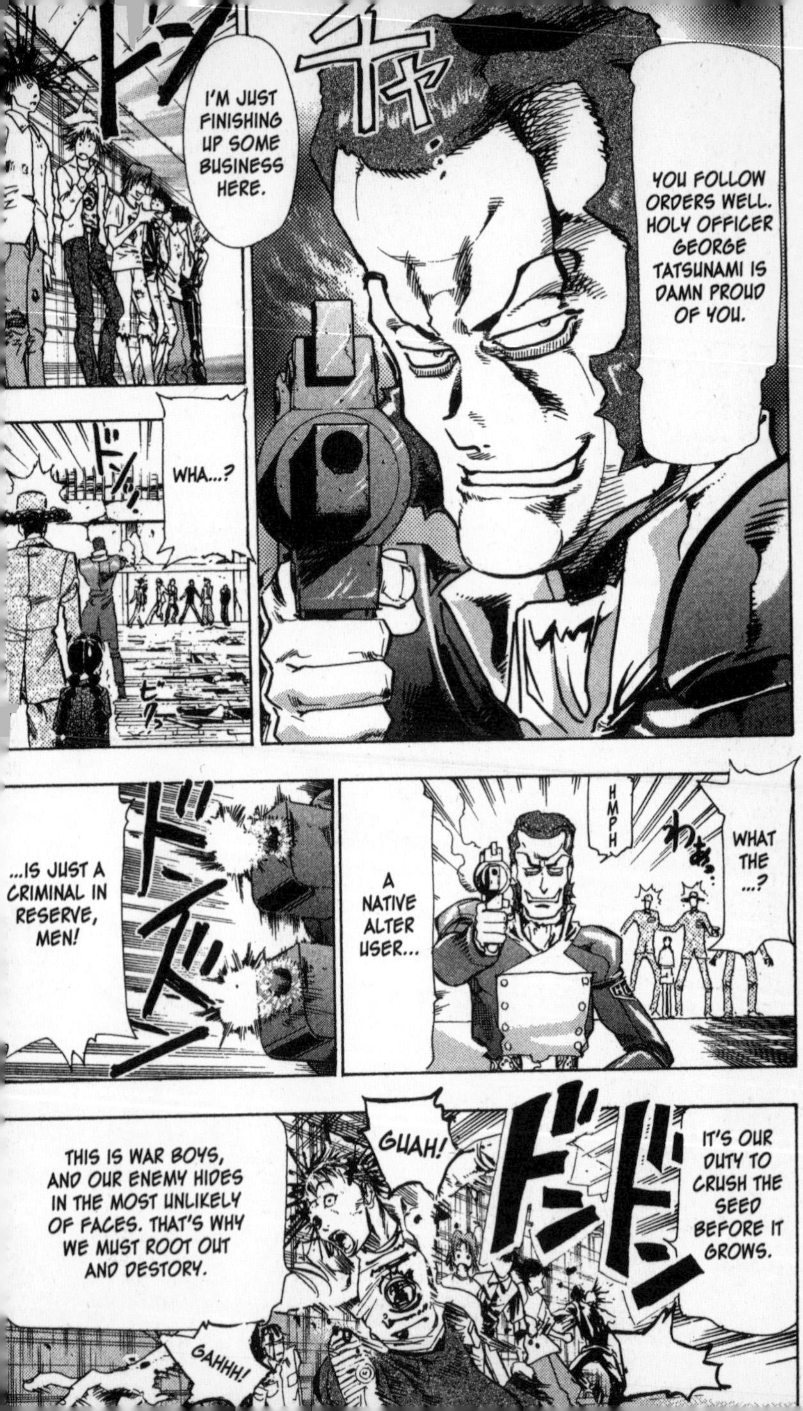
YOU FOLLOW ORDERS WELL. HOLY OFFICER GEORGE TATSUNAMI IS DAMN PROUD OF YOU.
I'M JUST FINISHING UP SOME BUSINESS HERE.
WHA...?
WHAT THE ...?
HMPH
A NATIVE ALTER USER...
...IS JUST A CRIMINAL IN RESERVE, MEN!
IT'S OUR DUTY TO CRUSH THE SEED BEFORE IT GROWS.
GUAH!
THIS IS WAR BOYS, AND OUR ENEMY HIDES IN THE MOST UNLIKELY OF FACES. THAT'S WHY WE MUST ROOT OUT AND DESTORY.
GAHHH!

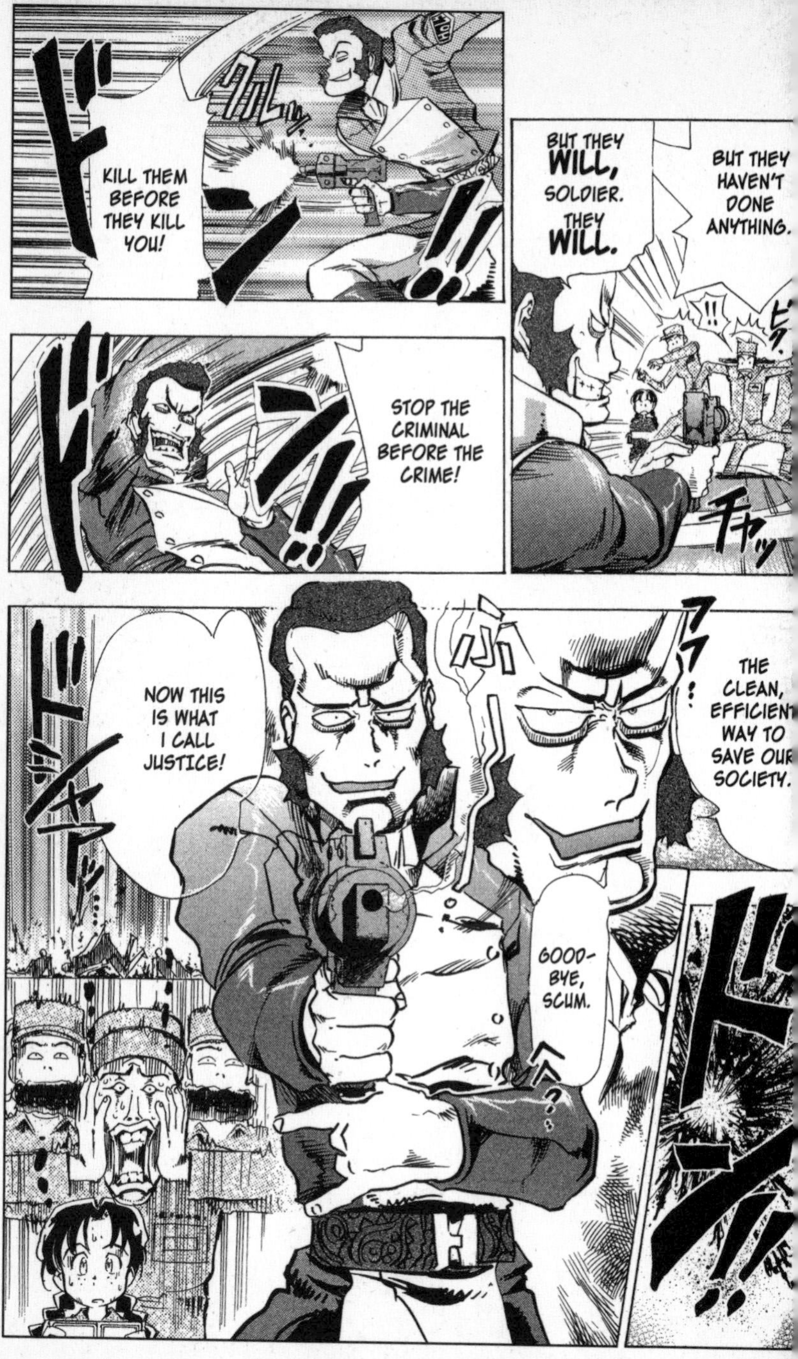
BUT THEY HAVEN'T DONE ANYTHING.
BUT THEY WILL, SOLDIER. THEY WILL.
KILL THEM BEFORE THEY KILL YOU!
STOP THE CRIMINAL BEFORE THE CRIME!
THE CLEAN, EFFICIENT WAY TO SAVE OUR SOCIETY.
NOW THIS IS WHAT I CALL JUSTICE!
GOOD-BYE, SCUM.

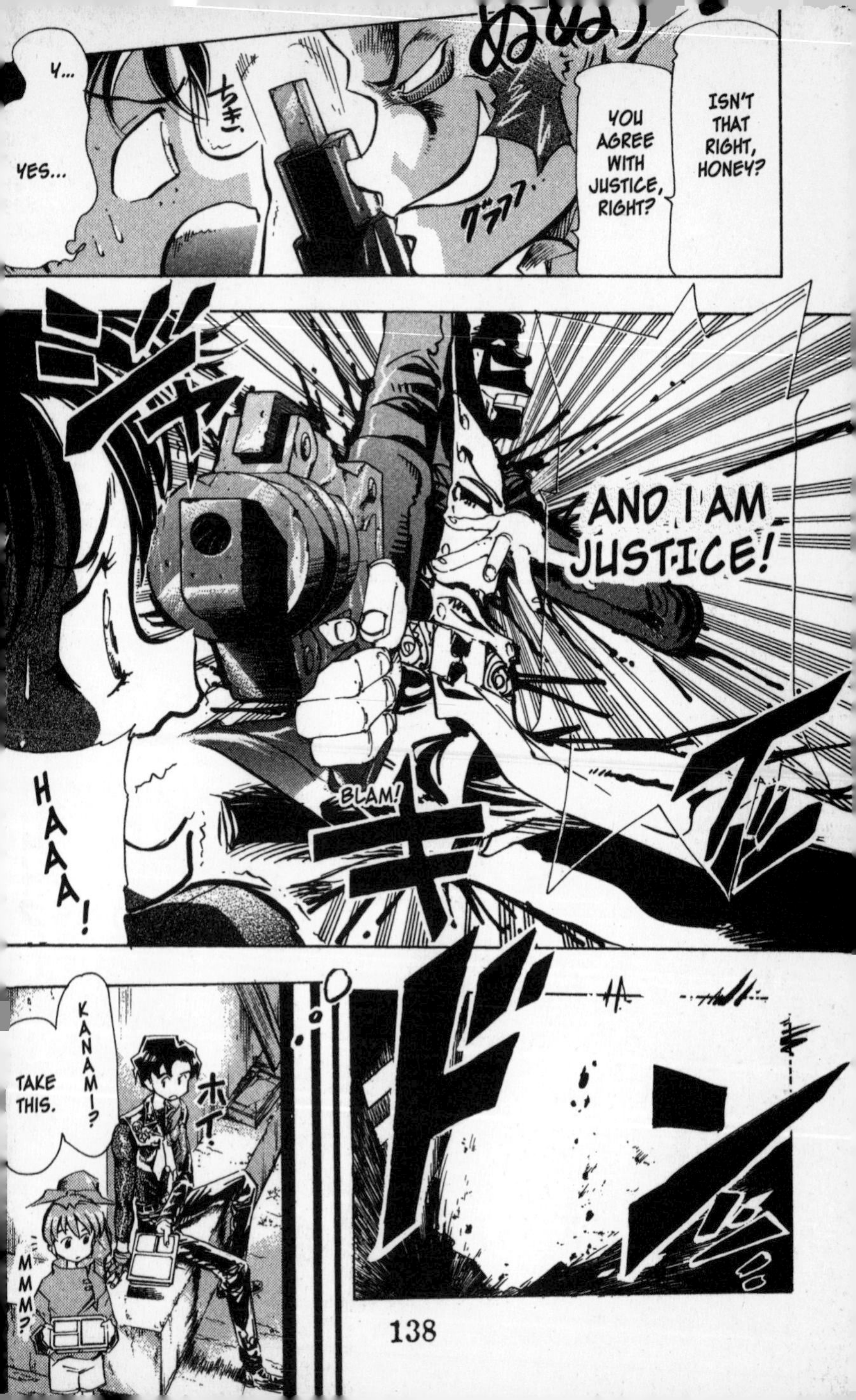

ISN'T THAT RIGHT, HONEY?
YOU AGREE WITH JUSTICE, RIGHT?
Y...
YES...
AND I AM JUSTICE!
BLAM!
HAAAA!
KANAMI!?
TAKE THIS.
MMM?

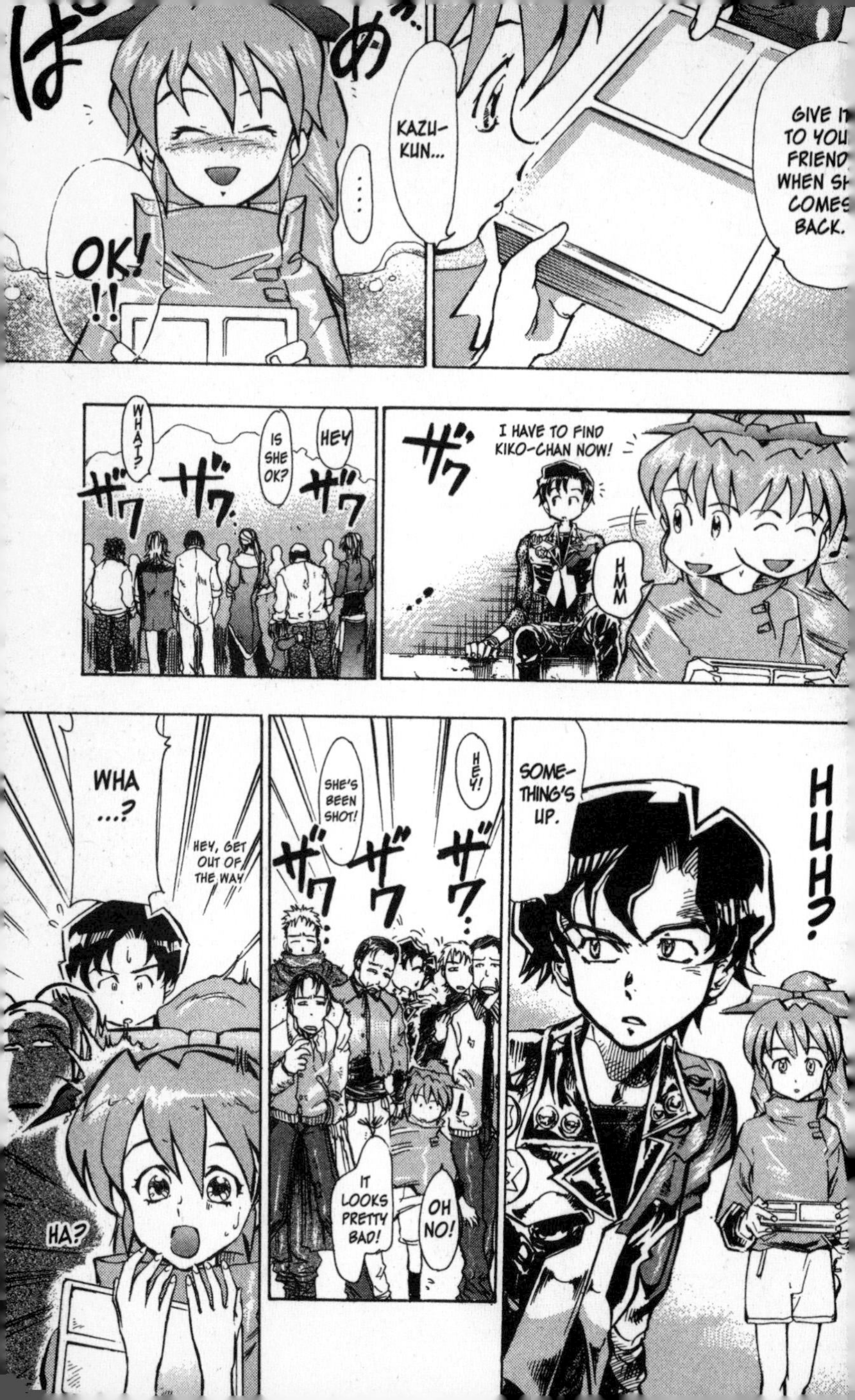
GIVE IT TO YOU FRIEND WHEN SH COMES BACK.
ぱ あ
KAZU-KUN...
....
OK!!!
ザワ
I HAVE TO FIND KIKO-CHAN NOW!
HMM
HEY
IS SHE OK?
WHAT?
ザワ ザワ ザワ
HUH?
SOME-THING'S UP.
HEY!
SHE'S BEEN SHOT!
ザワ ザワ ザワ
OH NO!
IT LOOKS PRETTY BAD!
WHA ...?
HEY, GET OUT OF THE WAY
HA?

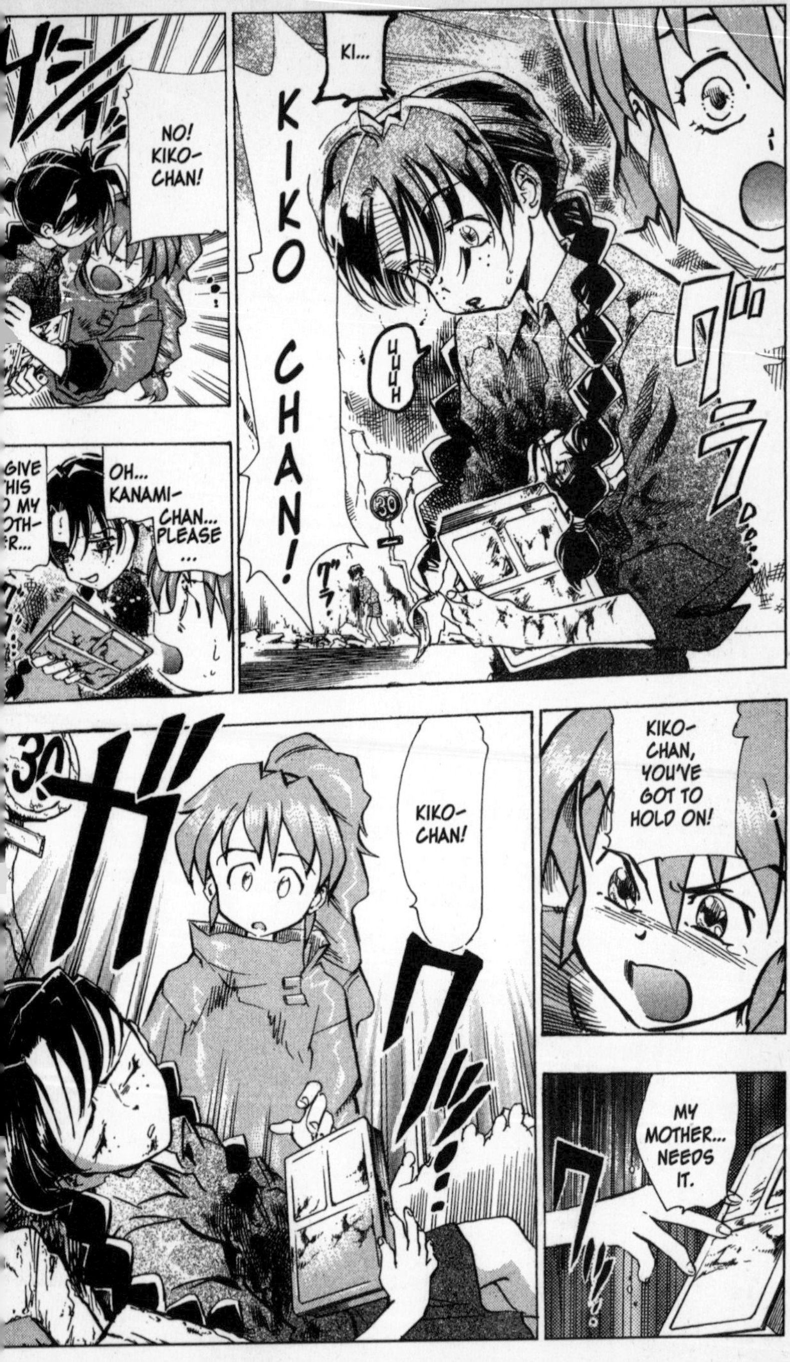
KI...
KIKO CHAN!
UUUH
NO! KIKO-CHAN!
OH... KANAMI-CHAN... PLEASE ...
GIVE THIS O MY OTH- ER...
KIKO-CHAN, YOU'VE GOT TO HOLD ON!
MY MOTHER... NEEDS IT.
KIKO-CHAN!

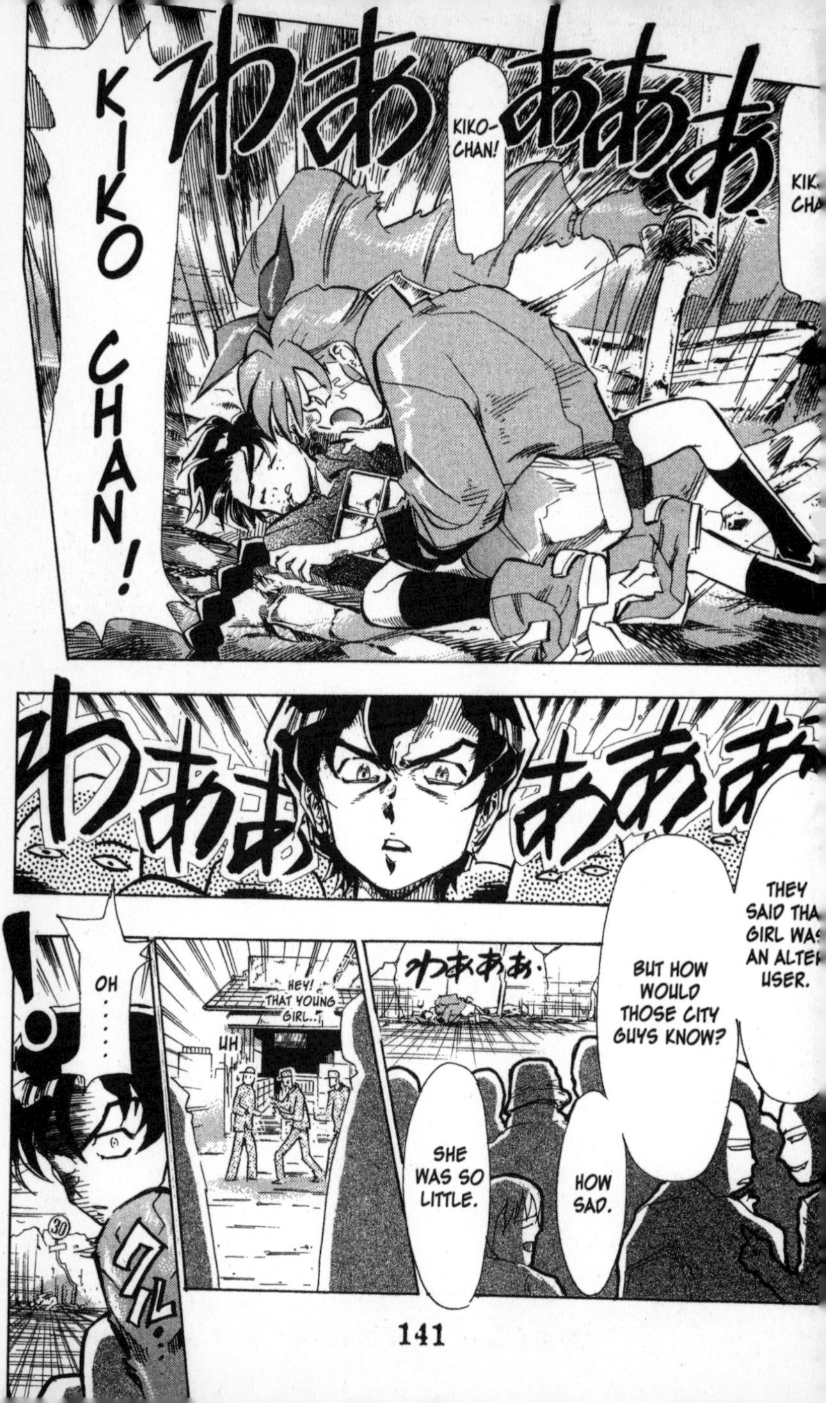
わあああああ
KIKO-CHAN!
KIKO CHAN!
わあああああ
THEY SAID THA GIRL WAS AN ALTE USER.
BUT HOW WOULD THOSE CITY GUYS KNOW?
HOW SAD.
SHE WAS SO LITTLE.
わあああ
HEY! THAT YOUNG GIRL...
UH
OH ......
!
クル...

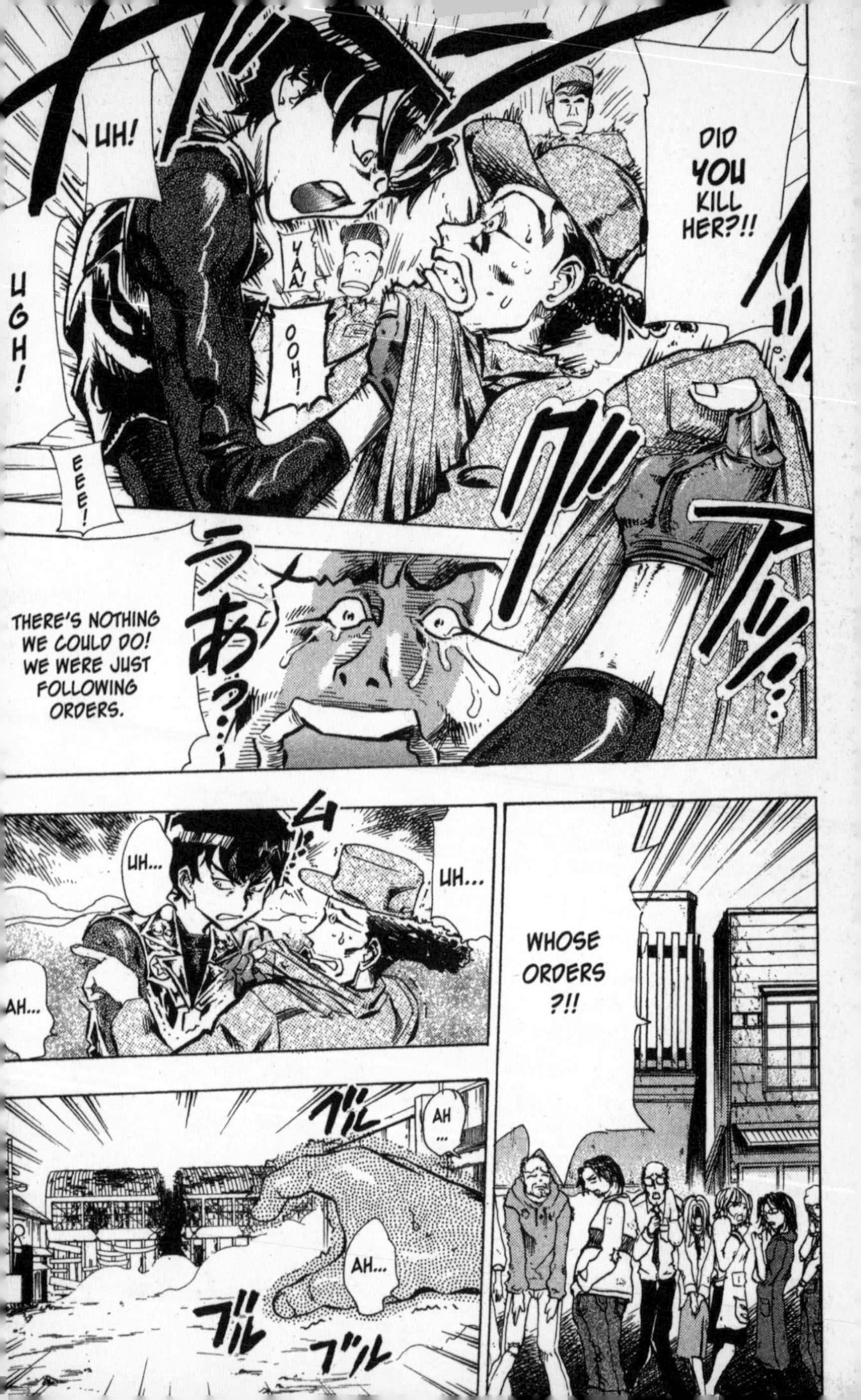
DID YOU KILL HER?!!
UH!
YAA!
OOH!
UGH!
EEE!
THERE'S NOTHING WE COULD DO! WE WERE JUST FOLLOWING ORDERS.
WHOSE ORDERS ?!!
UH...
UH...
AH...
AH ...
AH...

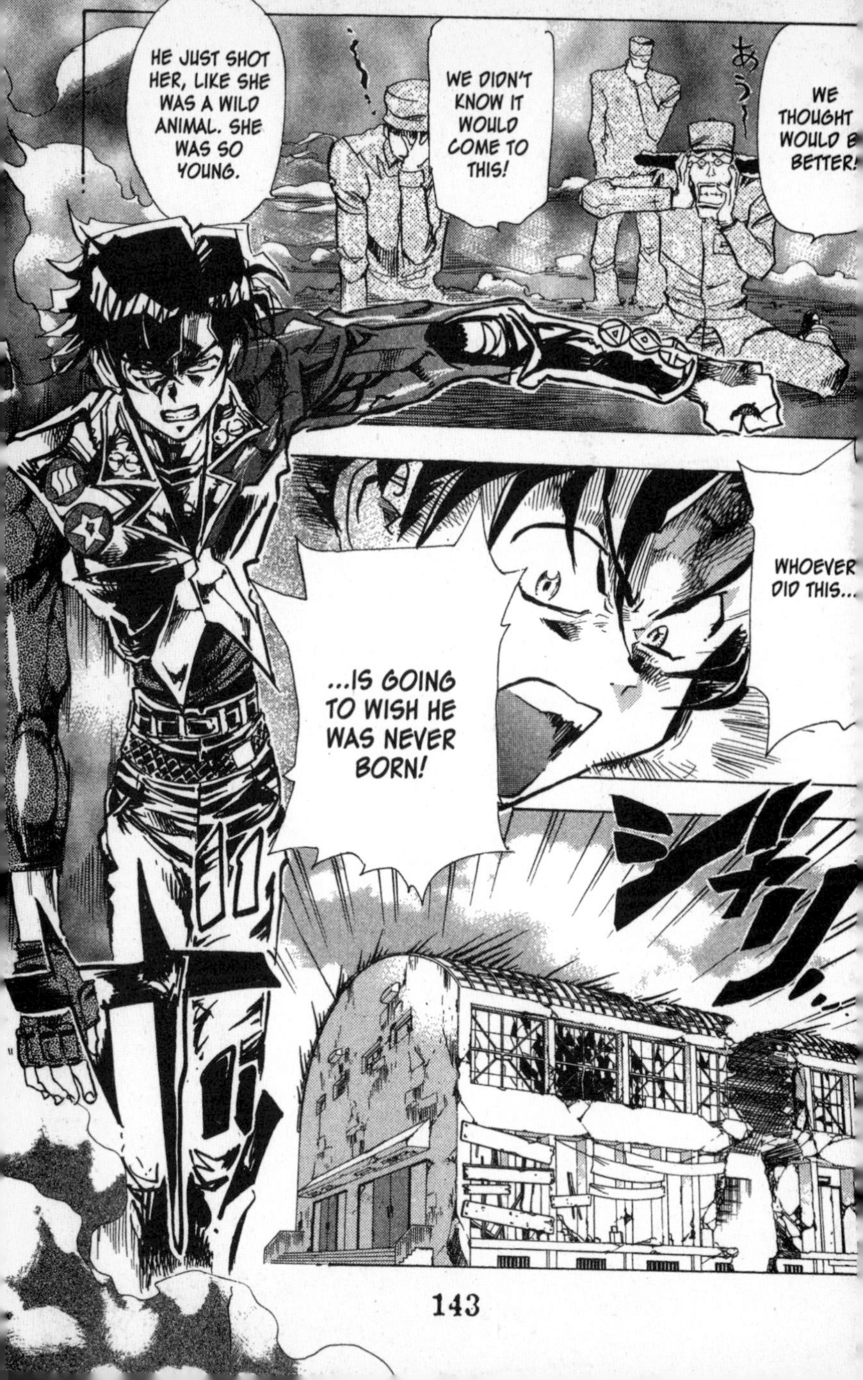
WE THOUGHT WOULD B BETTER!
あう～
WE DIDN'T KNOW IT WOULD COME TO THIS!
HE JUST SHOT HER, LIKE SHE WAS A WILD ANIMAL. SHE WAS SO YOUNG.
WHOEVER DID THIS...
...IS GOING TO WISH HE WAS NEVER BORN!

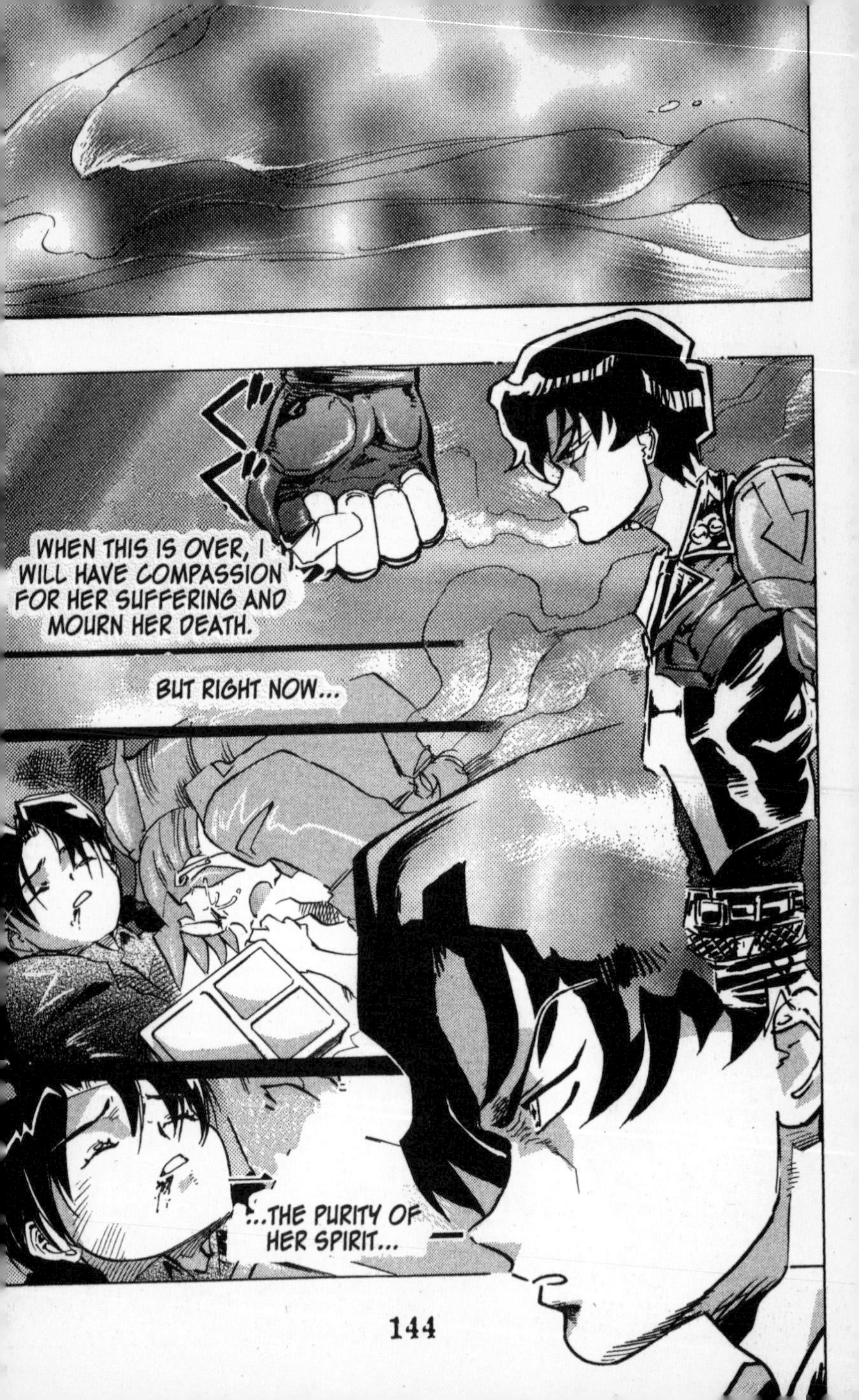
WHEN THIS IS OVER, I WILL HAVE COMPASSION FOR HER SUFFERING AND MOURN HER DEATH.
BUT RIGHT NOW...
...THE PURITY OF HER SPIRIT...

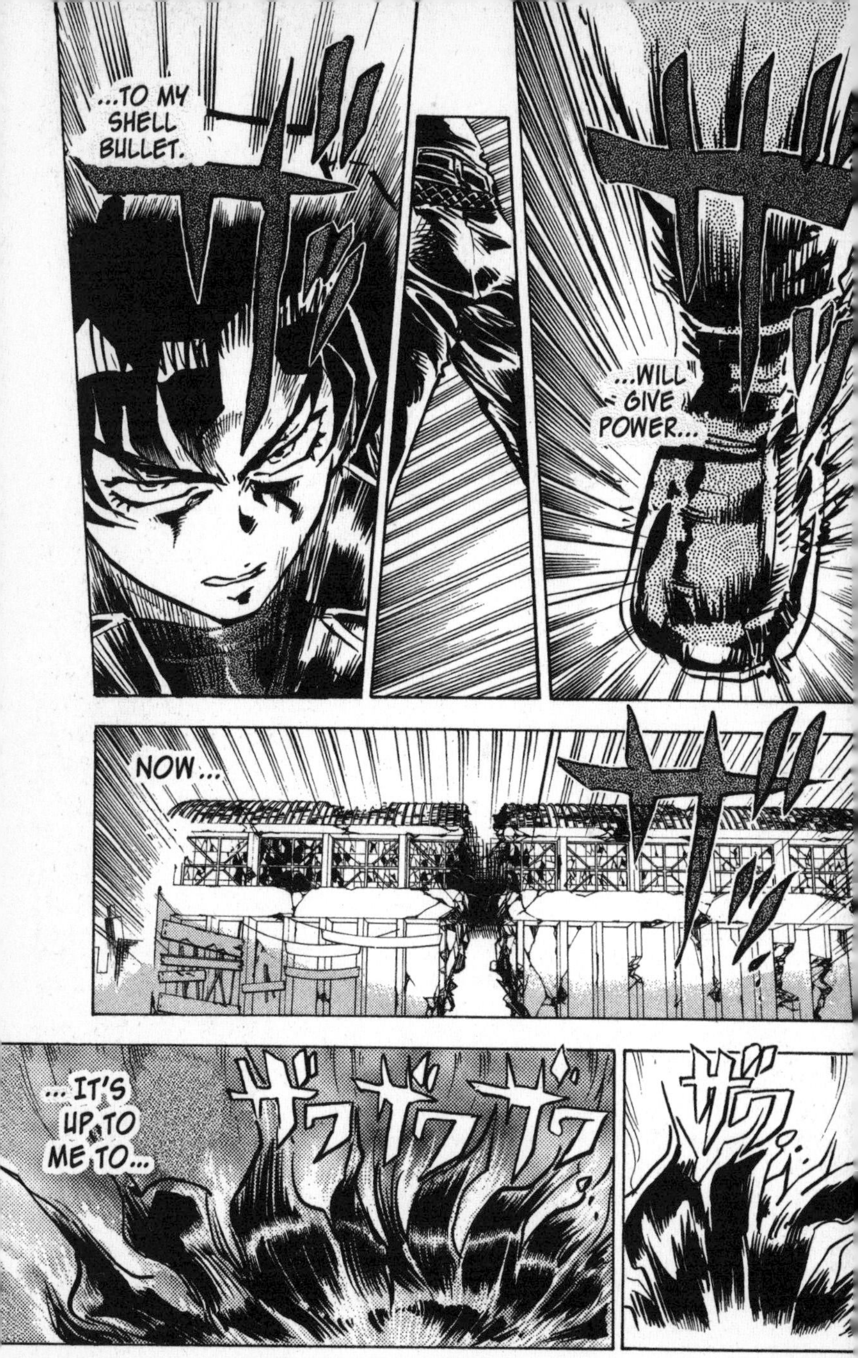
...WILL GIVE POWER...
...TO MY SHELL BULLET.
NOW...
ザワ...
ザワザワザワ
...IT'S UP TO ME TO...

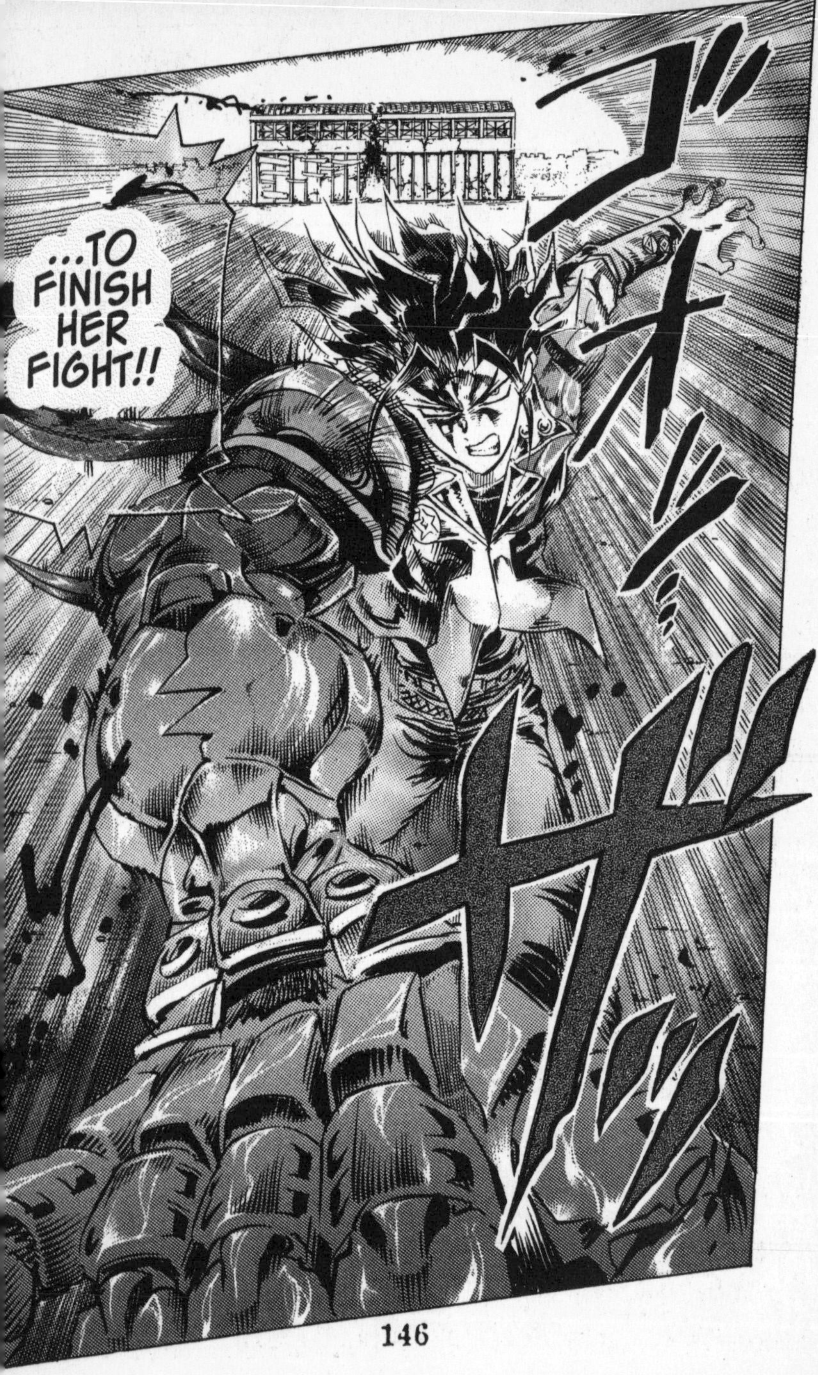
...TO FINISH HER FIGHT!!

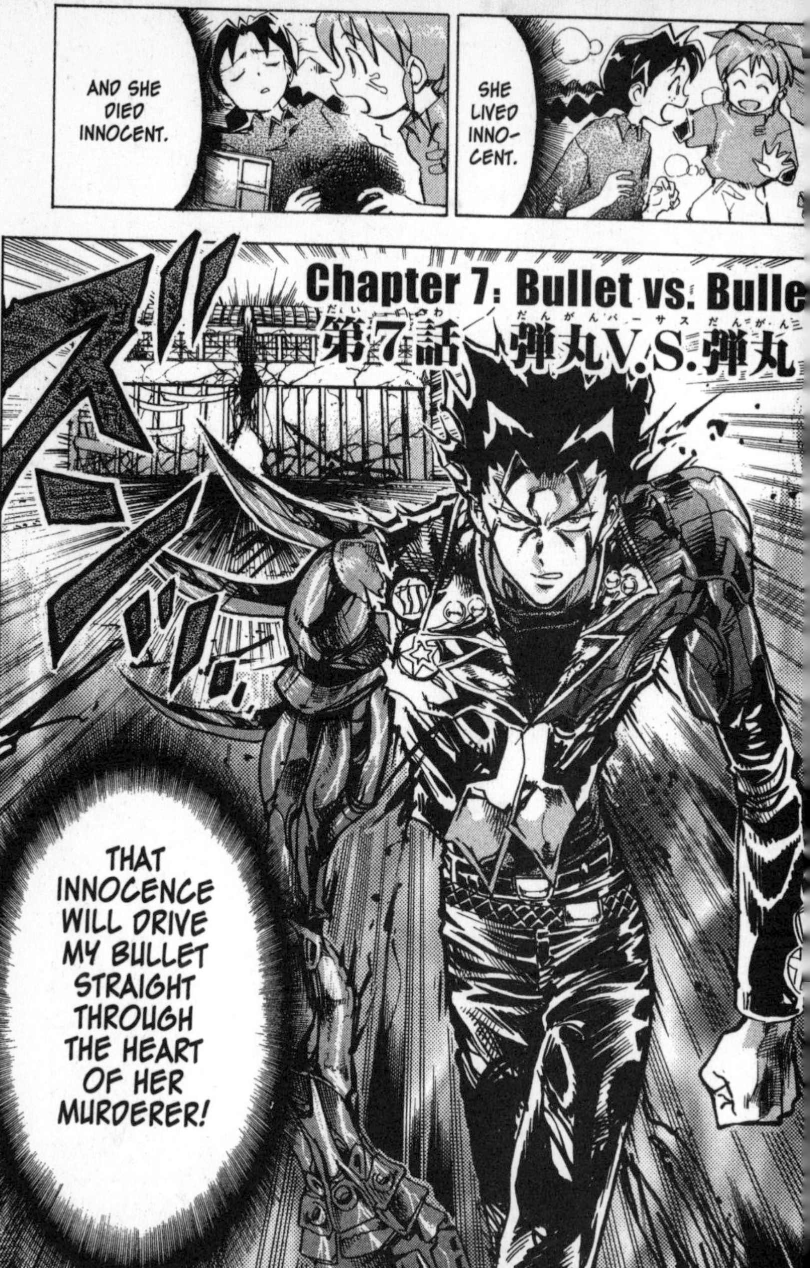
SHE LIVED INNOCENT.
AND SHE DIED INNOCENT.
Chapter 7: Bullet vs. Bulle
第7話 弾丸V.S.弾丸
THAT INNOCENCE WILL DRIVE MY BULLET STRAIGHT THROUGH THE HEART OF HER MURDERER!

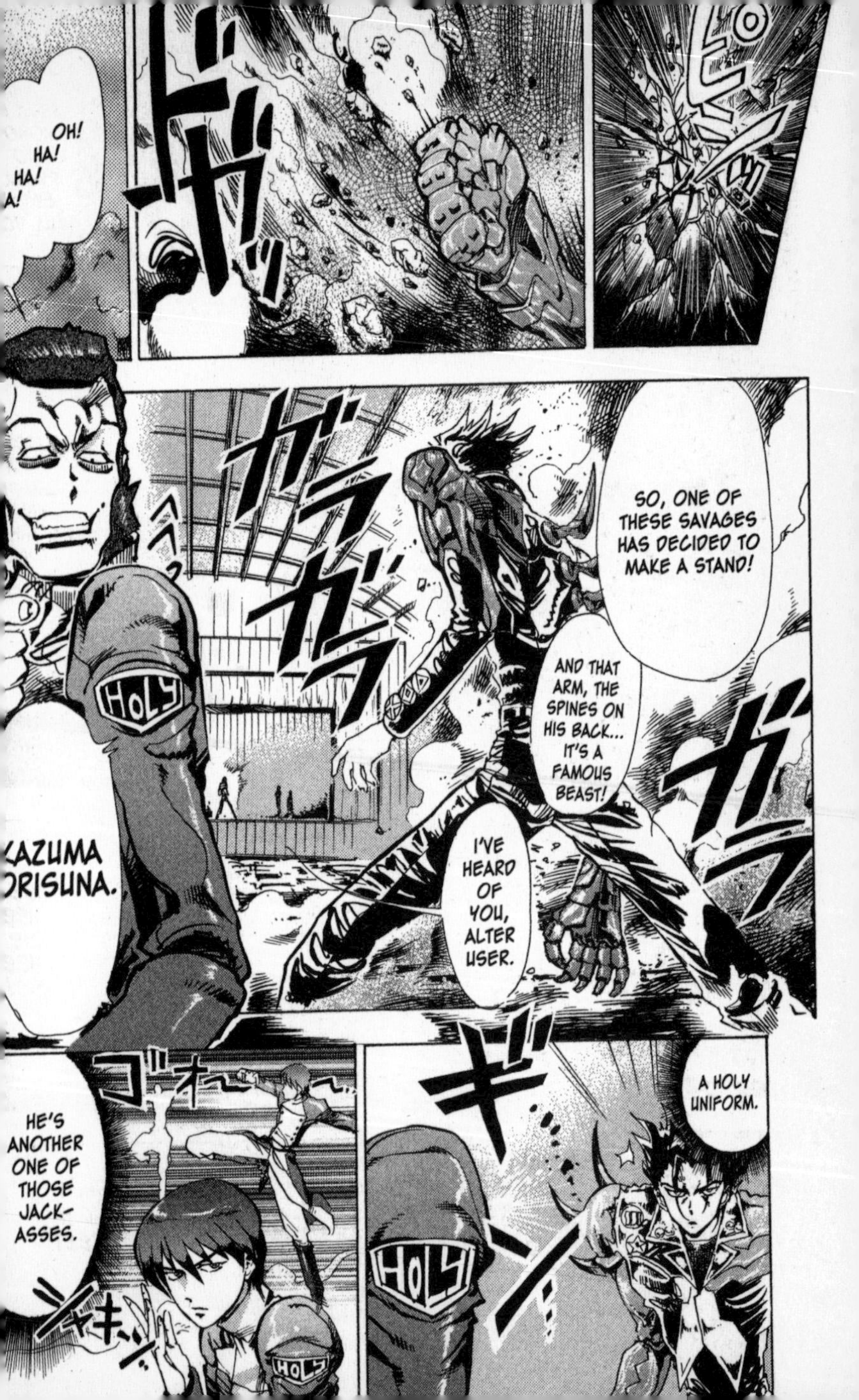
OH! HA! HA! A!
SO, ONE OF THESE SAVAGES HAS DECIDED TO MAKE A STAND!
AND THAT ARM, THE SPINES ON HIS BACK... IT'S A FAMOUS BEAST!
I'VE HEARD OF YOU, ALTER USER.
HOLY
KAZUMA ORISUNA.
A HOLY UNIFORM.
HOLY
HE'S ANOTHER ONE OF THOSE JACK-ASSES.
HOLY

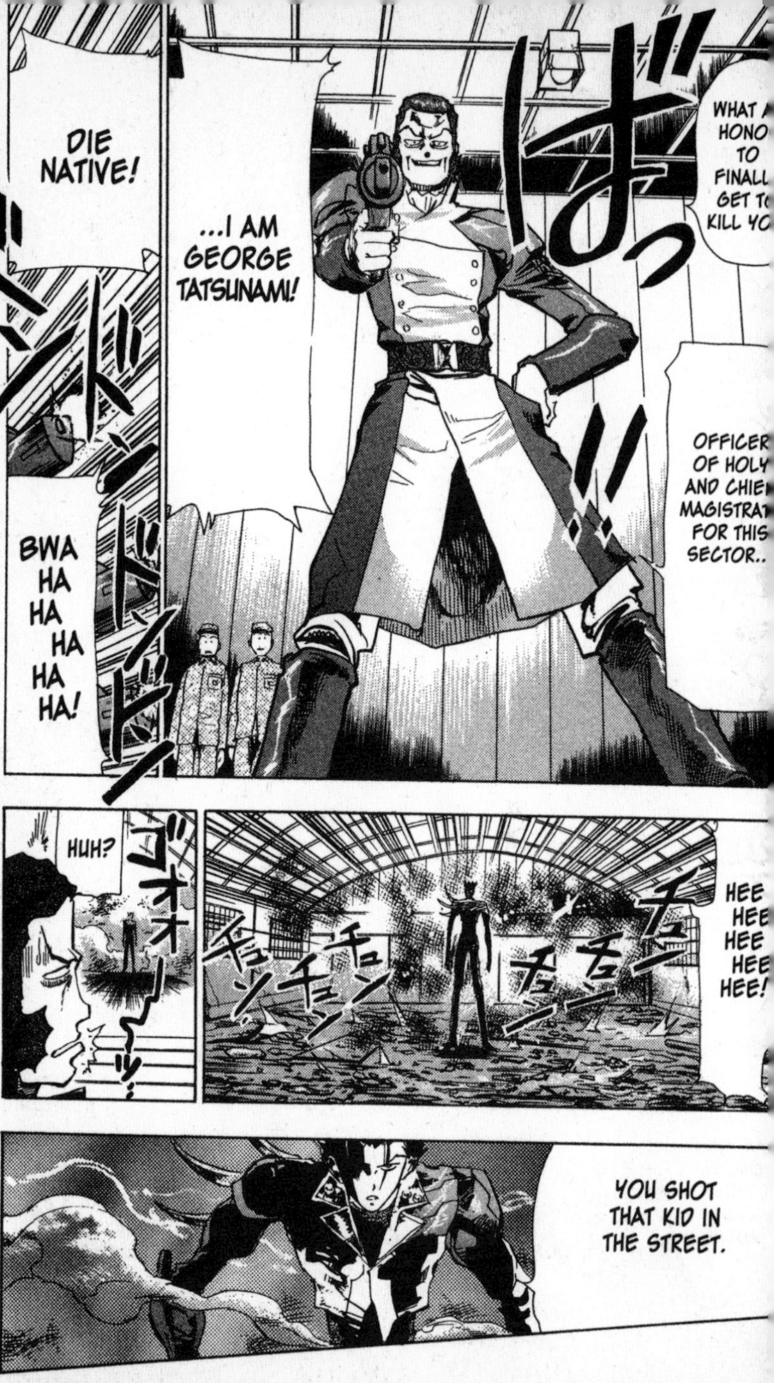
WHAT A HONO TO FINALL GET TO KILL YO
OFFICER OF HOLY AND CHIE MAGISTRAT FOR THIS SECTOR..
...I AM GEORGE TATSUNAMI!
DIE NATIVE!
BWA HA HA HA HA HA!
HEE HEE HEE HEE HEE!
HUH?
YOU SHOT THAT KID IN THE STREET.

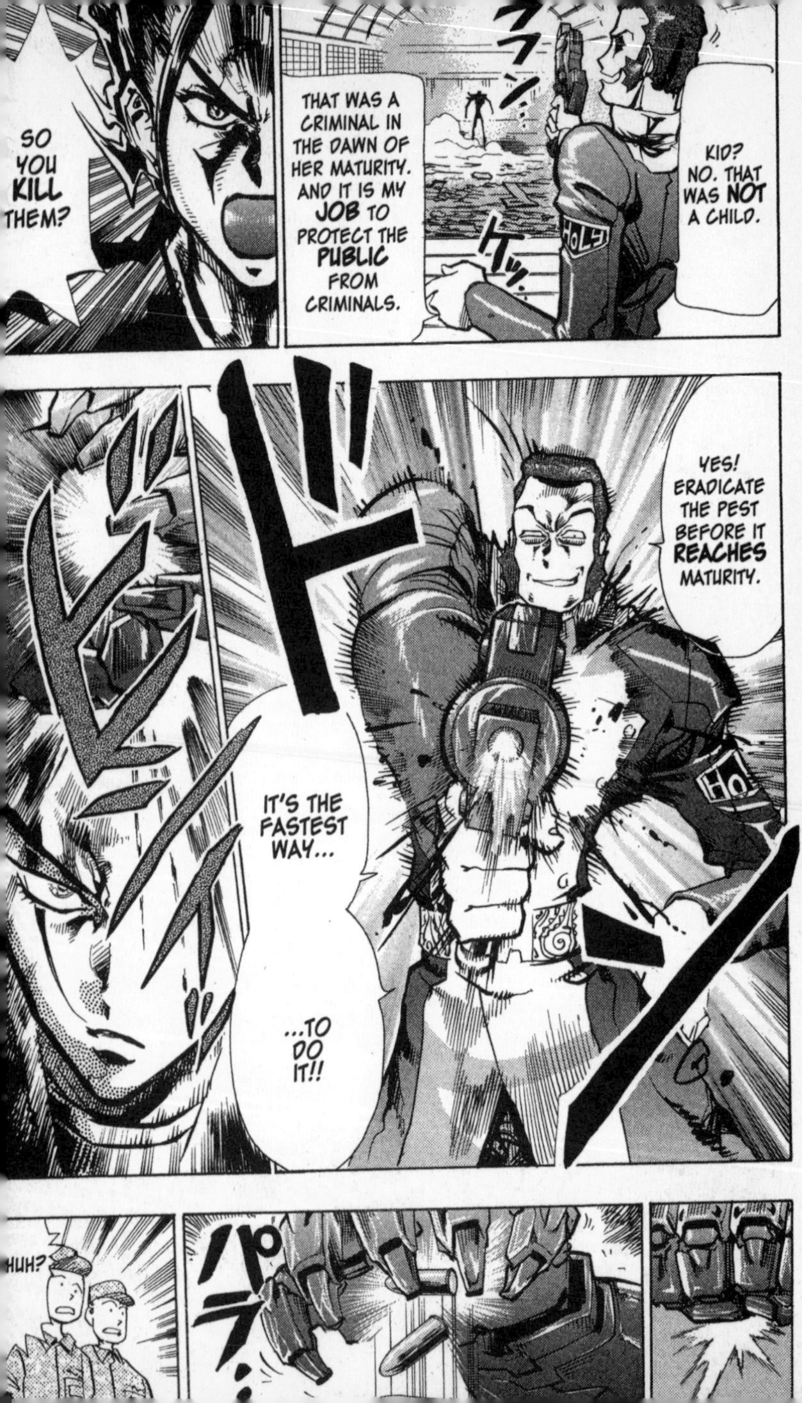
KID? NO. THAT WAS NOT A CHILD.
THAT WAS A CRIMINAL IN THE DAWN OF HER MATURITY. AND IT IS MY JOB TO PROTECT THE PUBLIC FROM CRIMINALS.
SO YOU KILL THEM?
YES! ERADICATE THE PEST BEFORE IT REACHES MATURITY.
IT'S THE FASTEST WAY...
...TO DO IT!!
HUH?

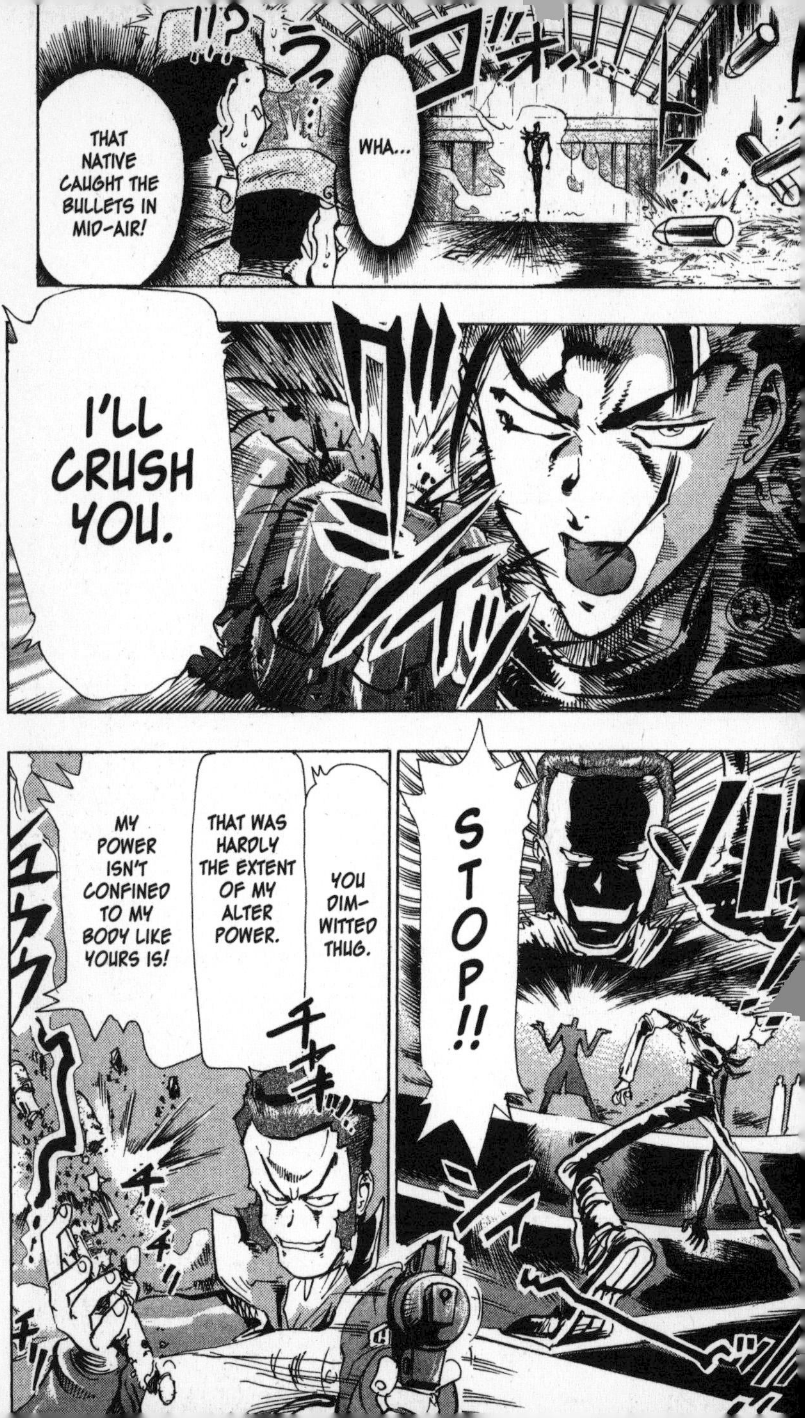
WHA...
THAT NATIVE CAUGHT THE BULLETS IN MID-AIR!
I'LL CRUSH YOU.
STOP!!
YOU DIM-WITTED THUG.
THAT WAS HARDLY THE EXTENT OF MY ALTER POWER.
MY POWER ISN'T CONFINED TO MY BODY LIKE YOURS IS!

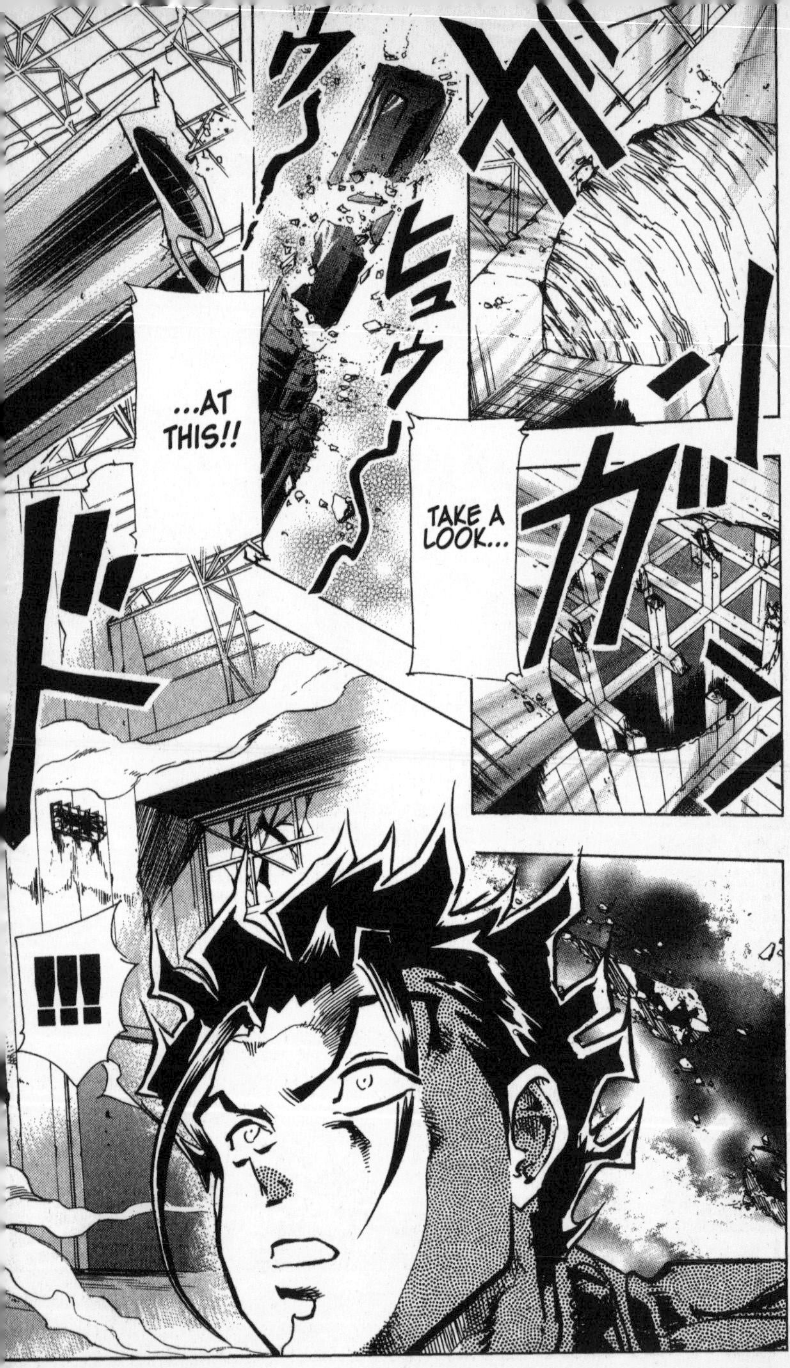
TAKE A LOOK...
...AT THIS!!
!!!

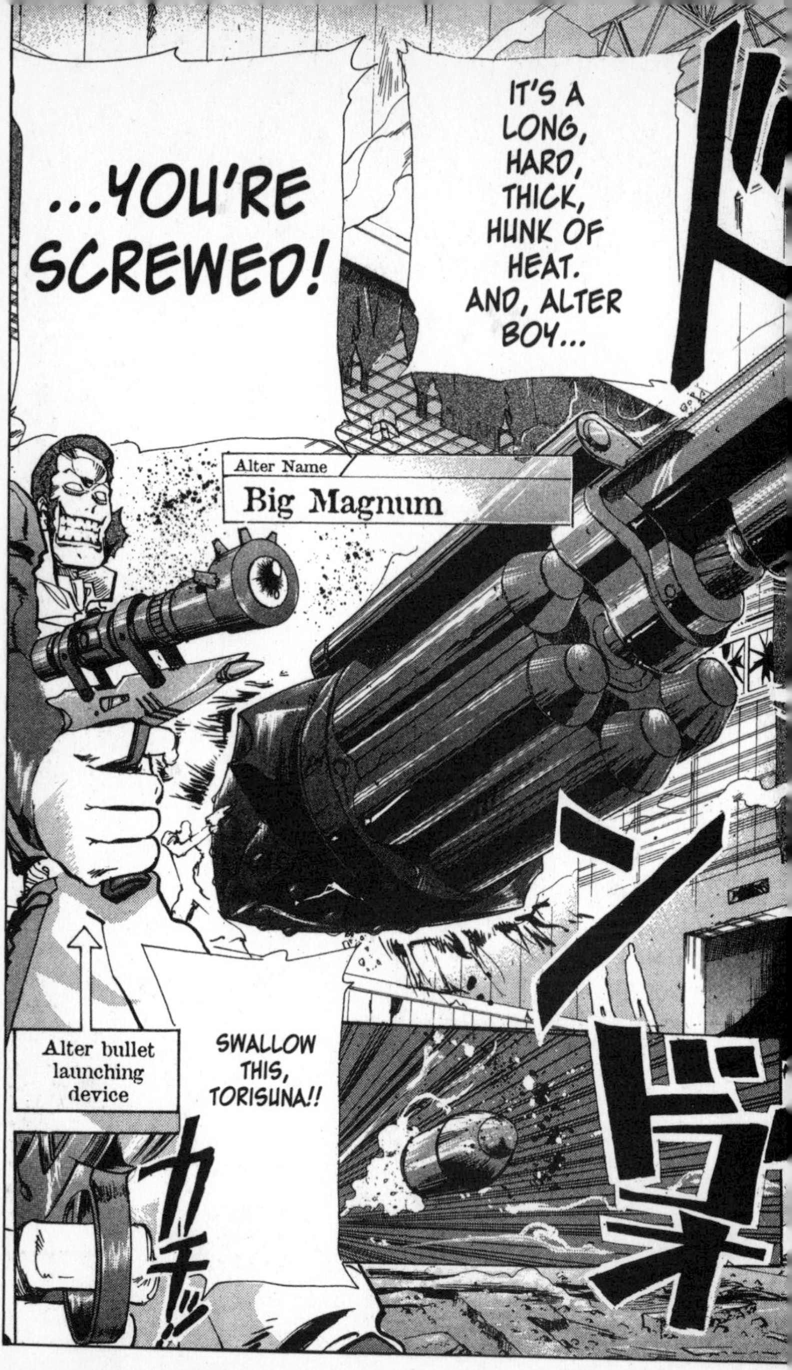
IT'S A LONG, HARD, THICK, HUNK OF HEAT. AND, ALTER BOY...
...YOU'RE SCREWED!
Alter Name
Big Magnum
SWALLOW THIS, TORISUNA!!
Alter bullet launching device

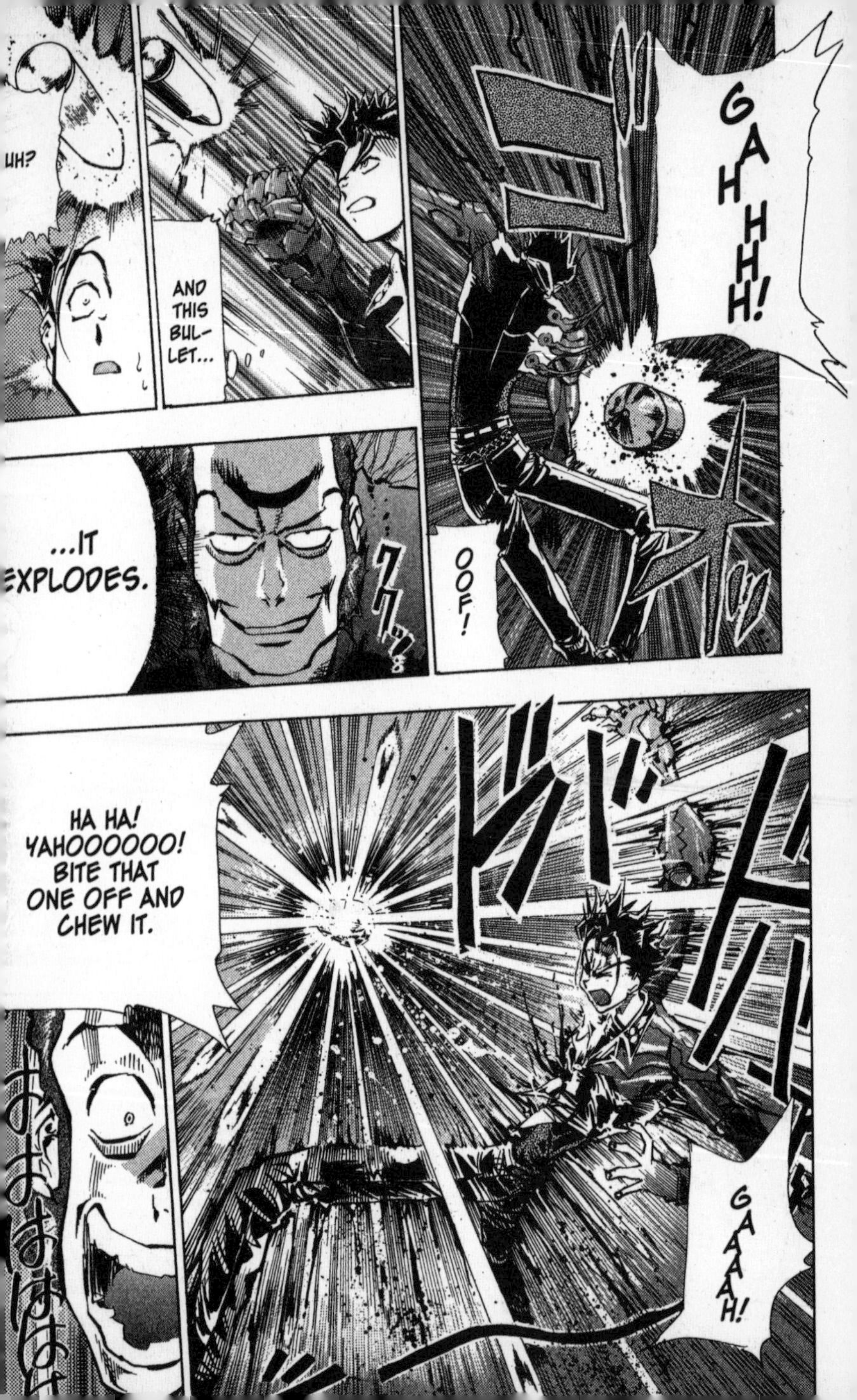
GAHHHHH!
OOF!
AND THIS BULLET...
UH?
...IT EXPLODES.
GAAAAH!
HA HA! YAHOOOOOO! BITE THAT ONE OFF AND CHEW IT.

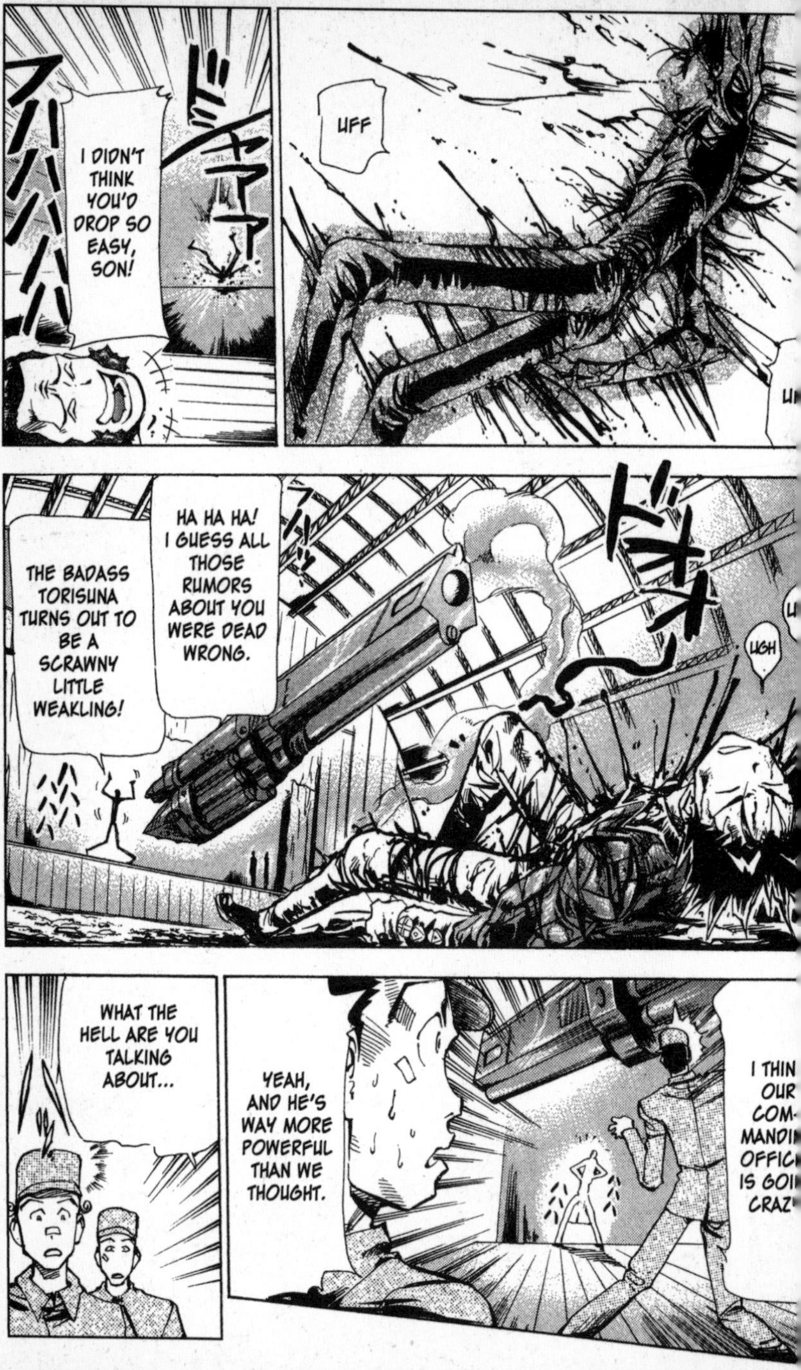
UFF
I DIDN'T THINK YOU'D DROP SO EASY, SON!
UGH
HA HA HA! I GUESS ALL THOSE RUMORS ABOUT YOU WERE DEAD WRONG.
THE BADASS TORISUNA TURNS OUT TO BE A SCRAWNY LITTLE WEAKLING!
YEAH, AND HE'S WAY MORE POWERFUL THAN WE THOUGHT.
WHAT THE HELL ARE YOU TALKING ABOUT...

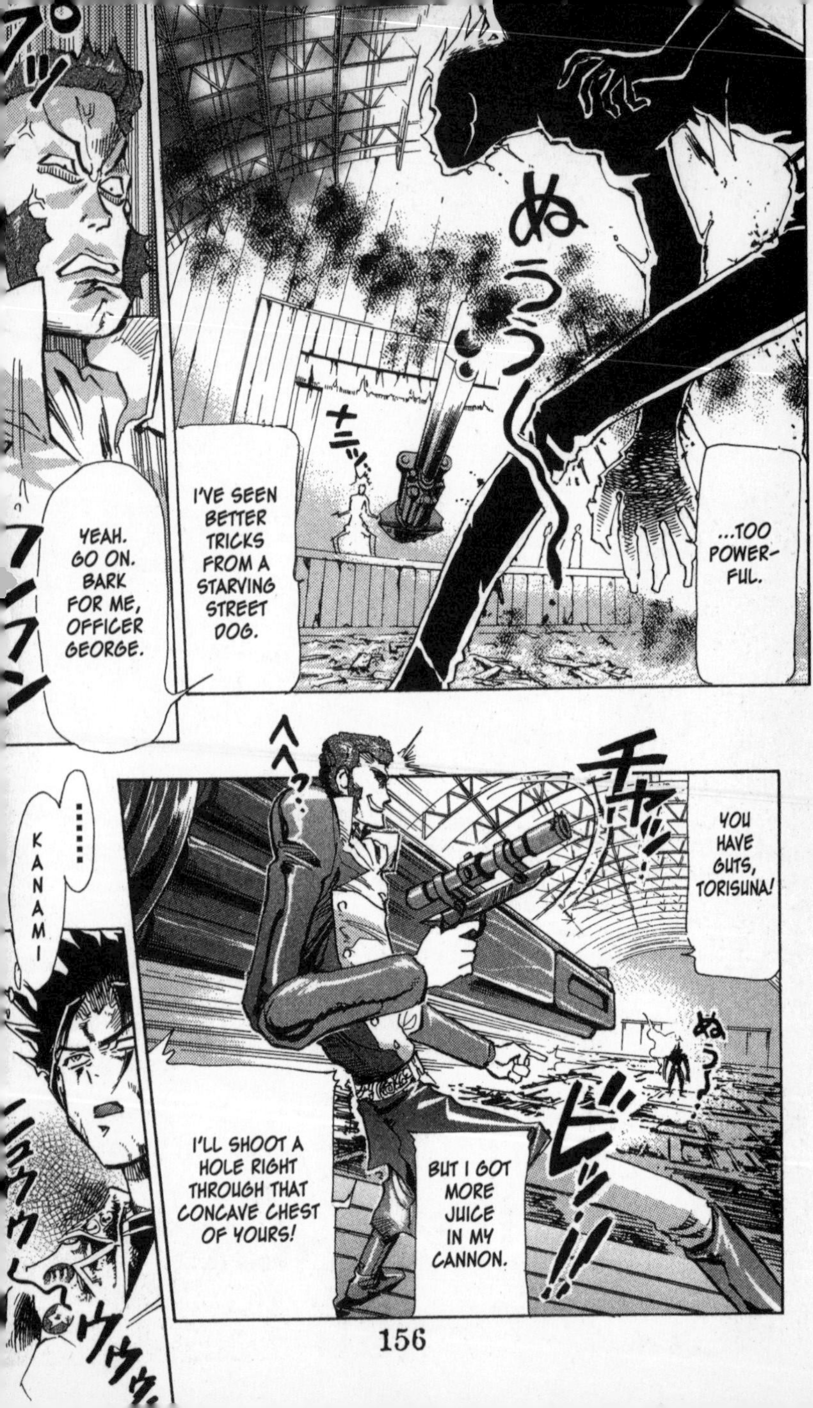
...TOO POWER-FUL.
I'VE SEEN BETTER TRICKS FROM A STARVING STREET DOG.
YEAH. GO ON. BARK FOR ME, OFFICER GEORGE.
YOU HAVE GUTS, TORISUNA!
BUT I GOT MORE JUICE IN MY CANNON.
I'LL SHOOT A HOLE RIGHT THROUGH THAT CONCAVE CHEST OF YOURS!
...... KANAMI

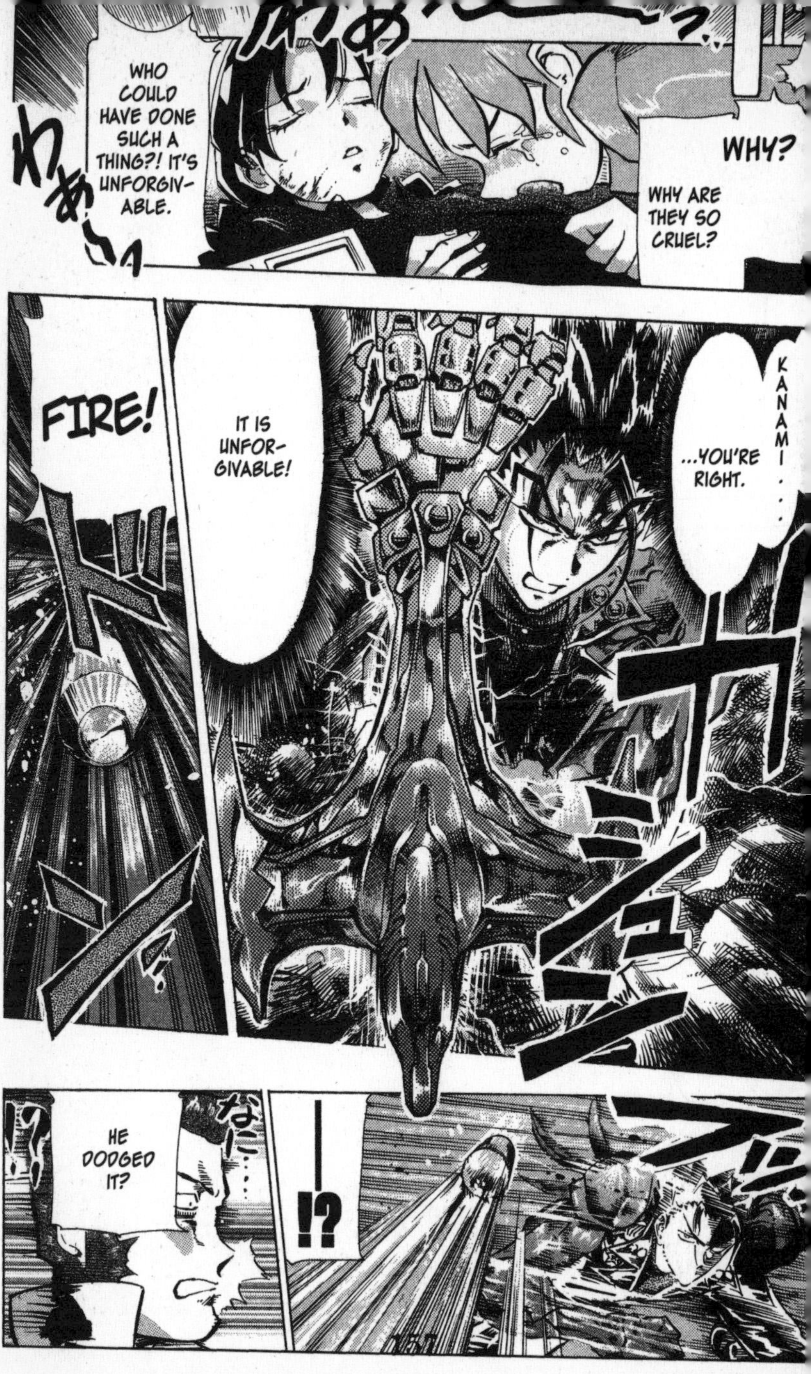
WHY?
WHY ARE THEY SO CRUEL?
WHO COULD HAVE DONE SUCH A THING?! IT'S UNFORGIVABLE.
KANAMI...
...YOU'RE RIGHT.
IT IS UNFORGIVABLE!
FIRE!
—!?
HE DODGED IT?

That girl's spirit is too strong for Kazuma's alter.

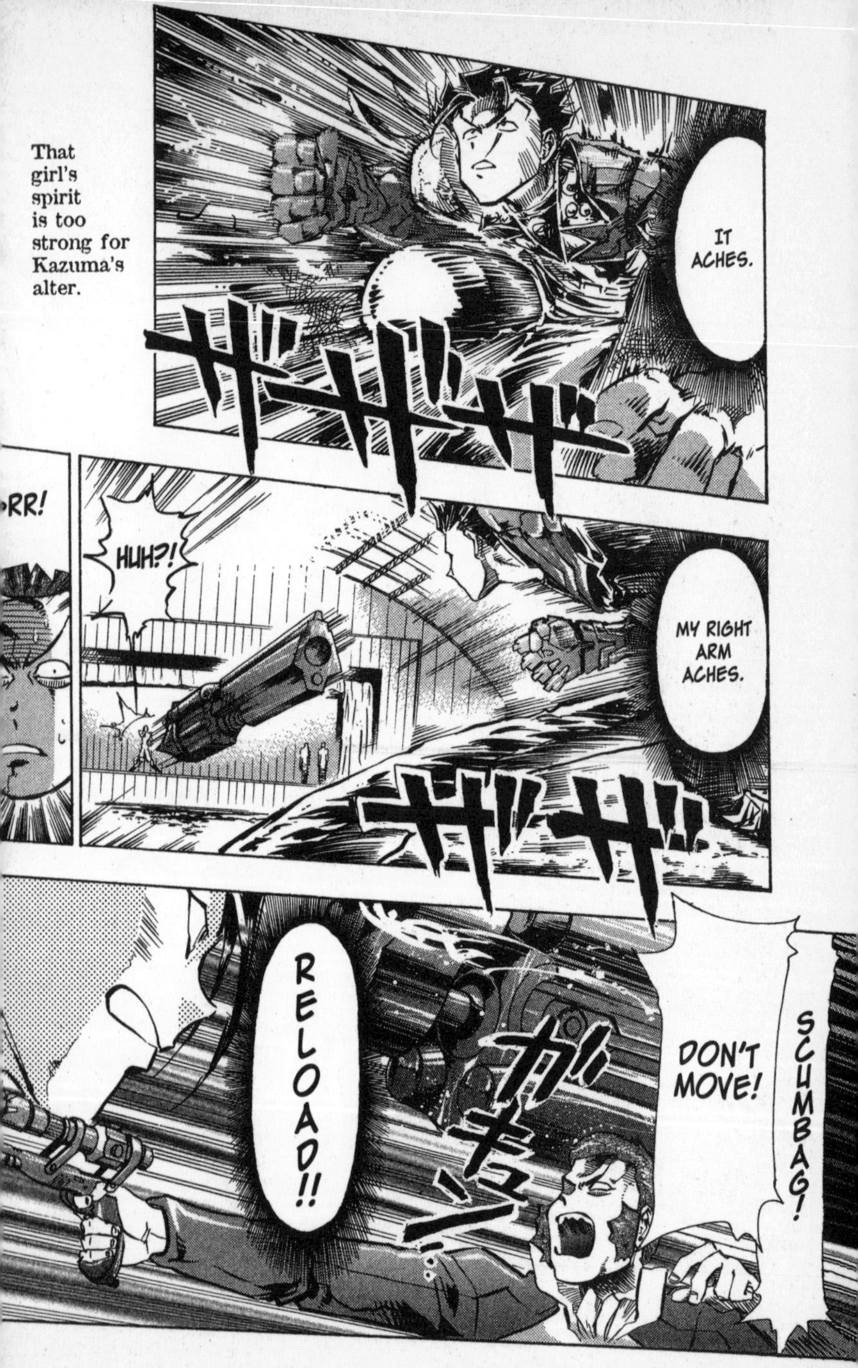
IT ACHES.
MY RIGHT ARM ACHES.
HUH?!
SCUMBAG!
DON'T MOVE!
RELOAD!!

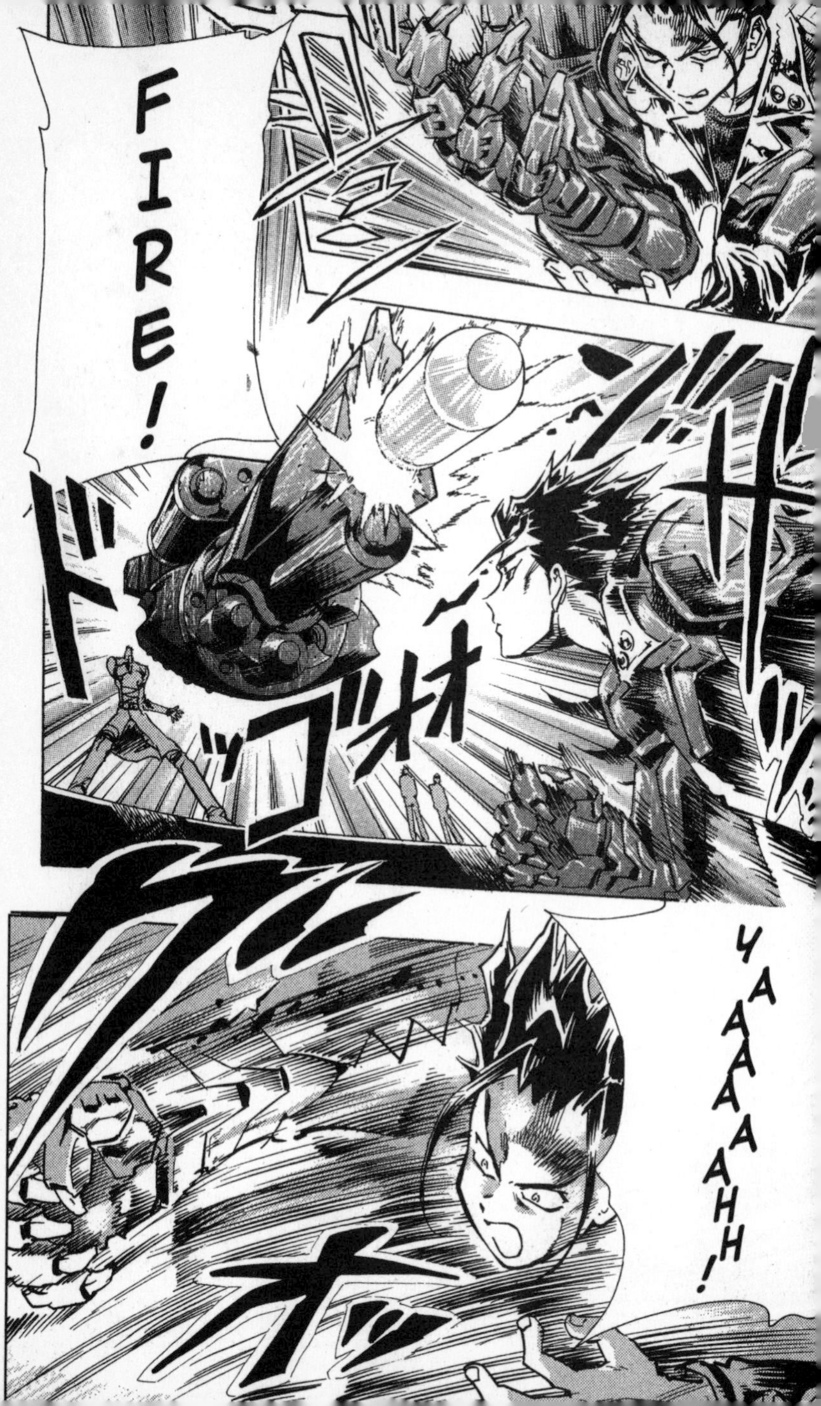
FIRE!
YAAAAAAHH!

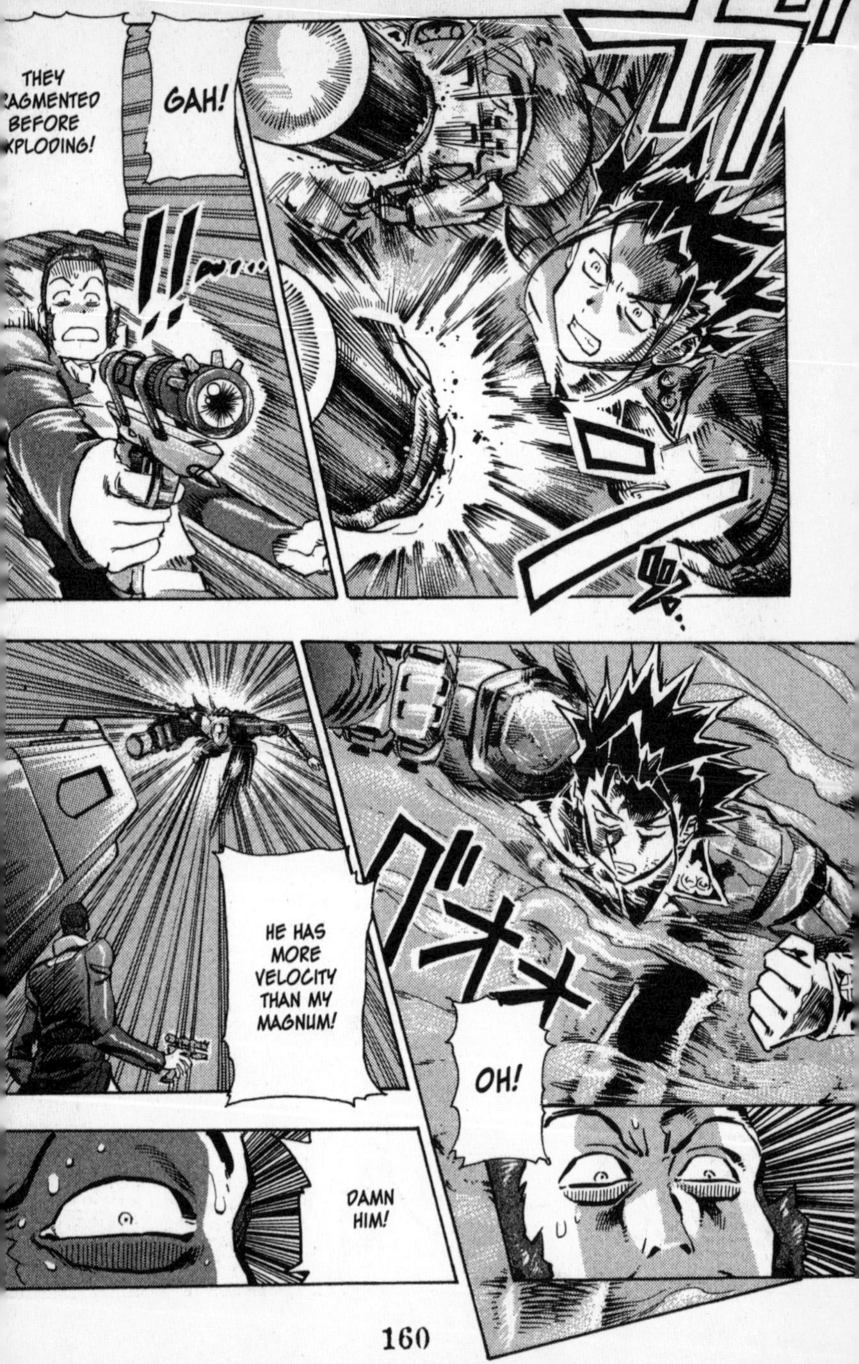
GAH!
THEY
RAGMENTED
BEFORE
XPLODING!
OH!
HE HAS
MORE
VELOCITY
THAN MY
MAGNUM!
DAMN
HIM!

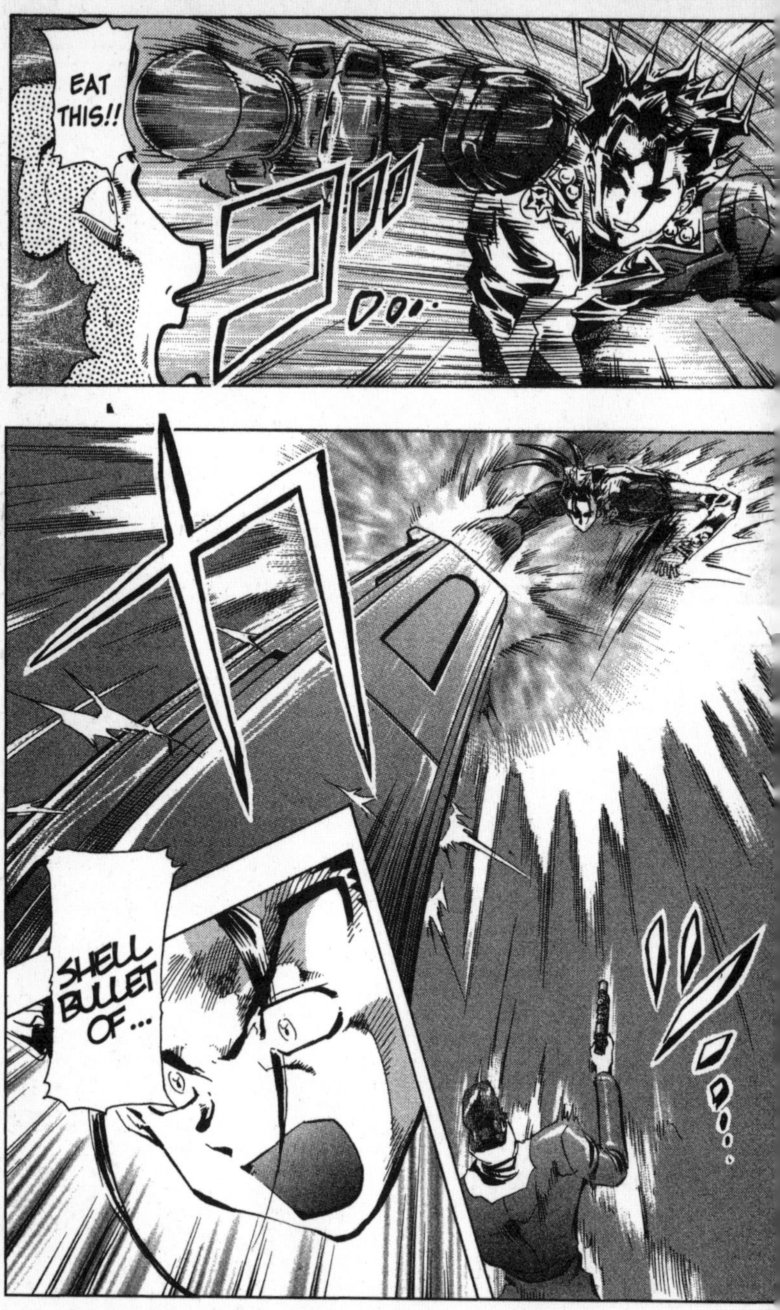
EAT THIS!!
SHELL BULLET OF...

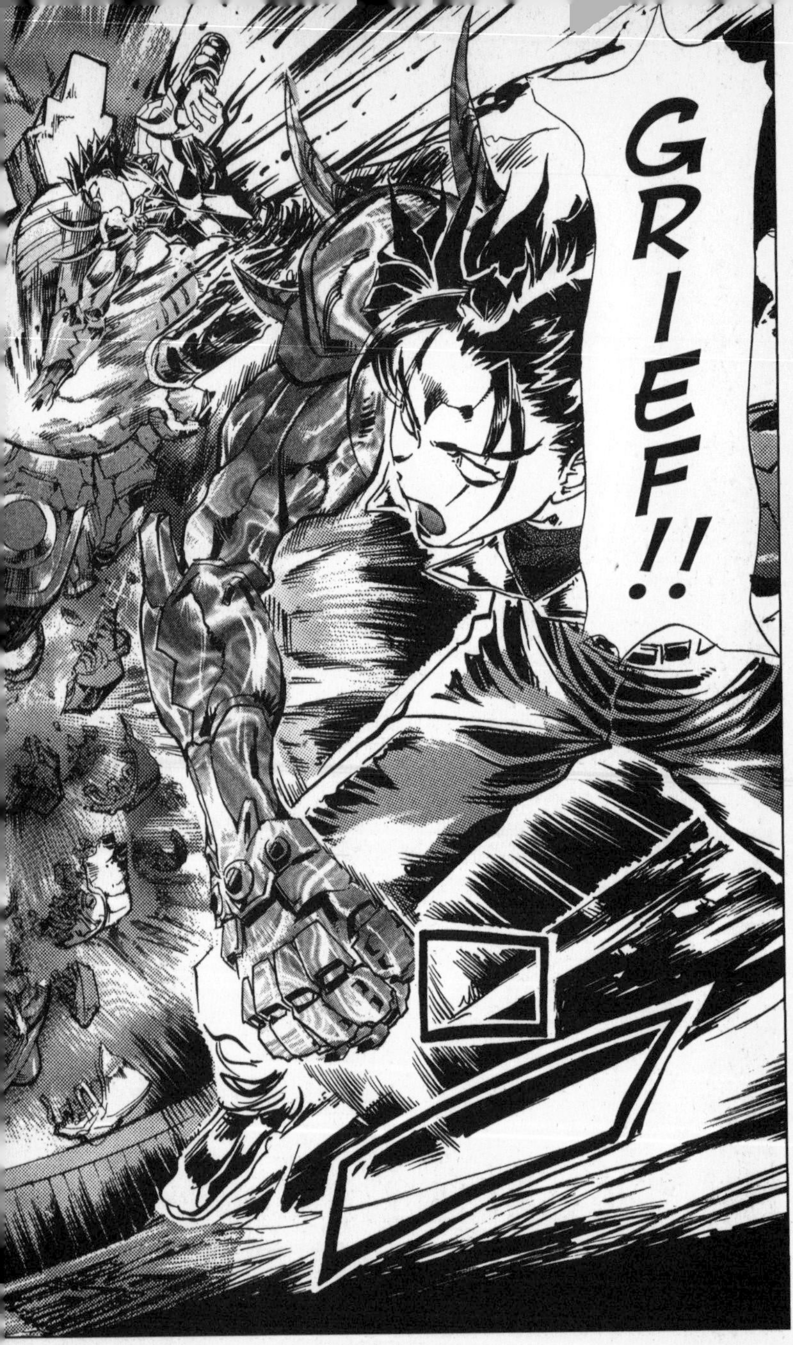
GRIEF!!

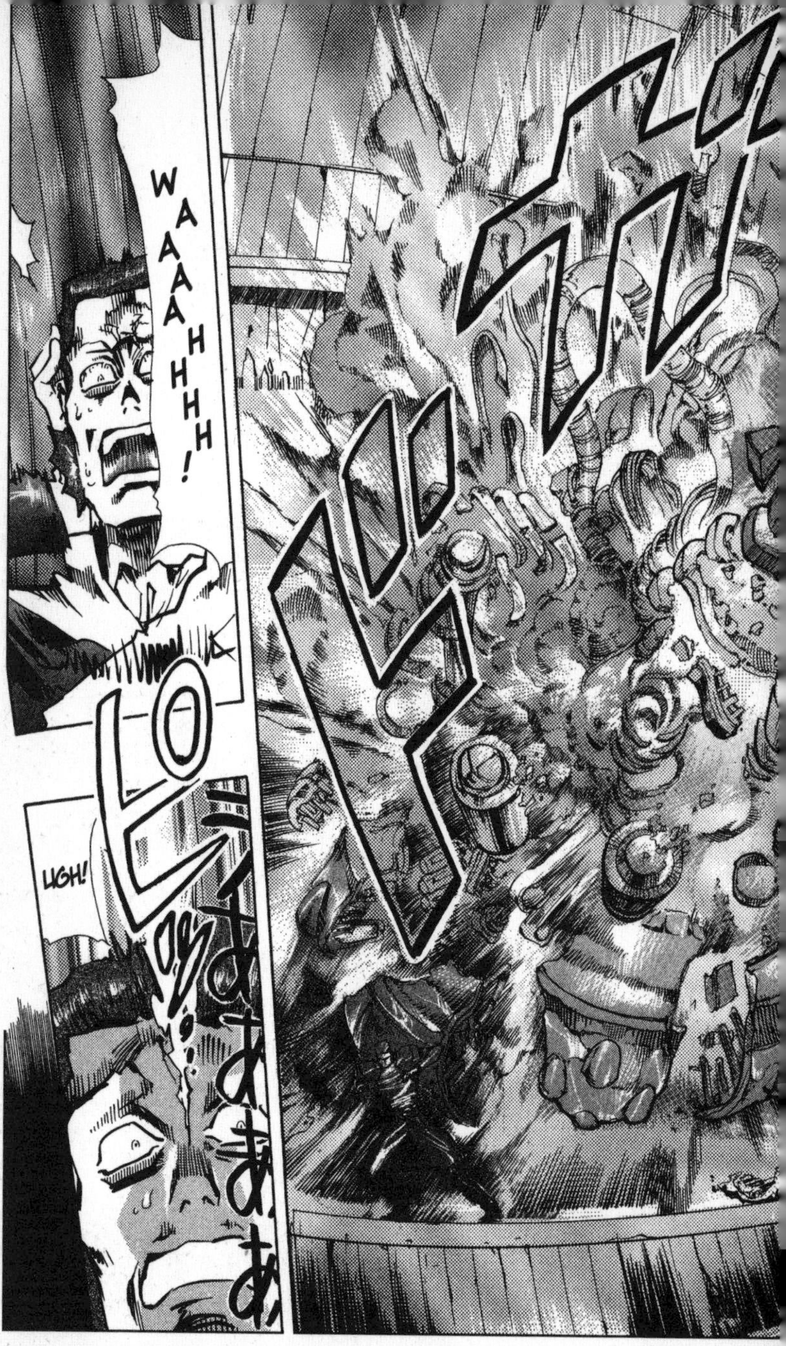
WAAAAHHHH!
UGH!

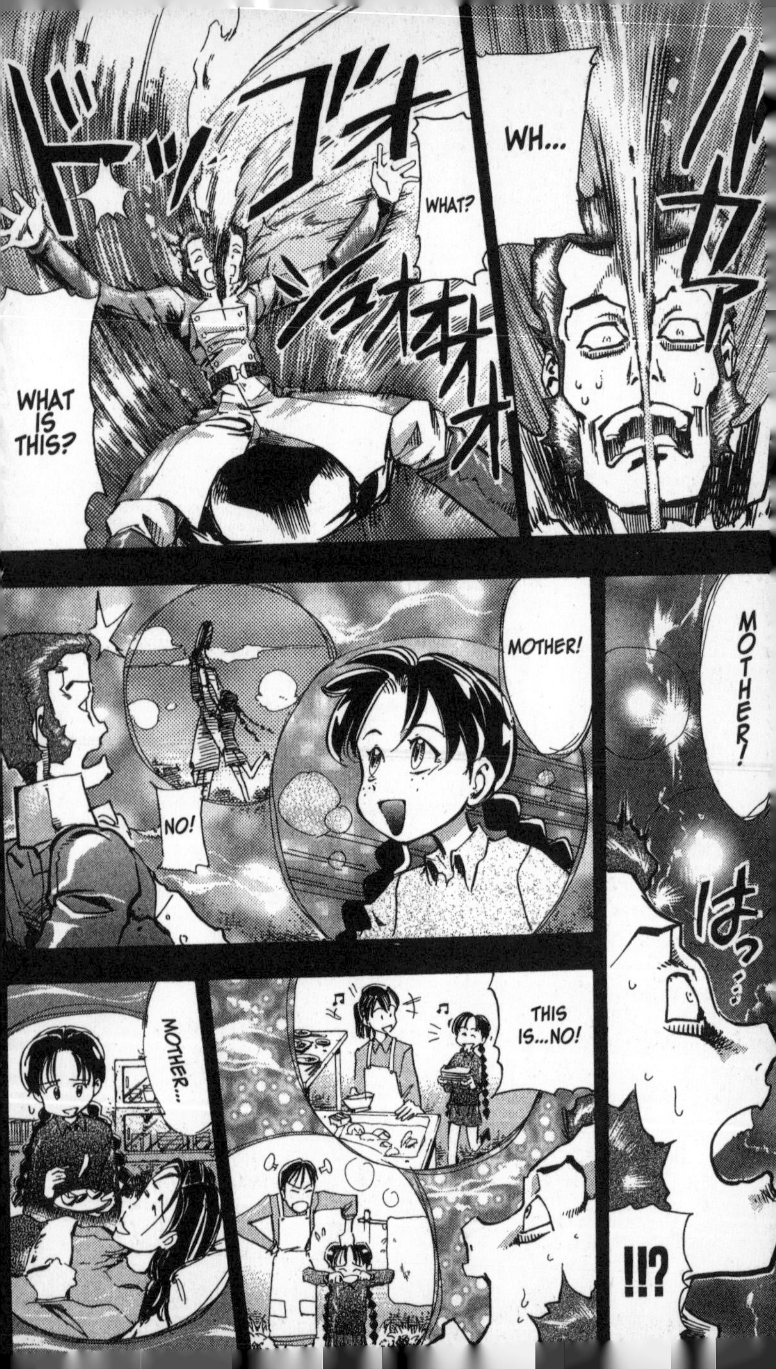
WH...
WHAT?
WHAT IS THIS?
MOTHER!
はっ...
!!?
MOTHER!
NO!
THIS IS...NO!
MOTHER...

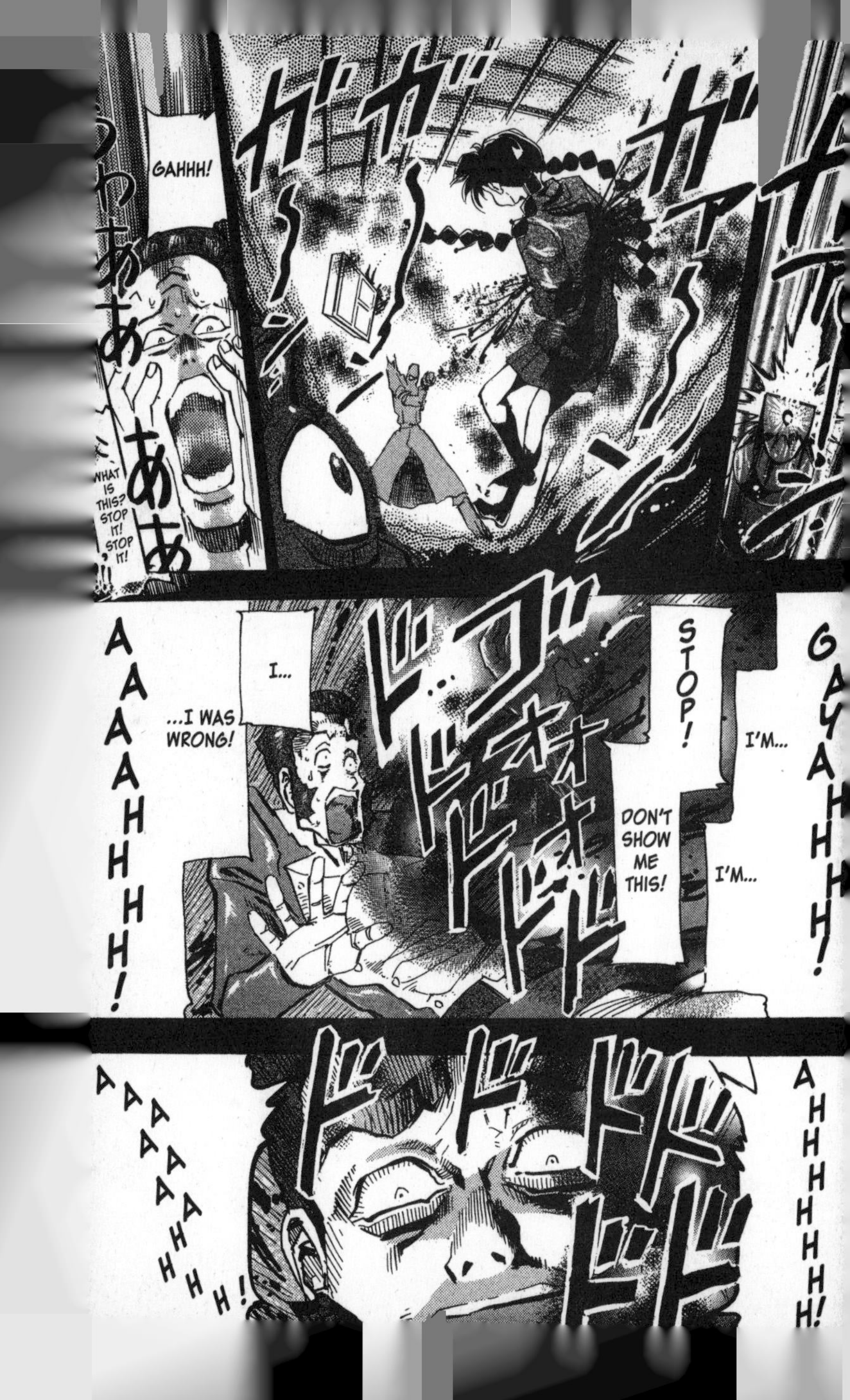
GAHHH!
うわあああ
WHAT IS THIS? STOP IT! STOP IT!
GAYAHHHHH!
I'M...
I'M...
STOP!
DON'T SHOW ME THIS!
I...
...I WAS WRONG!
AAAAHHHHH!
AHHHHHHHHH!
AAAAAAAAHHHH!

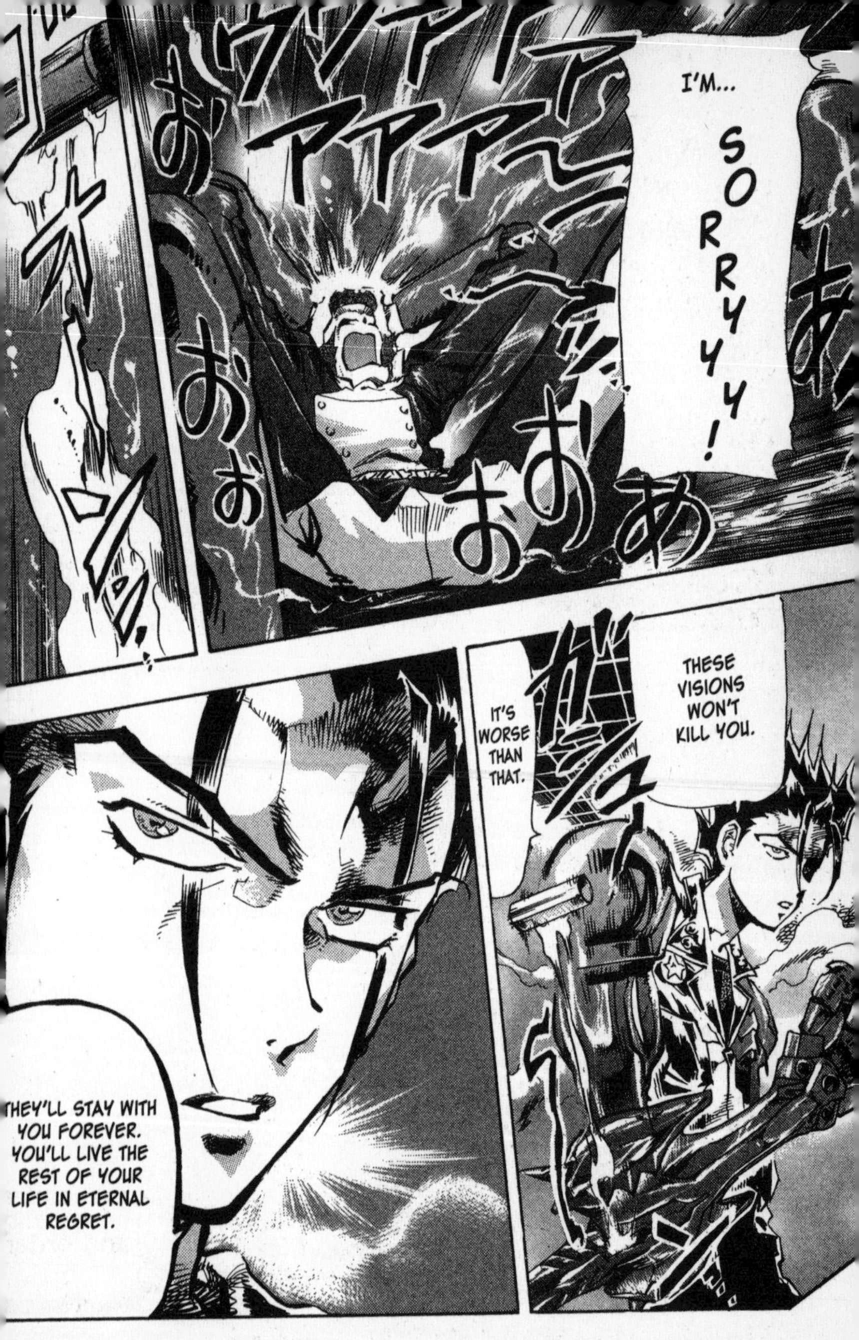
I'M... SORRYYYY!
THESE VISIONS WON'T KILL YOU.
IT'S WORSE THAN THAT.
THEY'LL STAY WITH YOU FOREVER. YOU'LL LIVE THE REST OF YOUR LIFE IN ETERNAL REGRET.

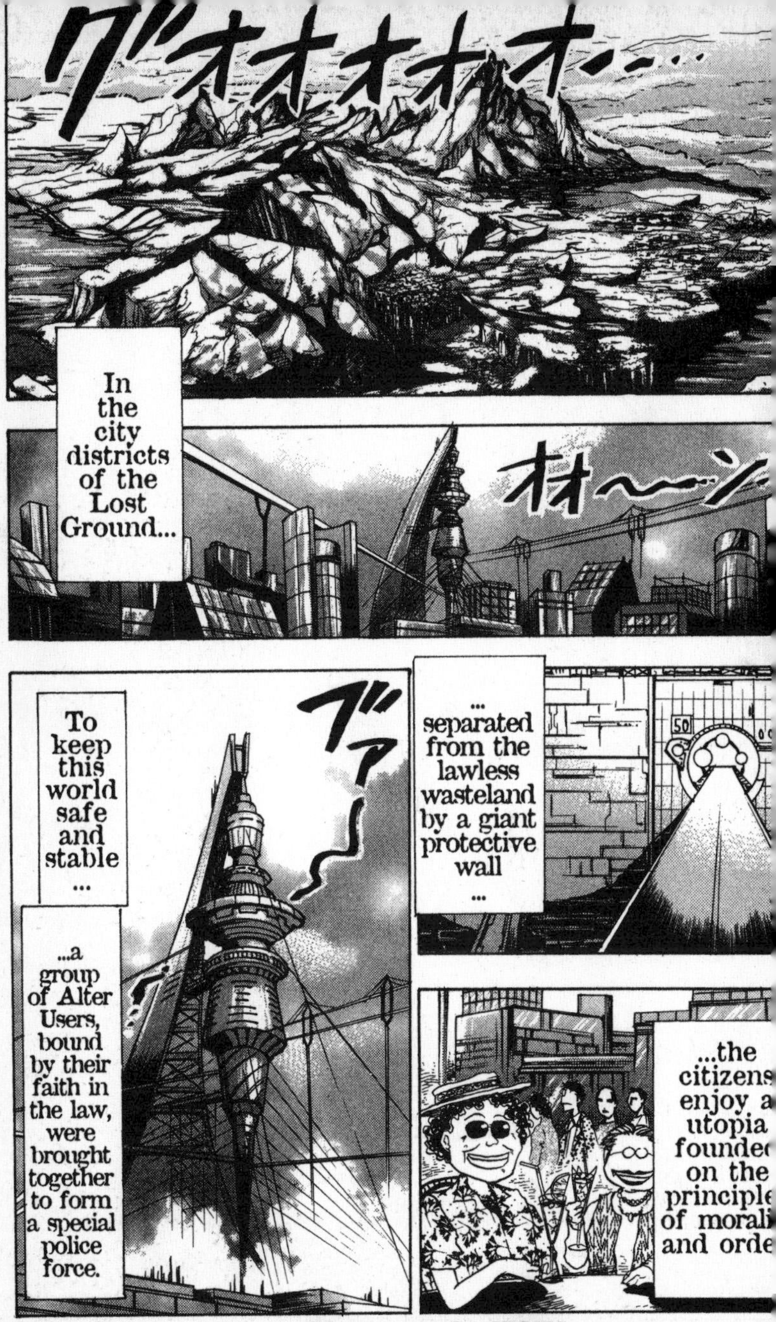
グオオオオオー…
In the city districts of the Lost Ground...
オオヘ〜ン
... separated from the lawless wasteland by a giant protective wall ...
...the citizens enjoy a utopia founded on the principle of morali and orde
ブァ〜
To keep this world safe and stable ...
...a group of Alter Users, bound by their faith in the law, were brought together to form a special police force.

第8話／ホーリー Chapter 8: HOLY

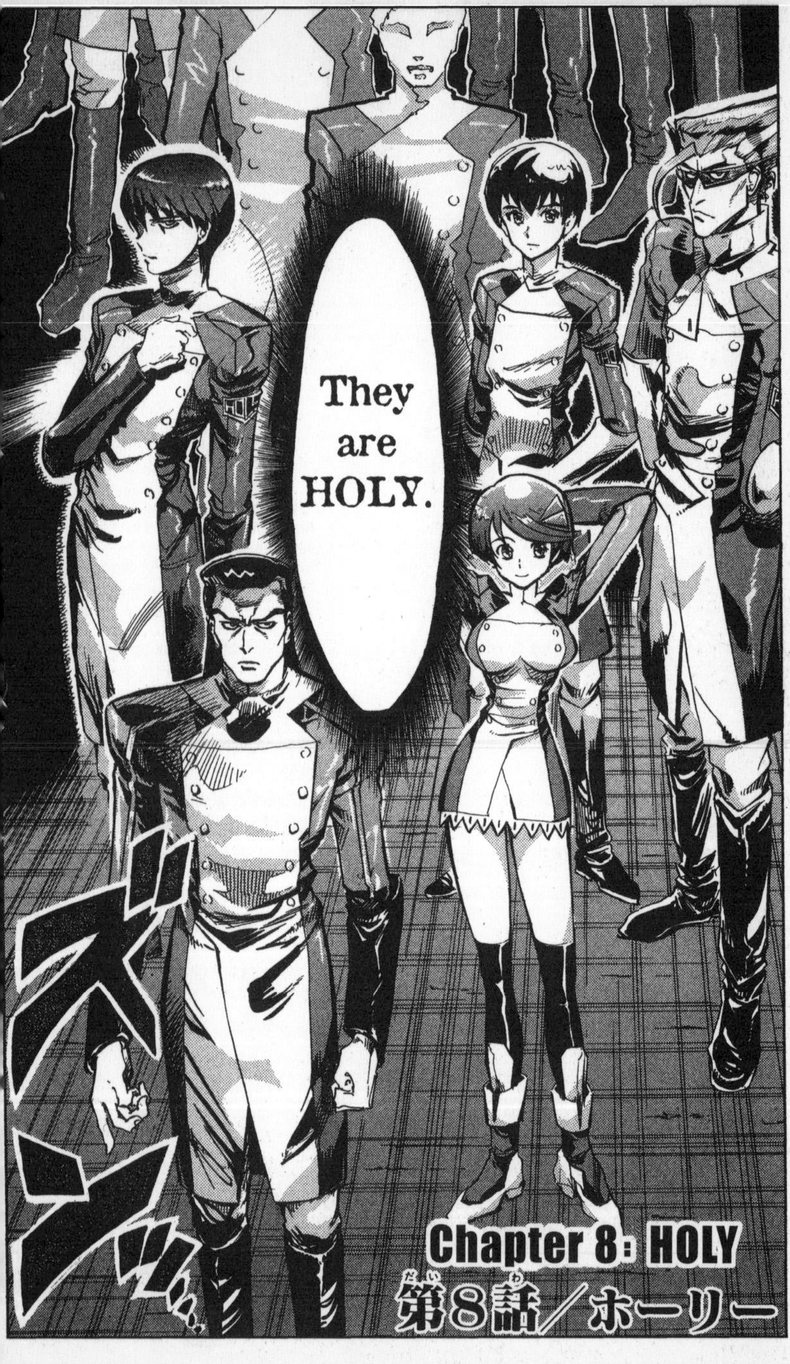
They are HOLY.
Chapter 8: HOLY
第8話／ホーリー

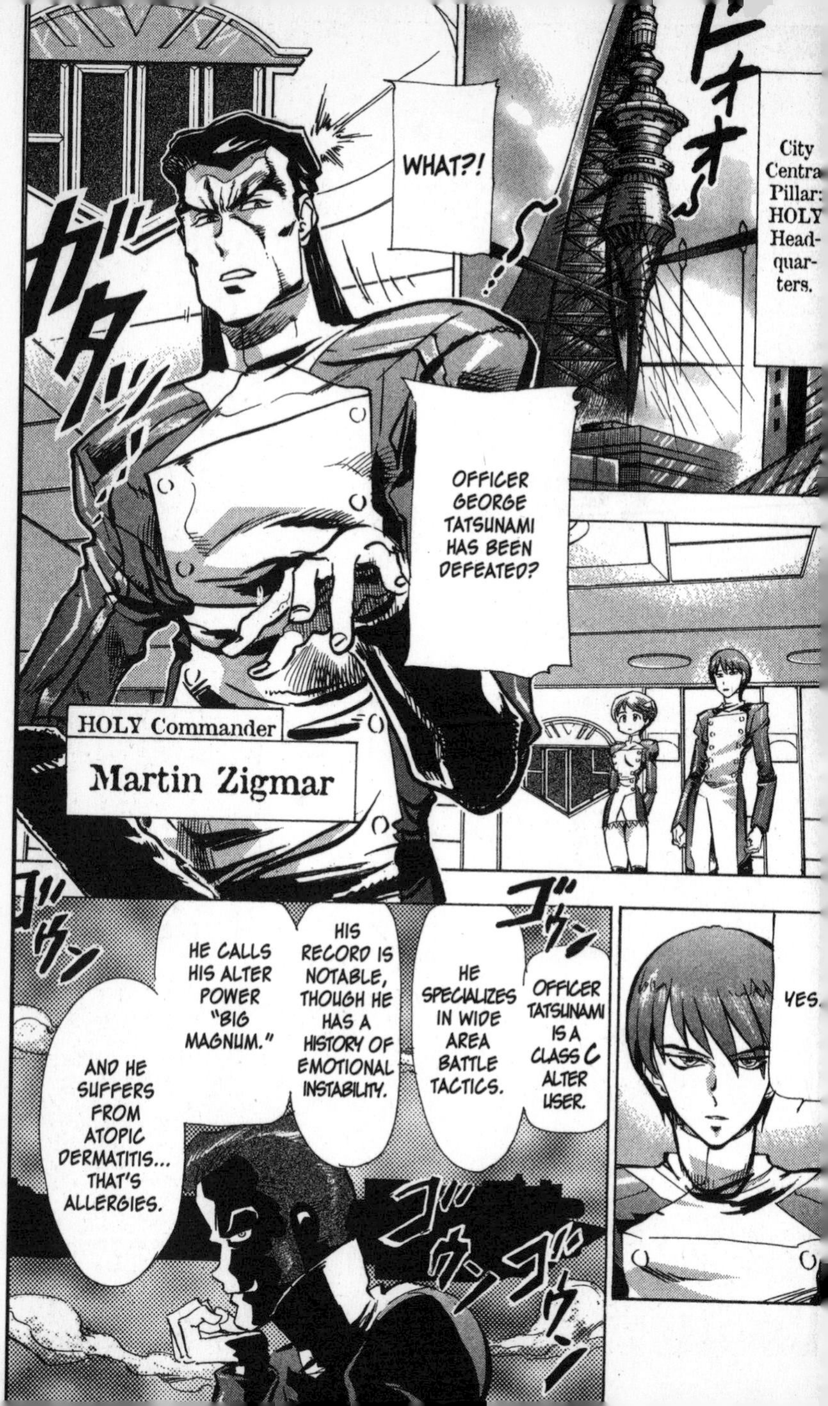
City Centra Pillar: HOLY Head-quar-ters.
ドォオ〜〜
WHAT?!
ガタッ
OFFICER GEORGE TATSUNAMI HAS BEEN DEFEATED?
HOLY Commander
Martin Zigmar
YES.
ゴウン
OFFICER TATSUNAMI IS A CLASS C ALTER USER.
HE SPECIALIZES IN WIDE AREA BATTLE TACTICS.
HIS RECORD IS NOTABLE, THOUGH HE HAS A HISTORY OF EMOTIONAL INSTABILITY.
HE CALLS HIS ALTER POWER "BIG MAGNUM."
ゴウン
AND HE SUFFERS FROM ATOPIC DERMATITIS... THAT'S ALLERGIES.
ゴウン ゴウン

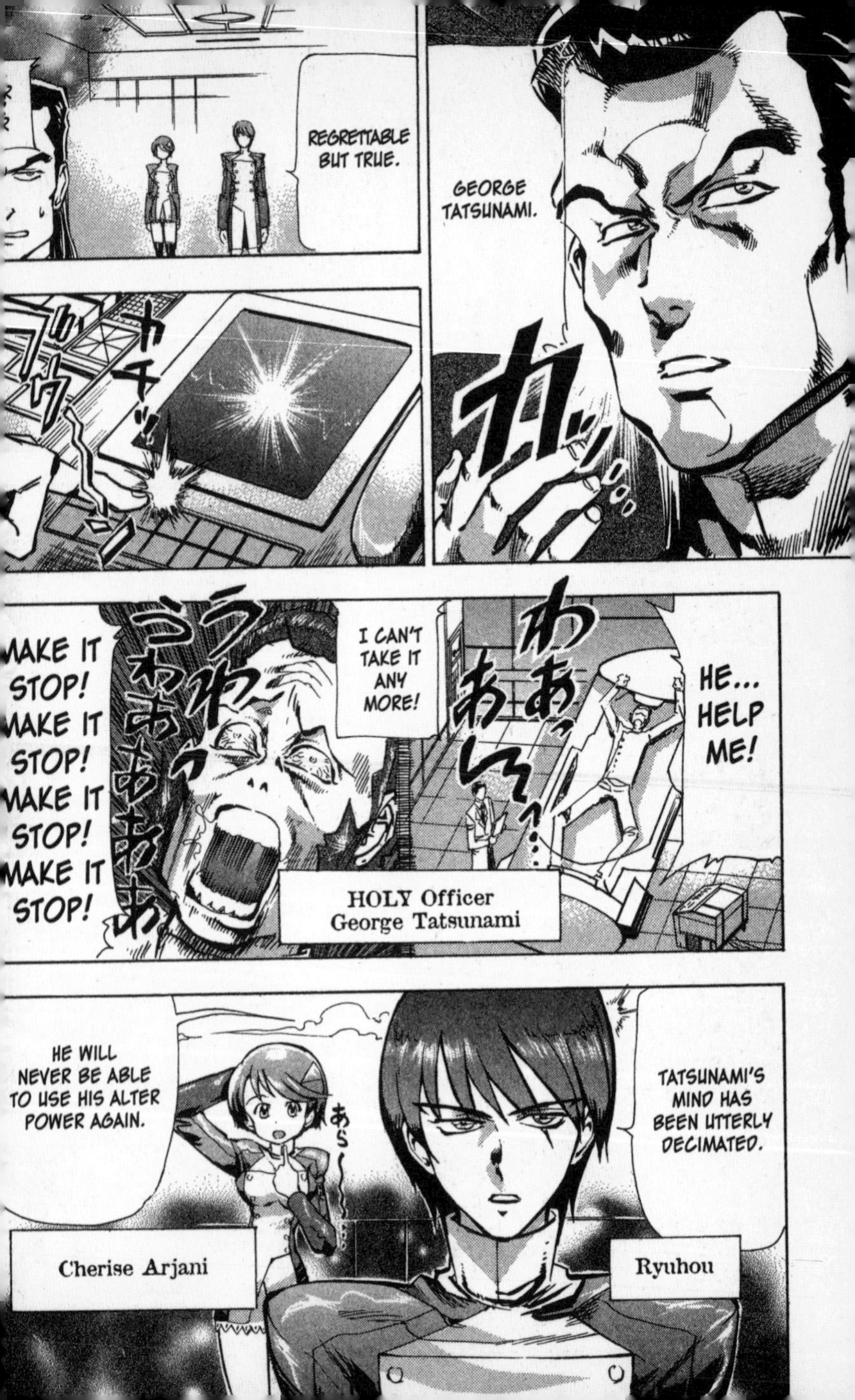
GEORGE TATSUNAMI.
カッ
REGRETTABLE BUT TRUE.
HE... HELP ME!
HOLY Officer George Tatsunami
I CAN'T TAKE IT ANY MORE!
MAKE IT STOP! MAKE IT STOP! MAKE IT STOP! MAKE IT STOP!
TATSUNAMI'S MIND HAS BEEN UTTERLY DECIMATED.
Ryuhou
HE WILL NEVER BE ABLE TO USE HIS ALTER POWER AGAIN.
あら～
Cherise Arjani

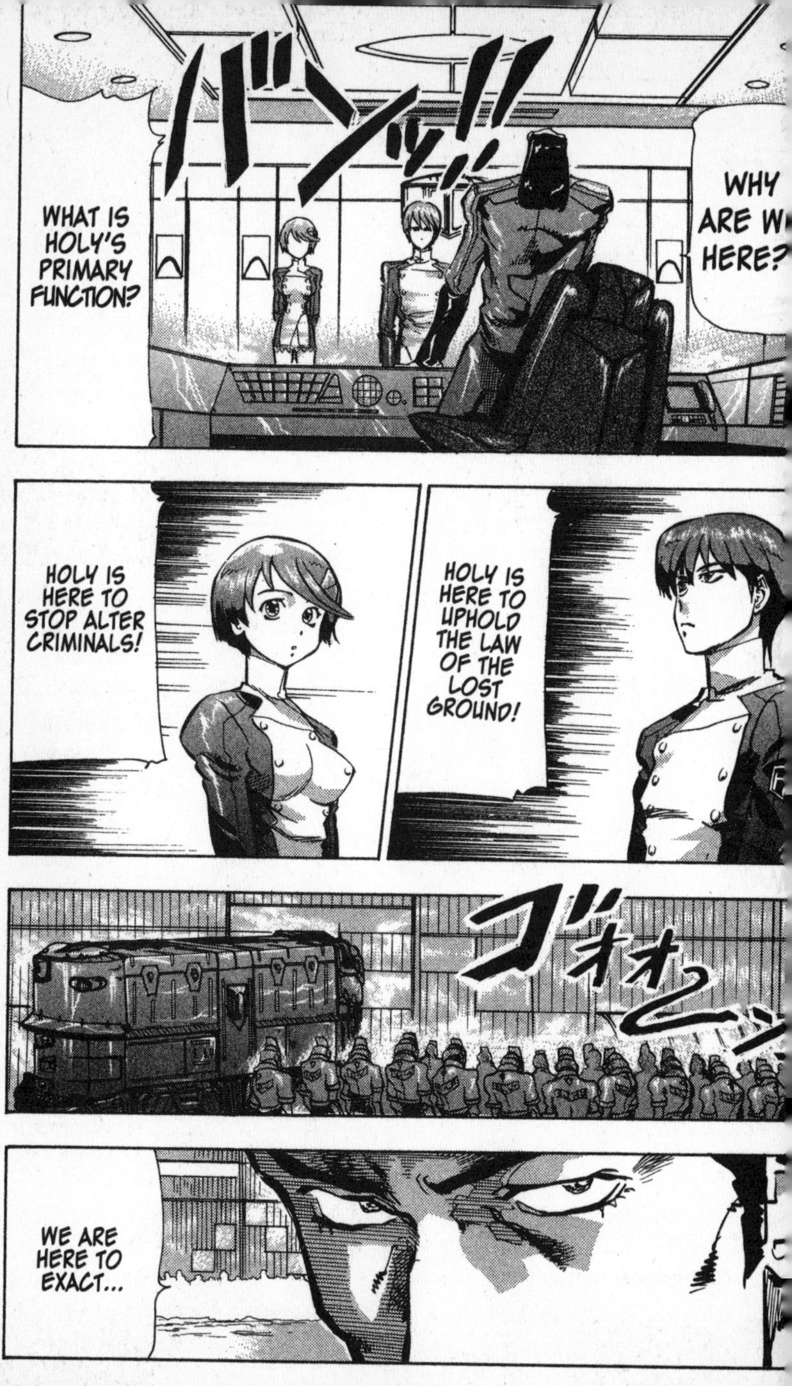
バンッ!!
WHY ARE W HERE?
WHAT IS HOLY'S PRIMARY FUNCTION?
HOLY IS HERE TO UPHOLD THE LAW OF THE LOST GROUND!
HOLY IS HERE TO STOP ALTER CRIMINALS!
WE ARE HERE TO EXACT...

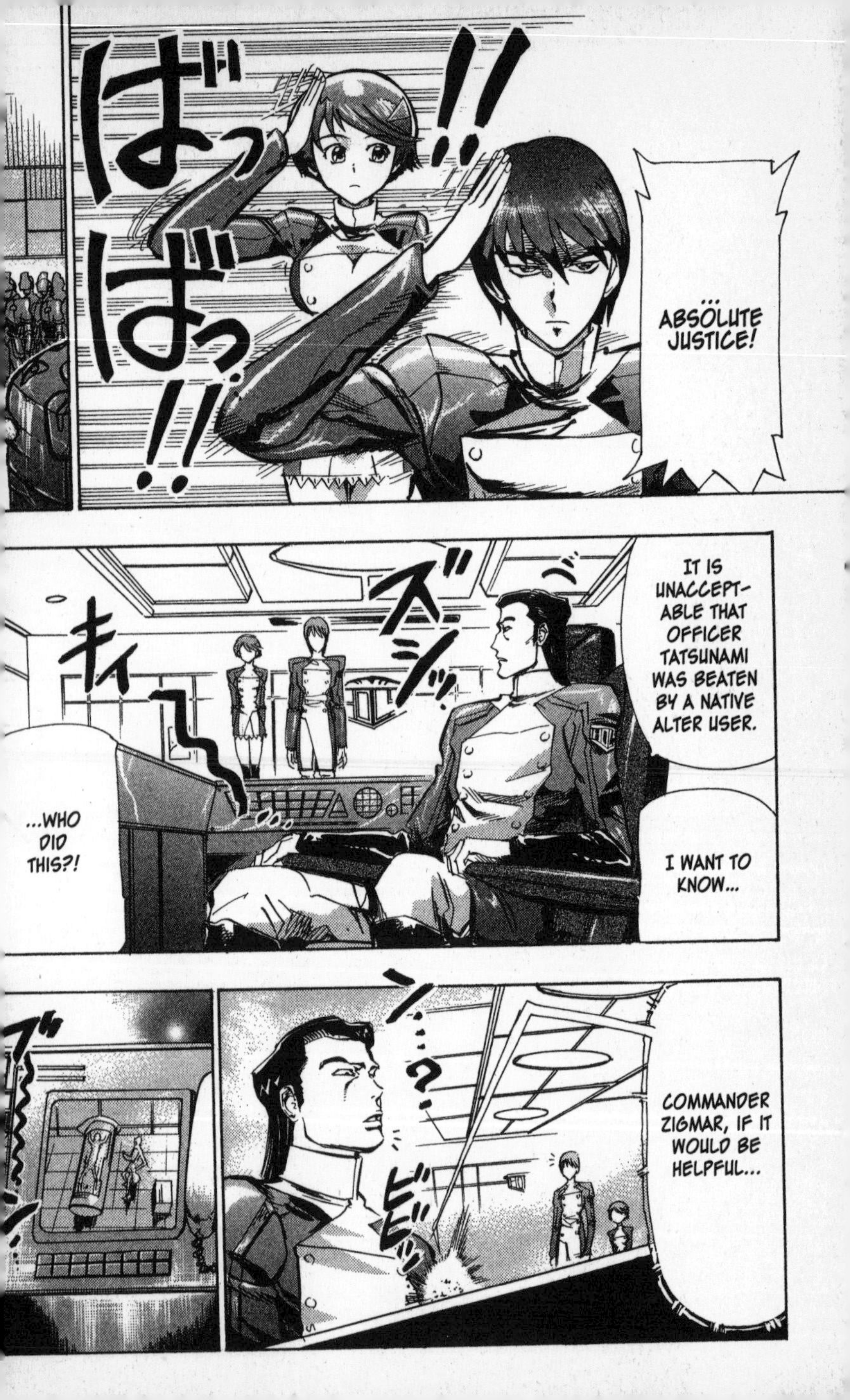
ばっ!!
ばっ!!
...ABSOLUTE JUSTICE!
IT IS UNACCEPTABLE THAT OFFICER TATSUNAMI WAS BEATEN BY A NATIVE ALTER USER.
ズシッ
I WANT TO KNOW...
キィ〜
...WHO DID THIS?!
COMMANDER ZIGMAR, IF IT WOULD BE HELPFUL...
...?
ビビッ
ブ〜

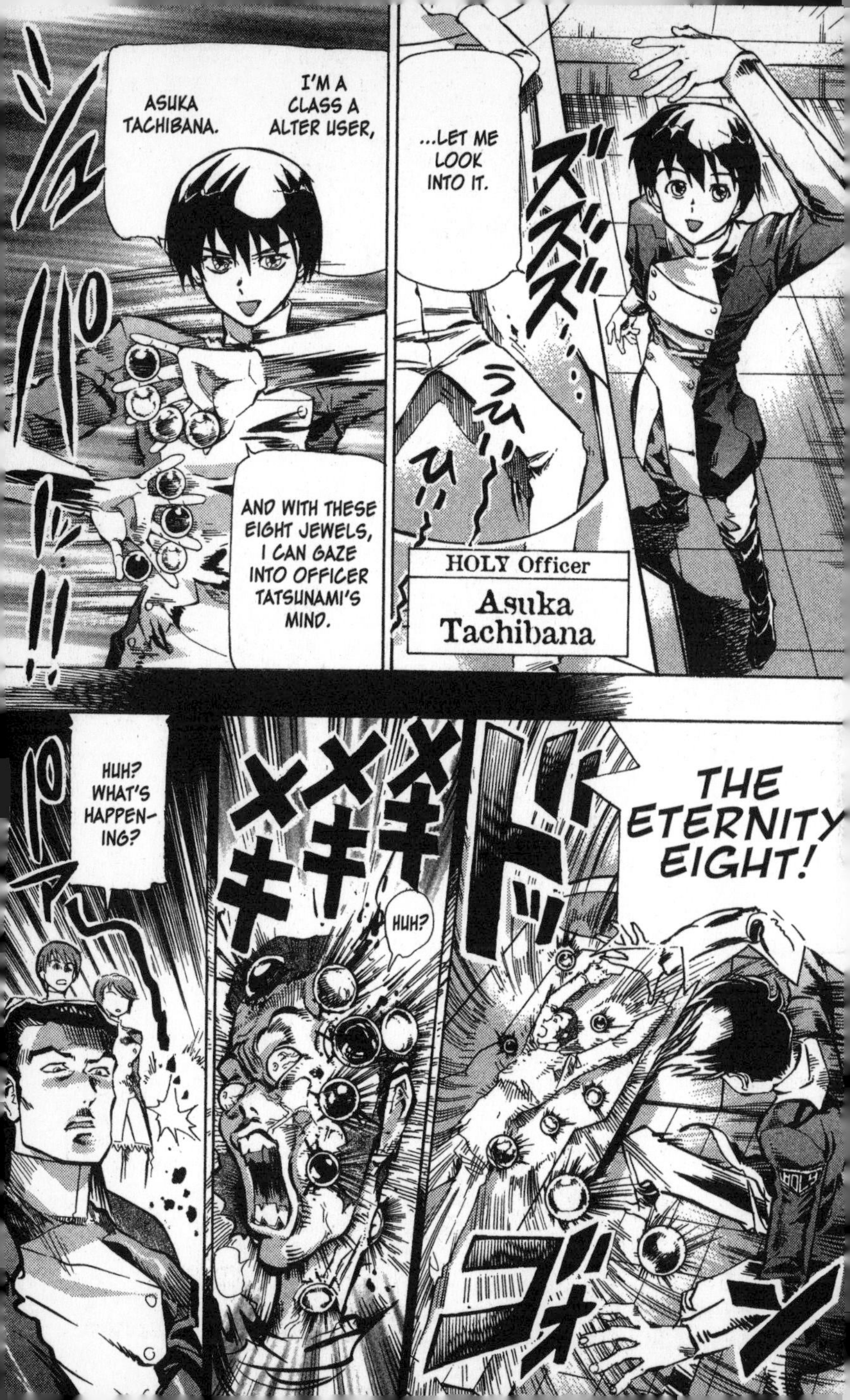
...LET ME LOOK INTO IT.
HOLY Officer
Asuka Tachibana
I'M A CLASS A ALTER USER,
ASUKA TACHIBANA.
AND WITH THESE EIGHT JEWELS, I CAN GAZE INTO OFFICER TATSUNAMI'S MIND.
THE ETERNITY EIGHT!
HUH?
HUH? WHAT'S HAPPEN-ING?

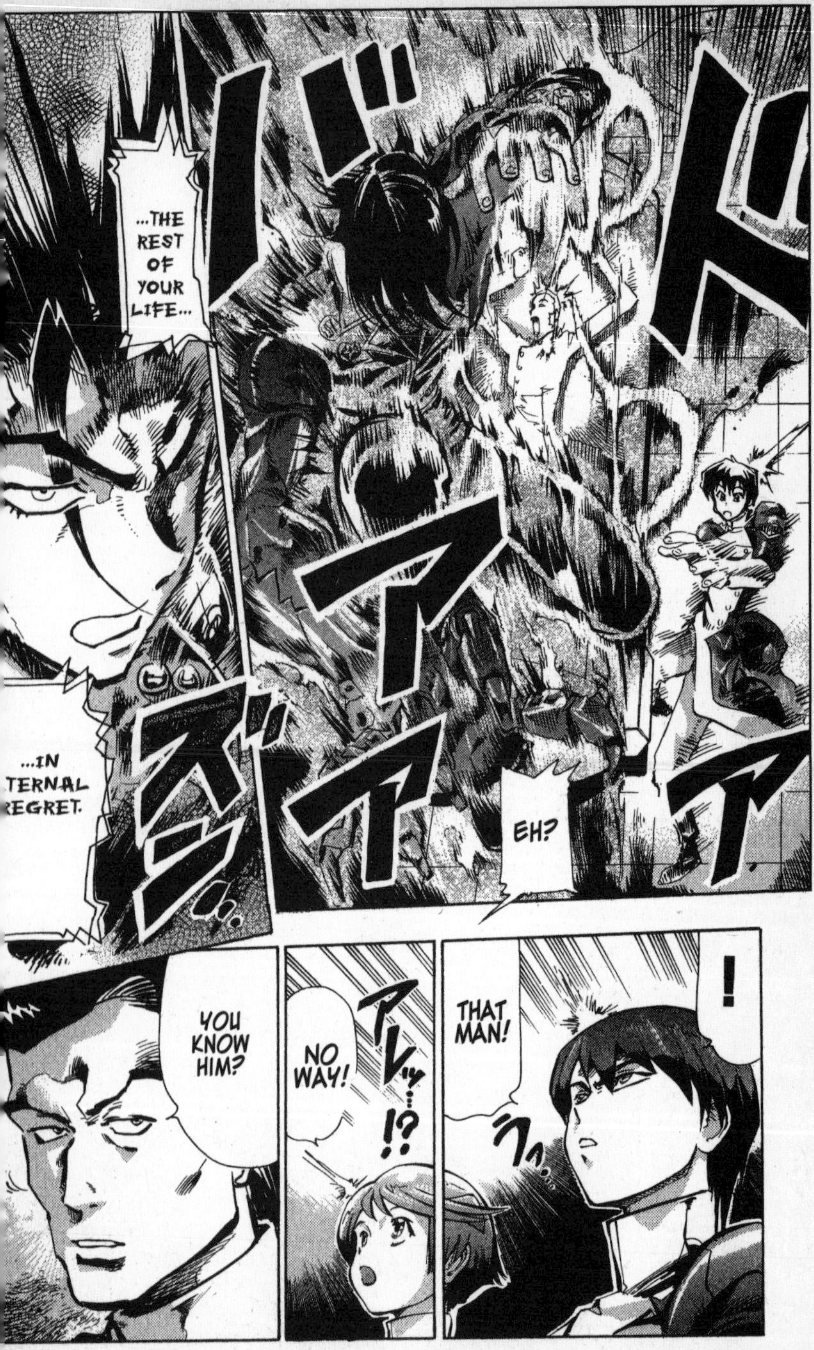
EH?
...THE REST OF YOUR LIFE...
...IN TERNAL REGRET.
!
THAT MAN!
NO WAY!
アレッ…!?
YOU KNOW HIM?

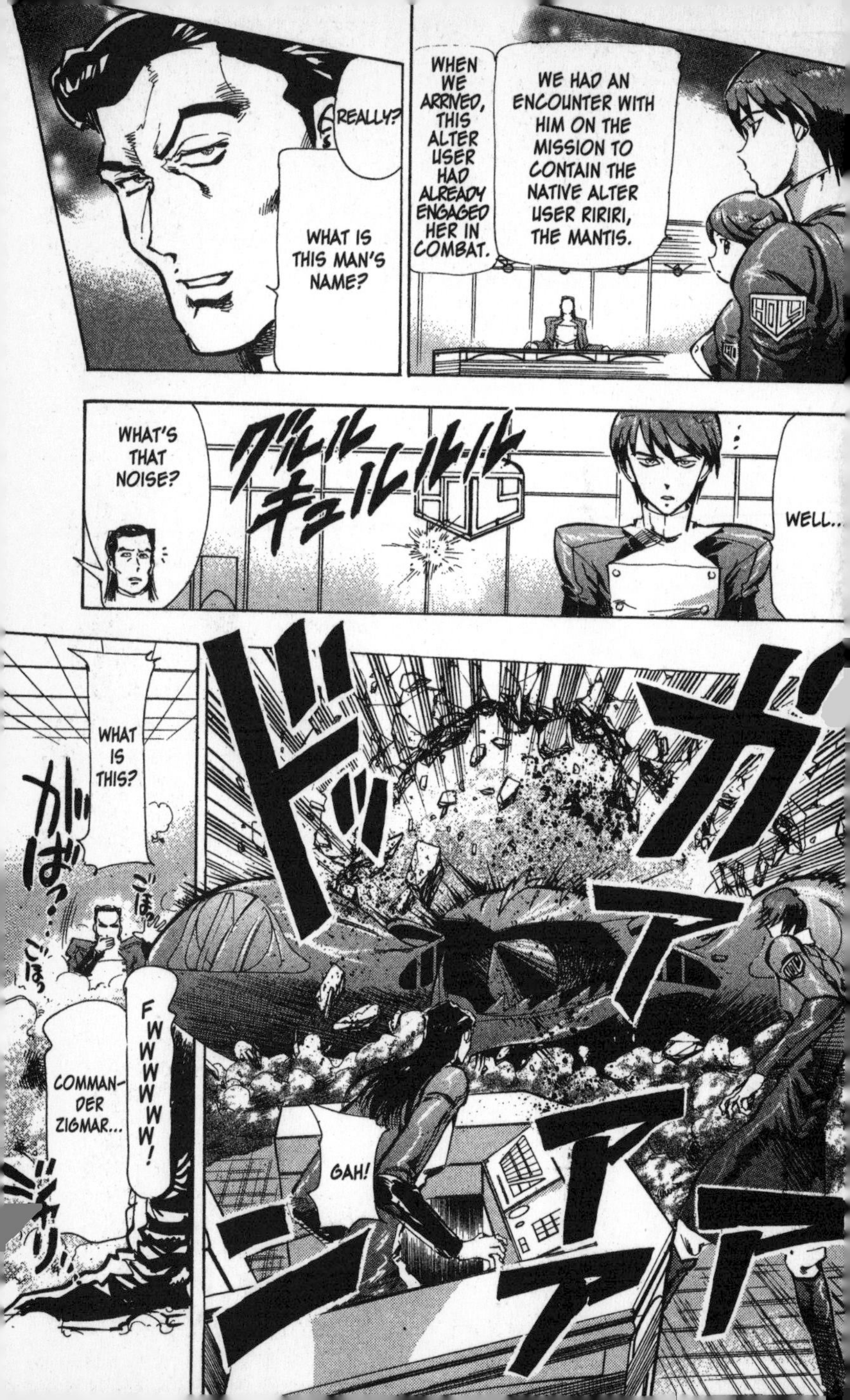
WE HAD AN ENCOUNTER WITH HIM ON THE MISSION TO CONTAIN THE NATIVE ALTER USER RIRIRI, THE MANTIS.
WHEN WE ARRIVED, THIS ALTER USER HAD ALREADY ENGAGED HER IN COMBAT.
REALLY?
WHAT IS THIS MAN'S NAME?
WELL...
WHAT'S THAT NOISE?
WHAT IS THIS?
FWWWWWWW!
COMMAN-DER ZIGMAR...
GAH!

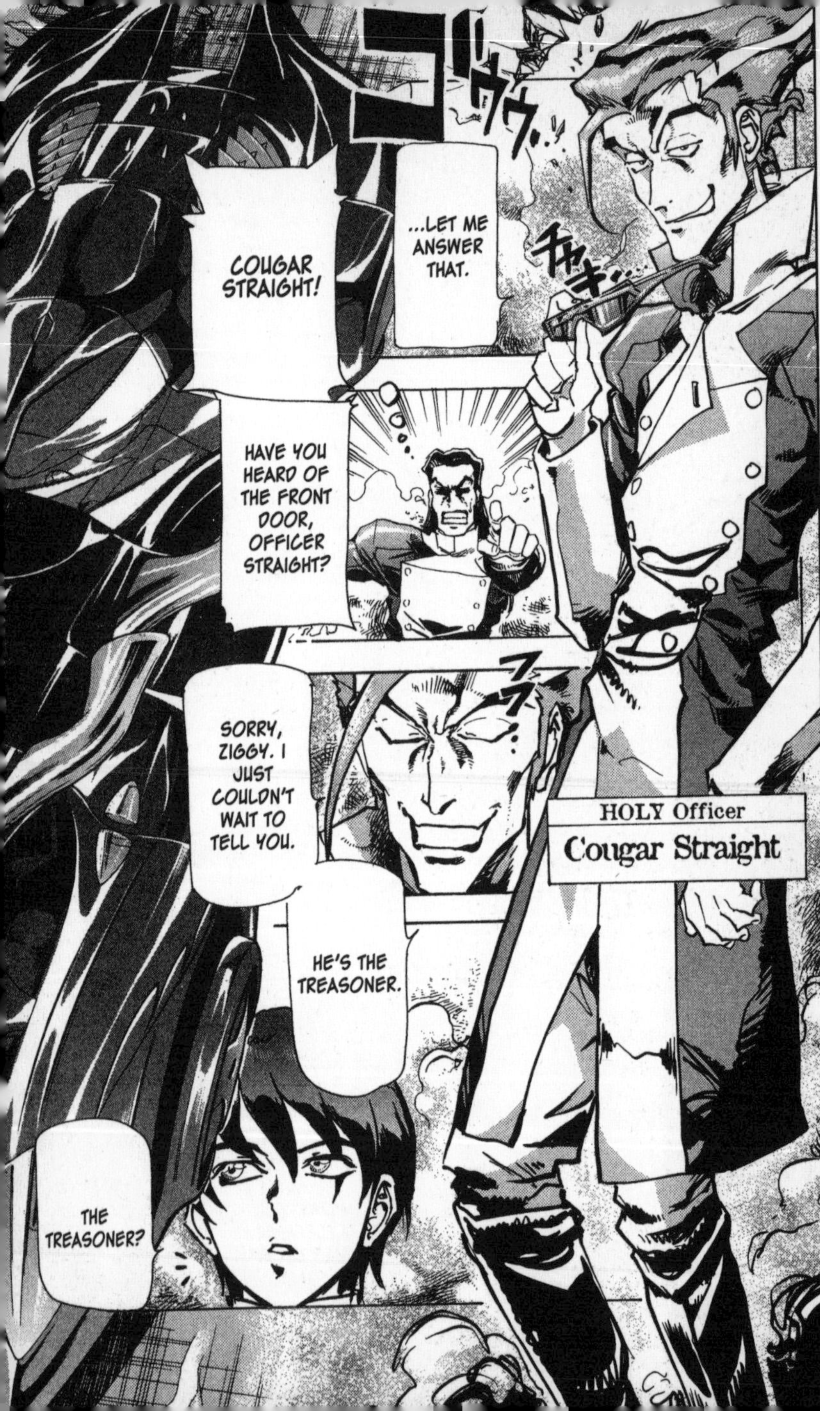

...LET ME ANSWER THAT.
COUGAR STRAIGHT!
HAVE YOU HEARD OF THE FRONT DOOR, OFFICER STRAIGHT?
SORRY, ZIGGY. I JUST COULDN'T WAIT TO TELL YOU.
HOLY Officer
Cougar Straight
HE'S THE TREASONER.
THE TREASONER?

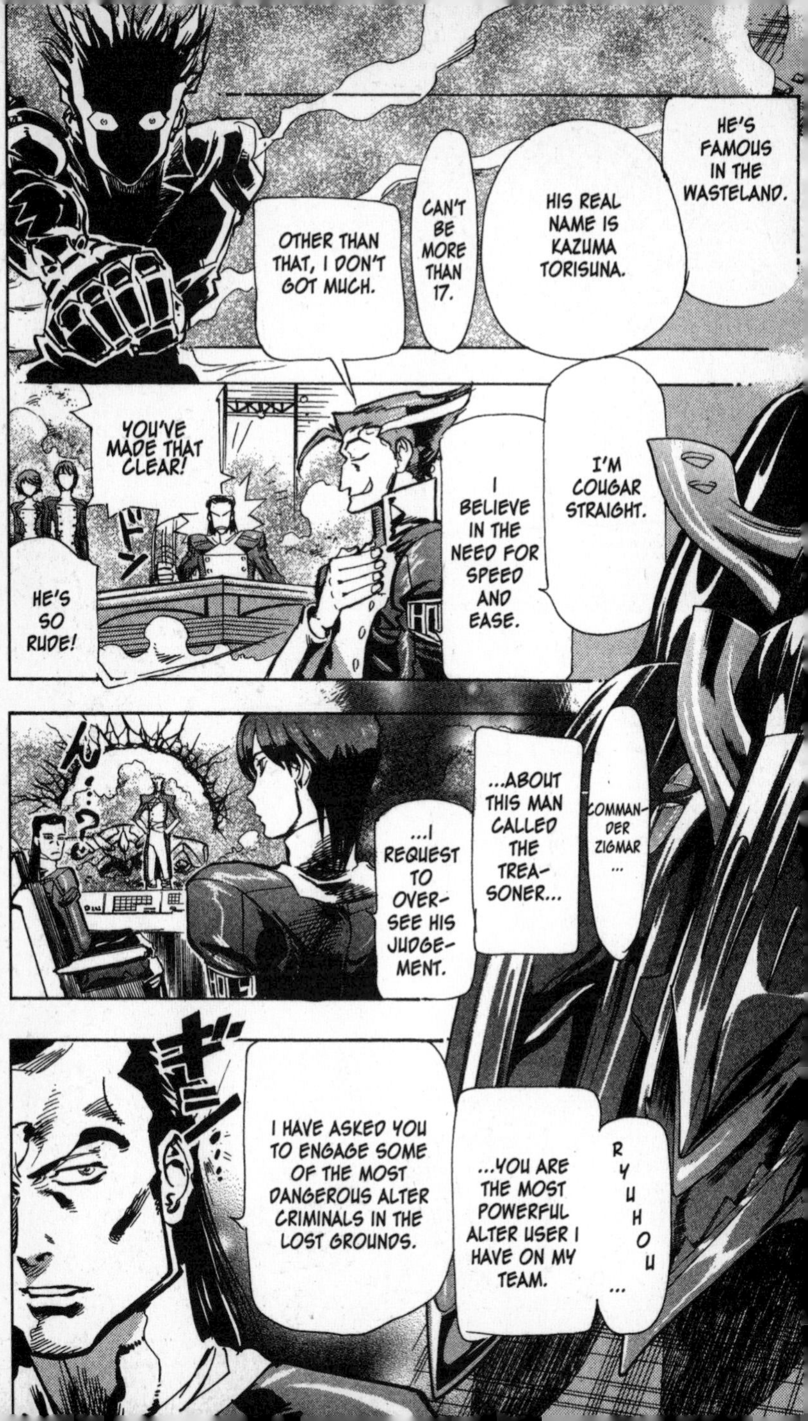
HE'S FAMOUS IN THE WASTELAND.
HIS REAL NAME IS KAZUMA TORISUNA.
CAN'T BE MORE THAN 17.
OTHER THAN THAT, I DON'T GOT MUCH.
I'M COUGAR STRAIGHT.
I BELIEVE IN THE NEED FOR SPEED AND EASE.
YOU'VE MADE THAT CLEAR!
HE'S SO RUDE!
COMMANDER ZIGMAR...
...ABOUT THIS MAN CALLED THE TREASONER...
...I REQUEST TO OVERSEE HIS JUDGEMENT.
RYUHOU...
...YOU ARE THE MOST POWERFUL ALTER USER I HAVE ON MY TEAM.
I HAVE ASKED YOU TO ENGAGE SOME OF THE MOST DANGEROUS ALTER CRIMINALS IN THE LOST GROUNDS.

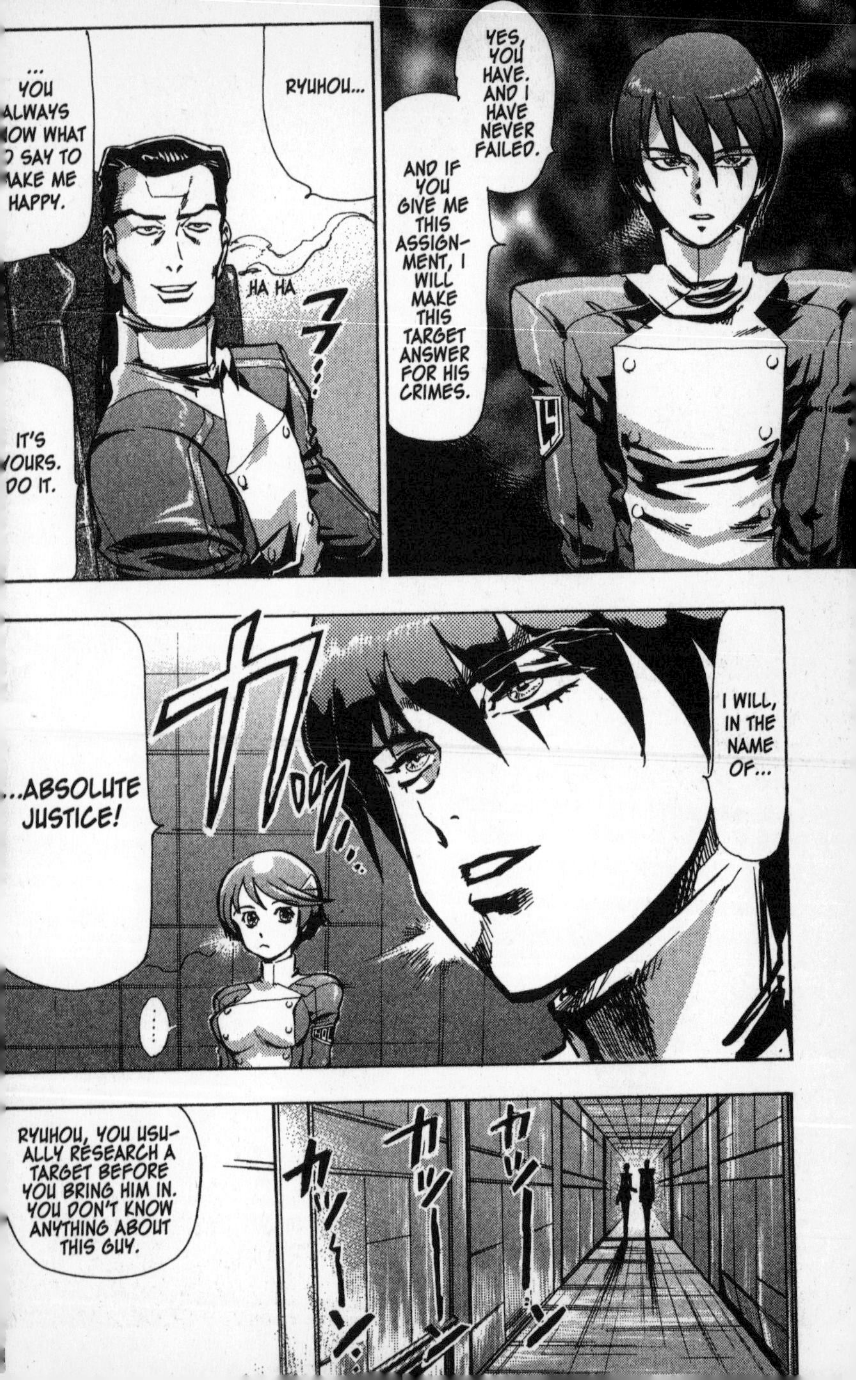

YES, YOU HAVE. AND I HAVE NEVER FAILED.
AND IF YOU GIVE ME THIS ASSIGNMENT, I WILL MAKE THIS TARGET ANSWER FOR HIS CRIMES.
RYUHOU...
HA HA
フフ...
... YOU ALWAYS NOW WHAT O SAY TO AKE ME HAPPY.
IT'S OURS. DO IT.
I WILL, IN THE NAME OF...
カッ...
...ABSOLUTE JUSTICE!
......
カツーン
カツーン
カツーン
RYUHOU, YOU USUALLY RESEARCH A TARGET BEFORE YOU BRING HIM IN. YOU DON'T KNOW ANYTHING ABOUT THIS GUY.

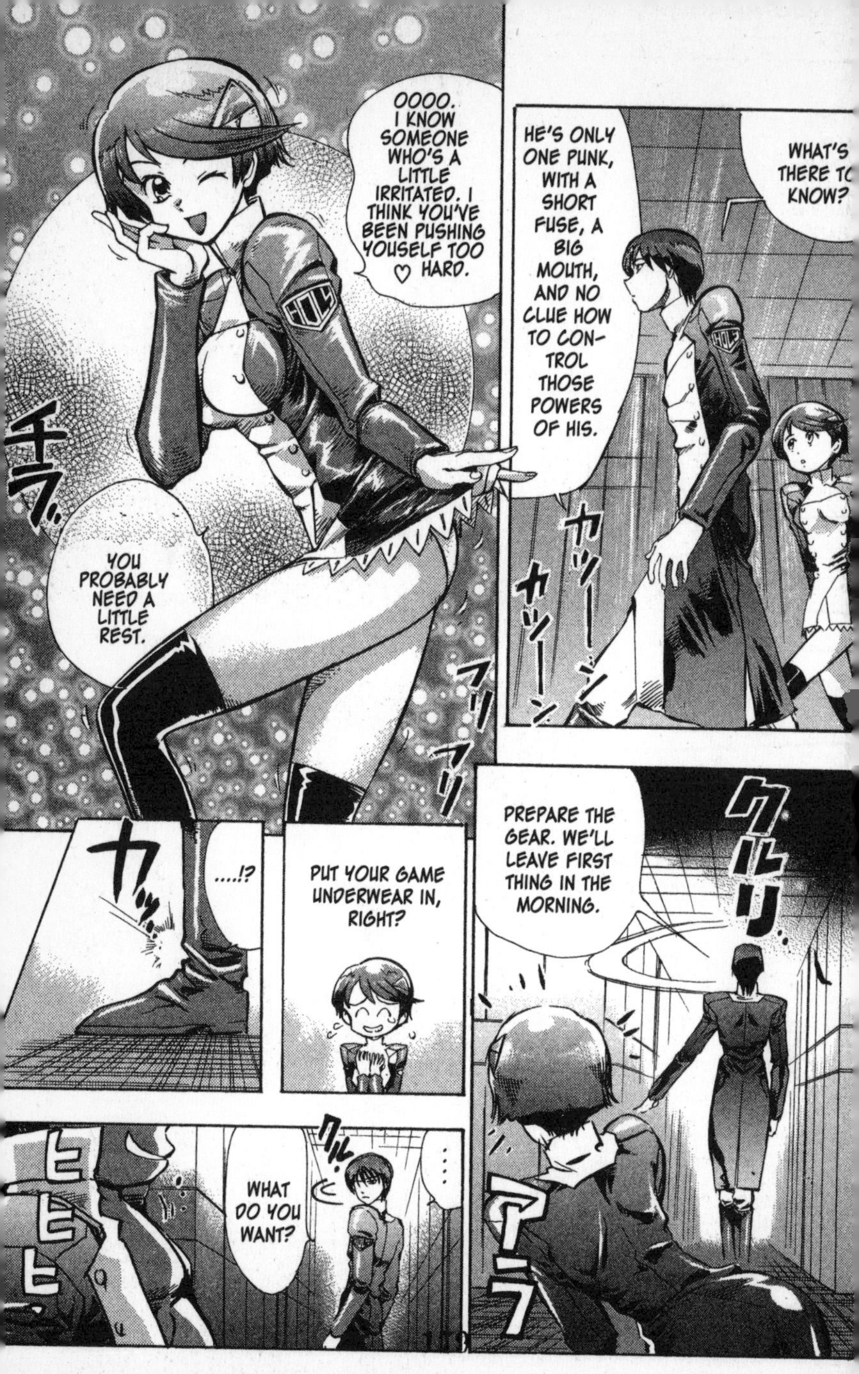
WHAT'S THERE TO KNOW?
HE'S ONLY ONE PUNK, WITH A SHORT FUSE, A BIG MOUTH, AND NO CLUE HOW TO CON-TROL THOSE POWERS OF HIS.
カツーン
カツーン
OOOO. I KNOW SOMEONE WHO'S A LITTLE IRRITATED. I THINK YOU'VE BEEN PUSHING YOUSELF TOO ♡ HARD.
チラ
YOU PROBABLY NEED A LITTLE REST.
クルリ
PREPARE THE GEAR. WE'LL LEAVE FIRST THING IN THE MORNING.
アラ
PUT YOUR GAME UNDERWEAR IN, RIGHT?
カッ
....!?
....
クル
WHAT DO YOU WANT?
ヒヒヒ

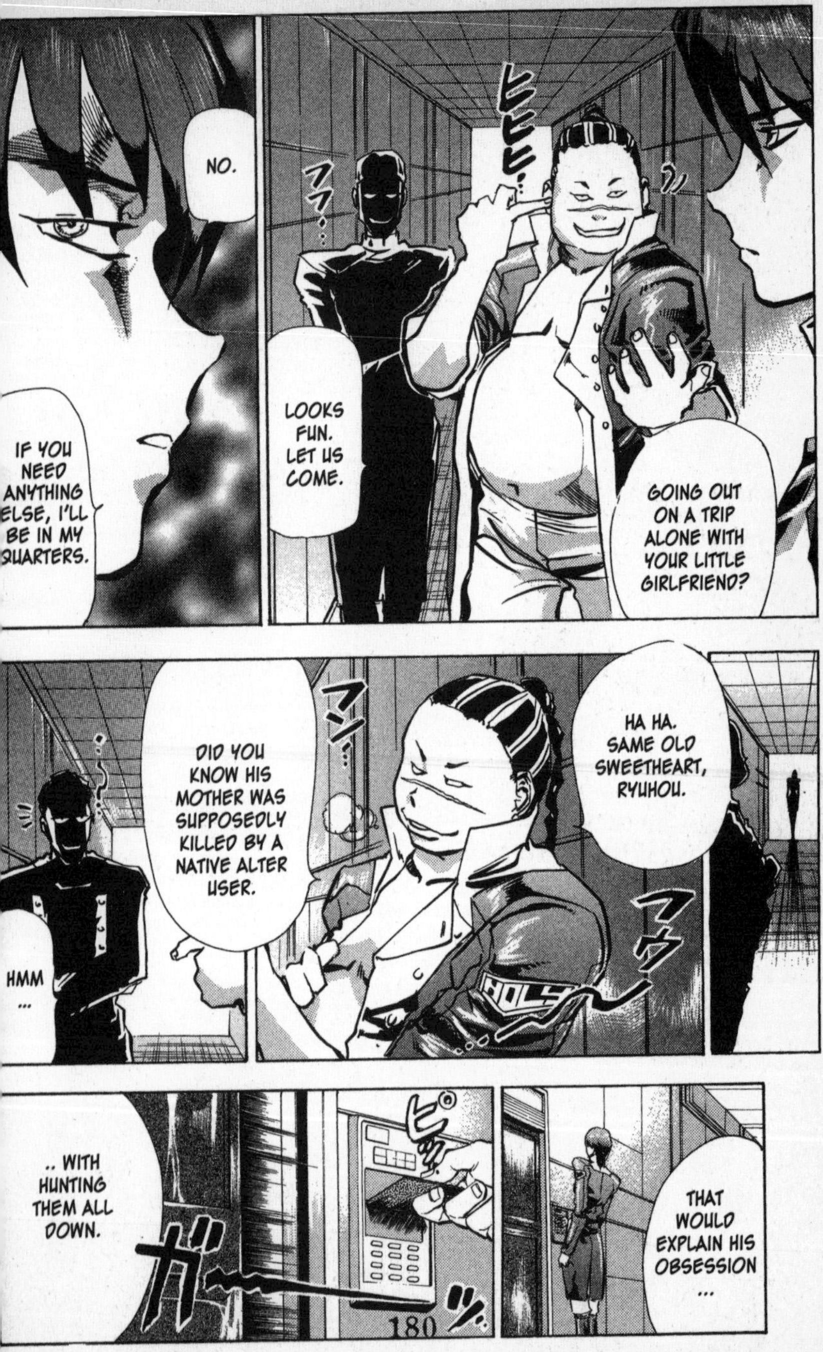
GOING OUT ON A TRIP ALONE WITH YOUR LITTLE GIRLFRIEND?
LOOKS FUN. LET US COME.
NO.
IF YOU NEED ANYTHING ELSE, I'LL BE IN MY QUARTERS.
HA HA. SAME OLD SWEETHEART, RYUHOU.
DID YOU KNOW HIS MOTHER WAS SUPPOSEDLY KILLED BY A NATIVE ALTER USER.
HMM ...
THAT WOULD EXPLAIN HIS OBSESSION ...
.. WITH HUNTING THEM ALL DOWN.

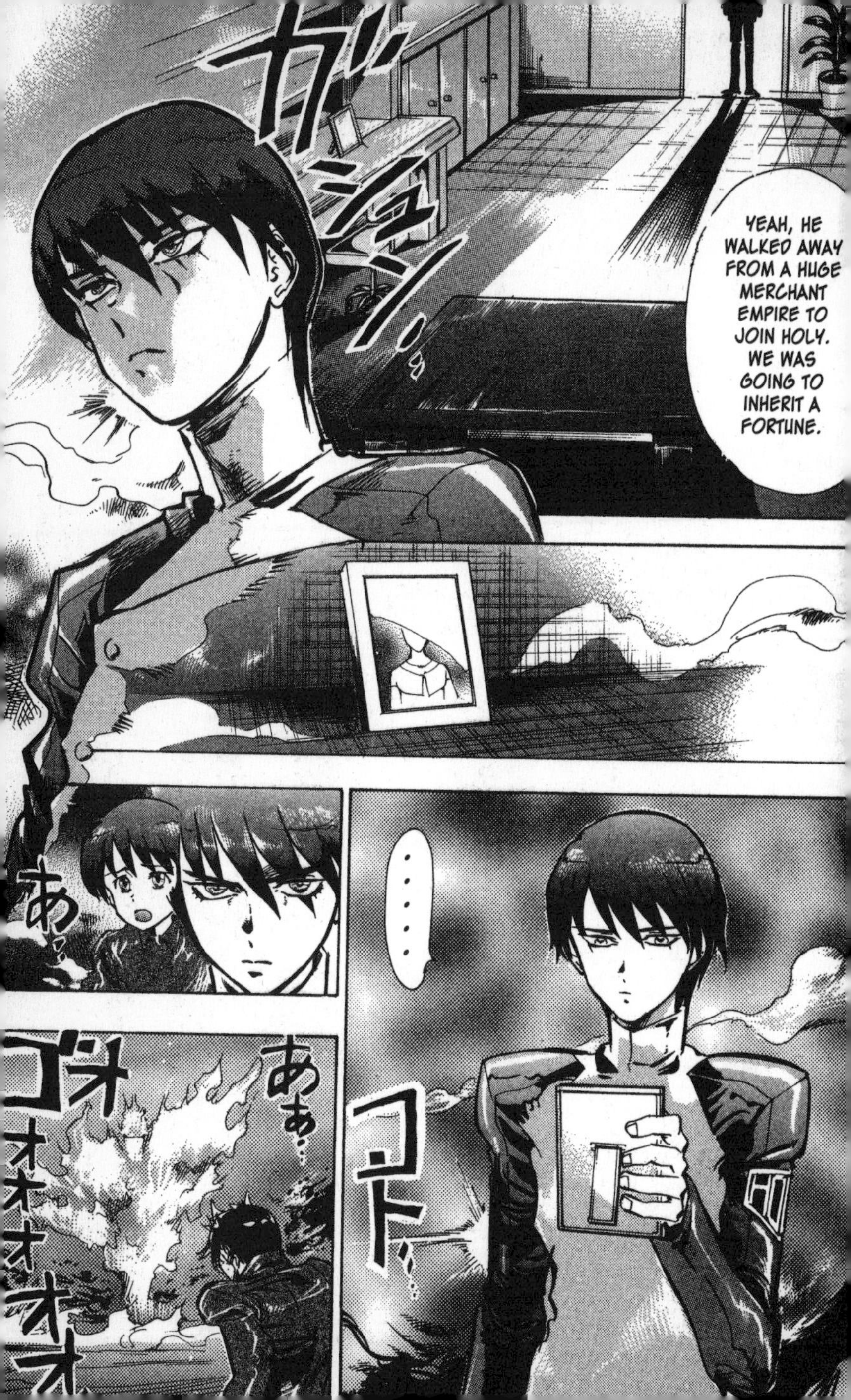

ガシュン…
YEAH, HE WALKED AWAY FROM A HUGE MERCHANT EMPIRE TO JOIN HOLY. WE WAS GOING TO INHERIT A FORTUNE.
......
コトッ…
あっ
ああ…
ゴオオオオ

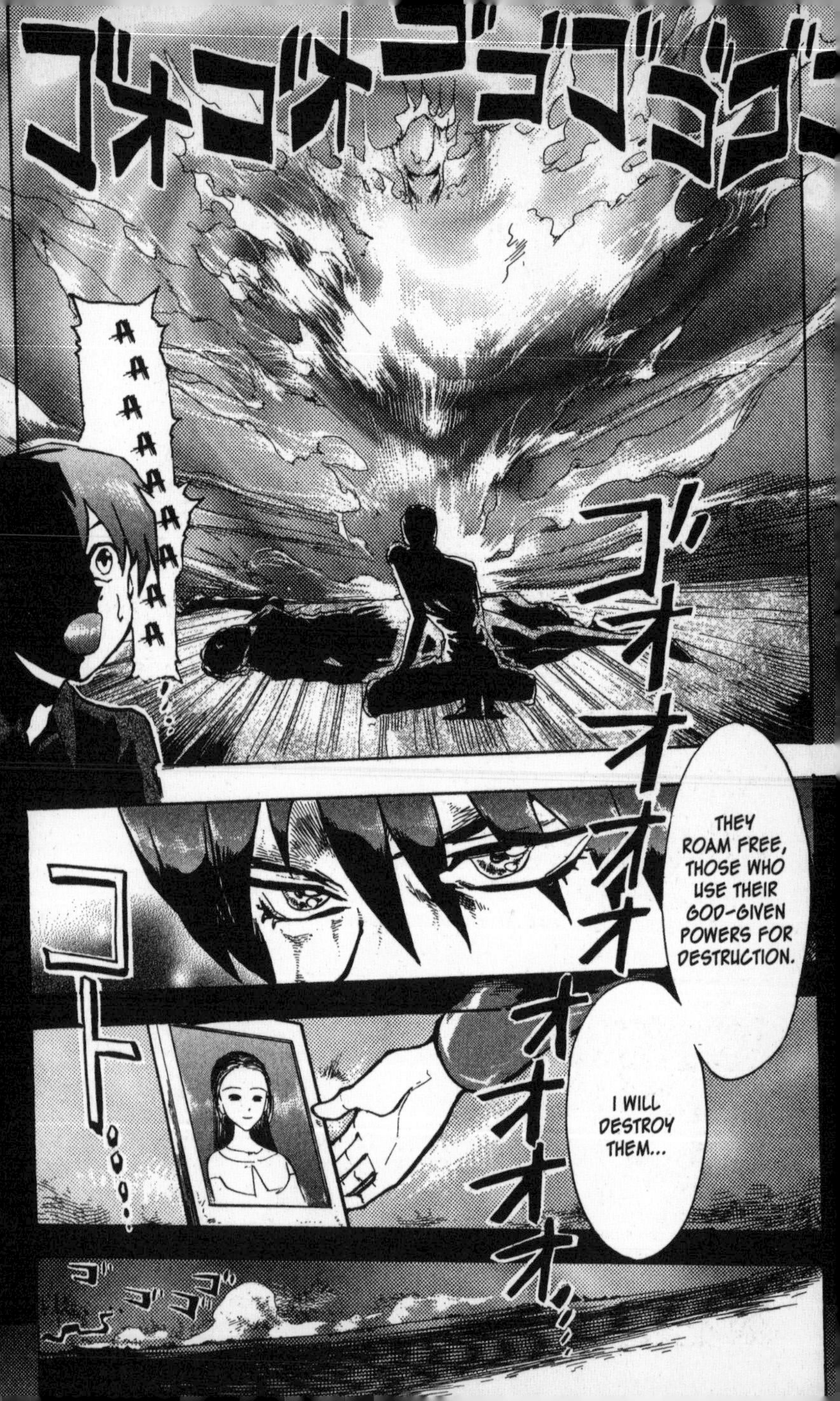
ゴォゴォゴゴゴゴ
AAAAAAAAA...
ゴォオオオオオオオ...
THEY ROAM FREE, THOSE WHO USE THEIR GOD-GIVEN POWERS FOR DESTRUCTION.
I WILL DESTROY THEM...
コト...
ゴゴゴ

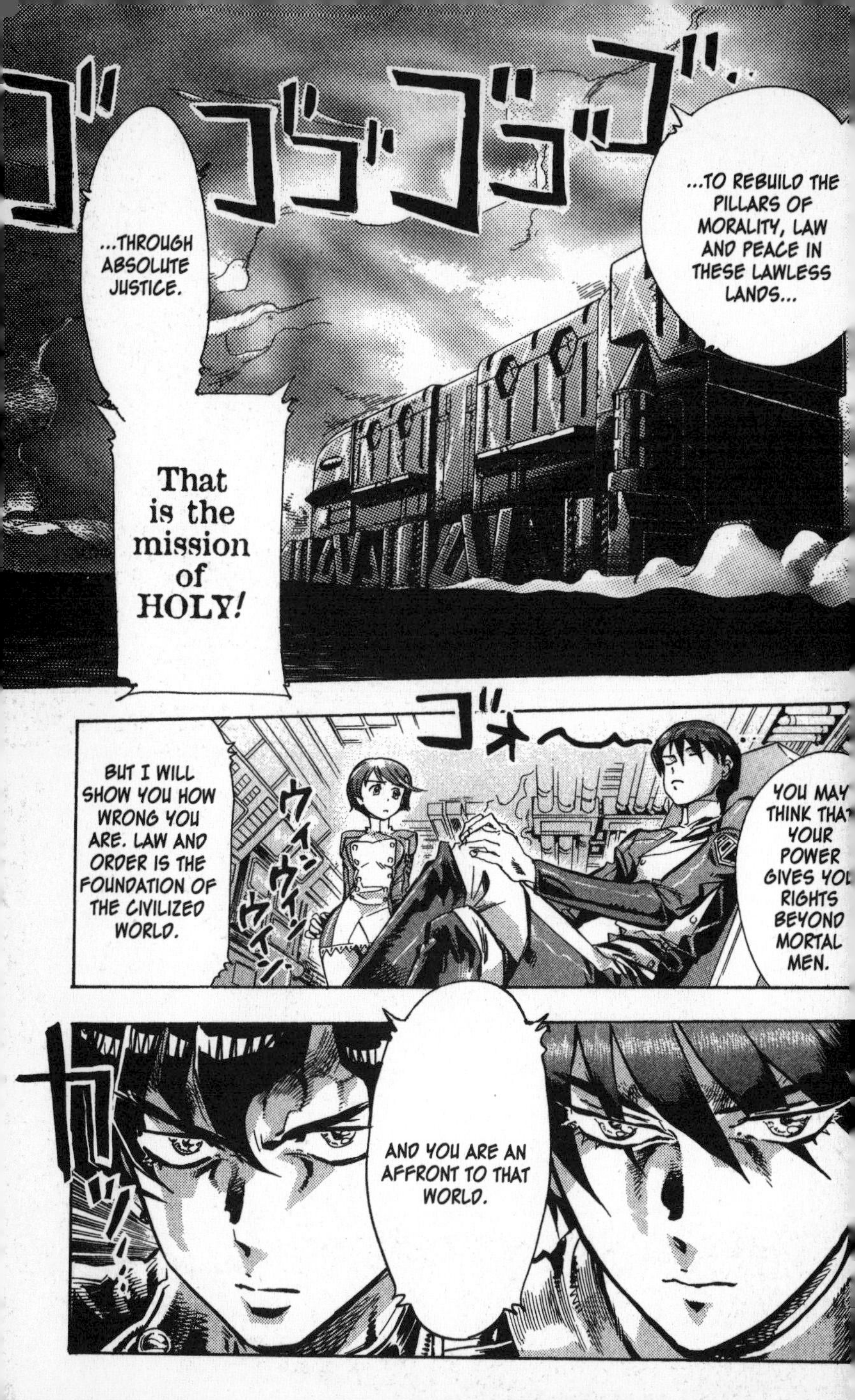
...TO REBUILD THE PILLARS OF MORALITY, LAW AND PEACE IN THESE LAWLESS LANDS...
...THROUGH ABSOLUTE JUSTICE.
That is the mission of HOLY!
YOU MAY THINK THAT YOUR POWER GIVES YOU RIGHTS BEYOND MORTAL MEN.
BUT I WILL SHOW YOU HOW WRONG YOU ARE. LAW AND ORDER IS THE FOUNDATION OF THE CIVILIZED WORLD.
AND YOU ARE AN AFFRONT TO THAT WORLD.

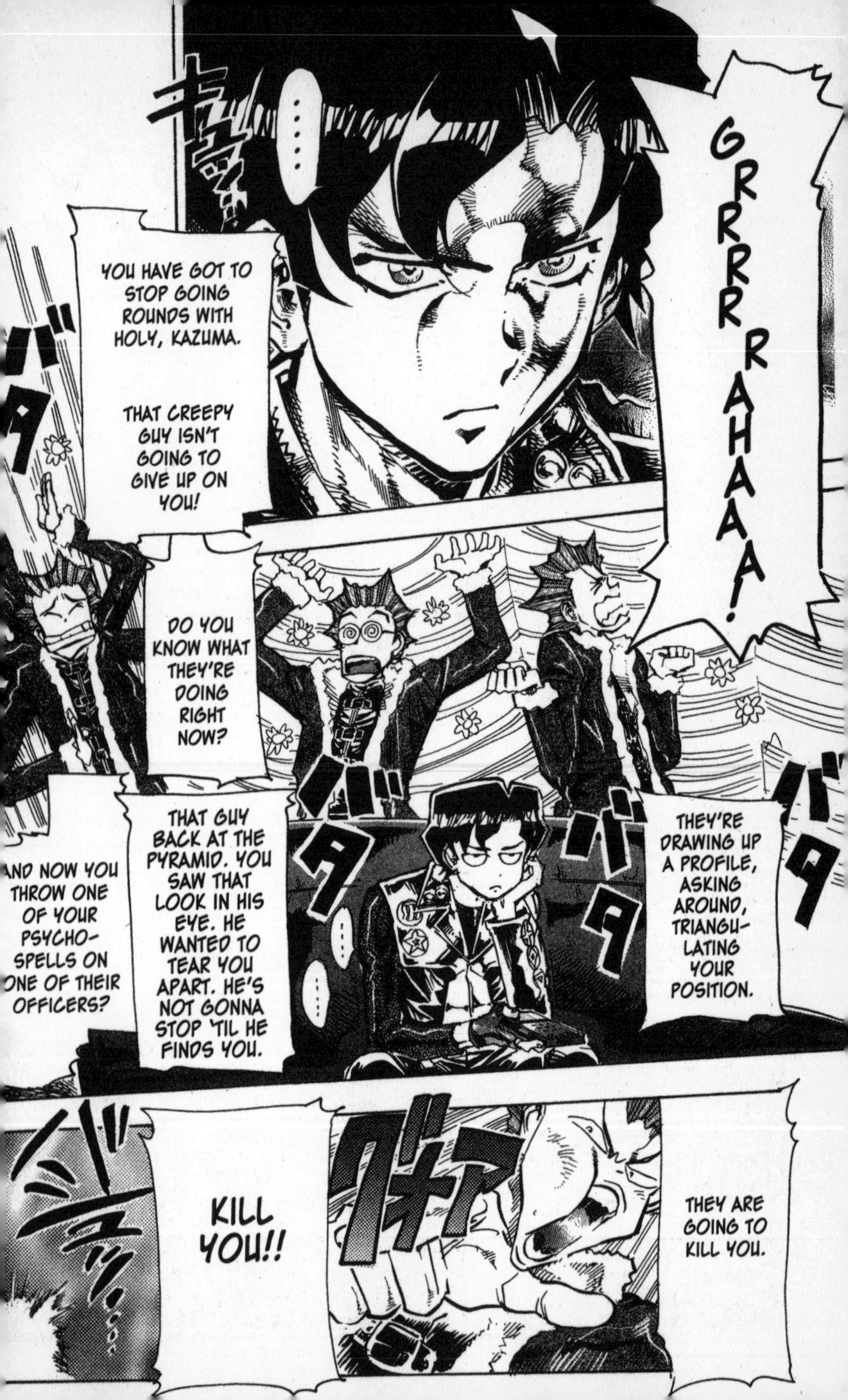
GRRRR RAHAAA!
...
YOU HAVE GOT TO STOP GOING ROUNDS WITH HOLY, KAZUMA.
THAT CREEPY GUY ISN'T GOING TO GIVE UP ON YOU!
バタ
DO YOU KNOW WHAT THEY'RE DOING RIGHT NOW?
バタ
THEY'RE DRAWING UP A PROFILE, ASKING AROUND, TRIANGU-LATING YOUR POSITION.
バタ
バタ
...
...
THAT GUY BACK AT THE PYRAMID. YOU SAW THAT LOOK IN HIS EYE. HE WANTED TO TEAR YOU APART. HE'S NOT GONNA STOP 'TIL HE FINDS YOU.
AND NOW YOU THROW ONE OF YOUR PSYCHO-SPELLS ON ONE OF THEIR OFFICERS?
THEY ARE GOING TO KILL YOU.
KILL YOU!!

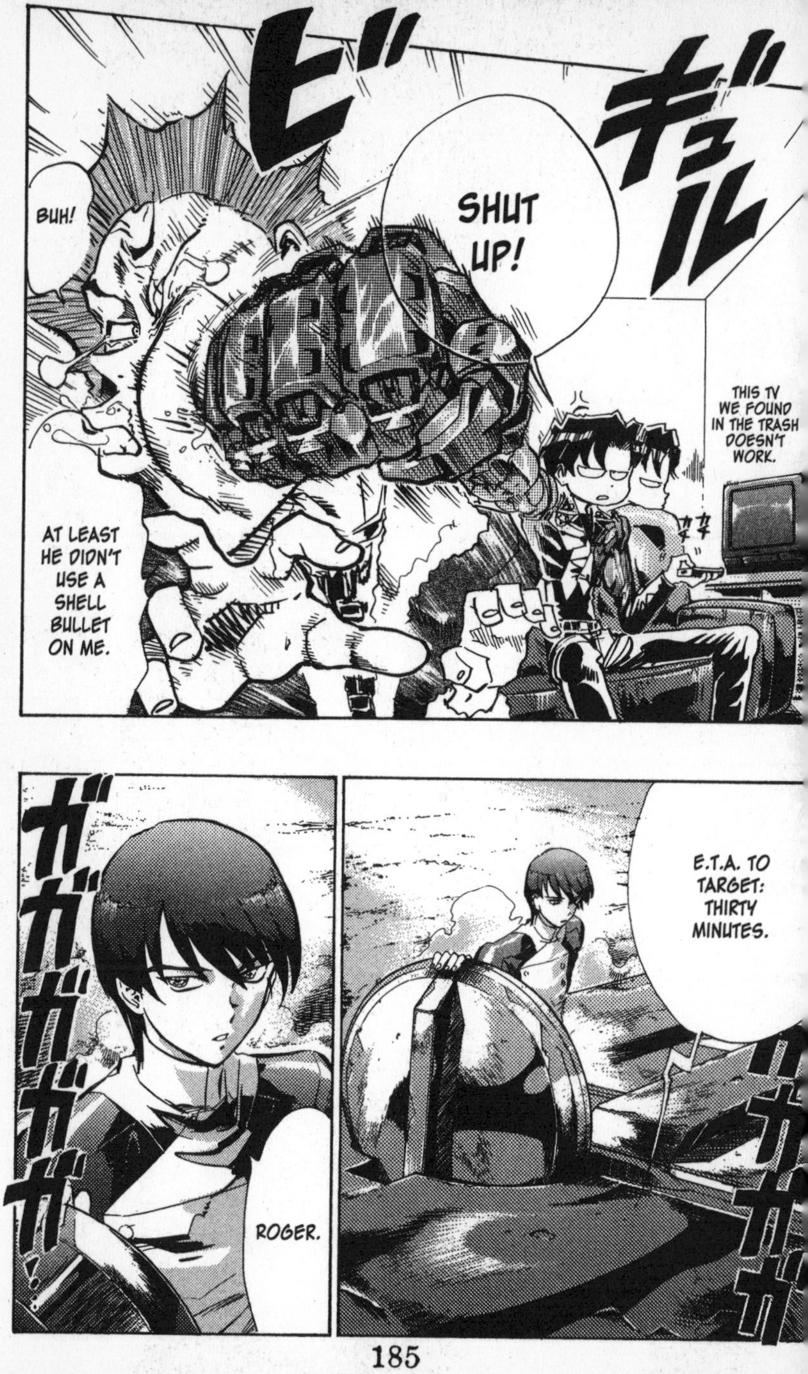
ギュル
SHUT UP!
ビ
THIS TV WE FOUND IN THE TRASH DOESN'T WORK.
BUH!
AT LEAST HE DIDN'T USE A SHELL BULLET ON ME.
E.T.A. TO TARGET: THIRTY MINUTES.
ガガガ
ガガガガガ…
ROGER.

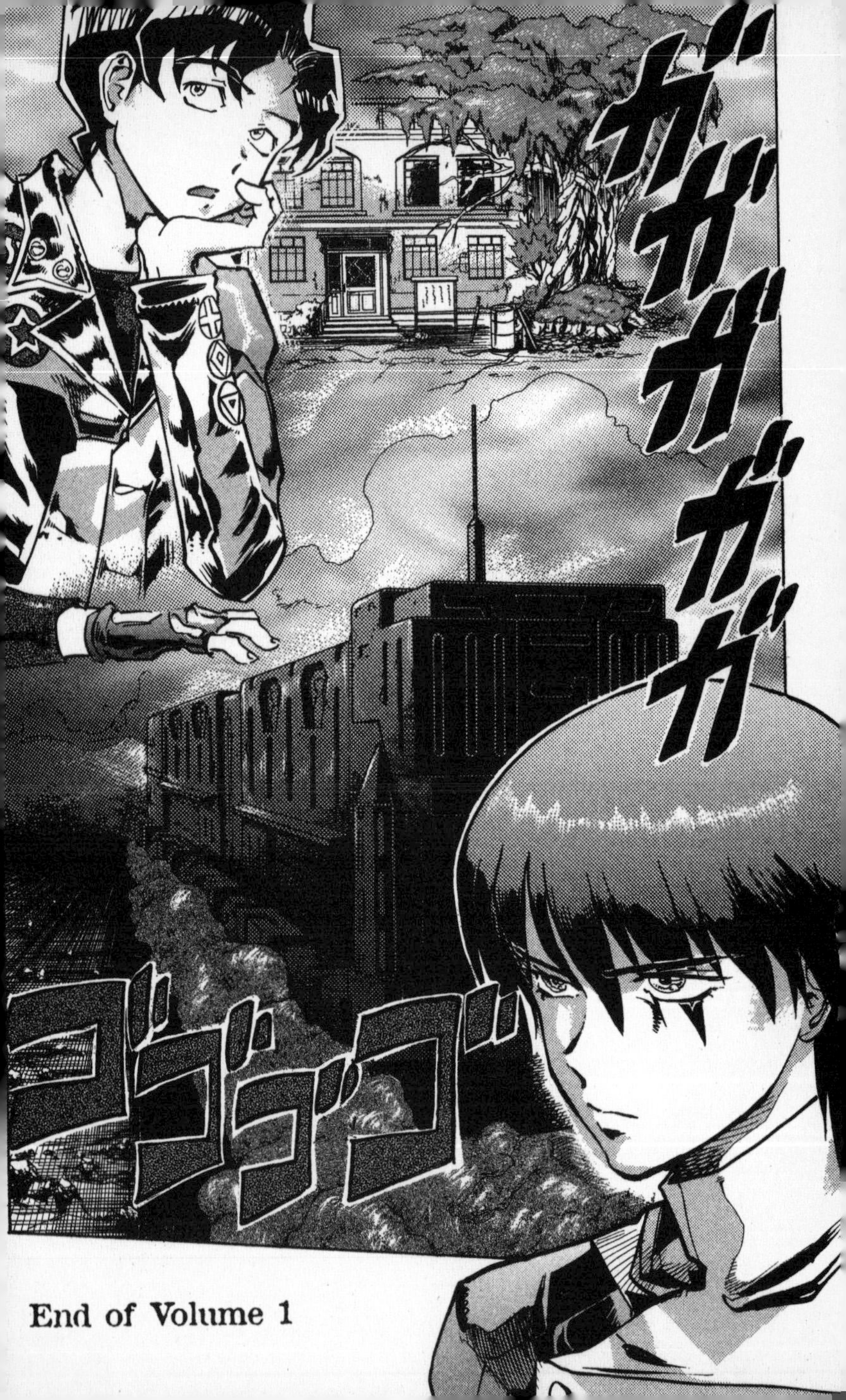
ゴゴゴゴ

End of Volume 1

SCRYED

Vol. 2 Preview

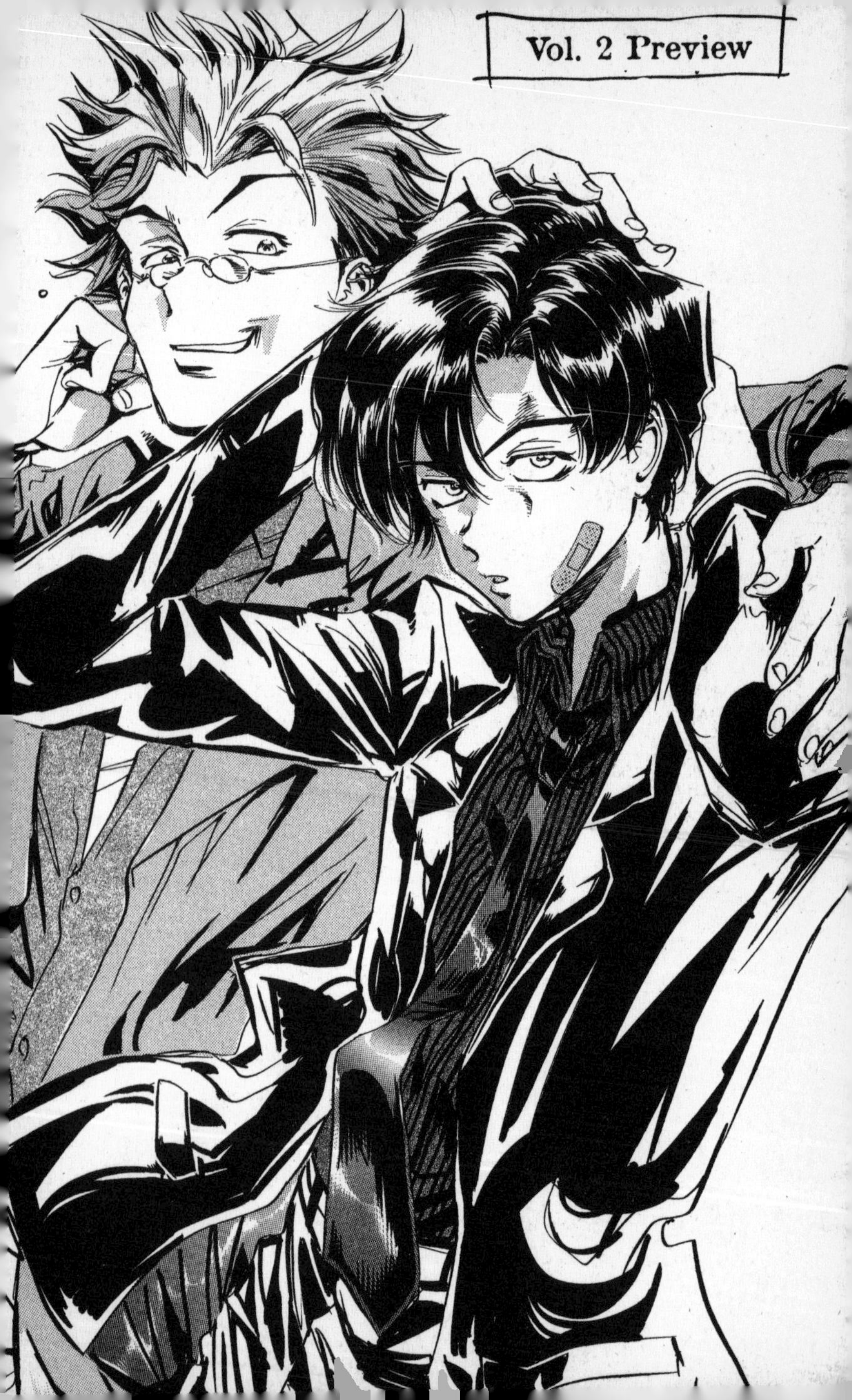

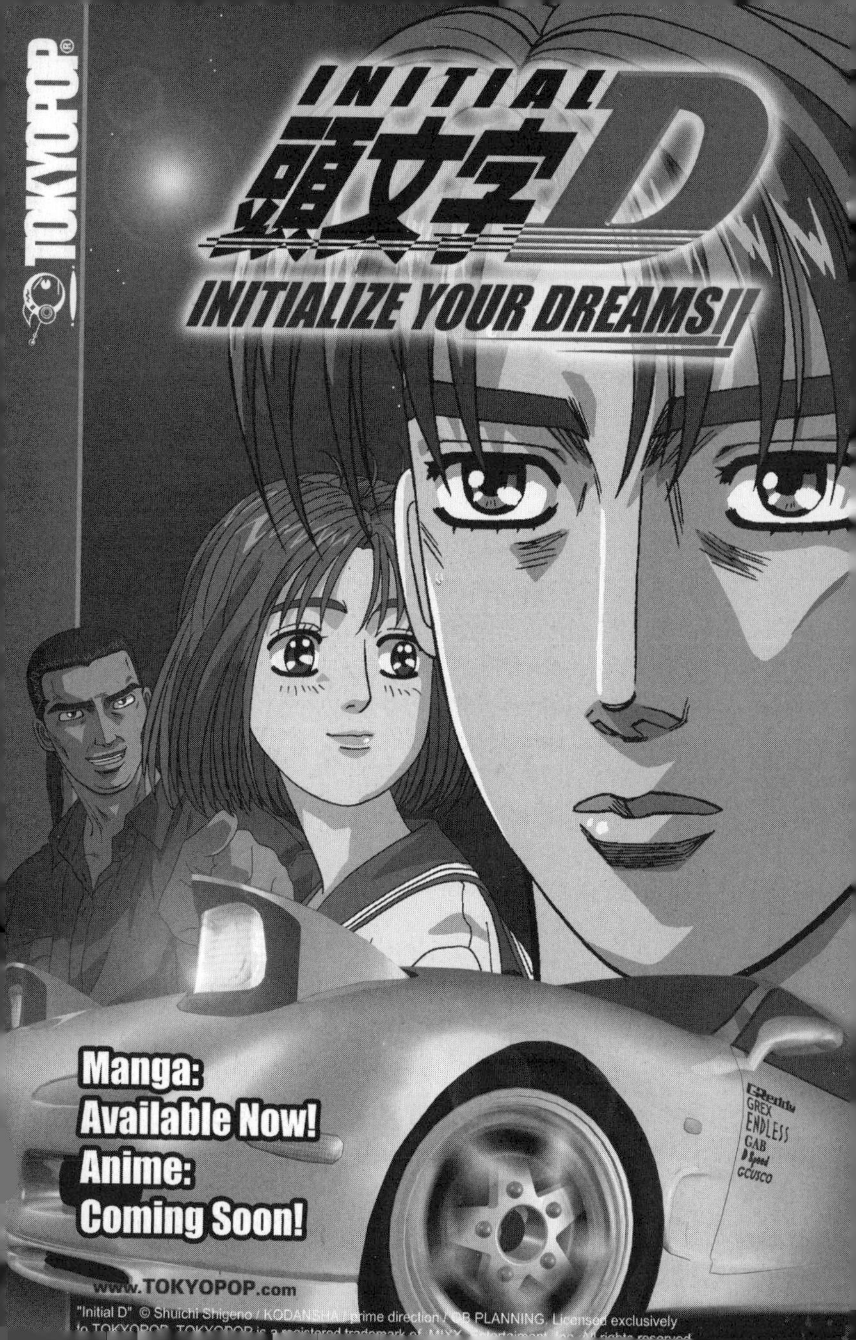
TOKYOPOP
INITIAL
頭文字D
INITIALIZE YOUR DREAMS!!
Manga:
Available Now!
Anime:
Coming Soon!
GREX
ENDLESS
GAB
D Speed
GCUSCO
www.TOKYOPOP.com
"Initial D" © Shuichi Shigeno / KODANSHA / prime direction / OB PLANNING. Licensed exclusively

STOP!

This is the back of the book.
You wouldn't want to spoil a great ending!

This book is printed "manga-style," in the authentic Japanese right-to-left format. Since none of the artwork has been flipped or altered, readers get to experience the story just as the creator intended. You've been asking for it, so TOKYOPOP® delivered: authentic, hot-off-the-press, and far more fun!

DIRECTIONS

If this is your first time reading manga-style, here's a quick guide to help you understand how it works.

It's easy... just start in the top right panel and follow the numbers. Have fun, and look for more 100% authentic manga from TOKYOPOP®!